Megachurch Accountability in Missions

Korean Global Mission Leadership Forum participants
November 2015

Megachurch Accountability in Missions

Critical Assessment through Global Case Studies

Editors

Jinbong Kim
Dwight P. Baker
J. Nelson Jennings
Jae Hoon Lee
Steve Sang-Cheol Moon

WILLIAM CAREY LIBRARY

www.missionbooks.org

Megachurch Accountability in Missions: Critical Assessment through Global Case Studies

ISBN: 978-0-87808-630-6

Published by William Carey Library
1605 E. Elizabeth Street
Pasadena, CA 91104 | www.missionbooks.org

Seulgi Lee, cover designer
Rose Lee-Norman, indexer

William Carey Library is a ministry of Frontier Ventures
Pasadena, CA | www.frontierventures.org

Printed in the Republic of Korea
20 19 18 17 16 5 4 3 2 1 DP 2000

Contents

Foreword

Accountability has deep roots in the Bible. Joseph held himself accountable not only to his employer but also to his God (Gen. 39:8–10). Samuel held himself accountable for his honest exercise of public office, with God and the people as his witnesses (1 Sam. 12:1–5.). David held himself accountable for stewarding the gifts of his people with integrity (1 Chron. 29:14–17). Paul held himself accountable in the eyes of God and man for his handling of money entrusted to him by other believers (2 Cor. 8:16–21).

Sadly, many successful Christian leaders behave differently. Unlike Joseph, they imagine that God will not see and that sexual favors are perks of the job. Unlike Samuel, they think there are no witnesses of their dishonest actions. Unlike David, they treat the gifts of God's people as their personal bank balance. Unlike Paul, they refuse to have other people present and involved in their handling of church finances. Tragically, because of such lack of accountability, they create for themselves a pit of wrongdoing, lies, and concealment and then fall into it in public disgrace. When that happens, not only do they suffer devastating loss of ministry credibility, but also the church and its mission suffer, and the name of Jesus Christ and his Gospel are dragged to the gutter.

Accountability is a matter of humility. It means taking seriously the reality of sin and temptation. It means knowing how vulnerable each of us is in the absence of the mutual checks and challenges that the gift of accountability provides for one another in Christian ministry. Accountability is also a matter of integrity. It means being what we are as men and women who have been redeemed by Christ and are called to walk worthy of our calling. It means living by different standards from those of the corrupt culture that surrounds us.

The call to such accountability, humility, and integrity was one of the major emphases of the Cape Town Commitment, the statement arising from the Third Lausanne Congress on World Evangelization (2010). The following quotations all come from its part IIE, "Calling the Church of Christ back to Humility, Integrity, and Simplicity" (www.lausanne.org/content/ctc/ctcommitment).

> When there is no distinction in conduct between Christians and non-Christians—for example in the practice of corruption and greed, or sexual promiscuity, or rate of divorce, or relapse to pre-Christian religious practice, or attitudes towards people of other races, or consumerist lifestyles, or social prejudice—then the world is right to wonder if our Christianity makes any difference at all. Our message carries no authenticity to a watching world. . . .
>
> Since there is no biblical mission without biblical living, we urgently re-commit ourselves, and challenge all those who profess the name of Christ, to live in radical distinctiveness from the ways of the world, to "put on the new humanity, created to be like God in true righteousness and holiness." . . .
>
> In our fallenness and sin, power is often exercised to abuse and exploit others. We exalt ourselves, claiming superiority of gender, race, or social status. Paul counters all these marks of the idolatry of pride and power with his requirement that those who are filled by God's Spirit should submit to one another for Christ's sake. . . .
>
> We call on all church and mission leaders to resist the temptation to be less than totally truthful in presenting our work. We are dishonest when we exaggerate our reports with unsubstantiated statistics, or twist the truth for the sake of gain. We pray for a cleansing wave of honesty and the end of such distortion, manipulation and exaggeration. We call on all who fund spiritual work not to make unrealistic demands for measurable and visible results, beyond the need for proper accountability. Let us strive for a culture of full integrity and transparency. We will choose to walk in the light and truth of God, for the Lord tests the heart and is pleased with integrity.

This wide-ranging KGMLF volume is a very commendable attempt to respond to that challenge and commitment. May its multiple examples, as well as the lessons drawn from them, serve to awaken other parts of the global church, especially in its mega-church manifestations, to take this issue of accountability with the biblical and missional seriousness it clearly deserves.

Christopher J. H. Wright
International Ministries Director
Langham Partnership
London

Foreword

I have been especially impressed with the ministry of the Overseas Ministries Study Center, New Haven, Connecticut, in two respects. The first is the way its approach stands in contrast to that of the Korean churches. Though the Korean church has sent out an immense number of missionaries over the past several decades, its lack of preparation for missionary retirements and sabbaticals has been glaring. OMSC, however, provides an inviting environment for missionaries to spend their time of rest meaningfully. Essentially, OMSC has been footing the bill for what the Korean churches should be doing for their own missionaries. For that ministry I am deeply humbled and grateful. Second, I am moved by OMSC's efforts to foster a more academic approach toward missions. Such an effort models a potential new approach for the Korean church in doing missions. By hosting joint conferences, OMSC has connected directly with the Korean churches and has made great strides in disseminating information. Participation in these efforts has encouraged me to do my own part as well.

The publication of *Megachurch Accountability in Missions* is a fruit of this effort. This volume will be a valuable reference not only for the churches of Korea but also for Korean diaspora churches worldwide, not to mention *all* parts of Jesus' "one flock" (John 10:16). Over the past quarter century, the trend has been for churches to become ever larger and for megachurches to end up monopolizing missional resources. This phenomenon can be expected only to increase with time. At this point it is essential to define clearly the missional duties of megachurches and the role they must play for the benefit of the larger mission community. Furthermore, megachurches not only must fulfill the responsibilities given to them but also, as this book urges, must be objectively evaluated by outside parties to determine whether they have been faithful stewards of their resources.

As a pastor who dreams of building a mission orientation within his Korean immigrant church in the United States, I have been led by the materials within this book to reflect deeply on the topic. Though we are at the low end of the megachurch scale, I believe that we must carefully and thoroughly study the topic of accountability in missions, particularly because the diaspora churches themselves are the fruit of missions.

I am confident that the readers of this book will find that it contains useful resources on the topic of accountability in missions. I see four valuable contributions the book makes. First, several chapters present specific ways that churches with missional resources can carry out their missionary responsibilities. Second, readers will be challenged by the chapters that introduce the missional programs undertaken by renowned churches in Korea, such as Onnuri Community Church and SaRang Church, as well as by the chapter "Hillsong Megachurch Network," a must-read case study of how a globe-encircling supermegachurch exercises missional accountability. One can experience a push, an intrigue, or even a sacred exhilaration in reading of a single church taking up a worldwide calling of vibrant mission.

Third, beyond megachurches, readers can also become acquainted with mission models of midsize churches in Hong Kong, Korea, and the United States. This information is especially valuable for pastors of Korean diaspora churches. In fact, any materials that can guide the hearts of pastors and inspire dedication in leaders to participate more effectively in world missions is greatly appreciated. Fourth, several chapters provide important information on the conduct of megachurches and the responsibilities they assume as they operate missions in Brazil, Africa, Japan, and other parts of the world.

This book introduces, in a balanced manner, churches that have approached their missional responsibility in various ways. Pastors and mission leaders have the privilege here of seeing within one book an array of current trends in world missions.

Kyusam Han
Chodae Community Church
Norwood, New Jersey

Foreword

Every church on earth, at whatever cost might be involved, has the mission to implement Christ's Great Commission: "Make disciples of all nations!" (Matt. 28:19). Over the centuries, local churches big and small, as well as mission organizations, have labored to carry out this mission responsibility. And now recently we have seen the emergence worldwide of megachurches. Many of these churches are also heavily involved in missionary efforts, many doing so, however, without close ties with other churches or with independent mission agencies. Megachurches typically have ample human and financial resources for whatever tasks they wish to undertake, and they can easily assume that they have little need to work closely with other entities. In the one body of Christ, however, we cannot forget Paul's teaching in 1 Corinthians 12:12–26 about how fellow members in the body are to view and treat each other. No part of the body is to consider its own role insignificant relative to that of others (vv. 15–20); conversely, no part of the body is allowed to say to any other part, "I have no need of you" (v. 21). Within the one family of God, all members must "have the same care for one another" (v. 25). In light of such a perspective, we can say that no single church, even the biggest megachurch, possesses all the gifts necessary to carry on missionary work independently. Churches in our global world must pursue cooperative, partnered ministry with other churches and mission organizations in order to truly carry out, in God's way, Jesus' Great Commission.

As this volume points out in various ways, megachurches must use their resources wisely and must not discourage the missionary spirit of ordinary-looking small- and mid-sized churches. Likewise, the more powerful or charismatic the leader of a megachurch may be, the more that leader and church need to be accountable for personal integrity in life and mission. Wisdom suggests that megachurches need to be careful not to make churches overseas dependent on them, not to try to control the churches they support, not to demand that local churches in the field conform themselves to the megachurches, which would ultimately deprive national churches of their autonomy. Sharing of resources and collaboration should be the tone among churches large and small, as well as with organizations devoted specifically to mission.

Welcome to the publication of the materials presented at the third KGMLF forum, once again led by OMSC, this one focusing on the accountability of megachurches in mission. This publication is the fruit of many brothers and sisters worldwide who, at the meetings in Korea in November 2015, humbly and candidly shared their experience in megachurches and in mission. The overall tone bodes well for clarifying the benefits and pitfalls of megachurches in mission. Though focused more explicitly on our largest churches, this book has insight and encouragement as well for mission organizations and for countless smaller churches.

Timothy Kiho Park
Professor of Asian Mission
School of Intercultural Studies
Fuller Theological Seminary
Pasadena, California

Preface

Now faith is confidence in what we hope for and assurance about what we do not see.

—Heb. 11:1 NIV

"Will we be able, in 2015, to hold the Korean Global Mission Leadership Forum (KGMLF) in Korea for the first time?" "The Overseas Ministries Study Center (OMSC) does not have sufficient resources to cover the cost of KGMLF 2015, so how will we secure finances for it?" These were two of the questions that I faced as coordinator for KGMLF 2015. In looking at the circumstances, it was uncertain whether this forum, planned to deal with the theme "Megachurch Accountability in Missions: Critical Assessment through Global Case Studies," would be able to convene, let alone be successful. Believing, however, that problems are really blessings in disguise, I would wake up at dawn and confess my unbelief.

Remembering the men and women in Hebrews 11, I would pray that the third KGMLF meeting, to be held in the mountains of South Korea, would be as beautiful and wonderful as the Korean autumn. Each year in mid-fall the beauty of Mount Seorak, near which KGMLF was to meet, is at its pinnacle. Was it a mark of God's blessing that in 2015 the scenery was its most beautiful during the week of KGMLF? God responded. All the financial needs of the forum were fulfilled and everything went smoothly.

Through this event I saw the vision and faith concerning KGMLF that God had given me in 2008 become a reality. Some people have misunderstood, thinking that KGMLF is a forum only for the Korean church and its missions. The case studies from around the globe and research on twenty-first-century mission trends carried out by persons associated with missions throughout the world proved otherwise. Participants got to know each other and challenged one another, making it clear that KGMLF deals with topics that concern all churches and missions everywhere.

PLANNING MEETINGS

To plan for the forum, twenty people gathered on November 28, 2013, at the Seoul Club, in Seoul, South Korea. This meeting was made possible by the support of Young Hyun Jung and his wife, Sook Hee Kim, who had made similar meetings possible in 2010 and 2012 at the same location. The participants from OMSC were Jonathan J. Bonk, executive director emeritus, J. Nelson Jennings, then executive director, Dwight P. Baker, former associate director, and myself. Attendees from megachurches were Jae Hoon Lee, senior pastor of Onnuri Community Church, Peter JaeHyeok Chin, senior pastor of Global Mission Church, and Dong Whee Lee, emeritus pastor of Antioch Church and founder of Paul Mission International.

Also in attendance were Steve Sang-Cheol Moon, executive director of Korea Research Institute for Mission (KRIM), various mission organization leaders, and missiology professors who have worked in close partnership with KGMLF since its first meeting in 2011. Several scholars expressed opposition to holding a forum in Korea focused on megachurches. In light of several Korean professors who were known to have a negative view of megachurches, the group feared that the topic would be too contentious. Nonetheless, Jae Hoon Lee stated his humble desire to learn how Onnuri Community Church is doing in mission today—as viewed by outsiders—thirty years after it was planted. Furthermore, OMSC's leaders observed that, since social trends have figured in the worldwide rise of megachurches, a presentation of case studies from around the globe could provide fruitful insight into the range of factors significant in their growth and thus suggest ways of conducting their ministries with greater accountability.

DISQUIETING QUESTIONS

In preparing for the KGMLF 2015 meeting, I kept in mind the questions (really, they were criticisms) voiced by one Korean American megachurch pastor: Do megachurches really need to work with mission organizations? Since many megachurches have their own ideas about people, finances, spirituality, and missions, is it necessary for them to view mission organizations as significant partners in mission? Furthermore, why don't mission organizations discuss important decisions concerning missionary personnel or change in mission field direction with the churches that have sent the missionaries?

In his book *The Church Is Bigger Than You Think*, Patrick Johnstone of WEC International writes about the relationship between churches and mission organizations. According to Johnstone, the priority of the local church should be world missions, but mission organizations often shoulder more than their fair share of this work. He suggests that these organizations should humbly serve local churches and work closely with them.[1]

Another unsettling question: Can there be world mission if local churches are not growing? All observers agree that the growth of Korean missions has been a consequence of the exponential growth of the Korean churches. In 1989 in the church in Seoul where I was a missionary candidate, a person who did not give any mission offering could not hold an office in the church. In addition, any church that did not send or support missionaries was considered to be failing to fulfill its role as a church.

According to Steve Sang-Cheol Moon, in 1979 there were only 93 Korean missionaries serving in countries outside Korea, a number that jumped to 1,645 by 1990.[2] The continued growth of the Korean church in the 1990s led to a 25 percent annual increase in the number of Korean missionaries. But then in the 2000s, the Korean church experienced a decline in its rate of growth, with a corresponding drop in the increase of Korean foreign missionaries to 7.6 percent per year. From December 2013 to December 2014, the increase was only 1.9 percent. In terms of total numbers, between 2002 and 2004 the Korean church sent out 2,452 new missionaries; between 2013 and 2015, only a little over 1,000.[3]

1. See Patrick Johnstone, *The Church Is Bigger Than You Think* (Fearn, Ross-shire, U.K.: Christian Focus Publications, 1998), chap. 19.

2. Steve Sang-Cheol Moon, "The Protestant Missionary Movement in Korea: Current Growth and Development," *International Bulletin of Missionary Research* 32, no. 2 (April 2008): 59.

3. See Steve Sang-Cheol Moon, Hee-Joo Yoo, and Eun-Mi Kim, "Missions from Korea 2015: Missionaries Unable to Continue Ministry in Their Country of Service," *International Bulletin of Missionary Research* 39, no. 2

During research for my recently completed dissertation, entitled "Rethinking Retirement and Creative Aging among Korean Protestant Missionaries," I found that more than half of Korea's missionaries are in their fifties, and 10 percent are in their sixties or older. Moreover, more than 90 percent of those who completed the survey answered that they would like to retire between the ages of sixty-five and seventy. In other words, many Korean missionaries can be expected to retire in the near future, with more than half of the present Korean missionary force returning home by the year 2030. The missionary outreach of the Korean church will be only as strong as the Korean church itself. An enormous influx of new missionaries will be necessary to sustain the present size of the Korean missionary force. Unless a radical change occurs and revival and growth come to the Korean church, it is difficult to envision that the Korean missionary force will be able to sustain even its present numbers through the coming decade.

ACKNOWLEDGMENTS

In this important time of change, with the demands it imposes, not only did many megachurch pastors and missionary pastors attend KGMLF 2015, but so too did several pastors of middle-sized and small churches. Furthermore, the presentations, discussions, and group debates by leaders of mission organizations and missiological scholars were animated. The rapid changes taking place in Korean society certainly provide part of the reason for the high level of engagement. But even more important may be the concern of churches and mission organizations around the world to reflect on missions from a perspective that is objective, open to the input of other churches and mission agencies, and ultimately pleasing to God.

KGMLF 2015 was held November 3–6, 2015, in Kensington Stars Hotel, Sokcho, South Korea. God responded to the pleas and prayers of his children in remarkable ways, and the forum was a success. Seventy-seven persons attended, coming from Africa, Asia, Australia, Europe, North America, and South America. The

---

(April 2015): 85; and Steve Sang-Cheol Moon, "Missions from Korea 2014: Missionary Children," *International Bulletin of Missionary Research* 38, no. 2 (April 2014): 85.

presenters and respondents dealt with thirteen subtopics. Each morning opened with a Bible study, led by presenters from Japan, Australia, and Ghana; in the afternoons the participants divided into eight small groups for discussion. During the final afternoon, presentations by six panelists stimulated discussion and questions. Overviews of the conference by Hyung Keun Choi and Dwight Baker concluded the forum. Thus, this third KGMLF book has been made possible, thanks to the effort and dedication of the forty-three authors who have contributed to it.

I often hear that KGMLF is unique and special. The reason can probably be found in the respect that the participants have for one another. The forum did not showcase some famous mission scholar from the West trying to teach the Korean church, nor was it an occasion for well-known megachurches to boast of their achievements. Attenders from all over the world came to humbly learn from one another. In the words of one, "This was a forum anointed by the Holy Spirit." I concur; the success of this KGMLF is to be credited solely to the grace of God.

God works through those who believe and obey his Word. When I was worried and did not know what to do, God provided many spiritual mentors and coworkers. In particular, the leadership of Jae Hoon Lee, senior pastor of Onnuri Community Church, which joyfully cohosted this convention, and the thoughtful cooperation between Onnuri Community Church and OMSC struck me as God's personal and encouraging gift to us all. The many details of this KGMLF were cared for through the dedicated efforts of Onnuri staff and volunteers under the leadership of Hong Joo Kim, head mission pastor of Onnuri Community Church, and mission pastor Il Young Kang. The service that Sonia Yim and Jeong Joon Kim provided to facilitate communication with foreign guests must receive special acknowledgment. Steven Cha, lead pastor of Onnuri Community Church's English ministry, and his team set aside their busy schedule and willingly served at the forum. I would also like to thank CGNTV for filming the entire forum and preparing the program "Global Talk" with five of the attending scholars. Finally, the Lord's blessings be on the "EZER" team, who prepared gifts, snacks, and drinks for all who attended the forum.

I would like to thank Nelson Jennings, who chose the KGMLF 2015 topic and invited most of the non-Korean participants, and for whom I have the deepest regard. Additionally, I would like to thank Jonathan Bonk. He has always been available as a spiritual mentor to help and encourage me, as has Won Sang Lee, my spiritual mentor. I appreciate the encouragement and support of all the pastors in the Connecticut Korean Church Council and their prayers on my behalf so I might better be able to serve the KGMLF. Especially I note the encouragement and advice of Sun Man Kim, senior pastor of the First Korean Presbyterian Church, Hartford, Connecticut. He and First Korean Presbyterian Church have sponsored the KGMLF since its beginning in 2011.

SPECIAL APPRECIATION

Many churches and organizations united in support of KGMLF 2015. I cannot list here all the ways in which they have helped, but I thank them by praying that God will bless them abundantly. These include the New Haven Korean Church (Dae Joon Roh, pastor), Harrisburg Korean Presbyterian Church (Song Joong Kang, pastor), Hong Kong Korean Exodus Mission Church (Hyung Joong Yoon, pastor), Yoido Full Gospel Church (Young-hoon Lee, pastor), Hwangji Presbyterian Church (Jong Eon Kim, pastor), Asian Mission (Jae Chul Chung, director), and the Mission Board of Korean Methodist Church (Dong Hwa Tae, vice–general secretary).

My thanks go to Ho In Choi, who joined OMSC's staff part time to help out with the preparations for KGMLF, and to Pastor Chun Lee and his wife, Sook Young Chang, who came to OMSC as residents, for their help. I would also like to thank the staff of OMSC for its great effort and dedication in support of KGMLF.

Support provided by the mission experience that had been accumulated over the years at OMSC and the cooperation of OMSC's staff made it possible to launch KGMLF, a new type of international forum. I also wish to thank my wife, Soon Young Jung, who has helped me in many ways behind the scenes.

PUBLICATION

An important consideration in starting KGMLF as a new type of forum was the publication of a well-edited book that would present the contents of the forum, a volume that could take its place, for example, in the library of Yale Divinity School, located near OMSC. Dwight Baker, Craig Noll, Rona Johnston Gordon, and Lois Baker, long-time members of the editorial team for the *International Bulletin of Missionary Research*, worked with dedication to turn this vision into reality. Special mention should be made of the advice and help Dwight Baker gave me concerning the preparations and progress of KGMLF. My sincere thanks go also to Abe Kugyong Koh, who translated the English edition for simultaneous publication in Korean.

Since 2011 the First Korean Presbyterian Church, Hartford, Connecticut (Sun Man Kim, pastor), and SaRang Church, Seoul (Jung-Hyun Oh, pastor), have generously sponsored publication of each of the English books (2011, 2013, 2015). Also, with the sponsorship of Onnuri Community Church, which began in 2013, we have been able to publish the Korean editions for 2013 and 2015 through Duranno Press. This press is a precious gift for the world mission enterprise.

I would like also to thank Debora Nam, Mi Young Song, and Joo Sun Park for their extensive, though hidden, efforts to edit, publish, and distribute previous Korean editions of KGMLF books, and to express appreciation to Pastor Yong Bum Park of the copyright team. I especially wish to express my heartfelt thanks to Hyung Ki Lee, who is in charge of Duranno Press, for his encouragement and cooperation.

THANKS TO GOD ABOVE ALL

By God's grace, plans are for KGMLF 2017 to be titled "Migration, Human Dislocation, and Accountability in Missions." The forum is set for November 7–10, 2017, again in Korea.

May the most recent KGMLF and its two published volumes be instruments in the hands of the Lord for furthering these worthy aims! *Soli Deo gloria!*

Jinbong Kim
Director of International Church Relations
and Coordinator of KGMLF
Overseas Ministries Study Center
New Haven, Connecticut, USA

1

To Whom Is a Megachurch Accountable? A U.S. Case Study

Scott Thumma

The religious landscape in the United States has changed dramatically in the last fifty years as the nondenominational reality erodes traditional religious organizations, and as parachurch and independently networked groups proliferate. Since 1965, many denominations have lost significant membership. Increasingly, Americans—especially younger generations—require their social commitments to be personally meaningful, tangible, and physically engaging. Likewise, the world has shrunk through greater mobility, increased personal wealth, and, most of all, Internet technologies. This context has led to a shift from a complete reliance on denominational mission groups, or even on parachurch mission agencies, toward "hands-on" local congregational mission activities.

During this same period, the proliferation of Protestant Christian megachurches—defined as churches with at least 2,000 attendees in weekly worship—has created a new religious reality in the United States and, increasingly, globally. In 1965 there were fewer than 50 megachurches in the United States. Today there are roughly 1,650 dominating the religious landscape and reshaping what "church" means, with contemporary worship, cutting-edge technology, multiple locations, celebrity clergy with charismatic personalities, and quasi-denominational networks of like-minded churches.[1]

1. All information about U.S. megachurches is taken from the author's

Yet megachurches are only the most obvious sign of the rapidly changing size of American churches. Over the past 100 years, the data from nearly every denomination show a dramatic concentration of its membership in ever-larger churches. Currently, the top 10 percent of American churches—roughly 35,000 congregations with 350 attendees or more—are home to more than half of the nation's religious citizens. At the same time, at least 60 percent of U.S. churches have fewer than 100 weekly attendees.[2] The implications of this striking size shift, when combined with other societal and cultural changes, are considerable for mission efforts.

What do mission activities look like in the nation's megachurches? Additionally, to whom and in what ways are they accountable? The missions approaches of megachurches are as diverse as the phenomenon itself. No single model of missions is distinctive to these large churches. In twenty-five years of studying the U.S. megachurch movement, I have found that mission activity is consistently a complex mix that may include partnerships with denominational agencies and nondenominational parachurch organizations, a focus on local and international missions, active engagement with mission trips, and other innovative and unique outreach efforts. Each particular megachurch's work is typically grounded in its distinctive vision and the interests that guide the church itself.

In this chapter, I explore the case of a Connecticut megachurch with a significant commitment to local and international missions. By highlighting this case, however, I do not mean to imply that it is a representative example of the nation's megachurches. Yet this case does demonstrate the breadth of mission efforts that can be accomplished by a large church, and the system of accountability that is at work.

---

research and can be found at "Megachurches," http://hirr.hartsem.edu/megachurch/megachurches.html, on the Hartford Institute for Religion Research website.

2. Information about the religious profile of the United States is drawn from "Fast Facts about American Religion" located on the Hartford Institute for Religion Research website, http://hirr.hartsem.edu/research/fastfacts/fast_facts.html.

CROSSROADS COMMUNITY CATHEDRAL: A MODEST MEGACHURCH

At first glance, Crossroads Community Cathedral, in East Hartford, Connecticut, probably would not be recognized as a megachurch. In contrast to the usual stereotype—that megachurches are flashy and extravagant—Crossroads' physical structure suggests a reserved demeanor. It is more horizontal than vertical, set back from the road, and anything but ostentatious. In fact, its low profile accurately embodies its bearing as well as its appearance. The church is mostly inconspicuous in the religious landscape of Connecticut, even though it is one of only a handful of megachurches in New England. Its sanctuary seats 900, roughly half the size of an average megachurch's primary sanctuary. Attendance at its four weekend services totals around 2,200 adults and children; it is one of the 40 percent of megachurches that fall in the 2,000–3,000 weekly attendance range.

The church began in 1951 as a mission venture of the Assemblies of God (AG). Thirty years later, Terry Wiles came to this congregation, which then had approximately 150 attendees. By 1990 the church had moved to its present location and began worshiping in a gym reconfigured as a temporary sanctuary space. Though the church is affiliated with the Assemblies of God, a visitor would not readily perceive this association, given its name and lack of identifiable AG logos, symbols, or literature.

The overall culture of Crossroads Community Cathedral is marked by an emphasis on discipleship and mission service, with a serious and authentic congregational culture. This approach has produced gradual, steady growth during the thirty-four-year tenure of senior pastor, now bishop, Terry Wiles, and it continues with his son, Sean Wiles, who is the primary congregational leader and executive pastor. Most church members are lower-middle-class professionals or service and blue-collar workers. The church's services are energetic, with a contemporary worship style and a solidly evangelical theology.

Perhaps the most noteworthy feature of the congregation is

its multiracial membership, represented for the last twenty years in almost equal percentages of Caucasian, Latino, and African American families, as well as a smattering of Asian American and African families—many of whom are first- and second-generation immigrants from a number of different countries. Additionally, worship services are translated into Spanish, and the leadership of the church increasingly reflects the congregation's racial diversity.

A MISSIONS-MINDED PASTORAL VISION

Since the arrival of Terry Wiles, the church has purposefully demonstrated his dedication to missions, which he often articulates simply as "reaching the lost." Fifteen years ago, Wiles told a group of my students at Hartford Seminary, "We have a mission, and that's what we consider ourselves to be doing, to serve God and man by reaching nonreligious people and turning them into fully devoted followers of Christ." More recently, after a powerful retelling of the encounter with God that shaped this commitment, he related, "I came [to the church] with a missions mind-set. . . . One of my major objectives has been to promote mission, . . . both home and world missions. . . . I wanted to build a missions church." Indeed, this purpose has been realized throughout his ministry—powerfully shaping the church's culture of evangelism and outreach activities.

The early years of the senior pastor's tenure focused primarily on local mission work and expanding the church itself, while also contributing significant monetary support to a large number of AG missionaries. In fact, field notes from my first encounter with the church seventeen years ago describe a long hallway covered with the photos of nearly two dozen foreign missionaries the church was supporting. From the beginning of his ministry at Crossroads, Pastor Wiles has committed himself to preach a mission-focused message every second Sunday of the month. Early on, these efforts also included occasional mission trips, along with the consistent support of a number of home missionaries. Reflecting on their mission outreach history, Wiles commented, "Initially we were operating in various countries like Mexico, Brazil, Honduras, and Guatemala. We were going down, working with Assemblies of God missionaries who were down there, and then we got away from that and started doing things on our own. Now everything we do outside the United States is disconnected from the AG."

This gradual shift away from the Assemblies mission structure was a pivotal change in the church's outlook. It began in the 1990s with an independent focus on Guatemala when the church established a long-term commitment to a particular region of the country. This change occurred by creating a partnership with an existing megachurch, Elim Central Church, in Guatemala City, and through the establishment of the ministry Cocina del Amor (Kitchen of Love), started by a Crossroads member who was a native Guatemalan. Since then, Crossroads has built more than forty churches and trained and developed relationships with more than 250 pastors.

This focused mission approach was expanded through the influence of another former AG missions-oriented megachurch pastor. In the early 2000s Charles Blair, then the senior pastor of the nondenominational megachurch Calvary Temple, in Denver, Colorado, was receiving attention for his efforts to plant 1,000 churches in Ethiopia. Blair described this mission effort as the "Ethiopian Call." In 2004 Pastor Wiles and his wife, Nita, traveled to Ethiopia to participate in this effort.

Not long after this mission trip Pastor Wiles had a "Peruvian Call"—a vision of replicating Blair's effort in the Loreto region of the Peruvian Amazon. "God directed me to build 100 churches and train 100 pastors," Wiles recalled. At the time, he was nearing sixty years of age and celebrating twenty-five years of ministry, while Crossroads was in the midst of building its 900-seat sanctuary and had by then expanded to around 2,000 attendees at its multiple worship services. Wiles realized he had accomplished many of the goals he had set for himself as a local pastor and was actively exploring God's direction for the coming ten years of his ministry—a direction he increasingly perceived as involving direct international mission work.

Today, Bishop Wiles estimates that 70 percent of his time is spent on missions. "I may be the senior pastor, but I am also the church's missions pastor," he said. As he transferred the church's daily leadership to his son, he noted that he received a clear message from church members: "We want to free your hands to do more of this [mission work]." His shift away from the everyday responsibility of running the church allowed him to express his mission vision and passion more intently. He created the Crossroads Community International Fellowship (CCIF), an oversight and accountability network of seventy-five clergy and seven churches in the United States, became more engaged in training pastors and planting Peruvian and Central American churches, and was elevated to the office of bishop in the International Bishops Conference, USA. The shift to an active mission status also led Bishop Wiles to drop his AG credentials.

THE CHURCH'S PRESENT MISSION ACTIVITIES

Currently the church contributes 20 percent of its $3.7 million annual income to missions. Of that total amount, 11 percent, or $407,000, goes to international missions. In the past five years, this amount increased by 42 percent, while average attendance has increased by only 21 percent. The autonomous CCIF, a 501(c)(3) organization, adds another $300,000 to the international missions effort. In addition, support for individual missionaries comes separately through a November Missionary Month fund drive that in 2013 raised an additional $184,000 (an increase of 31 percent in the previous five years) to partially fund over 45 individual missionaries, of whom three-quarters are affiliated with AG. Approximately 400 church members, or 18 percent of regularly attending adults, have taken at least one mission trip. The majority of these trips are two weeks long and support the church's continuing efforts in Guatemala through a medical mission, prison ministry, feeding program, youth ministry, and clergy support and training efforts. Twice a year, Bishop Wiles takes small work teams to assist in the Peruvian ministry, in addition to his other trips there.

Since 2009 the church's primary mission in Peru has consisted of establishing churches in the Amazon jungle's "unreached places," creating a system of religious education and establishing a network of pastoral support and organization. As a part of this effort, the church purchased 180 acres and cleared 10 of these to construct conference and training-camp facilities. The church established an accredited Peruvian educational organization with an academic dean and obtained the printing rights to a quality Spanish-language Bible-based curriculum. Thus far, this effort has graduated 150 ministers, with 200 additional students currently enrolled; and it has planted 65 churches with dedicated buildings, each with at least 15 active adult participants, for a total weekly attendance of more than 4,000. But the goal was not to make the mission wholly dependent on Crossroads Community Cathedral's efforts or money, and so the ministry has also instituted a system of internal leadership among the trained indigenous clergy. Crossroads leadership are insistent about making a commitment for the long term. "The only way we can establish [this permanently] is if it is a Peruvian organization. . . . If it is going to keep growing and thriving . . . , they need that permanent connection [with each other]." Additionally, Crossroads' effort in Peru has been augmented by two of the CCIF congregations. "As the church grows, it expands what we can do . . . but we can also expand with the network partners." Most recently they have begun work on equipping the educational facilities and church plants in the Peruvian villages with solar power, sources of fresh water, and basic medical supplies.

Crossroads has created its own ways of being engaged in mission—an approach not unlike the missions of many smaller congregations in the United States, but certainly on a grander scale. It has shown that a church can generate significant revenue, focus on a particular situation, harness social and political capital in this and other countries, and recruit highly skilled, passionate participants from within the congregation and across its networks of influence. The mission of this church is shaped by its vision and corresponds to the interests and talents of the people who participate. It is intentionally designed to generate intimate, long-lasting relationships between those engaged in the mission and those who benefit from the efforts.

RELATIONAL ACCOUNTABILITY

Given the seeming autonomy of Crossroads Community Cathedral's efforts, what systems are in place that provide accountability? In actual practice, no highly successful megachurch is accountable to anyone—not to a denominational executive, a mission agency, or even its own members and missionaries—unless it chooses to be. The integrity of a megachurch is directly dependent on the integrity of its leaders and their willingness to be held accountable. This is a "voluntary accountability" based on the relational ties created and forged with others who ideally hold the megachurch responsible for its mission efforts and agenda.

By their very nature, all forms of accountability are relational. Whether codified by laws or contracts or not, to be accountable means to answer for or justify one's actions to other parties. A megachurch's leadership is ideally answerable to those whom its mission efforts touch and benefit. In the case of Crossroads Community Cathedral, the church has intentionally shaped its missions efforts to forge multiple partnerships—with church members, the people it serves, and organizations it establishes or partners with—to hold it accountable.

Primarily, the church's mission efforts are beholden to congregational members. Bishop Wiles did not impose a mission agenda on the people; rather, he shaped the church culture to reinforce a missions mind-set and helped members internalize the vision of reaching others with the Gospel message. The result is a congregation that cares about outreach, wants to see it happen, and is willing to contribute significantly to support these efforts. "All this works because the congregation . . . has embraced the vision." While their activity was initiated by the senior pastor's vision, the people accept it, support it, and have made it *their* vision. This accountability is also reinforced by the immigrant population of the church, who themselves have significant ties to their countries of origin and who undoubtedly contribute to the physical and spiritual support of persons in those countries through prayer, visits, and financial contributions.

The configuration of the church's mission efforts, likewise, contributes to a system of accountability. Bishop Wiles's decisions to focus on a long-term relationship with a few mission locations and to intentionally involve church members through mission trips created the possibility for relational ties to develop with those who benefit from the evangelistic efforts. As a mission staff person said, "We want them to work, but we also want them to get out in the community, meet the children, be with the people—we want them to make a connection. This connection piece is very, very important."

These relationships between church members and those reached through the missions contribute to sustaining the program. Friendships are created, lives are changed, and commitments are solidified through firsthand encounters. One staff member commented, "[You] literally fall in love with the culture and the people, and that is what prompts [your] continued involvement. We have an investment in their lives; we are part of them now." In other words, "Our people have developed a relationship with the missionaries that are there. They look forward to going back out and seeing the people they have been working with and the pastors in the area. . . . We have created a community where they have relationships in missions." The more church members directly experience the mission efforts, the less likely they are to allow them to collapse through lack of funding or interest. This intimate connection is further reinforced by direct evidence of the fruits of their labor; as one person who has been on several mission trips suggested, "I have a connection with them . . . and now I see what the money and effort is doing over time." This happens vicariously through videos and stories shared with the congregation when mission trip participants return home, but it occurs most powerfully by direct contact and continued interaction in the mission field.

The mission is also held accountable by the network of pastors and churches developed through the collaboration of churches and ministries in the CCIF. These partners in mission—from diverse denominations, ethnicities, and geographic locations—help shoulder the burden, but they also contribute to the effort by sharing ideas and solutions. The increased number of mission participants improves the chance of sustaining the mission efforts across time. As Bishop Wiles commented, "We created partnerships so we could say, 'We are going to be here forever.'"

The church's plan, adopted early on, of working with established churches and mission efforts in the country, such as Kitchen of Love, provides another system of accountability. Supporting and augmenting the existing work means that the efforts are not entirely dependent upon one congregation's commitment, and that they will continue even if the church's participation does not. Additionally, by promoting an internal network of self-governance and oversight among the mission churches, the mission provides the indigenous system with some level of autonomy. Hiring, training, and supporting an internal infrastructure to carry out and accomplish tasks when Crossroads' members are not in the field is a way the church further contributes to this autonomy. As a missions staff person stated, "If you do not build a foundation [to support] the churches, then it's a good trip for you and your group, but there is nothing sustainable; it will not exist long."

There is no doubt that the mission efforts of Crossroads Community Cathedral are making a significant impact. The church's focused commitments are accomplishing positive changes in the physical and spiritual lives of thousands of people. The question remains, Do these relational ties provide accountability? Megachurches, by the very nature of their size, abundant resources, and charismatic leadership, can overshadow their partnerships. Their sincere commitments keep them engaged currently, but if those impulses shift, what keeps the ministries supported? Crossroads has made great efforts to establish partnerships and an autonomous indigenous system that will survive its involvement, but can this system be a truly independent partner, given the economic and resource inequities? Finally, what will happen when the senior pastor can no longer champion the mission effort? Clearly, the church's identity is profoundly influenced by its mission work in Central and South America. It would be difficult to envision this commitment disappearing after Terry Wiles is gone. The mission work is intimately intertwined with the culture of the congregation. It seems apparent that, no matter who the leader is, as long as this church exists, it will be involved in missions. As Bishop Wiles said, "It's my vision, but it is their project, and it has become their vision too." But even if that were not the case, the trained clergy, planted churches, and indigenous organization would continue to exist. And ultimately, the church is accountable to God's Great Commission—passionately spreading the Gospel and working to save souls for the kingdom.

QUESTIONS FOR REFLECTION

1. Given that much of the mission activity of megachurches is based on the vision of the senior pastor and is dependent on this person's continued commitment to support it, what might be the consequences for the mission effort if this individual's vision shifts to new interests?
2. Who has the authority to hold a megachurch accountable? If accountability is based on relationships, can the relationships be equitable, given the power imbalance inherent in them?
3. Are the structures of relationships, such as found in Crossroads Community Cathedral, strong enough to hold a megachurch accountable without its willing consent?
4. Recognizing the significant size and abundant resources megachurches are able to pour into their mission efforts, how can megachurches guard against, in any given context, overwhelming the efforts of smaller churches or mission agencies?

2

Response to "To Whom Is a Megachurch Accountable?"

N. Yong Sung

In his chapter "To Whom Is a Megachurch Accountable?," Scott Thumma discusses changes in missions in the last fifty years, noting that local churches now prefer to participate in missions directly rather than working through traditional denominational mission boards or mission agencies. In the past, local churches were not able to gain the information needed to engage effectively in mission work without the help of mission agencies. Now, however, local churches often do not have to rely on the assistance of mission agencies to become active in mission work. Because of greater mobility, the communication revolution, and the social media generally, there are now very few differences between professionals in missions and amateurs with respect to their understanding of mission fields. Local churches have accumulated information through their own personnel and have become well equipped with specialists. Although in the past only commissioned and sent-out missionaries were considered to be involved in missions, local church members now commonly see themselves as able to participate fully in missions.

We do not need to resist this trend in missions. Rather, we need to find ways to assist local churches with their missional aspirations. In order to do so, local churches should think in terms of empowering professional mission agencies so that they can function like conductors, leading a quality "orchestra" of mission workers. Likewise, by developing holistic and systematic strategies, discovering the deepest needs of mission fields, and letting those missional needs be known to the churches, mission agencies should become channels through which local churches participate in missions. In this model, mission agencies do not need to mobilize local churches for the agencies' ministries; rather, mission agencies should become helpers, assisting local churches with the churches' own mission activities. To consider another comparison: the mission agencies' role should be like that of a portal site on the Internet. In such a relationship, local churches would partner more closely with mission agencies because the local churches would be able to find more effective ways to participate in various missions activities.

I comment here on five issues raised or implied in Scott Thumma's thoughtful chapter.

CHURCHES AND GOD'S CHURCH

Thumma discusses churches and their relation to missions, using the example of the Crossroads Community Cathedral, in East Hartford, Connecticut. This church separated from its own denomination and, in partnership with a megachurch in Guatemala City, Guatemala, started forty churches in Guatemala and trained and developed relationships there with more than 250 pastors. The pastor who spearheaded missions in this manner was influenced by Calvary Temple in Denver, a megachurch that planted a thousand churches in Ethiopia.

These ministries of Crossroads and of Calvary are commendable and serve as good examples from which we can learn. We can ask, however, whether the local churches planted at such a distance are realistically sustainable. Do they represent healthy communities of faith? Do they enhance and empower the life of the existing church, or do they in effect work against it? Also, it would be good to know how the churches planted in this manner are counted. Was it by the number of church buildings or by the number of pastors being paid by these U.S. megachurches?

I know a number of cases in which missionaries have claimed to have planted churches but really were counting the number of local pastors on their payroll. One missionary reported that he had started 200 churches, but this figure was actually the number of local pastors that he was financially supporting. Some missionaries advertise the cost of a church building in their mission field and then try to find supporters for such buildings. The number of buildings erected through such efforts then is counted as the number of churches planted.

Biblically, however, the church is a spiritual building that God, the master builder, constructs, using the people of the church as the building materials (Eph. 2:20–22). It is joined together and rises (v. 21, present tense), and is being built together (v. 22—again, present tense) to become a holy place (lit. "holy temple") in the Lord. It is being built into a spiritual house, with Jesus Christ as the living stone, or cornerstone (1 Peter 2:4–6). The glory of God resides in such a spiritual house. The reason God's glory resides in the church is that the people of God are willing to participate in the glorious suffering of Jesus Christ (John 1:14; Rom. 8:17).[1] Without participating in this suffering in their attempt to build local churches, how can we help them experience the glory of God?

SEPARATE VS. COOPERATIVE WORK

Pastor Wiles created a new denomination, the Crossroads Community International Fellowship (CCIF), an expansion of his own church, and he became a bishop who supervised other pastors within his church. Is it possible that by separating himself in this manner, he is fostering the division of the church, not its unity? It seems that he illustrates the weakest point within the Protestant church, which is the tendency we have to be endlessly divided, to promote denominationalism.

It is not surprising, or even necessarily wrong, that there will

1. By faith, John the Apostle knew that Jesus was God incarnate and that he was the Christ to suffer on the cross. The glory mentioned in John 1:14 refers to the glory of God returning to the temple, as prophesied by the prophet Ezekiel (Ezek. 43:4–5). The temple filled with the glory of God is the glory of Jesus Christ who came to earth as the temple (John 2:19–21) and who suffered and died on the cross. From the beginning, the glory of God resided on the atonement cover of the ark where the judgment of God and the grace of God met together (Ex. 25:22; 40:34)— this is the same glory as that through the cross of Jesus Christ. The glory that John saw was this glory.

be a kind of competition among churches, divisions of churches, or great numbers of theological institutions. For the sake of elevating Christ, however, the church as a whole should do all it can to strengthen unity and cooperation among churches. We need to guard thoughtfully against excess competition in our mission efforts, including unnecessary raising of funds to support duplicate ministries.

The Korea World Missions Association (KWMA) has often tried to relocate missionaries to respond to specific needs and demands on mission fields. It has been largely frustrated in such efforts, however, because of individualism among Korean churches. Harmonious ministries in missions are possible when all churches unite together and submit their own agendas to the effectiveness of the larger cause of Christ. Would Pastor Wiles's ministries have been more effective had he worked together with his denomination and with other mission agencies?

PREPARATION FOR SHORT-TERM MISSION TRIPS

Approximately 18 percent of Crossroads church members have taken at least one mission trip. They have participated in medical missions, prison ministry, feeding programs, youth ministry, and efforts involving clergy support and training. Twice a year, Pastor Wiles leads small work teams on mission trips. I believe that the direct participation of church members in missions benefits not only those who participate but also the whole church community. Is there a way other local churches could share in some of these types of experiences? Such partnership might go a long way toward making other local churches more missional.

The impact of short-term mission trips, however, depends on proper preparation for ministry. The trips mentioned above seem not to require a great deal of preparation. SamKwang Presbyterian Church, where I serve as a pastor, also sponsors mission trips. We choose one or two mission fields a year, from mission works both within and outside of the country. For the foreign mission field ministries, we train mission participants for about six months. We have a general mission-training course for three months, followed by sessions focusing on the specific mission field for another three months.

Both mission participants and the missionaries who receive them seem to be satisfied with the contributions of these mission participants. We have many ministries, yet we tend to emphasize programs for children. Participants in our programs sense that in this way they are contributing directly to the future of the receiving countries.

RELATIONS BETWEEN MISSION AGENCIES AND LOCAL CHURCHES

Thumma mentions that the goal of Crossroads's mission efforts is not to make churches in mission fields dependent on them. The church expects local churches in the mission fields to grow on their own. To this end, care must be taken to promote relationships of mutual understanding among the various churches.

Harold Fuller, a former director of SIM in Nigeria, wrote *Mission-Church Dynamics* (William Carey Library, 1980), in which he explained the relationship between SIM, an international mission agency, and ECWA, a fellowship of churches in Nigeria. He explained the relationship between the mission agency and the local church using the term "4P," which stands for the sequence of relations that the (foreign) mission agency has with the (local) churches and denomination: Pioneer, Parent, Partner, Participant. After Fuller left Nigeria, the churches in Nigeria demanded that the missionaries participate in various ministries under the leadership of ECWA. This demand led to a certain amount of misunderstanding and conflict. Eventually, however, the two sides agreed to have an interdependent relationship, each recognizing the other and working together on an equal basis.

Most mission agencies, however, expect local churches to be independent, with perhaps exceptions for certain core, decision-making issues, such as financial decisions. But such exceptions indicate that true independence has not been achieved. We are able to empower local church leadership only by giving up our own power.

PURSUING TRUE ACCOUNTABILITY

Thumma uses Crossroads to address the issue of a megachurch's missional accountability. He notes that Crossroads has forged multiple partnerships with church members, the people it serves, and partnering organizations in its attempts to ensure that the megachurch be held accountable. The writer correctly questions whether we can expect full accountability from people who are inextricably intertwined with the church in this way.

To the extent that megachurches maintain partnerships with others by giving, teaching, and governing unilaterally, it will be difficult, if not impossible, to develop true mutual partnership, in which other local churches evaluate current ministries and propose new ones. In such a climate, the local churches may find it difficult to have effective and future-oriented working relationships.

Regardless of the one-sided nature of financial contributions and their resulting influence, megachurches and their various partners need to work at cultivating relationships with equal rights and finding ways each side may hold the other accountable. For example, the sending countries of SIM gave up their signatory rights to form the international mission board of SIM, which now includes representatives from all SIM entities, including the traditional mission fields. SIM is trying to transform the structure of missions from below, without giving special place to the financial contributions and influence of the missionary-sending countries. We cannot predict the difficulties that might lie ahead for this arrangement, but such equal partnerships and healthy relationships of accountability give hope for fruitful, long-term mission growth.

3

Bible Study 1. The First Megachurch in the Bible: A Lesson from Acts 2

Eiko Takamizawa

Greetings in the name of Jesus Christ from the Japanese church.

Churches in Japan have been struggling with their minority status for more than half a century; evangelical Christians compose a mere 0.3 percent of the population. The membership of Yamato Calvary Chapel, Japan's largest church today, is 1,400. Therefore, I ask you to add one or two more zeroes for the sake of comparing it with Korean churches. This change in number will help you to realize that, in Japan, Yamato Calvary Chapel is considered to be a very big church indeed!

Even though its membership is small by Korean standards, Yamato Calvary Chapel stands as a megachurch in Japan. In terms of its outreach programs, nurturing and education programs, media ministries, social services, and so forth, it is one of the country's most active churches.

When we read Scripture, we find that the first church in the New Testament was also a megachurch, one similar in size to the Japanese one—3,000 members. Acts 2:41 reads, "So those who received his word were baptized, and there were added that day about three thousand souls."[1] This happened on the day of

1. Unless otherwise noted, quotations from the Bible in this chapter are from the English Standard Version.

Pentecost; therefore, we find that the first church in history was a megachurch. I would like us to turn to the Book of Acts to revisit this first megachurch to learn what today's megachurch should be and should do in terms of mission.

THE FOUNDATION OF THE MEGACHURCH: THE CROSS AND THE RESURRECTION OF JESUS CHRIST

The first church was born during the festival of Pentecost, seven weeks after the crucifixion and resurrection of Jesus Christ. This timing is important if we are to understand the foundation of the church, which consists of the apostles' teaching, the advent of the Holy Spirit, and the church as shaped and guided by the Holy Spirit.

The apostles' teaching. Because of the cross of Jesus Christ, all of humanity's sins are now covered by his redemption, and the curse of death has ended. In the forty days following his resurrection, Jesus appeared to his disciples on different occasions and showed that he truly had triumphed over death. On the cross Jesus recaptured all authority in heaven and earth, on the basis of which he later gave the Great Commission to his disciples (Matt. 28:18). Then Jesus ascended into heaven right before his disciples. Only ten days later, during the festival of Pentecost, the disciples experienced the outpouring of the Holy Spirit. Peter connected the two incidents in the one scheme of God's salvation plan, "Being therefore exalted at the right hand of God, and having received from the Father the promise of the Holy Spirit, he has poured out this that you yourselves are seeing and hearing" (Acts 2:33). The order in his explanation is important: the accomplishment of redemption, the resurrection of Jesus Christ, and his ascension were together the necessary conditions for the descent of the Holy Spirit.

The very core of the Gospel as described by Paul is "that Christ died for our sins in accordance with the Scriptures, that he was buried, that he was raised on the third day in accordance with the Scriptures, and that he appeared to Cephas, then to the twelve" (1 Cor. 15:3–5). Good Tidings to be carried to the end of the earth were the words of the witnesses of the death and resurrection of

Jesus the Messiah. The church was founded upon the witnesses of history. These witnesses are those who had seen and experienced certain incidents. It is not merely a story.

The Christian view of deity was totally different from that observed in the Hellenistic world. The pantheon found in Greek mythologies was much more reflective of human nature, which includes anger, jealousy, eros, hatred, betrayal, conflicts, revenge, and so forth.[2] Christian belief in the Creator God who, out of nothing, creates all that is, and in the incarnation of the wholly benevolent God in Christ, who died for human sin, was unheard of.

One value of the New Testament is that each book is the witness of people who experienced the Messiah. Scholars believe that either 1 Thessalonians or Galatians was the first book of the New Testament to be written. These epistles were composed as early as A.D. 48, less than twenty years after the resurrection. Witnesses to the resurrected Christ were yet alive, and the New Testament contains the record of witnesses who heard, saw, and experienced the teaching and power of Jesus Christ (1 John 1:1–4). Moreover, the disciples spread what they witnessed to both Jews and Gentiles at the risk of their lives. In this sense the New Testament is a trustworthy witness (see diagram 3.1).

The response: confession of sin and repentance. After the descent of the Holy Spirit on Pentecost, Peter preached to the Jews, focusing on their sin. He pointed out that the Jews looked to their ancestor King David as the source of their identity, even though they should have grounded their identity in Abraham, who listened to God's voice and obeyed. Abraham's act of faith was counted by God as righteousness (Rom. 4:22), and God established him and his descendants as God's covenant nation. Abraham received three kinds of blessings: (1) for himself and those who bless him, (2) for his offspring as a nation, and (3) for the nations through them. He and the nation descended from him were called to be a channel of blessing for the nations. At the time of Jesus Christ, the Jews were not mindful of this third promise. They identified

2. "Gods and Men in Greek Religion," http://faculty.gvsu.edu/webst erm/gods&men.htm.

more with their political ancestor, King David, who made great conquests in ruling over the Promised Land. The result was an attitude of elitism on the part of the Jews, based on their status as a chosen nation. Especially after a long period of political subjugation and exile among the Gentile nations, Jewish hopes were focused more in the political realm than the spiritual, and more on this world than on the kingdom of God. Peter therefore points out that the Jews' focus on King David was misplaced, for he was merely a human king. The real King, the Messiah, is the one whom David worshipped in the Psalms. Peter declares that Jesus Christ is the Messiah and that the Jews had killed him.

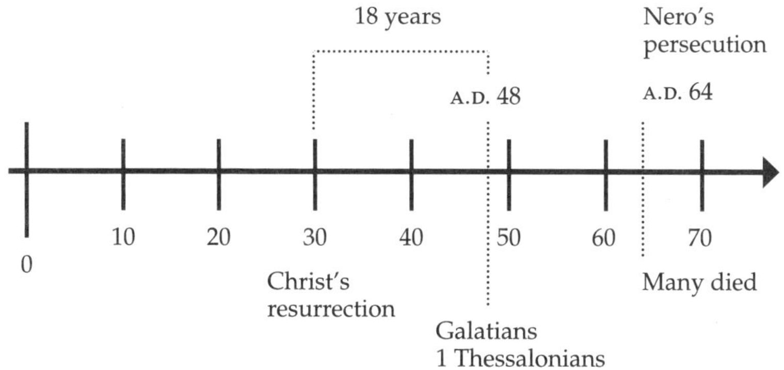

Diagram 3.1. New Testament witness to Christ's resurrection

We can understand the anguish of the Jews who were convicted by this accusation. They were guilty not just of homicide, but of murdering the Messiah, for whom all Jews throughout history had been waiting. Probably many of them could well remember the mob's shout "Crucify him!" in which they had joined. Now, listening to Peter's message, they clearly understood that the Messiah died because of their sin. In fact, Peter, the preacher himself, knew that Jesus died because of him, and his sense of guilt must have been even greater. He was the disciple closest to Jesus, having witnessed and experienced a number of the miracles that Jesus performed: he experienced the unexpected harvest in the Sea of Galilee, his mother-in-law was healed of a fever, he distributed bread and fish for 5,000, he walked on the sea when Jesus called, he saw Moses and Elijah on top of the mountain, and he had his feet washed by Jesus at the Last Supper. Yet, he denied Jesus three times, saying, "I don't know him!" Oh, the feelings of guilt that must have washed over him!

Now, however, Peter boldly preaches to the Jews and even accuses them of having killed the Messiah on the cross. The change in Peter proves that he is one who has had firsthand experience of the forgiveness of sin and of freedom after receiving the Holy Spirit. Listening to Peter, the Jewish people were convicted of their sin of rejecting God's covenant and killing his Son. They also understood, however, that on the cross Jesus made atonement for so grave a sin.

Christians today, too, are often tempted to focus on worldly things. To do so is the substance of idolatry. People depend on visible things, not on the invisible God. Christopher Wright points to power and pride, popularity and success, and wealth and greed as the three primary idols among the evangelicals. He calls for repentance and a radical return to God by changing our lives to ones of humility, integrity and simplicity.[3]

THE BIRTH OF THE MEGACHURCH: THE ADVENT OF THE HOLY SPIRIT

The advent of the Holy Spirit on Pentecost. The early church has its roots in Pentecost. After Jesus' ascension, the disciples were severely persecuted by the Roman government, as well as by the Jews. The apostles and 120 disciples gathered in one place and were praying. They must have been frightened, imagining that they might be captured next. The disciples who had witnessed Jesus on the cross, however, were no longer the same disciples who had left Jesus in the garden. Now, in the midst of high tension, they must have waited with strong faith and expectation until they were "clothed with power from on high" (Luke 24:49). Eventually, their prayers were heard, and a special event occurred on the Day of Pentecost.

Pentecost (Feast of Weeks) is celebrated after the barley harvest, at the beginning of the wheat harvest. A joyful time

3. Christopher Wright, "Confronting Idols," Lausanne Cape Town 2010, Plenary Session 2, www.youtube.com/watch?v=gZ57kCNQ6oQ.

of celebrating new blessings, it was thus a most appropriate day to expect new blessings. When the disciples were gathered in one place, praying with one another, there came from heaven a sound like a mighty rushing wind that filled the entire house. Divided tongues as of fire appeared to them and rested on each of them. They were all filled with the Holy Spirit and began to speak in other tongues. The sound rippled through the walls of the house, and the Jews who were outside came rushing up, wondering what was happening. From this narrative we learn that what had happened was not some sort of psychological phenomena that only the people inside of the house experienced. The sound physically reverberated to the outside. The people who gathered were "devout men from every nation under heaven" (Acts 2:5), that is, returning Diaspora Jews or Jews who were on pilgrimage. They must have been astonished to hear these people from Galilee (uneducated people with strong dialects) speaking in the languages of their current foreign places of residence. Nowhere had such an event been heard or seen. A new blessing, this was the start of a new age marked by the replacement of the law by the power of the Holy Spirit.

Removing the barrier. In one sense, language differences are a cultural barrier, but they are also political barriers. According to the Joshua Project (http://joshuaproject.net), the world contains approximately 9,700 people groups. Accepting other people from across linguistic, cultural, and political divides is often difficult, posing the risk of conflict. The root of this problem can be traced to the Tower of Babel, where humankind united in an effort to rebel against God. God divided their language and culture so as to prevent people from uniting to do evil. Once redemption had been accomplished through the Messiah, the barriers of language and culture could be removed once again through the Spirit of God. The event of Pentecost gave an eschatological glimpse of the day when all nations will bow down before the Lamb, worshipping in all tongues. Thus, humanity's history of conflict and aggression that began at the Tower of Babel was in effect declared to be at an end, through the Holy Spirit, who establishes unity in the midst of diversity, a feat only possible by God's promise of peace. Pentecost was the day when redemption was declared to all nations.

Pentecost was an event representative of and necessary for the building of God's kingdom by God's people. This miraculous experience indicated that God's redemptive plan will cover all nations, as attested to by the diversity of languages spoken by the disciples from Galilee. In Acts 2, a multitude of people gathered on the Day of Pentecost; they were "Parthians and Medes and Elamites and residents of Mesopotamia, Judea and Cappadocia, Pontus and Asia, Phrygia and Pamphylia, Egypt and the parts of Libya belonging to Cyrene, and visitors from Rome, both Jews and proselytes, Cretans and Arabians" (Acts 2:9–11).

Parthians came from the portion of Persia along the Caspian Sea. Medes were from current Iran, and Elamites lived along Iran's Persian Gulf coast. Mesopotamia was the region watered by the Tigris and Euphrates Rivers. Cappadocia, Pontus, Asia, Phrygia, and Pamphylia are encompassed by current Turkey and nearby countries. Egypt, Libya, and Cyrene, in North Africa, border the Mediterranean Sea. In addition, people were present from Rome, the island of Crete, and the Arabian Peninsula, as well as Jews from Judea. The people in Jerusalem during Pentecost were potential messengers to the world's diverse civilizations at that time (see diagram 3.2).[4] The miraculous work of God, which happened in a small region of Judea, during a traditional Jewish feast, spread beyond the Jewish cultural boundary to the ends of the world, sparking a dramatic leap forward in God's salvific plan.

To each one of them. The manifestation of the Holy Spirit was accompanied with a sound like a mighty rushing wind that shook the entire house, and with tongues of fire that rested on everyone in the house. The Holy Spirit rested on them, not as a group, but on the 120 disciples of Christ one by one. The result that day was a massive conversion of 3,000 people. The early church was founded on the disciples' experience of God and the pouring out of the Holy Spirit upon each saint.

Peter quotes Joel, who prophesied that, on the day of the Lord, God would pour out his Spirit on all flesh, the sons and the

4. See Noboru Yamaguchi, "Shitono Hataraki" [Acts of the apostles], in *Shin Seisho Chukai* [New Bible commentary], vol. 2, *Acts to Ephesians*, ed. Yoshio Masuda et al. (Tokyo: Inochino Kotobasha, 1986).

daughters would prophesy, and the old men would dream dreams (Joel 2:28). This verse does not indicate that the Spirit would be poured out based on some religious rank, such as priests or Pharisees, and neither would the pouring out of the Spirit be based on the tribes, such as Judah or Benjamin. The verse simply states that the Spirit would be poured out on sons and daughters, even on male and female servants, ignoring all human-made barriers. The

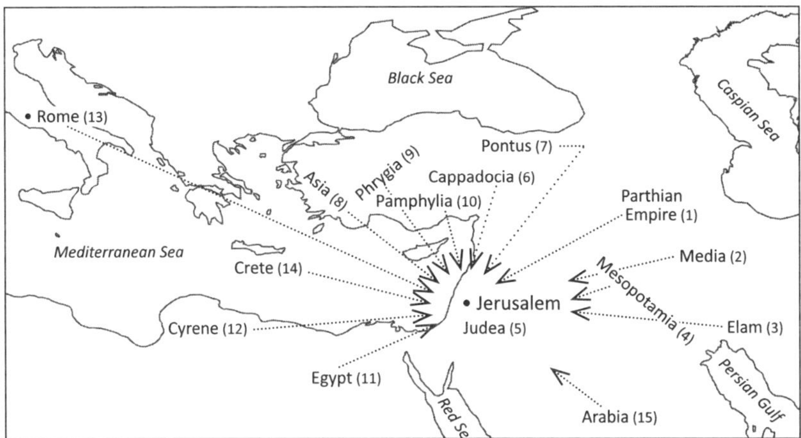

Diagram 3.2. Peoples and languages present at Pentecost

Note: The numbers in parentheses refer to the order in which the locations are mentioned in Acts 2:9–11.

Spirit of God is poured out regardless of geographic, ethnic, religious, or social divisions; all people will be given the mission of achieving God's purpose by his Spirit. Today we need to examine ourselves whether we are acknowledging this work of the Holy Spirit. When the church is becoming increasingly institutionalized, social success can become a great hindrance.

CHARACTERISTICS OF THE MEGACHURCH BORN OF THE HOLY SPIRIT

Let us look now at the characteristics of a church that is filled with the Holy Spirit.

Disciple-making. Acts 2:41 reads, "So those who received his word were baptized, and there were added [to the church] that day about three thousand souls." The 3,000 were made members of the group of "disciples" by being baptized and being taught to keep all that Jesus commanded to be done. In the final words of the Great Commission, Jesus used four verbs, "go," "make disciples," "baptize," and "teach" (Matt. 28:19–20). Among these four verbs, "make disciples" is the main verb; the other three are participles. Christ's Great Commission is not to build churches, but to make disciples. Therefore, all Christians and leaders have to focus on this point of making committed followers of Jesus. Now, just as the apostles and earlier followers of Jesus had learned about the attributes of God and the values of his kingdom, the new members needed to learn how to deal with opposition and persecution, how to fight against the temptations of this worldly wealth and greed, how to use social power and authority as good managers according to the Master's word, and how to prepare for the Last Day, when the Master returns (Luke 12).

Today, churches with huge numbers of members seem to spend a large amount of time and effort on providing better and better programs, events with good music, entertaining performances, service programs, appealing evangelistic campaigns, and so forth. In this trend, since megachurches require their ministers to prepare many programs, can they possibly have enough time for discipling people? The same problem can be seen in some charismatic churches. By focusing on certain aspects of the Christian faith, charismatic churches can run the risk of losing a holistic approach toward discipleship. The charismatic gifts need to be used for the purpose of building disciples of Jesus Christ. In his article "The Flaw of the Excluded Middle," Paul Hiebert analyzes Christian faith using a three-layered framework: other world/invisible, this world/invisible, and this world/visible. Hiebert points out that Western Christianity, which has been influenced by Greek philosophy, tends to view reality dichotomously and too often has excluded Hiebert's middle layer: this world/invisible (see diagram 3.3). Usually animists are concerned about things that belong to this middle layer. Charismatic movements that have a similar focus on the realm of this world/invisible are criticized as being Christo-paganism. When we consider, however, that Jesus focused on healing and delivering from evil spirits in his own and his disciples' ministries, we should see that these concerns are an important part of Christian ministry. So as to raise up balanced disciples, Christians must not neglect the top and bottom layers of the faith. In discipleship we should seek to prevent any reductionism that veers away from a complete view of Christian faith.

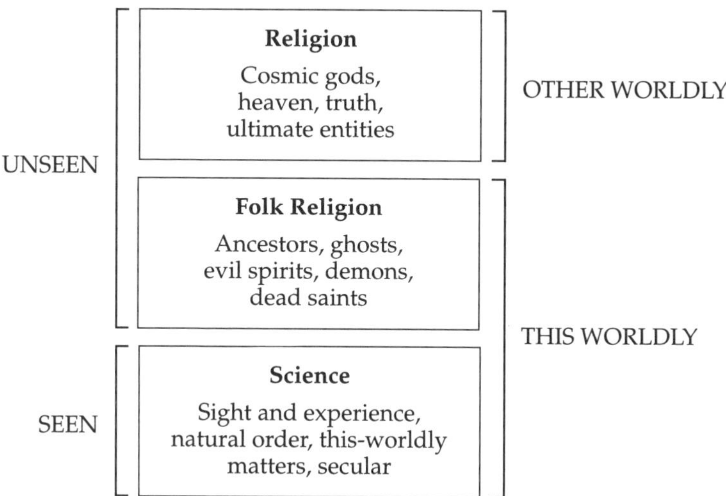

Diagram 3.3. Analytic framework for analysis of religious systems

Note: Adapted from Paul Hiebert.

Building ecclesia. The disciples, filled with the Holy Spirit, devoted themselves to what the apostles taught (Acts 2:42). Christian values, worldviews, ethical views, views of humans, perspectives on death and life after death, and so forth are all so different from what this world teaches. This difference eventually creates discomfort and hatred among non-believers. The people of this world have rejected Jesus Christ, and they do the same for his disciples.

Being based on God's truth, what Jesus taught his disciples was different from the teaching of other religions. This concern for the truth is Christianity's fundamental difference from the other religions in postmodernity. The denial of absolute truth leads to spiritual confusion and gives rise to the spiritual phenomena of our age. Postmodern spirituality privileges individualism, relativism, and pluralism, which leads to the ultimate idolatry of deifying human beings. Under such influences, Christianity, which upholds absolute truth, and the absolute God are rejected, and Christ's followers may be persecuted. Religion or ethics that eliminates the absolute standard lacks a proper moral axis and will go astray. Individual belief and preference are taken as personal truth. Christians may find themselves accused of being fundamentally conservative. To be a disciple of Jesus carries with it the danger of being rejected and persecuted by society. The Greek word for church, *ekklēsia,* comes from a word meaning to call out or choose. The church is a gathering of the chosen ones. If Christians are not different from people of this world, they cannot form a true ecclesia.

On three occasions since 2008, I have conducted street interviews in Seoul. Each time I interviewed approximately 200 nonchurchgoers, asking about their views of Christians and Christian churches. I discovered that more than 95 percent of those who were not churchgoers had negative views of Christians. The most common reason was the hypocritical lifestyle of church members. The second most common reason was the lack of any difference between the church and the world. Human competition and conflict were seen in the church just as they are in the secular world. Several asked, "If church is the same as the secular world, why should I go to church?" Christians are called to be different from the world as the salt of the earth and the light of the world (Matt. 5:13–16; Mark 9:48–50; Luke 14:34–35). The letter to Diognetus, written about 129 C.E., records the common view of Christians in those days:

> They live in their own countries, but only as aliens. They have a share in everything as citizens, and endure everything as foreigners. . . . They marry, like everyone else, and they beget children but they do not cast out their offspring. They share their board with each other, but not their marriage bed. It is true that they are in the flesh, but they do not live according to the flesh. They busy themselves on earth, but their citizenship is in heaven.[5]

5. Norman E. Thomas, ed., *Classic Texts in Mission and World Christianity: A Reader's Companion to David Bosch's* Transforming Mission (Maryknoll, N.Y.: Orbis Books, 1995), 5.

The early Christians were known for living differently from secular people, which bore witness to the indwelling Spirit of Jesus Christ.

Forming koinonia. Scripture describes the church as a body with Christ as its head. The church is an organic system to which each organ contributes, and all function together as a whole. This organic relationship within the church is called *koinonia,* practicing faith with personal fellowship, encouragement, sharing of burdens, confessing sins and forgiving one another, and serving together.

The most significant element of the early church's koinonia was "the breaking of bread" together. This phrase can be understood as a general sharing of the table or as keeping the Communion to remember their Master, as Jesus had instructed at the Last Supper. There can be no doubt that they took the meaning of the ritual seriously after witnessing the death and resurrection of Jesus Christ and the outpouring of the Holy Spirit. As they gathered again at the table of the Lord in spirit, all problems such as conflicts, hatred, and unforgiveness could be eased, and the fellowship of the forgiven sinners could be renewed.

Where the presence of his Spirit was, there were works of the Lord. "And awe came upon every soul, and many wonders and signs were being done through the apostles." (Acts 2:43). Jesus Christ had already demonstrated signs and wonders and had expressed his authority, power, and love to the people. Beginning from the miracle of changing the water into wine and going on to the great harvest in the sea, calming of the storm, and walking on the water, Jesus proved that he is the Creator of all of nature. His healing of the sick and raising of the dead back to life proved that he is the one who is above sin and its consequences. His deliverance of people from demons proved that he is the sovereign Lord in the spiritual realm. The koinonia, or organic relationship shared in the early church, was the fellowship of disciples who live in both the kingdom of heaven and this world, who can experience both the natural and supernatural.

Knowing that life in this world is a temporary journey, the Christians were able to detach themselves from worldly greed.

When some members were persecuted and their property was confiscated or when they were chased from their houses and livelihood, the koinonia helped them by sharing goods, distributing according to the needs of the people.

Today, many discuss the problem caused by what I call the "gap-widening society," that is, the spreading divide between the few who are well off and the many who do not have much. This problem is closely related to selfishness in human nature. God knew that people had this sinful tendency, and he made rules to solve the problem of gap-widening among his people, including canceling of debts every seven years and returning purchased land to the original owner in the year of Jubilee. In the Holy Spirit–filled koinonia of the early church, the disciples gladly shared their property with the most needy people in their community.

The disciples met together in the temple daily for worship and prayer. For the disciples the temple was not a commercial square. The temple was the place for prayer, as King Solomon of old had dedicated it, and as Jesus Christ claimed in his cleansing of the temple. The disciples, filled with the Spirit, gathered there with a genuine purpose of worship and prayer. No political and economic purposes were intertwined.

After worshiping at the temple, the disciples gathered together in homes for fellowship, which included the breaking of bread. The ritual instituted by Jesus was held during house fellowship, rather than in the temple itself. As there were no offices of ordained ministers at that time, it is possible that the Communion was served by informal leaders of the fellowship. The leading role possibly was taken by father figures present within the house fellowship. Through the Communion service, the family structure, especially the father's role, may have been enhanced. Members were able to be accountable to each other. With such mutual support, the Christians in the early church survived hardship and persecution. Rather than being overwhelmed by opposition, the early church as koinonia and ecclesia was actually a sign of hope for those who were seeking and waiting for the good news that brings all God's children to his kingdom.

CONCLUSION

The early church was built on the foundation of the Gospel: our redemption from our sin by the Messiah on the cross, and his triumph over death in his resurrection. Only when Jews recognized their sins and their need for salvation through Jesus Christ, were they ready to receive the Holy Spirit. On the day of Pentecost, the Holy Spirit came down on earth and manifested his sovereignty and power. By breaking down the barriers of language, the Holy Spirit revealed God's intention to save the whole world and equipped the church to carry the Gospel to the ends of the earth. The church became his instrument and was witness of God's sovereignty, power, and love. When the church proclaimed and demonstrated God's character and power in its life, people were attracted and joined the group of disciples. May we as the church in our day make certain of our standing on these foundations, obeying the call to make disciples of Jesus and living as his witnesses as we pray and work, always looking for fresh evidence of the Holy Spirit at work.

4

The Accountability of Megachurches in Missions: Onnuri Church, Seoul

Jae Hoon Lee, Daniel S. H. Ahn, and Tae Kyung Ham

When Yong Jo Ha, founding pastor of Onnuri Church in Seoul, began the church in October 1985, he envisioned merging the functions of a local church and a parachurch organization (i.e., a modality and a sodality), thereby giving birth to an all-new "missional church."[1] Though Pastor Ha was working independently, the vision of a missional church that he espoused had much in common with the view articulated by Roland Allen early in the twentieth century. Allen had argued that the functions of the local church and of mission societies had been unnaturally separated.

> We may compare the relationship of the [mission] societies to the [local] Church with the institution of divorce in relation to marriage. Just as divorce was permitted for the hardness of men's hearts because they were unable to observe the divine institution of marriage in its original perfection, so the organization of missionary societies was permitted for the hardness of our hearts, because we had lost the power to appreciate and to use the divine organization of the Church in its simplicity for the purpose for which it was first created.[2]

1. See Yong Jo Ha, *I, Yong Jo Ha, Have Dedicated My Life to Missions* [in Korean] (Seoul: Duranno, 2008). The language of modalities and sodalities comes from Ralph D. Winter, "The Two Structures of God's Redemptive Mission," in *Perspectives on the World Christian Movement*, ed. Ralph D. Winter and Steven C. Hawthorne (Pasadena, Calif.: William Carey Library, 2009), 244–53.

2. Roland Allen, *The Spontaneous Expansion of the Church—and the Causes Which Hinder It* (Cambridge, Eng.: Lutterworth, 2006; orig. 1927), 117.

Note that Roland Allen did not simply want churches to form their own mission societies in the sense that churches might provide for a department or division that saw to it that the church's missionary responsibilities were carried out.[3] He was advocating that the churches themselves be missional through and through. Onnuri Church, in a noteworthy manner, has combined the two aspects of modality and sodality from its very beginning. Within two months the church had begun supporting an international mission organization, and by 1992 Tyrannus International Mission (TIM) had been established, which sent out missionaries from Onnuri Church and from other local churches.[4] In 1994 Yong Jo Ha announced his vision of sending out 2,000 missionaries and established the "2000 Missions Headquarters," working to mobilize parishioners to go into mission fields.[5] Between 1996 and 1999, fifteen unreached people groups in eleven countries were adopted by the church and paired with various groups within Onnuri that focused on tribal missions. To facilitate cross-cultural mission training for short- and long-term missionaries, the Onnuri Mission Training Center was opened in June 1996. In 2002 it was rechristened the Onnuri World Mission Center, and then in 2010, the Acts29 Vision Village, each time with increased scope and scale.[6]

By 2015, its thirtieth anniversary, Onnuri Church had 111,000

3. Ibid., 117–18.

4. See Sungmo Moon, *The Story of Pastor Yong Jo Ha* [in Korean] (Seoul: Duranno, 2010), 197, and Onnuri Church, *Talk and Talk: Twenty-Five Years of Onnuri Church* [in Korean] (Seoul: Onnuri Church, 2010), 76. Although TIM was christened in 1992, its roots can be found in the gathering of eight families in July 1988 to begin intercessory prayer for missions (Moon, *Story of Pastor Yong Jo Ha*, 108).

5. In 1994, when Pastor Ha announced his vision of sending out 2,000 missionaries and 10,000 lay ministers, the church had a membership of between 6,000 and 7,000. As the main body of Onnuri missions, the 2000 Missions Headquarters connects the various mission groups within Onnuri, organizing and mobilizing mission resources, as well as implementing mission strategy.

6. Acts29 Vision Village is a missionary training center, a missionary academy, a place for missionaries on sabbatical to recharge and for parishioners to upgrade their ministry skills (Onnuri Church, *Talk and Talk*, 34–40).

registered members and an average weekly attendance of about 75,000. Pastor Ha died in August 2011, and Jae Hoon Lee replaced him as the church's second head pastor, opening a new era in the evolution of Onnuri's vision. In this chapter we assess the past thirty years of Onnuri's cross-cultural mission engagement. To produce one missionary, six "ingredients" are required: (1) human and financial resources, (2) training programs and facilities, (3) the development of professionalism on the mission field, (4) member care, (5) mission resources beyond Onnuri, and (6) self-missiologizing. We will look in turn at the issue of Onnuri Church's mission accountability in each of these six areas.

HUMAN AND FINANCIAL RESOURCES

Internal use of resources in missions. Megachurches clearly have significantly more internal human and financial resources than do ordinary local churches. They thus have a greater responsibility to be effective in mobilizing these resources for missions, something for which an approach uniting church and mission (i.e., uniting modality and sodality) is better suited than is a traditional "mission committee" approach.[7] A joint church-mission structure has greater ability to actually mobilize human resources, such as engaging members in giving mission-pledged offerings in addition to regular offerings. Mission organizations (sodalities) that are not connected with a local church find it difficult to rally material or human resources, and most seek manpower and financial support from local churches. Onnuri Church, in contrast, being founded as a missional church, has found it relatively easy to gather and mobilize financial and human resources for missions.[8] The head pastor's passion for missions and the congregation's structure uniting church and mission are conducive for motivating parishioners to support missions.

7. "Mobilize" and "mobilization" refer broadly to the process of motivating, recruiting, nurturing, training, and sending out.

8. Duranno Press, founded in December 1980, can be considered the precursor to Pastor Ha's "missional church." Ha spent three years (1981–1984) at John Stott's London Institute, where he focused on how to integrate the Gospel and society and developed his plan for a missional church (Moon, *Story of Pastor Yong Jo Ha*, 101–8).

A listing of the ministries launched by Onnuri indicates the scope of the church's engagement in mission. They include Duranno Press, which brings the Word of God into the everyday lives of Onnuri's congregation, as well as the lives of parishioners of other Korean churches. The church uses 2000 Missions Headquarters and TIM not only to recruit parishioners into missions but also to provide resources and ongoing support for them. A prime example is the annual special offering from the entire Onnuri congregation that is pledged during the first Sunday service each January in support of 2000 Missions Headquarters and TIM, as well as other cross-cultural missions.[9] As of January 2015, Onnuri Church had 854 cross-cultural missionaries in 70 countries, 423 of them being TIM missionaries. Since 2003, Onnuri Church has established branch churches in China, Japan, and the United States through Acts29.[10] In December 2006, using the U.S. branch church, or vision church, as a foundation, TIM mobilized missions focused on the Korean diaspora, leading eventually to the founding of TIMA (TIM America) in order to better serve the Latin American community.[11] TIMJ (TIM Japan), arising out of the vision church in Japan, followed in 2010. Since 2012, regional chapters have been steadily established throughout the Middle East–Africa region.

9. In January 2014 a total of 26,751 Onnuri parishioners pledged 10.96 billion KRW (US$9.96 million) to missions. Onnuri Church used these funds to provide $4.85 million toward the support of short- and long-term missionaries and scholarships for their children; $3.56 million toward the support of overseas mission pioneers, North Korean ministry, and immigrant ministry; $1.25 million toward partnerships between domestic and foreign organizations; and $0.30 million toward mission resource mobilization, schools, seminars, and similar activities.

10. The vision for Acts29 is to share Onnuri Church's evangelistic philosophy with churches in Korea. Pastor Ha summarized Onnuri Church's identity and the character of an Acts29 church as "a healthy church that reproduces churches," "a church that disperses to evangelize," and "a church that plants churches in the mission field" (Onnuri Church, *Talk and Talk*, 209–11).

11. Onnuri is a multi-site church. The seven Onnuri churches in Korea are referred to as "campus churches" and those in other parts of the world as "vision churches." By 2015 thirty vision churches were present in seven different countries. The term "vision church" means that we share the same vision for mission.

In 2005 the church founded Christian Global Network TV (CGNTV), with the goal of delivering quality Christian content to Korean missionaries and diaspora in every corner of the globe.[12] CGNTV partners with Better World (2010), Onnuri's international development NGO, and the church's Christian Medical Network (CMN) to deliver the Gospel.[13] In addition, it provides support to other cross-cultural missions such as Biblical Education by Extension (BEE) and the Society for World Internet Mission (SWIM).

Accountability to other churches and mission organizations. Many Korean churches have recently been experiencing a decline in their rate of growth, leading to congregations feeling overtaxed. The level of giving for missionaries in many local churches has declined, which has made it difficult for missionary candidates to find churches able to support them.[14] Megachurches therefore have a duty to provide human and financial resources to ordinary-sized local churches and to parachurch organizations.

Onnuri Church and TIM currently send out and support missionaries from other churches and organizations. They do so following a careful review process.[15] They also recommend internally chosen missionary candidates to suitable churches and organizations in need of personnel, effectively sending out Onnuri Church missionaries through outside mission organizations. The church supports outside mission organizations financially, in 2014 providing around US$1.26 million to sixty-four outside mission organizations. Despite these steps, Onnuri Church and TIM are widely perceived as focusing on their own internal mission mobilization and failing to provide significant financial and human resources to other organizations. TIM needs to break free of its image as being an arm of Onnuri Church and, instead, to become recognized as an interdenominational mission organization in its own right.

12. See Onnuri Church, *Talk and Talk*, 219.

13. Better World is dedicated to bringing unity to conflict areas around the globe. Launched in 2010, CMN is an evolution of Onnuri Church's medical missions organization, created in 1989.

14. Yoonsik Choi, *2020–2040: The Future Map of the Korean Church* [in Korean] (Seoul: Lifebook Life Press, 2013).

15. Moon, *Story of Pastor Yong Jo Ha*, 108.

TRAINING PROGRAMS AND FACILITIES

Mission training programs. Megachurches have an obligation to utilize their relatively greater human and material resources to create effective cross-cultural mission training programs and to make these available to other churches and mission organizations, which typically find it difficult to produce such programs.

Onnuri Church's Acts29 Vision Village, in cooperation with outside missionary training professionals, currently runs three training programs for field missionaries: Turning Point (TP) trains short-term missionaries, Onnuri School of Mission (OSOM) trains long-term missionaries, and Home to Home provides training for missionaries on sabbatical. Upon completion of OSOM, TIM missionaries enter three months of training through TIM Spirit Training. Intensive training continues for two additional years, with service as assistant missionaries in the field. The 2000 Missions Headquarters also establishes mission training programs suitable to the context of Onnuri Church, for example, the eight-week "Why Missions?" program designed to get laypersons involved with missions or, since 2011, short-term mission projects for college students through Frontier Agency. Additionally, 2000 Missions Headquarters is also on very close terms with fifteen mission organizations that have branched out from the church.

On the downside, Onnuri's rich internal missions infrastructure can impede utilization of similar or even better outside talent and know-how, which is a typical blind spot of missional megachurches. Satisfaction with in-house programs leads to failure to consider good programs developed by others.

Screening process for missionary candidates. It is of utmost importance that candidates for cross-cultural mission service be screened carefully regarding their calling, gifts, spirituality, emotional stability, and personality. International mission organizations utilize a stringent review process that includes exams, documents, psychological tests, and interviews based on objective criteria. Candidates who are not suitable for long-term mission service are either dropped from the program or reassigned to missions in their home country.

To meet its responsibility to commission sound missionary candidates, Onnuri Church uses objective criteria in setting standards that missionary candidates must meet and selects long-term mission candidates through its Missionary Review Board. A problem Onnuri faces, however—one that plagues most church-based mission organizations—is that the selection process can be compromised by lack of objectivity in evaluating candidates. If qualified missionaries are to be commissioned, it is imperative that the mission organization be granted a certain amount of independence in selection and training.

Long-term talent development is another important part of a megachurch's ministry. Onnuri needs to look ahead ten to twenty years and cultivate the development of outstanding missionary training professionals. Qualified missionaries proven through five to ten years in the mission field and who understand Onnuri's missionary spirit should be sent to educational institutions to learn advanced methods in mission studies, international development, and related fields. Such an investment would represent a contribution to Korean cross-cultural missions, as well as to world missions in general.

Mission facilities. Though Korea World Missions Association, Mission Korea, WEC, and others have used Onnuri Church's mission facilities, Onnuri must work to make these facilities more accessible to other churches and mission organizations. Acts29 Vision Village has large- and medium-sized chapels, classrooms, meeting rooms, a library, housing, a cafeteria, office space, and more. The natural surroundings are conducive to rest and restoration of missionaries. Well equipped for holding domestic and overseas mission conferences, forums, and mission training programs, if need be, it could also be used to host a graduate school of theology.

DEVELOPING PROFESSIONALISM ON THE MISSION FIELD

Megachurches have a responsibility to build up the expertise and professionalism of missionaries on the mission field. For this purpose, Onnuri Church must actively seek to learn from international mission organizations. When compared to the manuals, assessment tools, and application procedures developed by international mission organizations, those of Onnuri Church and of Korean mission organizations in general appear to be relatively weak.

Onnuri Church also needs to cultivate expertise in cross-cultural sensitivity and language proficiency among its long-term missionaries. Coming as they do from a largely homogenous country and culture, TIM missionaries face challenges in developing these skills (a problem that is not unique to Onnuri Church's missionaries). As a result, they often encounter difficulties when working in a mission field with other organizations or churches because of cultural conflicts or problems in communication.

In taking up this responsibility, Onnuri could explore engaging young overseas Koreans who have grown up in a multicultural environment as potential missionary candidates. For example, local chapters of TIMA (TIM America) could seek out Korean-Americans who are fluent in both English and Korean as possible missionary candidates. If the Onnuri Church missionary training process was then conducted bilingually, candidates could be put through prefield cross-cultural training and language education. Similar changes could be made to TP and OSOM training, which is compulsory for Onnuri Church missionaries as well as for missionaries from external organizations who are supported by Onnuri. OSOM training is currently sixteen weeks and takes place at Acts29 Vision Village. If the program could also include a subsequent three- to six-month multicultural, multilanguage, multiethnic, and multireligion intensive training period conducted in an international city (e.g., Kuala Lumpur, Bangkok, Chiang Mai, Singapore, Abu Dhabi, Amsterdam, or London), the trainees would be much better equipped for cross-cultural missions.

Particular attention should be given to the two directions missions takes—centrifugal (we go to them) and centripetal (they come to us). In the near future the number of immigrant workers coming to Korea from different countries, including unreached areas, is expected to rise to five million. This means that Korea will become a serious cross-cultural mission field. Onnuri M Mission for foreign immigrants was founded in 1994 and Onnuri M Center was set up in 2005 to respond to this trend toward centripetal missions.[16] Furthermore, in order to stimulate more active engagement in immigrant missions, a new Onnuri M complex, completed in March 2016, has been constructed.

MEMBER CARE

At home. Lifelong member care must be provided for long-term missionaries and their children, starting from the moment they are commissioned and continuing throughout sabbaticals and even into retirement. Smaller churches and mission organizations with limited resources may have difficulty providing sabbatical housing, medical check-ups, and assistance with missionary children's university tuition. These are challenges megachurches must address. For missionaries on sabbatical Onnuri Church currently provides member care in the form of housing for thirty-two families or households and medical care through memoranda of understanding with certain clinics. Onnuri also operates rest and recuperation programs such as Healing Camp and Home to Home, and it provides scholarships to missionary kids (MKs) when they enter tertiary education.

On the mission field. Missionary member care in the field is still quite insufficient. The nature of member care requires that those who provide it have an intimate knowledge of the mission field, along with spiritual, psychological, and pastoral maturity. For this role Onnuri Church needs to nurture the development of missionaries with field experience who will be capable of delivering high-quality member care and to call on the help of member-care organizations and experts.

In member care, prevention is very important, as are precautionary programs such as overseas mobile member care that can address concerns before they grow to become major problems. With wisdom gained through experience, international mission

16. Onnuri M Center is located in Ansan, a city in Gyeonggi Province with a high population of foreign workers. The center hosts church services for twenty-one foreign-worker communities, 850 immigrants in total, including Thai, Russian, and Sri Lankan services. Beyond simply sharing the Gospel, Onnuri M Center trains leaders who can plant churches in their home countries.

organizations almost never send a single missionary family by itself to any one mission field. Rather, each region has a team, and every team has a veteran field director to care for new missionaries. Onnuri Church would profit from adopting such a policy.

Professional care of MKs is critical, as it relates directly to the next generation of the Korean church and to enlisting the next generation of missionaries. At its core, MK care is related to identity concerns (as a Korean, as a Christian) and is not limited simply to issues related to education. Still, the matter of MK education—whether by establishing MK schools in the field, offering home schooling, having children attend public schools, or sending children to boarding schools—is a huge concern that missionary families face. As it seeks to improve in the area of MK care, Onnuri may find it desirable to develop closer ties with specialist organizations such as Missionary Kids Nest, a Global Missionary Fellowship affiliate, or with MK schools established by international mission organizations.

DEVELOPING MISSION RESOURCES BEYOND ONNURI

Megachurches have a responsibility to provide various mission resources and content to other churches and mission organizations. In this respect, Onnuri Church is seeking to serve Japanese missions through evangelical conferences such as Love Sonata, as well as through its partner organizations CGNTV and Duranno Press.

The Love Sonata conference is a premier example of Onnuri Church's holistic missionary work.[17] The conference requires considerable financial support and significant contribution of talent from internationally known actors, musicians, singers, and artists, not to mention an immense staff. The conference requires not only extensive stage, lighting, audiovisuals, and broadcast systems and equipment, but also suitable inspirational content capable of stirring the emotions of the audience. Above all, the cooperation of the wide network of local Japanese churches is needed.

17. In 2006 Pastor Yong Jo Ha recognized the importance of missions in Japan and Northeast Asia in general and in 2007 held the first Love Sonata conference in Okinawa. The twenty-second Love Sonata conference, held in Kyoto, took place in April 2015.

For these reasons, it would be difficult for independent mission organizations to produce this type of evangelical conference.

The first Love Sonata, in 2007, was met with a certain amount of skepticism by local church directors and Korean missionaries, who dismissed it as a one-time event held by a megachurch that just wanted to display its resources. That dismissive judgment is not common today. The change is due to the formation of regional executive committees that focus on Japanese pastors and the comprehensive preparation—a minimum of two years—needed to truly make each Love Sonata an evangelical festival "by the people of Japan, for the people of Japan."[18] The Love Sonata festivals are supplemented before and after by outreach programs, Quiet Time seminars, and more through Onnuri Church, CGNTV, and Duranno Press.

Another example is CGNTV, which broadcasts Christian programming in Korean, Japanese, and Chinese 24 hours a day, 365 days a year, to over 170 countries. Broadcasting by satellite, as CGNTV does, requires launching and maintaining a broadcast satellite, a high level of expertise in transmission technology, and significant financial backing. CGNTV also demands a constant supply of high-quality Christian content, which in turn requires a network of human resources. An independent mission organization would find such a many-sided and complex broadcast ministry nearly impossible to operate. CGNTV's ministry may be one of the most significant ministries Onnuri Church has taken on. With branches in the United States, Japan, and Indonesia, as well as production centers in Taiwan, Thailand, and the United Arab Emirates, CGNTV is at the vanguard of media missions.[19]

On another front, Duranno Press is supplying churches, mission organizations, missionaries, and regular churchgoers with the tools, documents, and programs needed for cross-cultural

18. There are Love Sonata Executive Committees in both Korea and Japan. The Korean committee is part of the Love Sonata Headquarters, which is part of Onnuri Church. The Japanese committee is headed by Tatsuhiro Mineno (of Yodobashi Church in Tokyo), with committees operating in each of the other Love Sonata locations.

19. A special case is Japan, where CGNTV within eight years of its founding had established linkages with 2,197 churches in 47 prefectures.

missions. In addition, it nurtures pastors, missionaries, and parishioners directly and indirectly through programs such as Duranno Bible College. Furthermore, in October 1995 Duranno Press opened the Duranno Father School,[20] which in 2000 expanded to an international ministry in thirty-nine countries, including China, Indonesia, Nepal, and Colombia, training fathers both inside and outside the local churches. Duranno Father School creates curricula in multiple languages besides Korean. Within Korea, Duranno Father School also operates English-language programs for foreign workers from places such as the Philippines, Vietnam, and Bangladesh.

Several challenges present in the provision of ministry resources need to be overcome. First, Onnuri Church is gradually weaning Love Sonata from the church's support, with the expectation that Japan's 8,000 churches will eventually supply the human and material resources needed to continue the program. Starting in 2018, Love Sonata in Korea is hoping to impact the next generation of leaders in Japan through a "younger Love Sonata," aimed more to younger Japanese Christians. For its part, CGNTV is striving to overcome being labeled as an Onnuri Church broadcast, rather than simply being known as a Christian ministry broadcast. Overall, broadcast content has been reorganized to contain less Onnuri content. As of December 2014, CGNTV China and Japan broadcast only 17.4 percent and 18.0 percent "Onnuri branded" content, respectively. With the large reach of the Korean and U.S. CGNTV broadcasts, CGNTV must acknowledge its identification with Onnuri and work toward more diverse sourcing for content.[21]

20. Duranno Father School was founded on the following idea: In order for the country to stand upright, the society must stand upright; and in order for society to stand upright, the household must stand upright; and in order for the household to stand upright, the father must stand upright.

21. As of December 2014, CGNTV's Korean channel (cable) was broadcasting 32.5 percent Onnuri content (including the Sunday service, 2014 Onnuri Celebration, CGNTV Vision Seminar, and QT Living Life). The figure for CGNTV in the United States was higher (42.6 percent) because of increased broadcast of the Sunday service from Onnuri Irvine and other vision churches. China and Japan CGNTV were broadcasting a lower proportion of Onnuri-branded content.

DEVELOPING SELF-MISSIOLOGIZING

Now, 130 years after the Gospel entered Korea, the Korean church overall has 26,677 missionaries working in over 170 countries.[22] The Korean church and Korean mission organizations have an extensive ministry infrastructure. It would not be an exaggeration, however, to say that compilation and development of distinctively Korean missiological literature—and the practices of self-theologizing and self-missiologizing—are for the most part nonexistent.[23] Taking this step is imperative if the non-Western church and Majority World missions are fully to move beyond the era of colonialism and imperialism.

In this context, megachurches such as Onnuri Church, with their rich human and material resources, have a responsibility to foster Korean self-theologizing and self-missiologizing and to participate by lending moral and financial support to the preparation of Korean theological literature. A possible next step would be for Onnuri Church to recruit missions experts (while commissioning its own) and to launch an institute for missiological research, development of missiological studies, and the preparation of missiological texts. The institute would cooperate with domestic and international seminaries and graduate schools of theology for the sake of developing a field-based theology for Korean churches, while at the same time introducing the latest missiological thinking and theological trends to Korea.

CONCLUSION

As a megachurch, Onnuri Church must maintain, support, develop, and improve the following critical points.

First, if until now Onnuri Church has poured its energy into missional action, the time has come for it to supplement that focus—which it must not lose—with like attention to the develop-

22. The figures come from statistics presented at the Korea World Mission Association annual meeting, January 8, 2015.

23. To the familiar tripartite principle for an indigenous church (that it be self-supporting, self-propagating, and self-governing), mission anthropologist Paul Hiebert advocates adding a fourth principle: self-theologizing. See Paul G. Hiebert, *Anthropological Insights for Missionaries* (Grand Rapids: Baker, 1985), 193–224.

ment of mission theology. If commissioning missionaries and seeing fruit develop in the field can be said to be the exterior walls of the edifice of mission, theology and missiology are the building's infrastructure. No matter how impressive the exterior, without a strong infrastructure and solid foundation, the eventual collapse of the building is inevitable.[24]

The Korean church has recently recognized the need for it to develop its capacity for self-theologizing and self-missiologizing.[25] Onnuri Church can participate in this movement in various ways. As mentioned, it could establish a missiological study center. It could hold self-theologizing and self-missiologizing forums throughout Korea and Asia in partnership with domestic theology graduate schools and mission organizations. It could gather the best papers from both Western and non-Western conferences on World Christianity and compile them into journals to keep our missiologists, mission practitioners, and missionaries abreast of global missiological trends. Doing so will encourage independent mission research and ultimately will provide a stepping-stone between the Korean church and the global mission community.

Second, while the missional-church format may feel confining at times, Onnuri Church must continue to maintain its chosen structure (a union of church and mission). The history of Christianity shows that mission movements have always been on the rise when modality and sodality join hands (when they have been remarried). When they have been separated or have acted independently (when they have been divorced from each other), a downturn in the mission movement has followed. After a repeated rise and fall in mission movements from the first through the mid-twentieth centuries, in the late twentieth century church-centered missions started to gain traction, and a new ecclesiology advocating a modality-sodality amalgamation began to emerge.

24. Daniel S. H. Ahn, "Historical Background of the Emergence and Development of Self-Theologizing and Self-Missiologizing" [in Korean], *Korea Mission Quarterly* 14, no. 1 (Fall 2014): 38–48.

25. Topics such as "Korean style missions," "self-missiologizing as Korean mission theology," and "continuities and discontinuities of Western and non-Western missions" have been addressed by a number of recent Korean missiological conferences.

Onnuri Church, which has been a missional church since its inception, must do its utmost to utilize its many various programs, even while striving to maximize their strengths and minimize their weaknesses. In doing so, it will be addressing the responsibilities of a megachurch in Korea.

QUESTIONS FOR REFLECTION

1. What features distinguish a modality (local church) from a sodality (parachurch or mission agency)?
2. In what ways might the roles of a modality and of a sodality differ?
3. Onnuri Church, in South Korea, has a unique modality-sodality structure. For example, the church has its own mission agencies: TIM, CGNTV, and Duranno Press. What strengths or weaknesses do you see in the structure of this church?
4. In the past, churches in the West generally focused on sending missionaries to unreached areas (e.g., to the so-called 10/40 Window). Today, however, great influxes of immigrants from unreached areas, especially from Islamic areas, are coming to the West and to reached areas, including South Korea. How can the churches of the world respond to this current trend in migration? What lessons can be learned from Onnuri Church's immigrant missions?
5. Missions has two dimensions: centrifugal (going) and centripetal (coming). What is a proper balance between these two dimensions? How would you assess the efforts of Onnuri Church to combine these two dimensions of missions?

5

Response to "The Accountability of Megachurches in Missions"

Wesley Granberg-Michaelson

The story of the Onnuri Church's commitment to global mission, presented by Jae Hoon Lee, Daniel S. H. Ahn, and Tae Kyung Ham, provides a compelling case study of one megachurch's accomplishments and ongoing challenges. The dimension of self-reflection and critique included by the authors is particularly helpful for this dialogue. But we should begin by recognizing the extraordinary missional achievements of the Onnuri Church in only the first three decades of its life.

To put this achievement into perspective: when first reading the authors' presentation, I was drawn to reflect on my time serving for seventeen years as general secretary of the Reformed Church in America and on its history of world mission. As the oldest Protestant denomination in the United States, with a continuing ministry going back to 1628, the Reformed Church in America (RCA) began its global mission about 150 years ago. Its historic accomplishments have borne lasting fruit. One of the first Western Protestant missionaries to China, David Abeel, was sent by the RCA. Some of the first Western missionaries to the Persian Gulf region of the Middle East were also RCA missionaries, and the now famous Christian Medical Center and Hospital in Vellore, India, was founded by a woman RCA missionary, Dr. Ida Scudder.

The RCA's missionary impact has also been felt, at least indirectly, here in Korea, where this forum is being held. Horace G. Underwood, the pioneer of Western missionaries to Korea, who established the Saemoonan Church in Seoul and is so widely revered here, graduated from the RCA's New Brunswick Theological Seminary. He received his call to mission while a student at New Brunswick. But when the RCA's mission board did not have sufficient funds (or faith?) to support him, Underwood found support from the Presbyterians. So, had my RCA ancestors been able to support their young seminary graduate with his call to be a missionary, all the Presbyterian churches in Korea today would more likely be called Reformed churches!

Though a relatively small U.S. denomination, with about 1,000 congregations and 170,000 confessing members in 2015, the RCA has had a remarkable impact historically on global mission. But when I began as general secretary, the challenges simply to maintain the RCA's global mission program were already evident. As with other denominations, our congregations wanted a more direct, firsthand involvement in global mission rather than simply trusting and supporting the denomination's mission program. We had to struggle continually to preserve our commitments and to increase ways for greater congregational engagement.

Today the RCA's global mission program has an annual budget of $6.7 million. It supports about ninety missionaries or missionary couples working in forty-three countries around the world. (Forty-four of the missionaries are personnel from local mission partners supported by the RCA.) Always, our work is guided by our local partners, working to support indigenous congregations. The policy of the denomination is not to establish RCA congregations outside of North America but always to work with partners in planting or nurturing locally rooted congregations and ministries.

CONTRASTING PICTURES

The contrast with Onnuri Church's global mission accomplishments, in terms of magnitude, becomes immediately clear. Presently, the Onnuri Church, according to Lee, Ahn, and Ham, supports 854 cross-cultural missionaries in seventy countries. Thus, the mission commitment mobilized by this single congregation far surpasses the global mission program of the Reformed Church in America, despite the long and historic commitment of the RCA to world mission.

The same is true in comparison with other U.S. denominations. The Presbyterian Church (USA), with a membership in 2014 of 1,667,000 in 9,862 congregations, is significantly larger than the RCA. It supports 162 mission co-workers throughout the world. And the Christian Missionary and Alliance denomination, known for its strong commitment to global mission and with 500,000 members in its U.S. congregations, supports 761 missionaries throughout the world—a number still less than those mobilized through the Onnuri Church.

Thus, the human and financial resources that have been mobilized by the Onnuri Church for cross-cultural global mission are a remarkable illustration of how the missional commitment of megachurches is dramatically changing the picture of how Christian mission is being carried out by churches around the world. Even recognizing that about half of these 854 missionaries have come from other congregations through the Tyrannus International Mission, all have been mobilized and supported through Onnuri's commitment to mission. Onnuri Church's example becomes even more dramatic when one takes into account its development of the Christian Global Network TV and the Duranno Press, along with other parts of its mission infrastructure.

THREE OPPORTUNITIES

With this recognition of Onnuri Church's contribution to global mission clearly in mind, let me offer three additional responses to the chapter by Lee, Ahn, and Ham, highlighting three areas of opportunity.

Development of Korean missiological reflection. First, the authors state that the "compilation and development of distinctively Korean missiological literature . . . are for the most part nonexistent" (44). They issue a strong call for Onnuri Church to develop an institute devoted to the development of indigenous Korean missional theology and reflection, in cooperation with other mission organizations and study centers. Such a call, in my view, should be strongly embraced and supported by other organizations and centers devoted to understanding theologically the nature of the *missio*

Dei in today's world and discerning the fresh responses required of the churches.

Such effort is crucial as we recognize that Christianity is emerging globally as a non-Western religion. Beginning in 1980, the majority of the world's Christians were found outside of the global North and West. That movement is accelerating, shaping World Christianity's future. Yet theological and financial capital remains centered in Europe and the United States. Thus, the development of theology in non-Western settings, and in particular with fresh missiological perspectives, is imperative.

Moreover, this effort can and should be undertaken ecumenically. New global platforms are emerging that can contribute to this task. Most notable, in my view, is the Global Christian Forum, which is successfully bringing together the recognized leadership of historic Protestant, Evangelical, Pentecostal, Catholic, and Orthodox churches and organizations around tables of shared fellowship. These efforts are beginning to open new doors of relationship and trust in the global body of Christ.

Other established global networks of missiological reflection are in place through organizations such as the Overseas Ministries Study Center, a cooperating sponsor of this gathering. The Commission on World Mission and Evangelism of the World Council of Churches, with Korean colleague Jooseop Keum as its director, is nurturing a number of theologically diverse reflections around the world that focus on its new statement on mission and evangelism, "Toward a Theology of Life." I do not underestimate the theological differences and tensions involved. But fresh missiological reflection in non-Western contexts needs to happen in ways that include the full diversity of Christ's global body today. Onnuri Church could make a historic contribution to this process.

Exploration of "missional" theology. Second, the chapter by Lee, Ahn, and Ham makes frequent reference to Onnuri Church as being a "missional church," and its footnotes include the work of David Bosch and Darrell Guder. These references take note of the growing missional theology and ecclesiology that has developed over the past two decades or so. But the meaning and implications of this term need to be explored in far greater depth. Indeed, in my country of the United States, the term "missional church" has evolved from being a fresh ecclesiological challenge into a term that has become so generic and popular that its actual meaning is hard to discern.

Reading this fine essay by Lee, Ahn, and Ham, I wonder if Onnuri Church's understanding of being a "missional church" means becoming a sending agency for global mission, organizationally centered in one congregation. In reality, the original development of missional theology went far deeper. Rooted, for instance, in Lesslie Newbigin's fresh insights when he returned from India as a missionary to his home in England, being "missional" meant not simply sending missionaries elsewhere, but participating in God's mission in the congregation's local setting and context. The congregation does not have a mission program; rather, its life and identity are rooted in its participation in God's mission, starting in its local culture.

Role of Korean churches in promoting global unity in the body of Christ. Finally, the narrative in this chapter raises more generally the potential role that the Korean churches may be called upon by God to play in the changing shape of World Christianity. As mentioned, we have witnessed in the last century the most dramatic shift in the geographic presence of Christians in the world that has occurred since the beginning of Christian history. In only a century, Christianity's dominant presence in the world has moved out of its comfortable Western center to the regions of Africa, Latin America, and Asia. Emerging churches in those regions, often fueled by Pentecostal spirituality and evangelical zeal, are highly contextualized to local cultures and are often isolated from the wider body of Christ.

Meanwhile, historic churches in the Global North, faithfully carrying the tradition of the church and nurturing ecumenical understandings of the body of Christ, struggle for a resonating witness within their own cultures. In my view, the separation between these two parts of Christ's body, expressed in many ways as a division between the Global North and Global South, or between "older" churches and "younger" churches, is the most serious and damaging division afflicting World Christianity today.

Who can mediate these differences and bridge this divide? Often I wonder whether the churches in Korea, whose place is found in neither the Global North nor the Global South and who now have resources and power independent from the West, might be given a crucial role in this task. The story of Onnuri Church as presented by Lee, Ahn, and Ham is another example that raises this possibility. Have the remarkable gifts and accomplishments of this church, and other megachurches in Korea, been given by God for a reason? And might that reason involve the service of these churches in building fresh and deeply needed expressions of unity in the global body of Christ today, for the sake of empowering God's mission in the world?

6

Várzea Paulista Assembly of God: A Case Study of a Brazilian Megachurch's Missionary Outreach

Tim Carriker

Because of its organizational structure, the Várzea Paulista Assembly of God (VPAG; in Portuguese: Assembléia de Deus—Várzea Paulista) presents an unusual case study of megachurch missionary involvement. Most members of the church participate in one of the sixty-two congregations that VPAG has planted in the surrounding area, while only 10 percent congregate in the mother church. VPAG's hierarchical organization and strong central leadership, however, create solidarity and maintain tight synergy between the mother church and the numerous daughter congregations in local growth, decision making, and missionary involvement in several countries.

VPAG, with approximately 8,000 members, is located in Várzea Paulista, a city of 115,000 that is approximately fifty kilometers north of São Paulo, Brazil's largest city. (With nearly 21 million inhabitants in 2014, São Paulo is the seventh largest metropolitan area in the world.) The church was founded in 1960 as a congregation of the Jundiaí Assemblies of God Church, four miles away. It was emancipated in 1996.[1] Presently, eight hundred VPAG members

1. Emancipation occurs when a congregation is no longer dependent on the mother church financially or in decision-making. Upon emancipation a congregation becomes a church and bears accountability to its regional ecclesiastical body (in this case to a convention) rather than to its founding church.

attend the mother church; the rest attend one of the sixty-four congregations, divided into seven sectors, planted by the mother church. The membership of these congregations varies widely, ranging from 50 to 500 members. Only two of them have over 500 members. Another eight congregations have around 300 members and the rest, some 3,800 members, are distributed among the other fifty-four congregations. The number of daughter congregations today is just over triple the twenty-one the mother church had planted previous to the arrival, in 2001, of the current pastor.

Even though much of its membership has ties to numerous local congregations, a common pattern for the Assemblies of God in Brazil, these congregations are strongly connected to the mother church.[2] VPAG thus can serve well as a case study of a megachurch with strong missionary involvement. Organizationally the Assemblies of God strongly concentrates church leadership in a single person; since 2001 Alberto Resende de Oliveira has served VPAG as both pastor and president.[3]

During the years 2001–14, the city of Várzea Paulista grew 24 percent, from 93,000 to its current size of 115,000. During the same time period the church, in contrast, grew 400 percent, from around 2,000 members in 2001 to 8,000 in 2014. Resende describes the church's situation in 2001 as financially critical, with members

2. Estimates of membership in the Assemblies of God throughout Latin America are difficult. For a brief introduction to the Assemblies of God in Brazil, see http://en.wikipedia.org/wiki/Assembleias_de_Deus and www.pewforum.org/2006/10/05/historical-overview-of-pentecostalism-in-brazil. According to official Brazilian government statistics, churches bearing the name "Assemblies of God" in Brazil had 12.3 million adherents (Instituto Brasileiro de Geografia e Estatística, 2010, www.ibge.gov.br/home/estatistica/populacao/censo2010/caracteristicas_religiao_deficiencia/caracteristicas_religiao_deficiencia_tab_pdf.shtm). According to official church publications, 27.3 million people attend more than 198,000 Assemblies of God churches in the region (http://worldmissions.ag.org/regions/latinamcab/overview.cfm), but this same publication gives an estimate for Assemblies of God attendance in Brazil of 21.5 million, nearly twice the figure given by the Brazilian government.

3. This case study is based on an interview with Pastor Alberto Resende de Oliveira, president and senior pastor of VPAG, and his son-in-law, Fabio Luis Rezende, the church's minister of evangelism. The church's website is www.advarzea.com.br.

deeply troubled over a debt that was sixteen times the monthly collections. Although he was aware that the church was in debt before he arrived, the magnitude of the debt became fully apparent only during his first forty days at VPAG, as creditors began to show up demanding payment. Resende's explanation of the situation is generous, suggesting simply that his predecessor lacked skill as an administrator.

Resende's previous years of experience as an administrator in the secular world was one of the reasons he was called to pastor VPAG. Before coming to VPAG, he also had successfully administered and pastored another Assemblies of God church, in Suzano, forty miles east of São Paulo. In Suzano he founded the Peru Missionary Project (PMP; in Portuguese, Missão Colheita, or "Harvest Mission"), a project he brought with him to VPAG. Adoption of PMP initially implied the support of seven missionary families beyond the large debt the church already had. At the time, members understandably protested: "Pastor, we can't even pay our own bills, how can we support others?" Resende's perspective was somewhat radical: "The *first* resources we receive will be used for the missionaries" (the seven PMP families, along with four families in Paraguay that VPAG was already supporting). Initially during the transition a few members left, who had also been strongly in favor of the previous pastor, but even these people soon returned.

STRATEGY

Upon his arrival, Resende immediately organized a Department of Mission and began to teach, preach, and explain in informal conversations his understanding that the monetary support of a strong mission program was the solution to the church's debt. At the time, he did not go into detail concerning the extent of the financial problems the church faced so as not to discourage the members further. Today, long after that debt has been resolved, his practice is quite different, maintaining public financial transparency. At the time of his arrival, church offerings averaged an equivalent of $30,000 U.S. dollars monthly, while the church's debt had risen to $500,000. Some members complained that church offerings were being invested outside the immediate geographic region of the church rather than being invested in local evangelization. Resende's typical response was to express his faith that giving away funds would become the means by which they would receive. "If we give our resources away, it is from the outside that we will also receive. Our only escape from this financial crisis is through our engagement in mission." Therefore, the church began immediately to increase the size of the missionary force they were supporting. Debts were renegotiated with creditors, and the church even began to purchase more property to build a larger facility with a seating capacity of 3,500 to accommodate the 750–800 worshipers that currently gather at the mother church as well as many of the members of the numerous daughter congregations. Worship services were held on Sunday, Monday, Wednesday, and Friday evenings, with Bible School classes on Sunday morning. Growth, Resende observes, has been constant, not in spurts, and he attributes much of that growth to the specific goals established among the various leaders of the whole church (the mother church and the congregations).

When Resende moved to Várzea Paulista, he brought with him a significant amount of experience. Besides his secular work as an administrator, he had successfully pastored a large church in Suzano for five and a half years. With 1,200 members and twelve congregations, two of which met in homes, it too had previously been a troubled church. Its four previous pastors had been problematic and had tarnished the image of a pastor. But during Resende's tenure there as pastor and president, the church grew to approximately 7,300 members with sixty-two congregations. During his final year alone, 1,649 members were added. In the same period of time, the population of Suzano tripled, from some 40,000 to 120,000. By means of community collaboration, church buildings were raised in as little as forty days. Congregations typically began in rented storefronts. When the worshipers could no longer fit, members of all the congregations and the mother church would come together to build a church. They built more than twenty church buildings during those five and a half years and would baptize 120 to 140 persons every two months.

Resende attributes 90 percent of membership growth at VPAG to new arrivals in the area who see in this church "something different and attractive." More than 90 percent of these new member are transfers from Assemblies of God churches in other areas. Interestingly, Resende does not attribute the church's success to his own preaching style. He says he prefers to speak more informally and naturally with the membership rather than use the familiar Pentecostal hardline style of preaching. Well-known guest preachers are frequent, and the leadership works hard to create an attractive atmosphere with excellent services, notably children's and young adult programs, and there are abundant parking facilities. They also invest heavily in the formation of workers. Each year some 450 to 500 persons enroll in an eleven-month course for ministry preparation that meets once a week for four hours.

As of 2014, VPAG had thirteen church sites under construction, each of them with a clear emphasis on how children will be taught and encouraged in their faith. As an example of the pastor's concern for the satisfaction of members and the quality of ministry, when members want to leave, he invites them to his office to pray for them, bless them, and ask why they are leaving, in order to make improvements. Monthly meetings are held with all of the leadership, which is organized on three levels, directors, assistants, and youth leaders—all in all, 250 leaders. During these administrative meetings, specific goals are developed for each area of ministry. All leaders are held accountable, including the pastor himself. At the administrative meetings, the leadership typically deals with some twenty items of business. Some of these items are recurrent, others occasional. The meetings are three to four hours long. Though criticism often arises, the pastor does not get discouraged.

Nearly all of these leaders are new; from the group of directors before Resende's arrival, only two remain. The rest were simply not able to keep up. These leaders are the pastors, elders, and deacons and one cooperator (assistant to an elder) who guide the congregations. Among them is one woman who leads one of the congregations. In 2014, after thirteen years, these younger leaders who were once recent graduates of the leadership program are mature men and women thirty to forty years old. Resende focuses his attention on this group. The Sunday School class he leads is for young families, and he considers the children's and young couples' the most important classes in the Sunday School program.

THE CHURCH'S MISSIONARY VISION

The PMP, mentioned above, began in Suzano, seven years before Resende's move to Várzea Paulista and before he became pastor there. Inspired by the kibbutz communities in Israel, the project initially established a base and erected a large church building in Puerto Maldonaldo, deep in the Peruvian Amazon forest. Originally, the objective was to have Brazilian missionaries spend six months in training at the church's Mission Training School in Brazil and then another six months of internship at this mission base in Peru. Today, however, they train Peruvians at the mission base for ministry in Peru, and churches have been planted in eight of Peru's twenty-four states. The church in Arequipa is the largest and has a Paraguayan pastor. A Peruvian is pastor of the church in Ayacucho, because, due to climate and cultural conditions, it is difficult for Brazilians or even coastal area Peruvians to adapt there. Lima has one of the newest churches, and it has already planted a number of smaller congregations.

VPAG takes into consideration that Peru is composed of three distinct peoples with three different major languages: the forest peoples, the mountain peoples, and the coastal population. The indigenous peoples in the forest and the mountains take longer to train. Students from these two groups are able to study for free, and the base training school (called PETRI for "Programa de Estudo Teológico em Regime de Internato") accommodates eighteen to twenty-four students during eight months of the year. To support these students, Brazilian churches and individuals adopt a student for approximately $120 a month, which covers room, board, and school expenses. Other AG churches in Brazil partner with VPAG to support this mission and contribute to student scholarships. Besides this mission to Peru, VPAG fully supports five missionary families or single persons in five countries in southern Africa, another in Spain, and two missionary families in the United States (Florida and Boston).[4] Altogether, VPAG supports thirty-three missionary families and two single missionaries.

4. VPAG's church in Boston has 150 members and is already fully supporting a ministry to evangelize, educate, and house 500 children in Guinea-Bissau.

To maintain interest in and support of the mission, selected members of VPAG and other partner Assemblies of God churches make annual trips in July by bus and airplane to the mission field in Peru. Approximately sixty persons participate in these trips, which also bring together the leadership of all twenty-four of the churches planted in Peru. Twelve of these churches are in Puerto Maldonaldo, four in Lima, two in Arequipa, four in Piura, and one each in Ica and Trujillo. The year 2014 saw 180 people (60 from the Brazilian churches plus some 120 Peruvian leaders) come to the base to promote an annual Bible school. Besides the Bible school, the annual trip includes street evangelism and visits to all the churches. Through this recurring ministry, the missionary vision of VPAG and its partner churches throughout Brazil is renewed annually. The vision is also renewed through the monthly reports required from all of the missionaries. Finally, interest in local mission in Várzea Paulista is maintained as some of the missionaries to Peru return to Brazil and are integrated into the leadership of the congregations of VPAG.

EVALUATION AND CONCLUSION

A number of factors have contributed to the unusual growth of VPAG and its missionary projects. The first is strong central leadership. All VPAG leaders—pastors, copastors, youth leaders, and missionaries—are subordinate to the president, Pastor Alberto Resende. Strong central leadership facilitates decision making and also fits well with Latin American culture. Central leadership, whether political, religious, or commercial, has been the key to success throughout Brazil's history. This generalization has been especially true of religious leaders who have generated transforming social movements—as long as they have been perceived as being holy, trustworthy, and socially engaged.[5] In spite

5. While the "strongman" is a well-documented feature of Latin American culture, the religious version of this phenomenon is not as widely known. See, for example, the literature on messianic movements in Brazil, especially Duglas T. Monteiro, "Um confronto entre Juazeiro, Canudos e Contestado," in *História geral da civilização brasileira* 3, no. 2, ed. Boris Fausto (Rio de Janeiro: Difel, 1978); Lísias Nogueira Negrão and Josildeth Gomes Consorte, *O messianismo no Brasil contemporâneo* (São Paulo: FFL-CH-USP/CER, 1984); René Ribeiro, "Brazilian Messianic Movements," in

of his predecessor's inadequacies, Alberto Resende, because of his deep, personal spirituality, was able to win the trust and allegiance of church leaders and members alike. Within Latin culture, strong central leadership, when recognized to be wise and altruistic, has been the key to rapid advancement, especially when coupled with abilities in strategic planning.

Second, as crucial as central leadership has been, the complementary skills of administration and goal-setting that Resende brought with him only increased the growth of the local ministry and of the missionary projects VPAG supports. VPAG's tight administration is maintained and reinforced through the lengthy three- to four-hour monthly meetings in which all leaders of all the congregations participate. In this manner, expectations are reinforced and the activities of all the congregations and ministries are communicated among all the working parts of the organization.

Third, the annual eleven-month leadership training program (Preparation and Formation of Church Workers Course, or in Portuguese, "Curso de Preparação e Formação de Obreiros") serves the dual purpose of providing personnel to direct new churches, ministries, and missionary projects and at the same time replenishing the ranks of the previous older leadership with younger leaders now trained under Resende's guidance. In this way his vision and modus operandi for ministry are consolidated.

Fourth, several times during my interview with him, Resende highlighted the role played by establishing clear and specific goals and holding all leaders, including himself, accountable for reaching those goals. Interestingly, no conflict was seen between setting specific goals and the traditional Pentecostal view of the spontaneous guidance of the Holy Spirit. Tensions between the two are resolved through the view that the same Holy Spirit holds especially the leadership of the church responsible. Church growth studies are consistent in recognizing the significance that establishing clear and specific goals has for the subsequent growth of the church.

Millennial Dreams in Action: Studies in Revolutionary Religious Movements, 2nd ed., ed. S. L. Thrupp (Nova Iorque: Schocken Books, 1970), 55–69; and the extensive documentation in C. Timothy Carriker, "As contribuições do Messianismo para uma hermenêutica missiológica," in *Evangelho e cultura: Leituras para a antropologia missionária*, lulu.com (2008), 177–99.

Fifth, practice of spiritual disciplines, along with the regular presentation at VPAG of inspiring messages by well-known Christian leaders from throughout Brazil, contribute to the sense of direction and solidarity possessed by members that is essential to the ongoing development of the local church and its missionary projects. Resende's constant inclusion in the pulpit of nationally known Christian leaders reinforces and contributes to the goal of excellence that he understands to be essential for attracting and maintaining church membership. He seeks diligently to offer a high level of life enhancing personal and social programs and ministry that both meets perceived needs and challenges laziness. Rather than simply granting church transfers to members who wish to leave, he shows concern to identify points of perceived weakness in programs and ministry and to correct them, rather than belligerently insisting on his own perspective or style.

Other factors also contribute to both the growth and the prosperity of VPAG's local ministries and the expansion of its ministry into Peru, the United States, Southern Africa, and Spain. The preceding five factors, however, are key. At this point we should note the insight provided by the last thirty years of sociological studies on the entrance and exit of persons into and out of religious organizations. Rodney Stark's books on the rise and growth of Christianity from its inception to its current state well summarize this research. The significance of Stark's work is only beginning to receive recognition among church historians and missiologists but is massive enough to be conclusive.[6]

Many of Stark's findings are conveniently summarized in the final chapter of one of his more recent books, *The Triumph of Christianity* (2011). The case study presented in this chapter both illustrates and confirms one of his major findings, namely, that

6. Stark's theories are elaborated in numerous books and articles. Especially important for our discussion are Rodney Stark and William Sims Bainbridge, *A Theory of Religion* (New York: Lang, 1987), and Rodney Stark and Roger Finke, *Acts of Faith: Explaining the Human Side of Religion* (Berkeley: Univ. of California Press, 2000). For a summary of Stark's many studies on Christianity, see especially *The Triumph of Christianity: How the Jesus Movement Became the World's Largest Religion* (New York: HarperCollins, 2011).

"religious competition increases the level of religiousness prevailing in a society. In the long run it also results in norms of religious civility."[7] Although stated simply, an immense amount of data confirms this finding. It speaks effectively to the growth of institutions that "compete" successfully. This statement sums up well VPAG's overall strategy and implementation of ministry: a desire to serve better, to offer better Bible reflections and inspiring messages, to serve the community better with more churches and better equipped leaders, and to expand this offering to the world through their mission engagement.

QUESTIONS FOR REFLECTION

1. How does church leadership style positively or negatively affect the church's missionary outreach? What styles of leadership are biblically appropriate to use as models in the furtherance of the Gospel? What limitations or parameters would you put on these styles?
2. What types of leadership training programs would you suggest to further the missionary witness of the local church? Describe possible scenarios in terms of content, duration, objectives, and other considerations.
3. What is the relationship between establishing clearly defined goals and the role of the Holy Spirit in the leadership of the local church and in the goal of greater missionary effectiveness?
4. In your experience what are the benefits and the risks of religious competition for the growth of the local church and its missionary effectiveness?

7. Stark, *Triumph of Christianity*, 418.

7

Response to "Várzea Paulista Assembly of God"

Han Young Lee

Having grown up in Brazil from my first year of elementary school all the way to college, I often introduce myself as "Korean by birth but Brazilian by heart." This background may be my only real qualification for sharing the following comments about the research that Timothy Carriker has presented. It is with much awareness of the limits of my knowledge and with more a spirit of apprenticeship that I present a brief response to his account of the Várzea Paulista Assembly of God (VPAG).

PERSONAL BACKGROUND

My father was one of the first few Korean pastors who had an opportunity to serve the Korean expats who migrated to Brazil during the late 1960s and early 1970s. As far as I remember in the early 1970s, *crente* (literally "believer") was a sort of nickname used to designate the Protestant minority in Brazil. But sometimes the term became a sarcastic label for this socioeconomically marginalized group. From 1940 up to 1991, the Brazilian census classified the religious population into a compressed set of only four major groups, "Católicos," "Evangélicos," "Sem-Religião" (without religion), and "Outros" (Others). But later censuses have subdivided Protestant churches ("Evangélicas") in more detail, with categories such as Igreja Evangélica Luterana, Presbiteriana, Metodista, Batista, Congrecional, Igreja Assembléia de Deus, and so forth, which reflects an exponential growth of non-Catholic churches in the last twenty years. The 1960 and 1970 census tables, for instance, show the category "Evangélicos," which accounted for only 3.7 percent and 5 percent of the population, respectively, compared with 22.2 percent in 2010.[1]

Now, more than thirty years since my departure from Brazil, I found reading Carriker's account of the missionary outreach of the VPAG to be personally eye-opening. Carriker provides a valuable update on the current state of the Brazilian evangelical churches, which now comprise the largest body of Protestants in Latin America and the fastest growing group of evangelicals in the world, a group marked with fervor for global mission.[2] As we are constantly reminded by the Great Commission, mission is essentially not what we initiate or do but what God does. That is, mission is part of the very nature of God's calling and of the church. As such, I think Thomas Breidenthal is correct when he writes that all churches have potential for growth, "if only they will stop focusing on survival and start on being the [missional] church."[3] With this in mind, and in light of what Carriker has presented in his case study, we can view the VPAG as an example of what a church can and should do in response to what God has already done for it.

THE VPAG STORY

VPAG grew exponentially during the years 2001–14, especially under the leadership of the new pastor, Alberto Resende de Oliveira. Upon his arrival, despite the church's poor finances and its daunting debt, which understandably had discouraged the congregation from undertaking further mission commitments, he

1. René D. Decol, "Mudança religiosa no Brasil: Uma visão demográfica," *Revista Brasileira de Estudos de População* 16, nos. 1/2 (January/December 1999): 123, www.abep.nepo.unicamp.br/docs/rev_inf/vol16_n1e2_1999/vol16_n1e2_1999_8artigo_121_137.pdf.

2. In the 2010 census, "Evangélicas" (Protestant churches) account for 22.2 percent (42,275,440) of the population. See "Tabela 1.4.1," ftp://ftp.ibge.gov.br/Censos/Censo_Demografico_2010/Caracteristicas_Gerais_Religiao_Deficiencia/tab1_4.pdf.

3. Thomas E. Breidenthal, "Formation for Mission," *Anglican Theological Review* 96, no. 1 (Winter 2014): 148.

challenged the congregation in concrete and systematic terms with a vision for restructuring the church's leadership organization and training. The challenge was for VPAG to be not a grown-up church doing mission, but a church that grows out of and for mission. Giving priority to the Great Commission and mission has become the driving force behind the church's growth.

Disregarding significant opposition and aspersions while establishing close and consistent rapport with VPAG's new leaders, Pastor Resende carried forward with integrity the Peru Mission Project that he had begun seven years before he moved to Várzea Paulista. He later expanded the mission beyond the borders of Peru with outreach to other countries as well. During the years 2001–14, VPAG grew considerably and is now a megachurch with approximately 8,000 members. It supports over 100 missionaries outside of Brazil, and some returnees are integrated into VPAG's ministry leadership.

In his evaluation and conclusion, Carriker pinpoints the following five major factors that contributed to VPAG's mission success:

- strong central leadership, maintaining scrupulous honesty
- efficient, systematic, and accountable administration
- focus on mission in training the next generation of leadership
- setting specific goals and targets
- continuously developing competitive educational curriculums and programs.

Timothy Carriker ends with a quotation from Rodney Stark: "Religious competition increases the level of religiousness prevailing in a society. In the long run it also results in norms of religious civility" (62).

QUESTIONS AND MISGIVINGS

Based on my understanding of VPAG as outlined above, I would like to express some of the questions and doubts that a careful reading of this chapter has raised for me. First, the chapter seems to be more a treatment of the church's growth per se than it is a discussion of the specific mission strategies VPAG employs as a megachurch. Since numerically many more small and midsized churches than megachurches are engaged in mission, I expected to see more attention given to the specific characteristics of megachurches' approach to mission. The chapter provides generalized concepts such as emphasis on mission priority, strong and accountable leadership, effective administration, continuous education, and so on, but it lacks, for instance, information on what VPAG as a megachurch can or cannot do in terms of mission vis-à-vis other, smaller, churches.

Second, from a socioeconomic and historical point of view, the question can be raised of a connection between the growth of VPAG's mission and the overall economic growth in Brazil, more specifically during the booming years of 2001–14. Church growth, as well as mission movements in Brazil, has not been confined to VPAG during this period of time; it has been quite pervasive and general, as indicated in the 2010 census.[4] The same was true in Korea in the 1970s and 1980s; exponential church growth took place along with national industrialization, leading to a prosperity theology within the church. Has VPAG been portrayed in this chapter as being too faultless? Are further details needed to round out the story and provide a more multidimensional and accurate evaluation?

Third, taking into account the social debate at the 1974 Lausanne Congress, that is, that "evangelicalism was not sure whether social concerns were also gospel concerns,"[5] this case study could have explored the socioeconomic aspects of mission at VPAG as a megachurch.

Last, not the least, the chapter could perhaps have been strengthened by discussing whether VPAG might be repeating some of the mistakes made previously in the history of mission, such as denominational narrowness, a too short training time for missionaries, lack of active networking and cooperation with other independent mission organizations, possible insensitivity

4. See "Tabela 1.4.1."

5. Justin Thacker, "Opening Address at the World Evangelical Alliance," *Journal of Latin American Theology* 5, no. 2 (2010): 8.

to paradigm shifts in modern mission strategies, and privileging imperial and material values or criteria over incarnational aspects of mission.[6]

CONCLUSION

I trust that VPAG is on the right track as it continuously pushes forward and expands its efforts beyond its own locale. But dynamism should not overlook the need to pause for serious historical reflection. In Korean churches, I have often witnessed a neglect of social justice and of the importance of Christian individual ethics (Micah 6:8). Unfortunately, such neglect is too often justified by an ostensible evangelical mission zeal that in practice is deeply rooted in the sands of prosperity theology. Apart from the above questions and doubts, words cannot express all that I have gained from this insightful study by Timothy Carriker.

Reportedly forty new churches open every week in Rio de Janeiro alone, attracting "consumers looking for service."[7] So there is much to be learned from VPAG's efforts as it strives to reshuffle the church's dynamism and then to nurture and transform churchgoers from being mere church shoppers into becoming higher-level, purpose-driven visionaries and missionaries.

6. See Ruth O. Oke, "Paradigm Shift in Mission from Biblical Perpectives," *Ogbomoso Journal of Theology* 15, no. 1 (2010): 147–57, for the paradigm shift in mission, especially in Africa.

7. Jason Byassee, "Purpose-Driven in Brazil: Perspectives on Church Growth," *Christian Century*, April 4, 2006, p. 8.

8

Hong Kong Korean Exodus Mission Church: A Model for the Diaspora Church

Jinbong Kim

Back in 1990, I heard the saying, "If two or more Chinese meet in a foreign land, they open a Chinese restaurant; if two or more Koreans meet in a foreign country, they plant a church." Soon after as I was searching for the mission field in which God would have me to serve, I realized there was some truth to the saying. Opportunities for mission service abroad came relatively more easily for me if the positions were for service in a diaspora Korean church. At one point I seriously considered accepting a missionary position at a Korean church in Abidjan, the largest city and financial hub of Côte d'Ivoire, West Africa. This church had been planted by three Korean Christian families, one the family of a dentist who had been invited by the government of Côte d'Ivoire. This Korean diaspora church has grown steadily and is now doing active mission outreach.

The size of the Korean diaspora is significant, and so is the number of Korean churches located around the world. In 2015 about 7 million Koreans were estimated to be residing outside Korea, nearly one-tenth the size of the current population of North and South Korea together.[1] According to the *Korean Christian*

1. The Overseas Koreans Foundation lists the figure of 7,010,000 Koreans living in diaspora in 2015; see www.okf.or.kr/portal/OkfMainView.do.

Press, there are 4,150 Korean churches in the United States, with an additional 1,299 Korean churches located in seventy-eight other countries, for a total of 5,449 Korean diaspora churches around the world.[2]

What is the mission of these Korean diaspora churches? Do they exist just to satisfy the cultural and spiritual needs of Koreans living abroad? The best answer to these questions is something Christopher Wright wrote in his book *The Mission of God*: "In the New Testament, . . . while it is certainly true that the centrifugal commission of Jesus to go to the nations is a radical new departure, consistent with the dawning of the new age of salvation, the purpose of that *going out* is so that the nations might be *gathered into* God's kingdom, in fulfillment of the scriptural vision."[3] That is, whether in the United States or in Hong Kong, the purpose of the Korean diaspora churches should be to serve all the people in their vicinity who are in need of the Gospel. Therefore, all diaspora churches of mature faith have to invite both those who speak Korean and those in their neighborhood who do not into the church of the Lord. Hong Kong Korean Exodus Mission Church is an extraordinary diaspora church that is a good example of a church that is carrying out this mission.

A MULTICULTURAL, MULTILINGUAL, AND UNITED DIASPORA CHURCH COMMUNITY

Planted in 1985 as Hong Kong Choonghyun Presbyterian Church, the new church began as a branch of Choonghyun Presbyterian Church in Seoul, where Chang In Kim was the senior pastor. With a calling for missions in Asia and North Korea, Kim and his congregation sent Chi Yong Oh to Hong Kong to found the new church. In 1997 Hyung Joong Yoon was installed as the second senior pastor and, in 2005, following his missional vision for Hong Kong, the former Hong Kong Choonghyun Presbyterian Church was renamed

2. For Korean diaspora church statistics, see www.chpress.net/detail.asp?id=8667&cate=search.

3. Christopher J. H. Wright, *The Mission of God* (Downers Grove, Ill.: IVP Academic, 2006), 523.

the Hong Kong Korean Exodus Mission Church (HKKEMC).[4] Under Yoon's excellent leadership the church not only overcame several difficult situations but also revived and grew in number and in spirit. Today it stands as a rare example of a mission-oriented diaspora church.

Hong Kong itself is a hub for trade, finance, logistics, traffic, and tourism in Asia. Of the city's population of 7 million, about 10 percent is estimated to be Christian.[5] Korean residents number about 13,000, or 0.19 percent; there are twelve Korean churches in Hong Kong, attended by some 2,000 Korean believers.[6] Cantonese and English are the official languages of Hong Kong. Since the late 1980s, however, with increased communication with mainland China, the use of Mandarin has also become widespread.[7]

Hong Kong Korean Exodus Mission Church has existed for years as a diaspora church in this multicultural and multilingual city. It embraces four different language groups under one roof. About 500 members attend the Sunday worship services each week. Hyung Joong Yoon, head pastor, and two assistant pastors serve the Korean-language service with a congregation of 350, including children and youth. Pastor Wong Chi Leung Peter leads the Cantonese language service for about 100 members. Wong Hoi David serves as pastor for the Mandarin language service, with about 60 members in attendance. Michael A. Klumpp, who is from the United States, ministers to about 40 English-speaking members of the church.

The four different language groups have different services with different ministers, but they operate as one body, with one session of elders under the leadership of Yoon, who functions as presider. When I visited HKKEMC and met all the pastors in February 2014, I was impressed with the excellence of their work.

4. Hong Kong Korean Exodus Mission Church is no longer officially related to Choonghyun Presbyterian Church in Seoul.

5. See http://en.wikipedia.org/wiki/Hong_Kong.

6. See Korean Residents Association H.K., http://kra.hk/new/home/kra/index.php.

7. For further information on Hong Kong, see http://en.wikipedia.org/wiki/Hong_Kong.

Each pastor was self-motivated and worked autonomously; at the same time, all members of the pastoral staff exercised their pastoral gifts and ministries in the service of the one church body. Despite the diversity of languages and cultures, they all collaborate to achieve one missional vision for the church. Pastor Yoon proactively reaches out to the leaders of other Christian groups in Hong Kong and seeks to create opportunities for participating in joint ministry with them.[8] When I asked about the need for a ministry specifically focused on Korean-speaking individuals, Yoon responded, "I'm convinced that God has called me to Hong Kong to serve Korean-speaking believers, as well as all the nations here."[9]

A DIASPORA CHURCH ESTABLISHES A MISSION AGENCY

In 1998 lead pastor Hyung Joong Yoon and HKKEMC established Life Road Mission (LRM), which is independent of the church, for specialized missions. Two years later, LRM organized a professional praise ministry team called Life Road Singers. In 2002 LRM opened Life Road Mission Training Center to train, dispatch, and care for missionaries. Since its founding, LRM has trained and sent sixty missionaries to lead cross-cultural ministries. Significant features of LRM are its mission policies, its distinctive mission strategy, and its approach to missionary member care.

Efficient and strategic mission policies. To gain the greatest benefit from Hong Kong's geographic and cultural advantages, LRM recruits missionary candidates who are willing to dedicate their

8. Since 1997 HKKEMC has worked with the Protestant churches of Hong Kong in a number of evangelism events and cultural ministries to reach the city's younger generation. In 1997 HKKEMC helped establish Life Road Mission. The ministry's four main purposes are to mobilize young adult Christians in Hong Kong for spiritual awakening, to start a nationwide revival for evangelism, to organize a therapeutic event for couples and families once a year, and to engage in a local ministry of mercy for those in need.

9. Hyung Joong Yoon, personal interview by Jinbong Kim, HKKEMC, February 8, 2014.

lives to serving the unreached tribal regions in China and Central Asia. Hyung Joong Yoon, who is also director of LRM, emphasizes the importance of the work in these areas:

> As I was looking at Hong Kong on a world map one day, God showed me the Silk Road and gave me the inspiration to evangelize the peoples along the Silk Road. Since the ancient time when merchants established the road, it has become the lifeline or "life road" for many across nations. With a clear conviction, I followed God's inspiration and founded Life Road Mission to accomplish the evangelization of China and Central Asia, despite my weakness.[10]

Once prospective candidates become qualified for missionary service with LRM, they are required to spend a year at HKKEMC in study of the local language and culture of their mission field. They also develop relationships of accountability with the officers of the mission center and the church members. Through this intimate community life, the new missionaries mature in their faith and confirm their calling for mission in the field.

In February 2014 I had the pleasure of being part of the commissioning service for four of the new missionaries, an experience that thrills me to this day. One of the elders of HKKEMC, who also served as a board member of LRM, was overwhelmed with emotion and shed tears while presenting a summary of the past year's training. The testimonies of the new missionaries followed.[11] Toward the end of the ceremony, all attendees, including the sixty LRM member missionaries, prayed for and blessed the newly commissioned missionaries. In my eyes, that moment was a time when heaven opened and the grace of the Holy Spirit rained down abundantly. God was with them, and they were with him.

Specialized and distinctive mission strategy. Timothy Kiho Park, a missiologist at Fuller Theological Seminary, has observed that "Korean

10. Ibid.

11. The missionaries were installed and sent off during the Wednesday evening worship service on February 12, 2014. Elder Jaesung Yang, head of HKKEMC's mission committee, reported on the training missionary candidates received in preparation for their ministry.

missionaries are sent to the mission fields to develop and enhance areas with which the target countries struggle."[12] A contemporary mission trend likewise calls for missionaries to focus specifically on ministries that the nations they serve might not have the capacity to carry out. For example, having observed the need for support in the area of Christian music in China, LRM continues to send the Life Road Singers to China for specialized musical ministry.[13] Since the Christian music industry in China is quite underdeveloped in comparison with the explosive growth of Chinese Christianity, Life Road Singers, composed of professionally trained vocal and instrumental musicians, meets a real need. Life Road Singers has helped to empower over 6,000 Korean missionaries in China and nearby countries to approach their ministries more strategically. Most of its twenty-two members have majored in voice at various universities in Korea and the United States. The group pursues ministries of record production, annual performances, church and mission field visits, and specialized programs for missionaries in the field. The members perform in Christian praise concerts across China and serve numerous Chinese churches as choir conductors and worship leaders. The ministry has prospered and has led to opening the Christian Music School and Seminary to train Chinese Christian musicians and worship leaders.

LRM consulted with many Christian leaders and experienced missionaries in launching the specialized Life Road Singers ministry for the purpose of evangelizing the Silk Road regions. In the process, LRM mobilized those leaders to support the Silk Road Mission Strategic Forum financially and with prayer. The Forum is held every two years with the involvement of several major churches. In this way, LRM will be able to identify and provide appropriate services for those in need as they work together with missionaries from diverse backgrounds.[14]

12. Timothy Kiho Park's observation was made during a lecture he delivered on January 2012 at the Overseas Ministries Study Center, New Haven, Connecticut.

13. Half of the Life Road Singers are now missionaries in China; the rest have professional jobs in Korea and in the United States.

14. In 2010, according to the Korean Mission Association in China and the Silk Road Research Team, more than 6,000 Korean missionaries were working in China and Central Asia.

LRM's unique care of member missionaries. My report "Korean Missionary Retirement Survey" was included as an addendum in the book *Family Accountability in Missions*.[15] It highlighted weaknesses in the level of missionary member care provided by Korean churches. Understanding this need, Life Road Mission has shown an extraordinary commitment to providing excellent care for its member missionaries.

A significant event related to member care that occurs yearly is the Strategy Conference and Retreat for Missionaries; it is organized by LRM and is held in the HKKEMC building. For this spiritual retreat program, all member missionaries and their families are invited to Hong Kong once a year to reflect upon their ministries and to recharge their heart, soul, and mind. LRM, which assists generously with participants' costs, has designed the program to meet the needs of adult missionaries in a conference format, as well as of MKs in a camp setting.

Missionaries and their families who have gone through the series of workshops and worship services have reported that the experience has brought healing and energy to their journey and helped in refining their calling. When I participated in this program for a week in February 2014, I was deeply impressed by the staff from HKKEMC, who served with sincere joy and wholehearted thanksgiving. The week was a one-of-a-kind experience that stands out in my entire journey as a missionary.

Pastor Hyung Joong Yoon also has a deep commitment to supporting female missionaries, most of whom are married, with their particular hardships. To support and encourage them, HKKEMC holds an annual program that offers seminars and counseling, with all expenses covered by the church.

Recently a mission pastor from a megachurch in Seoul shared his concerns with me, saying, "We have no plan for the retirement of 120 missionaries whom our church has sent. In the past we tried our best to cover for their children's education, but every day we are faced with a bigger financial challenge with new projects." I then remembered Hyung Joong Yoon's word of encouragement

15. Jin Bong Kim, "Korean Missionary Retirement Survey," in *Family Accountability in Missions*, ed. Jonathan J. Bonk (New Haven, Conn.: OMSC Publications, 2013), 259–73.

given in September 2014 at the Overseas Ministries Study Center (OMSC), and I thought that the steps taken by HKKEMC could provide a marvelous example for all churches.

> Since the director of international church relations at OMSC, Rev. Jinbong Kim, came to speak at our mission center last February, the issue of missionary retirement has seriously challenged me as the director of the center. As I was praying about it one day, we received a donation of a large piece of property in a suburban area of Seoul. We have recently finalized a construction plan, and we are moving forward to build a missionary residential complex in the upcoming year. This area will be operated with and for retired missionaries![16]

Having observed Hyung Joong Yoon and HKKEMC for over a decade, I can testify that he is a miracle worker of God and that God's hand is evident in all his work and plans.

LOOKING BACK AND LOOKING AHEAD

The leadership and ministry philosophy embraced by Hyung Joong Yoon has shown itself to be successful in developing a healthy and thriving diaspora church that can serve as a model for other such churches. Especially to be valued is the ministry of HKKEMC's Life Road Mission over the past decade and a half. In keeping with the motto he has kept close to his heart, "One person's dream is just a dream, but the dream of all is reality," Pastor Yoon strives to share the vision of mission with all of his church members wherever and whenever he can. He purposely looks not only upward toward the vision but also around him, as he cares for and empowers each member of the congregation every day.

Yoon reports that his immediate concern is not the work of mission, but that of pastoring as the senior pastor. Over twenty-one years ago when he first became the head pastor, he was convicted of the need for HKKEMC to go out to do mission and to give, even if they went bankrupt. The church has not gone bankrupt; rather,

16. Hyung Joong Yoon, "A Diaspora Story of a Missional Church: The Hong Kong Korea Mission Church Story," presentation given at the annual Korean Pastors Luncheon, held at OMSC in New Haven, Connecticut, on September 22, 2014.

they have sent sixty cross-cultural missionaries into the field without having a financial burden, and they plan to support three hundred missionaries in the future. Pastor Yoon now dreams of the future, thirty years from now, when the Silk Road, once built for trading, will become the "life road" for those who need the message of eternal life.

Yoon has the following word of encouragement for churches around the world: "Mission is not only a foundational reason for the church but also its essence. Believing that God is in charge and in control, I was able to come this far. Do not let your circumstances get in the way of doing God's work. Mission begins and moves with prayer and prayer alone."

QUESTIONS FOR REFLECTION

1. Wherever they are located, "the purpose of the Korean diaspora churches should be to serve all the people in their vicinity who are in need of the Gospel." How do these words apply to your church in today's multicultural societies? What changes might be entailed if they are taken seriously?
2. My chapter "Korean Missionary Retirement Survey" highlighted weaknesses in the missionary member care provided by Korean churches. Does your church or your mission agency have a member care team? What kind of care does your church or your mission agency provide for its missionaries?
3. "The leadership and ministry philosophy embraced by Hyung Joong Yoon has shown itself to be successful in developing a healthy and thriving diaspora church that can serve as a model for other such churches." If the present leadership of HKKEMC changes, how can it ensure that its current mission work continues? Is structuring the church as a sodality a healthy approach for doing mission work?

9

Response to "Hong Kong Korean Exodus Mission Church"

Peter Tze Ming Ng

I wish to thank Jinbong Kim for his chapter introducing us to the Hong Kong Korean Exodus Mission Church (HKKEMC), which can serve as a good model for today's diaspora church. This church is a good example of a Korean congregation actively serving missionally in Hong Kong. The Korean diaspora church must be viewed in relation to the Korean missionary movement as a whole. In 2008, Korean Protestant churches had the goal of sending out at least 1,000 new foreign missionaries each year. Such growth has made the Korean mission force one of the most rapidly growing national missionary movements in the world.[1] Even now, with its more than 17,000 Christian missionaries and preachers (evangelists) serving abroad, Korea is second only to the United States in the number of Christian missionaries it sends beyond its borders.[2] In his chapter Kim draws our attention to ways that one Korean diaspora church can serve as a model for missional churches today. The Korean diaspora mission is definitely a key subject in recent studies of Christian world mission.[3]

1. See Steve Sang-Cheol Moon, "The Protestant Missionary Movement in Korea: Current Growth and Development," *International Bulletin of Missionary Research* 32, no. 2 (2008): 59–64.

2. Culled from Wikipedia under the heading "Korean Christians in Hong Kong"; see https://en.wikipedia.org/wiki/Korean_Christians_in_Hong_Kong.

3. See, e.g., *Korean Diaspora and Christian Mission*, ed. S. Hun Kim and

HKKEMC: ITS DIVERSITY OF LANGUAGES AND MINISTRIES

According to the 2011 Hong Kong census, it was home to 5,209 Koreans, which represented 1.2 percent of the total ethnic minority population of 451,183 persons.[4] From Kim's report, approximately 2,000 of these Koreans were Christians. According to Kim, "The Korean diaspora churches should . . . serve all the people in their vicinity who are in need of the Gospel. . . . [They should] invite both those who speak Korean and those in their neighborhood who do not into the church of the Lord" (69).

Since Hong Kong is a multicultural and multilingual city, Korean diaspora churches located there have the opportunity to embrace various linguistic and cultural groups in their assemblies. This fact is very important for our understanding of Christian mission in diaspora churches today. As Kim reports, the 500 or so members of HKKEMC include four distinct, though not separate, congregations, each functioning in their own language: Korean (350 members), Cantonese (100 members), Mandarin (60 members), and English (40 members). Together, they provide a wonderful example of a church in which believers can use their own diverse languages to worship the same God, a God who understands and is willing to listen to the prayers of all and to accept their worship in whatever form of language or culture they are accustomed to using. Will this diversity characterize the heavenly kingdom of God? It certainly seems so: "I beheld, and, lo, a great multitude, which no man could number, of all nations, and kindreds, and people, and tongues, stood before the throne, and before the Lamb . . . and cried with a loud voice, saying, 'Salvation to our God which

---

Wonsuk Ma (Oxford: Regnum Studies in Mission Series, 2011). It would also be good to compare the study of Chinese diaspora churches in recent years; e.g., see Enoch Wan, "Mission among the Chinese Diaspora: A Case Study of Migration and Mission," http://missiology.org/missionchina/ChineseDiaspora-Missiology.pdf.

4. See the Census and Statistics Department, "Thematic Report: Ethnic Minorities," in *The 2011 Population Census* (Hong Kong: HKSAR Government Printing Office, 2011), available at www.census2011.gov.hk/pdf/EM.pdf.

sitteth upon the throne, and unto the Lamb'" (Rev. 7:9–10 KJV). If we are accountable to God, we should understand that God loves all peoples and accept their worship in whatever forms of language and culture they are accustomed to using.

In such a diversity of languages and cultures, the leaders of HKKEMC are working to formulate and achieve a unified missional vision for the church. In 1998 senior pastor Hyung Joong Yoon led in the establishment of Life Road Mission (LRM). Built upon a missional vision of the church, LRM works to train missionaries for cross-cultural ministry. Again, cross-cultural ministry is of great significance to Christian mission today. So far, as Jinbong Kim reports, LRM has sent out sixty missionaries equipped to lead cross-cultural ministries. In 2000 the church organized a professional praise ministry team, the Life Road Singers. This group comprises professional singers and musicians from Seoul and Hong Kong who give concerts to support the cause of Christian world mission. Music is indeed an excellent medium for offering witness to the Christian Gospel, because music can be expressed in any language or culture. Christian ministries such as the LRM are definitely avenues of ministry that diaspora churches can perform for the sake of world mission today.

HKKEMC has also developed other Christian ministries in the past decade, including the Life Road Mission Training Center, which trains, sends out, and cares for missionaries who serve in cross-cultural ministry. Today, Christian missionaries need to be equipped to serve in multiracial and multicultural environments. They need to develop healthy communities and centers of Christian fellowship among people of different races and cultures. "Prayer Meetings" and "Families" have been found to be very good strategic bases for Christian ministry in multicultural situations. For example, Korean churches commonly include morning prayers and "home-cell groups" in their ministries. Some churches, such as the Hong Kong Elim Presbyterian Church, have mountain prayers every Saturday morning. Church members climb up to "Jacob's Ladder" on Mount Parker at Hong Kong's Quarry Bay to pray for peace and harmony in the city. The Hong Kong Han Hwa Presbyterian Church has also introduced the practice of "family meadow" for the home-cell groups in the church. Family meadow seeks to promote family relationships and to provide a platform for different cultural groups, including both Christians and non-Christians, to help one another.[5] In Hong Kong such activities are valuable aspects of cross-cultural ministry.

Another important topic noted by Kim is that of missionary retirement. Elsewhere Kim refers to a report by the Korea Research Institute for Mission, which states that in 2011 some 19,373 Korean missionaries were active in 177 countries, and nearly one quarter (24.3 percent) of them were fifty years old or more.[6] It would be desirable to sponsor retirement centers or residential complexes for retired missionaries where workers from all over the world could find a home and create a new community. A benefit of the new community centers is that they would become excellent places for retired missionaries to share their valuable experiences of doing Christian ministry in different countries and cultures. These centers could contribute to our concern today for multiracial and multicultural world ministries.

HKKEMC: A TIMELY MODEL

Pastor Hyung Joong Yoon and HKKEMC have already sent sixty cross-cultural missionaries into the field, and they look forward to supporting three hundred missionaries thirty years from now. Well-trained and well-equipped missionaries who are capable of doing a variety of cross-cultural Christian ministries are precisely what the world needs today. Through its growth as a church that can accommodate multilingual and multicultural constituencies and its development of relevant Christian ministries such as the Life Road Mission and Life Road Singers, HKKEMC has provided a good model for diaspora churches. But let us not forget, as Pastor Yoon says, "Mission begins and moves with prayer and prayer alone" (76).

In reading Jinbong Kim's chapter, I was reminded of Chinese scholar Francis C. M. Wei (1888–1976), who in 1945–46 was the first

5. See, e.g., https://en.wikipedia.org/wiki/Korean_Christians_in_Hong_Kong.

6. Jin Bong Kim, "Korean Missionary Retirement Survey," in *Family Accountability in Missions*, ed. Jonathan Bonk (New Haven, Conn.: OMSC Publications, 2013), 259.

Henry W. Luce Visiting Professor of World Christianity at Union Theological Seminary in New York. In one of his lectures, he stated that, in order to realize the truth of Christianity as a world religion, we need to seek the expressions of our Christian faith made in different cultures and by different peoples of the world. He suggested that, rather than seeking to conquer non-Christian Asia, Western missionaries should seek help from Asian peoples, inviting them to join as partners in the worldwide Christian movement.[7] Wei was calling for us to pay more respectful attention to local contexts, including to the diversity of cultures and languages among the people we are serving, whether in the diaspora or any part of today's globalized world.

7. See Francis C. M. Wei, *The Spirit of Chinese Culture* (New York: Scribner's Sons, 1947), and also the discussion in Peter Tze Ming Ng, "'Globalization' as a Key to the Interplay between Christianity and Asian Cultures: The Vision of Francis Wei in Early Twentieth-Century China," *International Journal of Public Theology* 1 (2007): 104–15.

10

A Medium-Size Korean Church and a Small Korean Church in Mission

Jinbong Kim

In 2013 Christian Ethics Movement Korea (CEMK), an independent nonprofit research organization founded in 1987 by a group of Christian Korean professors, conducted a survey in South Korea on the topic of the social credibility of the Korean Protestant churches. The negative responses were more than double the number of positive ones. Of the 1,000 persons who took part in the survey, only 19.4 percent indicated that they trusted Korean Protestant churches, and fully 44.6 percent showed distrust toward the churches. The responses of nonbelievers to the CEMK survey are telling: 47.0 percent believe Catholicism is the most credible religion, 38.0 percent Buddhism, and 12.5 percent Protestantism.[1] Protestant church leaders should take this data to heart and carefully consider their implications.

Statistics released by the major Protestant denominations of South Korea in September 2014 indicated that, in that year, all Korean Protestant denominations were declining in membership.[2] In his comment on this decline in the CEMK report, Wonkyoo Lee,

1. See Christian Ethics Movement Korea, "Data of Opinion Research on Social Credibility of Korean Protestant Church 2013 (2014.2.5)" [in Korean], http://cemk.org/2008/bbs/board.php?bo_table=207_data_cemk&wr_id=347. Documents can be downloaded at http://trusti.tistory.com/938.

2. "2014 General Assemblies of Major Denominations of South Korea" [in Korean], *Kukmin Daily*, September 29, 2014, http://news.kmib.co.kr/article/view.asp?arcid=0922799465&.

professor of religious and social studies at Methodist Theological University in Korea, identifies serious challenges facing Korean Protestant churches.

> How can we interpret the phenomenon that Korean Protestant churches are more criticized from within than from the outside? Two trends seem possible: First, when self-critical voices cry out for church renewal, a new atmosphere welcoming church renewal could emerge. Second, the negative impression of Korean Protestant churches could grow stronger, leading more Protestant members to leave their churches, thereby accelerating Korean Protestantism's decline.[3]

Why have the Korean people lost trust in the Korean church? Similar answers are given by Christians and non-Christians: they expect the church to manifest a sense of honesty and conscience and to express love for neighbors in their services.[4] The future of the Korean church will be brighter insofar as the church seriously commits itself to carrying out the two greatest commands: "Love the Lord your God with all your heart and with all your soul and with all your mind," which Jesus called "the first and greatest commandment." The second is "Love your neighbor as yourself." As Jesus summarized, "All the Law and the Prophets hang on these two commandments" (Matt. 22:37–40 NIV).

In this chapter I consider two ordinary-sized Korean churches. The first is Hwangji Presbyterian Church, a medium-sized church that thoughtfully tries to shed Christ's light on its local community. It exhibits love for God and love for its neighbors, doing all it can to dispel the cold, even harsh, impression given off by Korean Protestant churches. The second is Juhyanghan Church, a small mission-minded church located in Seoul that meets in rented facilities.

HWANGJI PRESBYTERIAN CHURCH

Denominationally, Hwangji Presbyterian Church (HPC) belongs to the Presbyterian Church of Korea (Tonghap). It is located in Taebaek, a small city that lies 220 kilometers (135 miles) to the east of Seoul.

3. Ibid.
4. See Christian Ethics Movement Korea, "Data."

Starting with five to six believers in Hwangji Eup, in the area of Taebaek, where the coal mining industry was prospering, HPC began on March 29, 1951, as a prayer shelter.[5] As the region's coal mines developed, numerous jobs were created, which attracted many newcomers. Because of Hwangji Eup's popularity, the population swelled to over 110,000.[6] On July 1, 1981, the government recognized Taebaek as an official city. By the mid-1980s, however, the international price of oil had dropped, and South Korea followed the trend of switching its primary energy source from coal to petroleum. As the demand for coal decreased, multiple coal mines were closed, including those in Taebaek.[7] From a high of more than 120,000 in 1987, Taebaek's population dropped to 49,837 in 2012. Despite the city's decrease in population and its devastated economy, HPC maintained its membership and continued to grow. When Jong Eon Kim was installed as the church's senior pastor in 1999, the adult membership stood at 330 and the population of Taebaek at 60,000. By 2008 the church membership had reached 521, while the population of Taebaek had shrunk to 50,000. By 2012 the population of Taebaek had fallen below 50,000, but HPC continued to grow; in 2014 it had about 800 church members, of whom 607 were adults.[8] This church, which I have visited several times, witnessed a revival that went beyond simply the number of its members. HPC experienced healthy spiritual growth, just as the early church in Jerusalem did, and the membership of the church increased naturally as members truly became salt and light in their community. Several characteristics stand out as being crucial to the surprising growth of HPC.

Pastoral leadership and congregational service. At the head of the list of characteristics crucial to HPC's revival stand the integrity and

5. Jong Eon Kim, "The History of Hwangji Church and the Philosophy of Ministry of Jong Eon Kim" (e-mail responses, in Korean, to written interview questions from Jinbong Kim), November 20, 2014; in author's files.

6. For the population of Taebaek, see http://blog.daum.net/pm21234/15862358.

7. See Research Institute of Korean Studies, http://rikszine.korea.ac.kr/front/article/humanList.minyeon?selectArticle_id=74.

8. Jong Eon Kim, "The History of Hwangji Church."

the unconditionally loving leadership shown by Jong Eon Kim, who since 1999 has served the church as head pastor. These attitudes are evident in words he wrote about his ministry at HPC: "First and foremost, Rev. Jungkyoo Lee, the previous senior pastor of HPC, played an important role in building up the church as it is today. In my philosophy of ministry I take the ministries of the Word, prayer, service, and charity as my mission and believe that the church should be focused on nurturing people, not on doing businesses."[9]

In 2006–7 the HPC membership and church council enabled Jong Eon Kim and his family to have a one-year sabbatical in the United States. Their deep trust and full financial support for him were well justified. I personally appreciated sharing in community life with him and his family when they came to reside at the Overseas Ministries Study Center (OMSC) for the ten-month program year. During that time Pastor Kim showed that his character is grounded in honesty, integrity, care, and love.

Throughout its history HPC has not focused primarily on growth-oriented ministries, but on faithfully obeying the Lord's two greatest commands by getting involved with community-oriented ministries. The church continuously served the community by conducting social welfare work for thirty years, kindergarten ministry for fifty-five years, Kids' House for twenty-seven years, and Adult Middle School for thirty-seven years. These activities were not carried out as a means to grow the church's membership but in order to sincerely follow the instructions of Jesus Christ.[10] A result, as Kim has told me, is that the local community views the church very favorably: "When I walk around the town or engage in street evangelism, I hear many say, 'If I go to a church, it will be HPC.'"[11]

Kim also wrote about a special moment at HPC that touched the hearts of many staff and board members of OMSC. Upon the retirement of Jonathan Bonk, former executive director of OMSC, the center was working to form a special scholarship in his honor. When Pastor Kim heard the news, he arranged for the Women's Evangelism Group at his church to organize a fund-raising event to

9. Ibid.
10. Ibid.
11. Ibid.

benefit OMSC. They held a food bazaar on March 14–15, 2013, cooking and selling 567 chickens, from which they collected US$5,000. Another $5,000 was received through matching gifts from several members of the congregation. In the end HPC donated $10,000 to OMSC for the scholarship fund.[12] Pastor Kim has shown honorable leadership at HPC, and I hope that the example HPC has given of genuine service can be shared with churches in Korea, the United States, and around the world, for it shows the value of faithfully putting into practice the Bible's command to love our neighbors as ourselves (Matt. 22:39).

Ministry as the matrix of social welfare work in the local community. HPC has a long history of social welfare work in behalf of coal miners. An example is the Christian Coal Miners' Social Development Welfare Ministry, which the church founded in 1984. It provides services for the miners such as House of Rest, Taebaek Nursing Home, and Lunch Box of Love, which were later incorporated into the Taebaek Social Welfare Corporation of Taebaek City.[13] These services grew out of four practical objectives for coal miners that HPC adopted in 1980: to recognize the miners and their work, to encourage them, to improve their living standard, and to "inspire them to embrace hope." In order to achieve these objectives, the church initiated five ministries: an educational ministry, a medical ministry, a counseling ministry, a ministry to coal miners' families, and a ministry of leadership development in the mining community. In 1991 the church opened the Center for Miners' Disease for patients with pneumoconiosis (black lung disease). Medical ministry is accompanied by ministries of worship, Bible study, counseling, and literacy education. In 1991 they also opened the Free Silver Nursing Home for fifty elderly residents.[14] Formerly, each of these social welfare ministries was funded solely from donations by the church and individual donors. Under welfare laws enacted in 1984, the Korean government now contributes more than 80 percent of the expenses of these social ministries.

12. Ibid.
13. Ibid.
14. Ibid.

When Jong Eon Kim became senior pastor, he embraced HPC's foundational missional spirit, further developed the church's community-oriented service ministries, and supported engaging professionals in the operation of the social ministries. With the conviction that the church should continuously seek to develop outreach as well as activities for the benefit of the community, he invested more energy and effort in the ministries of worship, evangelism, and education than had previously been given to them.[15] Two full-time assistant pastors were hired with responsibility for visiting the parishioners, organizing better and more frequent fellowship events, looking after inactive church members, and leading a Thursday evangelism group for local nonbelievers. Two Christian education pastors have been employed by the church with full authority for the education departments. To challenge the idol-worshiping culture of the community, Kim has invested in cultural outreach. The church operates a small performance amphitheater, a music school, and classes for drama and worship dance. To enrich and extend the faith of soldiers in the area, HPC initiated an outreach program focused on military personnel. In 2003 this program was incorporated into the Armed Forces Outreach Committee under Taebaek's Christian Church Coalition.

Currently HPC engages in three major outreach ministries. The first is general evangelism ministries. This emphasis includes the New Life Festival (held for the entire month of May, it welcomes and registers about two hundred seekers) and Finding Lost Sheep (occurring in October, it reaches out to church members who have not attended worship services for a long time). HPC's second major outreach ministry is that of service ministries. These are cultural outreach, hospice services and volunteer training, relief ministries, scholarship fund, kids' house, kindergarten, and overseas missions that support financially and with prayer their commissioned missionary in Kyrgyzstan and additional missionaries and organizations around the world. The church's third major outreach is its ministry of evangelism among Korea's military forces; the Military Forces Outreach, initiated by HPC, is now conducted in cooperation with the Christian Church Coalition.

Since its founding, HPC has followed the Golden Rule

15. Ibid.

(Matt. 7:12) by doing its best "to accept and serve others." In 2014 the church cheerfully spent $200,000, about 25 percent of its annual budget, for community-oriented services and evangelism and for overseas missions.[16]

Evangelizing in accordance with the rapidly changing needs of the society. As mentioned, the population of Taebaek decreased from more than 120,000 in 1987 to less than 50,000 in 2014. When the region's coal mines shut down and the community's economy shrank, the government tried to revitalize the economy by introducing the leisure industry. Casinos and hotels soon began to appear and prosper in the area.[17] HPC makes constant efforts to accommodate the rapidly changing needs of the local community and to share the Gospel effectively. For example, English-speaking young people from affiliated Korean churches abroad have come to serve in the Summer English Camp that HPC began in 2008. The work of the camps has been well received by the community, and the youth visiting from abroad have positive reports about their experience in the area. Buoyed by these favorable responses to the English camp, HPC has been developing plans to build an English Bible school, complete with dormitories. The proposal is to recruit students from across Asia, supplying training based on biblical values.

A coffee shop is located inside the education center of the church building in downtown Taebaek. It provides coffee at an affordable price and attracts townspeople. All proceeds from the coffee shop go back to the community and to overseas missions. Compared to big cities such as Seoul, Taebaek is culturally impoverished. To contribute to the region's cultural enrichment, HPC built a new theater in which professional musicians and artists offer regular concerts and hold music schools, drama classes, and worship dance classes. The presence of these new services makes HPC exemplary as a church that carries out effective cultural outreach and addresses the needs of its community.

16. Ibid.

17. See *Monthly Chosun*, http://monthly.chosun.com/client/news/print.asp?ctcd=C&nNewsNumb=201004100052.

On the one hand, as we noted at the beginning of this chapter, Korean Protestantism is losing its once-high credibility, not only among the general public but also among those within the church. According to a survey conducted by CEMK in 2013, distrust of Korean Protestantism grows within the Korean populace when Korean Protestantism's words and deeds do not match (24.8 percent) and when corruption is present in the churches (21.4 percent). On the other hand, trust grows in the Korean Protestant church when it is seen as honest and has integrity (18.6 percent) and when the church provides social services (17.5 percent).[18]

HPC has been in Taebaek, a region now of deserted coal mines, for over sixty years. Despite the obstacles presented by a decreased population and shrinking economy, the church has offered sacrificial service and agape love for more than half a century. Serving with integrity and an honorable lifestyle, the current senior pastor, Jong Eon Kim, has impressed not only his church members but also nonbelievers in the local community. While other church communities are concerned that membership and budget are decreasing, in Taebaek HPC stands as the salt and light of Jesus Christ, gaining members every year. The church's story provides inspiration, encouragement, and hope for churches in other poverty-stricken areas.

JUHYANGHAN CHURCH

When in 1990 I first went as a missionary to Côte d'Ivoire, a French-speaking country in West Africa, only a handful of Korean missionaries were working in Francophone Africa. The number grew significantly, bolstered by the efforts of the Communauté Coréenne des Missions pour la Francophonie (CCMF), so that by the end of 2014 more than 200 Korean missionaries were ministering in Francophone Africa. Initially formed in Juhyanghan Church, CCMF has played a crucial role in informing Korean churches of the urgency of missions to French-speaking Africa, inspiring the churches to send many enthusiastic missionaries there.[19]

18. See Christian Ethics Movement Korea, "Data."

19. See www.iccmf.com, the website of the Communauté Coréenne des Missions pour la Francophonie.

Mongsik Lee, pastor of Juhyanghan Church, shared with me how he came to plant Juhyanghan Church as a church in Korea that was solely dedicated to Francophone missions:

> In 1991 I took an introductory French course taught by a professor who had studied in France. The course totally opened my eyes to the presence of French-speaking regions around the world and made me wonder why they were quite neglected as a mission field. This vision became the primary motive that led me to plant a local church solely dedicated to Francophone missions. During the following year a French-language study group evolved into a prayer meeting for French-speaking countries. After exploring France in 1993 and Francophone Africa in 1995, the prayer group sent its first missionary to the African country of Chad in 1997, five years after its formation.[20]

Juhyanghan Church became the base on which CCMF took form, and it still plays a central role in its operation. The church is located near the Geoyeo subway station in Seoul, where it leases space in a commercial building that contains small markets and offices. Since the church does not own the space, 30–40 percent of its annual budget goes for rent, something that is common for many churches in Seoul and beyond, which makes survival financially difficult. Making matters worse, many Korean Christians have been switching church membership, usually from small and midsized churches to megachurches. Unsurprisingly, many small churches located in commercial buildings eventually close because of financial pressures.

In his book *2020–2040: The Future Map of the Korean Church*, Yoonsik Choi well diagnoses the issues facing Korean churches:

> Small churches, which compose 80 percent of the Protestant churches in Korea, are falling into defeatism, for their church members keep moving to bigger churches perceived to be more comfortable, convenient, easy-going, and better-programmed. When megachurches launch satellite chapel buildings and invest several hundred million dollars in newly developed suburban

20. Mongsik Lee, pastor of Juhyanghan Church, interview by Jinbong Kim, January 11, 2013.

> areas, the small churches within a radius of several kilometers wither away.[21]

Though the number of small churches is declining, Juhyanghan Church stands strong on its calling from God. Pastor Lee insists that even though the church has relatively few members, it cannot turn away from God's mission.

> Many people think that big churches can afford [to be involved in] overseas missions, while small churches cannot. It may also be claimed that mission is all about sending missionaries and that overseas missions are done only by full-time missionaries. These notions, however, reflect a prejudiced view of the work of missions. This type of misunderstanding and ignorance of mission creates a real problem in this field. As a matter of fact, not all of the bigger churches are involved in missions, and not all of the smaller churches are incapable of missions. Regardless of the size or funding of a church, the important issues in mission lie within the truth of the Gospel and delivering that message.[22]

Ministry strategy of CCMF and Juhyanghan Church. CCMF is a nondenominational overseas ministry team, founded and dedicated specifically to evangelizing the entire Francophone world. The society recruits, trains, and sends missionaries to Francophone Africa, which for many years has been neglected by most Korean overseas mission organizations.[23]

Founded by Juhyanghan Church in 1992, CCMF started a missionary training program in 1997 that was focused on a Francophone population and sent its first missionary family to Chad in August 1997. In 2001 a French-speaking worship service began at Shinbanpo Church in Seoul (the pastor is president of the board of trustees for CCMF); a French pastor currently leads this ministry. CCMF's French-language program has continued from the

21. Yoonsik Choi, *2020–2040: The Future Map of the Korean Church* [in Korean] (Seoul: Word of Life, 2013), 75.

22. Lee, interview by Jinbong Kim.

23. This paragraph and the following two paragraphs draw on information available at www.iccmf.com.

beginning. After seven years of translation effort, CCMF published a French-Korean Bible in June 2013.

CCMF has four principal objectives: prayer, pioneer church planting in unreached areas, devotion, and cooperation. Under the title "The Sahara Project," CCMF explores ways to prevent the southward expansion of Islam from the Middle East and North Africa. The intent is to explore West African French-speaking areas, where many unreached tribes still remain, so as to plant churches and to establish a mission base in a region where few Korean missionaries (but many non-Korean missionaries) currently minister.

Juhyanghan Church's role in CCMF bears emphasis. The church gave the mission society full support by allowing its senior pastor to participate actively in the organization as its director. Well-trained and highly committed church members have served the community as staff members and have provided abundant resources for missions. But the most important support from the church is its intercessory prayer for Francophone missions; most church members actively participate as intercessors. In addition, Juhyanghan Church dedicates regular financial support to CCMF, and two families from the congregation serve as missionaries with CCMF.

Pastor Lee's vision for Juhyanghan Church and CCMF is expansive.

> Juhyanghan Church was born to serve Francophonic missions, so I pray that the church will continually grow in its conduct of missions in the Francophone world. I plan to organize a church-wide movement for Francophone missions and to produce many national Francophone ministers. Furthermore, I would like to invite more churches to do missions in the Francophone world. The most practical hope is that our church may establish a mission center in a French-speaking region in West Africa so that our church members may actively participate in it.[24]

With supporters such as Munsu Hong, senior pastor of Shinbanpo Church, this vision does not seem out of reach. Hong has shown overwhelming support for the community, having served as president of CCMF's board of directors since the board's first

24. Lee, interview by Jinbong Kim.

meeting. When CCMF published a French-Korean Bible, Shinbanpo Church made a large financial contribution for the project.[25]

A small congregation committed to African Francophone missions. Mongsik Lee and I graduated from seminary together. At that time I helped inspire him and the professor who taught him French to commit to a Francophone mission. For the past twenty-five years I have had the privilege of witnessing the amazing work of God in his ministry. Lee has been a Gospel-oriented, humble, and thoughtful pastor before God and his colleagues. Above everything else he, as a minister, has dedicated all of his heart, soul, and mind for Francophone missions. Though he neither majored in the French language nor had any experience of ministry in French-speaking Africa, as I did, his zeal and commitment to Francophone African evangelization are second to none. His unstinting commitment and effort in behalf of Francophone African missions have challenged Korean churches to get involved and have made Francophone African missions more fruitful.

Pastors often seek a larger and more comfortable space for their church as their ministry progresses. They purchase land or a facility to settle in where they can build up their ministries for many years to come. Who would not? Pastor Lee, however, chose a different course. He has remained dedicated to Francophone missions from the time when he planted Juhyanghan Church in a commercial building and had no ambition to move to nicer facilities. The church's congregation has remained just under 100 members, and it commits 20–30 percent of its annual budget solely for missions in Francophone Africa. When the cost of rent is deducted, it seems clear that the church gives more than 50 percent of its annual offerings for mission and relief.

As a senior pastor, Lee is not free from pastoral complaints and ministerial disagreements. New members especially may not completely understand the priority the senior pastor gives to Francophone ministries, which takes up resources that could be used for their own congregation. Most of the congregation, however, supports the vision of the church for Francophone missions and

25. See GoodtvNews [in Korean], www.c3tv.com/newsmission/news_view.asp?seq=54646.

takes pride in the church's proactive cooperation in this ministry. Many of them participate in the CCMF ministries and encourage Lee's service as director of CCMF.

Despite decades of accepting relative discomfort in a small space in a commercial building, Juhyanghan Church is happy to be part of the evangelization of French-speaking people around the world. The church and CCMF have overcome numerous obstacles to stay focused on Francophone missions, and Lee has played a major role in overseeing these organizations. Who, therefore, would label him only a small church pastor?

Mongsik Lee's words pose a thoughtful challenge to the small churches of the world: "People think that small churches cannot afford to carry out world missions because of their limited human and financial resources. Though our church is small, even from the beginning we have never thought that way. We never stop working for the message of the Gospel and the spread of the Gospel, for these are the reasons Christian churches exist."[26]

QUESTIONS FOR REFLECTION

1. In his book *2020–2040: The Future Map of the Korean Church*, Yoonsik Choi diagnoses the plight of many small Korean churches: "Small churches are falling to defeatism, for their church members keep moving to bigger churches, more comfortable, convenient, easy-going, and better-programmed." In light of this comment, what kinds of accountability do megachurches have toward smaller churches?
2. Mongsik Lee states, "Though our church is small, . . . [we] never stop working for the message of the Gospel and the spread of the Gospel, for these are the reasons Christian churches exist." How can small churches engage in mission? How can the leaders of small churches encourage their congregations to be involved in mission?
3. Even though it has sent more than 20,000 missionaries

26. Lee, interview by Jinbong Kim.

around the world, why has the Korean Protestant church lost the trust of the Korean people, including the trust of a number of Christians?

4. Hwangji Presbyterian Church has offered sacrificial service and agape love for more than half a century, and it stands as the salt and light of Jesus Christ. In what ways is it a model of a missional church? Can its experience be duplicated within the life of your congregation?

5. The story of Hwangji Presbyterian Church provides inspiration, encouragement, and hope for churches in other poverty-stricken areas. Are socially marginal people comfortable attending a church in an affluent area or in which most members of the congregation are rich or highly intellectual? How can a church become a holy place for everybody?

11

Response to "A Medium-Size Korean Church and a Small Korean Church in Mission"

Peter Tze Ming Ng

Reading Jinbong Kim's chapter "A Medium-Size Korean Church and a Small Korean Church in Mission" brought to my mind the exciting period in the 1980s when megachurches began to emerge in South Korea. In those days, more than 10,000 members were attending worship services each Sunday in Young Nak Church, Yoido Full Gospel Church, and many others like them. In this chapter Kim looks the other direction, calling our attention to the ministry of two more ordinary Korean churches—one small in size, and the other medium-sized.

These two churches provide a good illustration of ways that ordinary-sized congregations can be committed to mission, including overseas missions. The first, Hwangji Presbyterian Church, is a medium-sized church that has thoughtfully tried to shed Christ's light on its local community and has extended its concern to overseas ministries as well. The second, Juhyanghan Church, though small in size, from its very beginning has been mission minded and dedicated to overseas ministries.

HWANGJI PRESBYTERIAN CHURCH

Hwangji Presbyterian Church (HPC) is located in the city of Taebaek, 135 miles east of Seoul. Despite the fact that Taebaek's population was dropping drastically—from 120,000 in 1987 to below 50,000 in 2012—HPC's membership continued to grow, climbing from 330 in 1999 to 800 in 2014. As Kim reports, growth has been in more than just numbers; church members have experienced healthy spiritual growth and have become salt and light in their community.

The two senior pastors—Jungkyoo Lee and, since 1999, his successor, Jong Eon Kim—have guided the congregation toward becoming a missional church. Pastor Lee laid a good foundation for the church, on which Jong Eon Kim has built. Kim states, "I take the ministries of the Word, prayer, service, and charity as my mission and believe that the church should be focused on nurturing people, not on doing businesses" (85). Kim did not focus simply on numerical growth, but continued Lee's work by getting members of the church involved in outreach ministries. In particular, the church has focused on general evangelism, voluntary services, and evangelism among Korea's military forces. Pursuing these three ministries has led to substantial growth not only in its membership, but also in its outreach services to the local community—despite the region's declining population and the city's shrinking economy.

Besides the church's community-oriented service ministries, HPC has put much effort into the ministries of worship, evangelism, and education. It has supported cultural outreach in Taebaek, including building a small performance amphitheater, initiating a music school, and hosting classes for drama and worship dance. It was exciting to learn that HPC commits "about 25 percent of its annual budget . . . to community-oriented services and evangelism and for overseas missions" (88). HPC's vision extends far beyond its own setting. Jinbong Kim draws our attention to the church's link with the Overseas Ministries Study Center (OMSC) in New Haven, Connecticut, including a donation of $10,000 to support OMSC's scholarship funds. This example typifies HPC's practice of reaching out beyond itself that the church has developed over the years. The point was not simply a matter of a onetime cultural event of fund-raising to benefit OMSC; more important, it became an opportunity to educate church members about the church's concern and commitment to outreach and ministry overseas, as well as locally. Other examples include the summer English camp that HPC began in 2008 and its plans to build an English Bible school, complete with dormitories, that would recruit students from across Asia.

JUHYANGHAN CHURCH

Jinbong Kim's second example, Juhyanghan Church (JC), demonstrates the ability of a small-sized church to offer support for overseas ministries. Planted as a church that is specifically dedicated to Francophone missions in Africa, the church belies the common misconception that only big churches can become heavily involved in overseas missions. In fact, many larger churches are only minimally involved in overseas missions. Despite its financial constraints, JC is dedicated in particular to the support of the Communauté Coréenne des Missions pour la Francophonie (CCMF) and, more generally, to Francophone missions in Africa. Besides the work on which Jinbong Kim reports, Mongsik Lee, the church's pastor, has set up a Korean website "Prayer Calendar" (http://iccmf.com) to encourage church members to support CCMF by praying for French missionaries and their ministries. Church members are encouraged to support Francophone mission financially or by donations of materials such as books or clothing. To make its ministries more effective, the church has a vision of establishing a mission center in French-speaking West Africa.

JC demonstrates the importance of having a mission-oriented mind-set. Pastor Lee was already dedicated to Francophone mission when he planted JC, and the fact that he has continued his work there for the past twenty-five years proves that a church can adopt such a vision. His work poses a great challenge to others who are working in small churches. As he says, "People think that small churches cannot afford to carry out world missions because of their limited human and financial resources. Though our church is small, even from the beginning we have never thought that way. We never stop working for the message of the Gospel and the spread of the Gospel, for these are the reasons Christian churches exist" (94). What matters most is not the size of the church, but who is leading the church.

CONCLUSION

I appreciate Jinbong Kim's introducing us to these two churches. Both HPC and JC offer challenging examples. Their stories remind us that what is important in forming a missional church—a church which is accountable for Christian mission, either large or small in size—is whether a church's pastor has a mission-minded orientation and a vision for missionary outreach. What matters most, of course, is whether the pastor embraces and communicates the direction that Christ the great shepherd (1 Peter 5:4) has for the church. These churches remind us of the two great commands of Jesus: to "love the Lord your God with all your heart, and with all your soul, and with all your mind" and to "love your neighbor as yourself'" (Matt. 22:37, 39). And it is worth remembering that the Golden Rule (Matt. 7:12) has been paraphrased as "to accept and serve others." These are Christian truths given to us from the Bible.

The missional church described so far refers mostly to evangelism and being of service, whether locally or overseas. With these we do well to keep in mind Dana Robert's recent reminder that "friendship is a foundational practice in Christian mission."[1] Robert even suggests that "'global friendship' is possibly a more compelling motivation for mission than either evangelism or service."[2] Hence, no matter what size a church is, it needs to establish friendship with others, and such friendship should be seen as a foundational practice in its Christian mission. Especially if a church is to be dedicated to overseas missions it should be engaged

1. Dana L. Robert, "Global Friendship as Incarnational Missional Practice," *International Bulletin of Missionary Research* 39, no. 4 (2015): 180. See, also, Dana L. Robert, "Cross-Cultural Friendship in the Creation of Twentieth-Century World Christianity," *International Bulletin of Missionary Research* 35, no. 2 (2011): 100–107.

2. Robert, "Global Friendship as Incarnational Missional Practice," 180.

in developing global friendship, for as Robert states, "Friendship in the way of Jesus creates communities that point toward the kingdom of God."[3]

One of the most crucial legacies a pastor can bequeath to a church is to pass on a vision for outreach ministries, including the development of global friendship, to all members of the congregation. Indeed, the work a pastor does in educating church members, in nurturing them rather than just doing "business as usual," is supremely important for the church. During the past several years, the pastors of both HPC and JC have been exemplary in educating the members of their churches, in enlarging and sustaining a vision for their churches' role in overseas ministries, and in their extension of global friendship. These all constitute good examples—not only for small-sized and medium-sized churches, but also for megachurches—of doing Christian world mission today. They provide good models, not only for evangelism and service, but also for the development of global friendship as a foundational practice of Christian mission.

3. Ibid., 184.

12

African Megachurches and Missions: Mavuno Church, Nairobi, and the Challenge of Accountability

Mark Shaw and Wanjiru M. Gitau

Mavuno Church, located in metropolitan Nairobi, Kenya, is an African megachurch with regular attendance of nearly 3,000 worshippers during their two Sunday services.[1] Like many megachurches around the world, Mavuno is committed to a global strategy of urban church planting; since its beginning in 2005, it has been actively engaged in planting churches in gateway cities of Africa and Europe. Having itself begun as a church plant, Mavuno has a vision for evangelizing urban centers through the founding of culture-defining churches. The rapid growth of Mavuno's church planting mission—which in 2015 could count four congregations in Nairobi and one each in Uganda, Rwanda, Malawi, Zambia, and Germany—has been widely hailed by observers. Less attention has been given to the important question of accountability and the effectiveness of Mavuno's international church planters. In this case study we look closely at Mavuno's vision and practice of cross-cultural urban missions and assess the degree to which their oversight of their growing missions network has kept pace with the multiplication of their daughter churches.[2]

1. "Mavuno" and "Mavuno Church" are used in this chapter to refer to Mavuno Hill City Church located in suburbn Nairobi. In Swahili the word "Mavuno" means "harvest."

2. The information in this case study comes largely from interviews

The issue of accountability in mission is an urgent one. A recent voice calling the attention of Majority World missions to the task of accountability is that of Kiho (Timothy) Park.[3] Park's work is important not only because it comes from the Majority World but also because it responds to one of the great new facts of our time: the rise of Majority World missions. Lausanne 1974 marked a turning point for evangelical missions in which the mission of the church was no longer simply "from the West to the rest" but from everywhere to everywhere. Since that time, Majority World missions (through both migration and conventional mission action) have skyrocketed.[4]

Though Park is aware of the dynamism and vigor of Korean missions, he is concerned about the critical question of missionary accountability. What is the role or responsibility of sending churches and agencies for providing both support and structures of accountability to ensure missionary effectiveness? This question is related to Jonathan Bonk's prophetic call in *Missions and Money* to bring our mission practices into line with both the example of Christ and the practice of the early church.[5] Restoring spiritual and financial integrity is central to this call. The new megachurches "covet numerical growth and proudly cite their numbers as testimonies to spiritual relevance and success in evangelism," writes Kwabena

---

with Muriithi Wanjau, senior pastor of Mavuno Hill City (formerly Mavuno Church; interview conducted by Kyama Mugambi); Kyama Mugambi, executive pastor of Mavuno Hill City; Jerry and Cynthia Opiyo, pastors of Mavuno Kigali (Rwanda); Daniel and Nancy Fleschig, pastors of Mavuno Berlin (Germany); Wareru and Evie Njenga, pastors of Mavuno Blantyre (Malawi); and Antony Njoroge, pastor of Mavuno Kampala (Uganda), all conducted by Wanjiru Wangui. Additional information was obtained through participant observation and from ephemeral material such as church bulletins.

3. Kiho (Timothy) Park, "The Big Picture: Accountability from a Korean Missiologist's Perspective," in *Accountability in Missions: Korean and Western Case Studies*, ed. Jonathan J. Bonk (Eugene, Ore.: Wipf & Stock, 2011), 53–65.

4. Jehu J. Hanciles, "Migration, Diaspora Communities, and the New Missionary Encounter with Western Society," *Lausanne World Pulse*, July 2008, www.lausanneworldpulse.com/themedarticles.php/975?pg=all.

5. Jonathan J. Bonk, *Missions and Money: Affluence as a Missionary Problem . . . Revisited* (Maryknoll, N.Y.: Orbis Books, 2006).

Asamoah-Gyadu.[6] The sheer size of these churches, however, has often created administrative difficulties and made accountability problematic. Some megachurch leaders have become victims of their own success and have fallen into emotional and moral problems. As we will see, Mavuno Church has worked diligently to avoid such problems.

THE MAVUNO STORY

Mavuno Church was launched in 2005 as a daughter church of Nairobi Chapel; its founding pastor, Muriithi Wanjau, played a key role. The site chosen for the first meetings was in a residential area in the south of the city known as South B and South C that straddled Mombasa Road. In an interview, Muriithi noted that from its inception, Mavuno was focused on being a congregation of "apostles to the Gentiles." Although Nairobi was well populated with churches, most of the existing congregations were operating in what the Mavuno leadership described as a "cocooned Christian subculture." Muriithi and his leadership team of three other pastors, along with a significant group of volunteers, realized that emergent, postcollege urbanites were increasingly unresponsive to, if not alienated by, existing methods of evangelism in Nairobi. As the church leaders intentionally built friendships with this younger demographic, they listened closely to find out what this group thought about Christianity. They noted the needs and concerns mentioned in an effort to adapt their ministry to that audience. Based on those conversations, the Mavuno Church pastors designed services that engaged unchurched young adults, whom they referred to as a "sight and sound generation." Access to Mavuno's initial location proved inadequate. Growth was modest, but a foundation of prayer, outreach strategies, methods of preaching, and leadership was perfected and put in place. The goal was to develop a church that could evangelize, engage, and retain a previously unreached, upwardly mobile, young adult population. In June 2008 Mavuno Church moved to a more

6. J. Kwabena Asamoah-Gyadu, "Megachurches and Their Implications for Christian Mission," *Lausanne Global Analysis* 3, no. 5 (September 2014), www.lausanne.org/docs/LGA/Lausanne-Global-Analysis-2014-09.pdf.

accessible location off Mombasa Highway. During the next few years the congregation grew from 600 to nearly 3,000 in attendance. In 2014 Mavuno acquired and moved into its own permanent property in the developing middle-class suburb of Athi River. The headquarters of the Mavuno family of churches is now officially called Mavuno Hill City (or simply Mavuno or Mavuno Church in this chapter).

From 2000 to 2005, when Mavuno Church was founded, Muriithi was involved in twenty-one church plants. By 2005 he had developed a sharply focused understanding of the demographic group to which God had called him—educated, emerging adults in an urban context. This group is poised to become leaders, yet it is often neglected by traditional churches. In 2006 Mavuno Church began to plant daughter churches. These efforts were entrusted to Kyama Mugambi, who became the executive pastor in charge of church planting. Mavuno's initial church plant, in the city center, was known as Mavuno Downtown, a congregation that aimed to reach even younger emerging adults, particularly those in college and university.

In 2010 Mavuno's church planting strategy was redesigned and clarified. The executive team along with the management team,[7] under the leadership of Muriithi, clarified the church's mission and expressed its vision as follows: "Mavuno's Mission Statement expresses our overarching purpose or why we exist. Our mission involves reaching out to today's un-churched urban generation and through our discipleship process, the Mavuno Marathon, turning them into change agents who will influence the various sectors of society. It can be stated simply as, 'Turning Ordinary People into Fearless Influencers of Society.'"[8] Mavuno has come to identify six sectors of society that, collectively, every member of the congregation would have a

7. In Mavuno's organizational chart, management and the staff team represent different entities. The staff team is organized in an ascending scale from Discovery (internship), to Pastoral Trainees, to Management (heads of departments), to Executive (section assistants under the senior pastor), to Senior Pastor. This scale is referred to as the Leadership Pipeline.

8. *Mavuno Leader's Day Bulletin*, 2010.

role in fearlessly influencing: (1) church and mission, (2) media and the arts, (3) business and the economy, (4) health and the environment, (5) politics and governance, and (6) education and family.[9] The revised mission statement included a sharpening of the Mavuno Church's vision to plant churches:

> Our vision answers the question, What will the future look like if we are faithful in fulfilling our mission? We desire to do nothing less than to change the world in our generation beginning with Africa! We plan to do this by planting culture-defining churches in strategic capital cities. Mavuno's vision can be thus expressed as *"To plant a culture-defining church in every capital city of Africa and the gateway cities of the world by 2035."* Or simply put, "Change a City, Take a Continent, and Win the World."[10]

This vision—to plant a culture-defining church in all African capital cities and gateway cities across the globe—became the guide for the activities of Mavuno's outreach and expansion department. Mavuno decided not to set up a separate missions "sending board" but, rather, to incorporate missions into the leadership structure of the entire church. Church Planting is one of the Departments, and it is led by an Executive Pastor, Kyama Mugambi. This approach allows Mavuno's church planting vision to receive the same regular attention as all the other main ministries of the church.

HOW DOES MAVUNO ENGAGE IN CHURCH PLANTING?

Every year a team from Discovery, Mavuno's annual internship program for leadership training, goes for a short-term mission trip to a selected country, usually in Africa. Part of the goal for this trip is to conduct a "spy mission," to scout the possibilities of starting a Mavuno-style church in the new location. If their report is favorable, the Discovery team is followed by a team from the church planting department. This team is led by the expansions pastor, Kyama Mugambi, and consists of a few pastoral trainees, along with members of Life Groups (the church's small groups) that would have

9. See www.mavunochurch.org/new/content.php?id=50.

10. *Mavuno Leader's Day Bulletin*, 2010.

"adopted" that particular country as a focus for prayer. This team seeks out "men of peace" (see Luke 10:6), friends who are somewhat acquainted with Mavuno members. Relationships are built around young adults in the business community and in media and the entertainment industry. Relationships are also established with university students and sometimes with certain leaders of existing churches. From these relationships a core group is formed to start a Mizizi (Swahili for "roots") class, the main discipleship tool used by Mavuno. Mizizi classes consist of a ten-week discipleship course that utilizes a workbook with instructional material, practical group activities, weekly sessions, and a graduating rite of passage upon completion. The members of the graduating core group are then encouraged to invite their friends and families for a second and third round of Mizizi classes. Through this process a core group of people from the city is formed who are sufficiently familiar with Mavuno's vision, are connected with each other, and are growing in their Christian faith. They become the critical mass for starting a church plant. Using this method, Mavuno has planted churches in Kampala, Uganda; Kigali, Rwanda; Blantyre, Malawi; and Lusaka, Zambia, with similar plans for starting churches in other African major cities.

WHO ARE THE CHURCH PLANTERS?

Mavuno Church's first international church plant, in Kampala, is led by Antony Kigwi Njoroge. The church was officially begun in 2010 by Kevin Nderitu, a pastoral trainee. For a year Nderitu and a team of volunteers commuted to Kampala weekly to run Mizizi classes. In 2012 Njoroge relocated to Kampala with his family to become the lead pastor of the church. Thirty-four-year-old Njoroge, a graduate of East Africa School of Theology, had joined Mavuno Church as an intern in 2008 and, advancing through the leadership pipeline, had grown to become a departmental pastoral leader. Mavuno Kampala has flourished under his leadership and now has about five hundred members. The church's three other staff members are his wife, Gathoni, and two Ugandan pastoral trainees, who have responsibility for Greenhouse (the children's church) and for administration. A compelling leader, Njoroge possesses a charismatic personality.

Twenty-eight-year-old Jerry Rawlings Opiyo (JR) and his wife, Cynthia, are the planters and pastors of Mavuno Kigali. JR gave his life to Christ as a young boy in primary school. While studying engineering at the University of Nairobi, he joined and served in the student ministry of Mamlaka Hill Chapel, a sister church to Mavuno Church. As an engineering student, his career prospects were high, so his parents were initially not enthused by his decision to pursue church ministry after college (though they eventually came to support him). At the invitation of Pastor Muriithi, he joined Mavuno Discovery in 2009. Together with Cynthia, then his fiancée and a Mavuno intern, he hoped to pursue further theological training in the United States. As he prayed, and with encouragement from Pastor Muriithi, he sensed a leading instead to become a church planter with Mavuno. He did so, and in 2013 he and Cynthia were commissioned as a couple to lead the church in Kigali, which had already been holding Mizizi classes for more than a year. By the end of 2014 the church had about one hundred adults and expected to grow quickly in the following year.

Mavuno's church plant in Berlin is led by a German couple, Daniel and Nancy Fleschig. As newlyweds, they met Pastor Oscar Muriu of Nairobi Chapel, Mavuno's mother church. Pastor Muriu was preaching at a conference at Wiedenest Bible School in Germany. In 2008 he invited the Fleschigs to Nairobi Chapel for a year of internship. They were soon seconded to Mavuno Church to aid in a Mavuno relocation project, from the Sports Club to Bellevue. After their internship they continued with the pastoral training program, serving in Mavuno Church altogether for three years. In 2012 they relocated to Berlin and assumed leadership of a small congregation within a fellowship of evangelical churches in Germany. Through a network of relationships, this congregation had already built a friendship with Mavuno Church and had asked for help in reviving the church. Mavuno Berlin has involved remodeling this older congregation rather than starting a brand new one, which, according to Daniel Fleschig, has turned out to be more a matter of change management than church planting. The congregation currently has about fifty adults.

Waweru Njenga, known to his people as Pastor Wa, and his

wife, Evie, are pastors in Malawi of one-year-old Mavuno Blantyre. Originally they were pastors and church planters with Nairobi Lighthouse, a congregation with U.S. Southern Baptist roots. Waweru and Evie planted and led two Lighthouse congregations for ten years before they felt led to leave Lighthouse and move to Mavuno Church. In 2012, despite their long experience as church planters, they joined Mavuno Discovery along with young post-college recruits. Mavuno requires that anyone who joins the pastoral team should first join Discovery to learn Mavuno's culture, or DNA. This DNA includes Mavuno's mission, vision, and strategy, as well as its approach to leadership. Mavuno Blantyre has about fifty adults.

Mavuno Lusaka's path of growth is similar to that of the churches in Blantyre and Kigali. The church is under the pastoral leadership of James Muchai, who has been in the leadership pipeline of Mavuno since 2009. As of 2015, Mavuno Church has plans under way to plant further churches in Ethiopia, South Africa, Tanzania, and Zimbabwe, following the same Mavuno blueprint.

WHAT ABOUT ACCOUNTABILITY?

Technology plays a big role in keeping the church planters connected to Mavuno and to each other. Once a month the church planters are connected to a Mavuno Church staff meeting via Skype conferencing. They share ministry activities and prayer items, as well as hearing from Mavuno staff. Daniel Fleschig says that the Skype conference is usually his monthly highlight. He runs a monthly meeting with volunteers in Berlin, but those meetings are not the same as the Mavuno staff meetings. Mavuno prays and runs meetings with a passion that he does not experience in Berlin. The church planters are also connected to the church's central management team (or department heads) via e-mail. They receive notes about the weekly meetings, which consist of updates, upcoming events, and seasonal goals. This linkage, they say, helps them to remain focused, motivated, and connected. They are not alone, even if they serve at a physical distance.

The church planting pastors are also members of a "What's-

Up."[11] This What's-Up group is moderated by senior pastor Muriithi. Here the pastors share very intentionally about their family lives, interesting encounters, ongoing activity in the churches, challenges (and ideas to solve them), and prayer items. All this technology is expensive, so it becomes a major budget item for all the missionaries; they nevertheless regard it as worthwhile expense. The churches have factored in the cost of technology as part of the cost of making the movement work.

Another way of staying in touch is through visits to Nairobi. Those within East Africa come to Nairobi with some frequency. Njoroge says that after every "season" he takes time off with his family to come to Nairobi.[12] Some of those trips are part of the individual church plant's ministry budget, but some of the costs are met by the pastors themselves.[13] The annual Mavuno staff meeting brings all staff together for a week of relaxing, celebrating, and envisioning into the next year. Another activity hosted by Mavuno Church is the "Fearless Conference," a high-energy leadership

11. The What's-Up group is based on "WhatsApp," a popular app for forming private mobile phone groups. This cross-platform mobile messaging app enables real-time sharing, offering camaraderie and fellowship among pastors who are engaged in similar ministries.

12. Mavuno's annual calendar contains three "seasons," each lasting ten weeks: January to March, May to July, and September to November. Mavuno Church runs its discipleship classes, known as the Mavuno Marathon Classes—Mizizi, Ombi, Ndoa, Lea, Hatua, and Simama—according to these seasons. April, August, and December provide breaks from the classes, which gives the volunteers opportunities to rest and also allows for other outreach activities to be carried out.

13. All the church planters report their churches' financial giving to the central accounts department at Mavuno Central (Mavuno Hill City). Large budgetary items such as the salaries of all church planters and capital expenditures such as rent and purchase of large equipment are centrally determined from Mavuno Church's accounts department. The smaller regular expenditures of church plants are determined by the church planting pastors according to the local needs of their churches. For this purpose the church planters have discretionary funds at their disposal, though the disbursement of all funds in all church plants must still follow accounting procedures that undergo annual audits. The intent is that when the church plants mature, they will determine their own budgets and other ministry decisions.

training conference for church members that is also open to leaders from other churches around the country and from around the world. Church planters find this an empowering opportunity.[14]

ACCOUNTABILITY IN PERSONAL MORAL INTEGRITY

When interns are sent to pioneer Mizizi classes, they go in twos. They accompany each other in their tasks, but they also uphold each other in all areas of accountability, including moral integrity. All church planters at present are married; when they go to plant churches, they go with their spouses. Since the wives, too, are trained or have been volunteers with Mavuno, they also take on leadership responsibilities in the church plants. By working alongside their husbands, they turn church planting into a husband-wife team effort. Persons in pastoral ministry face the temptation to be out on ministry engagements every night. In terms of making pastoral visits or organizing evening events, the Mavuno model requires pastors to spend no more than three nights a week away from their family in ministry. The entire pastoral staff at Mavuno Church follows this principle, and the same expectation is applied to its church planters. Mavuno's practice of recruiting and training a large cohort of volunteer lay leaders in every department, who are able to take on some responsibilities that otherwise would press for the attention of the pastors, is part of what enables the pastoral staff to follow this guideline. The church planters themselves cultivate sensitivity to personal family needs.

FINANCIAL ACCOUNTABILITY

When it plants a new church, Mavuno pays the salaries of church planters and the current expenses of the new church plants for the first year. After that, the level of subsidy depends on how well the church is doing. Regardless of how finances are raised

14. The Fearless Conference is an Annual Leadership Training and Mobilization Conference hosted every June by Mavuno Hill City Church, the headquarters of the movement. Mavuno uses this conference to enhance the training of its church planters and also to share its ministry resources with other churches around the city and from around the world, particularly churches that, like Mavuno Church, are focused on reaching a postcollege demographic. All the Mavuno church planters return to Nairobi for this three-day conference.

and spent, all of the accounts of Mavuno churches are subjected to an annual audit by an independent auditor, and the results are made public on the church's website.[15] Both Mavuno Berlin and Mavuno Kampala are now fully independent financially, though they are still financially limited. In Kampala, Mavuno subsidized the salaries and costs of running the church up until August 2013. Mavuno Kigali and Blantyre are still receiving support from the mother church.

CONCLUSION: THE POWER OF RELATIONSHIPS

Can megachurches provide accountability in missions? The case of Mavuno suggests that while the challenges are many, effective oversight is possible. Relationships are the key. What would Mavuno Church do if one of the church planters went rogue, either in false teaching or in moral failure? Mavuno's response, according to Muriithi, would be to recall the pastor. This is a legal safeguard that Mavuno has built into the registration of each of its international churches.[16] The mother church reserves the right to revoke the license of the pastor and replace him. But such punitive action is a last resort. Mavuno does all it can to build and strengthen close personal ties between its missionaries and its senders. Muriithi describes it as a commitment "to not just export church planters but to plant 'sons.'" This strong relational tie transcends mere loyalty to a job or a contract. Muriithi acknowledges that this close, paternal accountability was not always in

15. Church Planting is one of the departments within Mavuno Church. Other departments include Children, Teens, Marathon (discipleship), Outreach, Worship (weekend services), and Operations (accounts and facilities). Each department, including Church Planting, is allocated an annual budget. The budget for church planting includes the costs of starting a new church, relocating the church planters, paying church planting pastors and staff, spy missions, and all other expenses that go into planting a church. The allocation continues until a church plant, such as Kampala or Kigali or Berlin, can meet some of its own financial needs. When churches reach that point, they are slowly eased off the central budget, but they still have to follow the accounting procedures that the entire Mavuno Church follows. All pastors are able to communicate their income and to report special needs with which they need help.

16. Muriithi Wanjau, interview by Kyama Mugambi, Nairobi, August 2014.

place but has developed through trial and error. How sustainable this model will be over time remains to be seen. But at this stage in Mavuno's ministry, relationships and not just regulations provide for effective accountability.

QUESTIONS FOR REFLECTION

1. Mavuno Church began as a church plant of Nairobi Chapel, another megachurch. How much of its model for doing mission reflects these church network ties? What are the strengths and limitations of doing missions within a network of churches? What strengths and drawbacks are found in replicating patterns of synergy and dependency between a daughter church and a mother church?

2. The case study notes Mavuno's success in planting churches in places such as Kampala, Uganda, and Berlin, Germany. Little was said about the failure of its church plant in Dar es Salaam, Tanzania. Those with whom the authors spoke believed that the cause of failure had more to do with insufficient understanding of the dramatically different urban culture found in Dar es Salaam from that of Nairobi than with factors such as missionary behavior, lack of funds, or conflict with the mother church. To what extent might this lack of cross-cultural sensitivity be due to the current method used in training (the apprentice model, with time on staff at Mavuno Church) and to the broad concepts of "gateway cities" and "culture-defining churches," concepts that tend to overemphasize similarities between cities and to downplay differences?

3. Key to the missionary accountability system of Mavuno is the belief in establishing "Paul-Timothy" relationships. Keeping these relationships of intimacy, encouragement, and accountability alive and effective requires a commitment to technology (weekly social networking), expensive annual conferences (Mavuno "Fearless" conferences), and time-consuming personal connections. In most cases the people responsible for maintaining the relationships with the missionaries are also heavily involved in local ministry.

Is this enough? Do megachurches need to formalize their missionary care by developing separate agencies or freeing pastoral staff to carry on the work of missionary care? Or are current patterns of relationship-building sufficiently effective and sustainable?

4. As one looks at the rise of cross-cultural megachurch missions in the book of Acts, the role of leadership networks, discipleship, and one-on-one training is apparent. How much does Mavuno reflect this apostolic pattern of missions and missionary care and accountability? What are some major differences?

5. Mavuno builds its ministry both at home and abroad around the "Mavuno Marathon." This philosophy of ministry involves "turning ordinary people into fearless influencers of society" by using seeker services, intensive ten-week training via a core curriculum called "Mizizi" (Roots), ongoing discipleship through small "ecclesia groups," and helping individuals to identify a "frontline" ministry in one of the key areas of a nation (such as governance, media and arts, education and family, money and economy, and church and culture). Gateway city church planters begin their work by creating a Mizizi group and eventually growing it into a congregation of several hundred that can begin to run the "Marathon." How realistic is this ministry framework and curriculum for the wide variety of global cities that Mavuno seeks to engage? How might this approach need to be adapted to face a variety of cross-cultural dynamics? What concepts are transferable to your current ministry and situation?

13

Response to "African Megachurches and Missions"

Stephen S. Park

We are always amazed to see God's miraculous intervention in particular ministries in our days. Divine intervention began in Acts 2 when the church was first launched in a hostile environment composed of a stubborn Judaism and a dominant secular Greco-Roman polytheism. Such divine interventions have appeared at various times in church and mission history ever since. It is a great encouragement that these divine interventions are more visible in our time, especially in various regions of Africa, the Middle East, and South America.

MEGACHURCHES AND MISSION: KOREAN AND KENYAN

During the last few decades, "miraculous church growth" is a term that has become familiar to Korean Christians and church leaders, for three of the world's largest megachurches are located in Seoul. These megachurches developed during a very brief period of time, from the mid-1970s to the mid-1990s.[1] Korean world missions grew in parallel with this rapid church growth and as a natural consequence of it. Interesting similarities are apparent in the church growth strategies of Mavuno Church, in Nairobi, Kenya, and those of the Korean megachurches, in South Korea: these churches are

1. See Ro Bon-Rin and Marlin L. Nelson, *Korean Church Growth Explosion: Centennial of the Protestant Church (1884–1984)* (Seoul: Word of Life Press; Taichung, Taiwan: Asia Theological Association, 1983).

urban oriented, focus on the younger and better-educated generations, invest heavily in contextualized training and communication skills, and have a centralized leadership structure.

Mavuno Church was planted in 2005, following extensive evaluation of the pros and cons of traditional church growth theories. Its successful launch was hedged about with various safeguards. In comparison with Mavuno Church's thorough approach and solid strategic foundation, Korean church growth theories in the 1970s and 1980s were poorly developed. For example, a competitive attitude, something that is contrary to biblical teaching, was rampant in urban churches in Korea during the mid-1970s to the mid-1990s. During that period the majority of local churches in big cities such as Seoul had a strong drive for rapid church growth, but they failed to provide for self-examination on issues related to accountability. Since by their nature church growth and world mission develop on parallel tracks, Korean world missions had the same weaknesses. They lacked a solid strategic foundation and showed a lack of accountability. Out of this particular cultural and spiritual context, Korean world missions began their cross-cultural ministries, and problems of accountability soon became apparent: a lack of accountability on the part of missionaries, of their supporting churches, and even of sending agencies

MAVUNO CHURCH DECISIONS

Mavuno Church has an excellent mission statement that is clear, feasible, and relevant: "turning ordinary people into fearless influencers of society."[2] If the first-century church had issued a mission statement, I am sure they would have formulated one similar to this for their witness within the secular Greco-Roman world.

Commissioning a pastor and his wife as a ministry team is not a common approach for the church in traditional, male-dominant African culture, yet Mavuno Church gives both husband and wife equal opportunity for training and ministry. In contrast, the Korean church does not give official ministerial positions or titles

2. *Mavuno Leader's Day Bulletin, 2010*; quoted by Mark Shaw and Wanjiru Gitau on p. 104 of this volume.

to a pastor's wife. Such a pioneering spirit in Mavuno leadership development has been effective for enhancing church growth.

MISSION ISSUES IN KOREAN MEGACHURCHES

Possessed as they were with ardent zeal for world mission, Korean churches typically initiated mission outreach through individual local churches, not professional mission agencies. This approach often led to a competitive spirit between neighboring churches. For this competitive spirit, Kwabena Asamoah-Gyadu's rebuke (as quoted by Mark Shaw and Wanjiru Gitau, p. 102) fits only too well: "[They] covet numerical growth and proudly cite their numbers as testimonies to spiritual relevance and success in evangelism."

Human nature, marred by sin as it is, only too easily succumbs to such tendencies. In any cultural setting the temptations that beset missionaries are more likely to lead to mistakes and failure in their ministry when they are overseen only by their individual supporting church rather than by an agency dedicated to world mission. Such missionaries tend to be more autonomous in their ministries, as well as in their finances, than their counterparts serving under an external mission board. Ministry efficiency, raising mission funds and spending them in appropriate ways, MK issues, missionary care, and dealing with missionary attrition are major challenges for a majority of Korean missionaries and their supporting churches. And of course even independent mission agencies with an outstanding record of ministry can face daunting problems. Unless the missionary support systems of individual churches and of mission agencies are constantly undergoing transformation, these issues will continue to be problems in the Korean church.

Missionary accountability has been a thorny issue in the Korean church, as Shaw and Gitau's reference to the work of Timothy Park makes clear (102). By the dawn of the twenty-first century the problem had become a major issue in Korea. Missionaries and supporting churches alike agree on the significance of the problems involved. These issues of accountability appear in major missionary conferences, forums, and articles, as well as in doctoral dissertations and even in seminary classrooms. Despite this great array of professional efforts, we have few indications that the problems are being alleviated. Are we missing something?

Korea is a country with 5,000 years of history in a compact land with a dense population. In land size it is the same as the U.S. state of Indiana. But while Indiana is home to a population of 6.8 million on a largely flat plain, South Korea has 50 million people, and two-thirds of its land is mountainous. Traditionally, Korea is a collective, relational society. With this particular cultural and geographic background, Korean missionaries maintain relationships with their supporting churches through traditional cultural ways, an approach that is preferred by the supporting churches as well. Accountability is relegated to the level of a secondary issue when missionary and supporting church are bonded together through close personal ties anchored in the traditional social structure.

CULTURAL CHOICES IN MAVUNO CHURCH MISSIONS

Each culture has its own way of defining accountability and understanding the practice of accountability. For example, the boundary between a gift and a bribe differs in every cultural setting. More task-oriented cultures such as those in North America and Western Europe have clear boundaries between gifts and bribes, while the more relationally oriented cultures in Asia, Africa, and South America typically have more fuzzy boundaries. Not uncommonly, differences between the two cultural value systems give rise to accusations and misunderstandings. Concerning this sensitive issue, Mavuno Church applies a hybrid system: it uses collective African cultural values in local ministry and efficiency-oriented Western cultural values in leadership training, finances, and debriefing.

Here we see Mavuno Church applying Western cultural values to issues of accountability, especially to accountability related to the finances of missionaries. In the African cultural context, this step is quite a pioneering strategy and can be a model more broadly for missions in the Majority World. Mavuno Church has achieved high efficiency through the use of a centralized audit system for local church ministries, for financial activities, for leadership development, and for debriefing as well. All these changes have proved effective and are made possible by Mavuno Church's centralized leadership structure.

GROWING WELL

My concern is that churches overly concerned about quick growth may encounter problematic side effects. Within the first decades of their ministry, many Korean megachurches experienced difficulties in church administration, in overseeing their pastoral staff, and even in their mission efforts. Major causes of the problems, in my perspective, were lack of experience, overenthusiasm, a macho complex, seeking worldly fame via media, and financial misconduct among top leaders.

Mavuno Church will continue its impressive development and solid ministry if it is sensitive to issues that have caused major megachurches elsewhere to stumble. It will continue to grow into a healthy megachurch if it maintains culturally relevant leadership development and accountability that reflect local cultural values.

14

Megachurch–Mission Agency Interaction: A Case Study of SaRang Church

Pil-Hun Park

I am grateful for the invitation to present a case study of the interaction between one particular megachurch and mission agencies, for it provides an opportunity to shed light on how megachurches have contributed to global missions. I believe that this forum will enable us to appreciate more fully the variety of ways megachurches have been engaged in mission work.

Megachurches enjoy an abundance of resources of many kinds. This abundance enables them to engage in global mission ministry on an expansive scale, including setting up mission bases in multiple fields, building cultural centers for missions, operating their own church missions departments, and providing financial support for projects carried out by other mission organizations. We must recognize, however, that the enormous amount of material resources flowing from megachurches could prove to be a good that gets in the way of the best. For example, it could tend to isolate megachurches, leading them to pursue independence rather than cooperation in ministry. The latter approach opens up access to the depth of experience and long-honed skills in mission strategizing that mission organizations possess. "Going it alone" in mission can prove costly.

Though this chapter looks only at ways that SaRang Church, in Seoul, has cooperated with other mission organizations, it is meant to serve also as a case study of ways that megachurches and mission agencies can establish relationships for the purpose of global missions.[1] This case study seeks to identify a model for cooperation between megachurches and mission agencies and to explore the ways that cooperation benefits both parties.

SARANG CHURCH'S COOPERATION WITH MISSION AGENCIES

As of September 2014, SaRang Church was cooperating financially with a total of 94 mission organizations.[2] Of these organizations, 18 were international mission agencies that began in other nations, 41 were mission agencies that originated in Korea but worked internationally, and 35 were organizations engaged in domestic mission ministry, such as reaching out to rural areas in Korea. These organizations include not only major missionary sending agencies but also mission research institutions (e.g., Korea Research Institute for Mission, Overseas Ministries Study Center, Unreached People Mission Alliance), joint movements in missions (e.g., Mission Korea), and professional institutions for member care (e.g., Missionary Counseling Center).

SaRang Church's practical cooperation with mission organizations can be considered almost as important as its financial support. SaRang understands that mission is carried out most effectively through partnerships, and it seeks to build mission synergy through cooperation with various mission organizations. In fact, what differentiates SaRang from other megachurches active in mission is its thorough cooperation with other mission organizations; in most cases, SaRang's missionaries are affiliated with domestic

1. John H. Oak, *Called to Awaken the Laity* (London: Christian Focus, 2006), 273. SaRang Church was founded in 1978 by John Han-Hum Oak with nine members; in 2014 attendance at SaRang services stood at around 30,000. John Jung-Hyun Oh serves as senior pastor, with 140 associate pastors and around 3,000 lay leaders committed to a fivefold vision: growing in truth, loving family, obeying God, volunteering in Christian life, and evangelizing the world.

2. A detailed overview of SaRang Church's mission ministry and its world mission department is given by Seung Kwan (David) Yoo, "Accountability in a Local Church's Ministry of World Mission: SaRang Community Church as a Case Study," in *Accountability in Missions: Korean and Western Case Studies*, ed. Jonathan J. Bonk (Eugene, Ore.: Wipf & Stock, 2011), 88–139.

and international mission organizations, instead of being sent out only by the church itself. The same is true for SaRang's cooperating missionaries; see table 14.1. (For SaRang Church, "appointed missionaries" are those who are sent by SaRang Church. "Cooperating missionaries" are missionaries who are sent by another church but who are supported in prayer and financially by SaRang Church. In tallying "missionary units," SaRang Church counts an unmarried or single missionary as one unit and also a missionary family as one unit.)

Mission agency	*Appointed miss'y units*	*Cooperating miss'y units*	*Mission agency*	*Appointed miss'y units*	*Cooperating miss'y units*
AAP	1	–	KPM	–	1
ANN	1	–	KWMA	–	1
ARILAC	1	–	LCI	–	1
CCC	3	3	MSS	–	1
Chonghae Mission	–	3	Nagusamenokoe	1	–
Compassion	–	1	Nations	1	–
DMS	–	1	NTM	1	–
ECMI	–	1	OM	7	9
FBDB	–	1	OMF	–	4
FMnC	–	2	Paul's Mission	2	–
GBT (Wycliffe)	3	4	PCKW	1	–
GCM	1	–	Pioneers	2	–
GMF	–	1	Russian Mission	–	1
GMP	7	4	SEED	2	3
GMS	2	7	Silk Wave	–	1
GP	–	2	SIM	2	2
GPTI	1	–	UPMA	1	–
HOPE	3	2	WEC	20	6
Int'l Volunteers of Love	2	–	WEM	1	–
			WEST	1	1
Interserve	15	2	World Diakonia	1	1
IOCK	1	–	YUST	11	3
KFHI	2	–	YWAM	1	1
KPCUSA	1	–	Without agency	25	17
			TOTAL	**124**	**87**

Table 14.1. SaRang missionary units with mission agencies: appointed or cooperating

In summary, we see that the 124 missionary units appointed by SaRang are affiliated with 31 domestic and international mission organizations, and its 87 cooperating missionary units are affiliated with 29 domestic and international mission organizations. Such an arrangement of dual-affiliation is a missional model that midsize and small churches can also follow; it is not limited to megachurches.

EXAMPLES OF COOPERATION

In this section we consider SaRang's partnership with four mission organizations: Operation Mobilization (OM), Worldwide Evangelization for Christ (WEC), SIM, and Interserve.

Partnership with OM. OM Korea was established in close connection with SaRang Church. In 1989 SaRang provided administrative support for the initial establishment of OM Korea by offering office space, and it provided crucial help that enabled the start-up phase to go smoothly. SaRang, as an influential and fast-growing church with disciple-making at the core of its ministry, supplied both workforce and funds essential for the Korean branch of this international mission organization to grow quickly. This mutually beneficial relationship continued to grow. *SaRang was able to mobilize its young adults group in missional activities, and at the same time OM Korea was able to grow in recruiting and appointing young, committed missionaries.*

Another reason that OM Korea was able to grow so quickly was the trust it earned through having a solid partnership with SaRang. Local churches in Korea were willing to trust this start-up organization thanks to the trust and confidence they had in SaRang. Furthermore, John Oak, a highly recognized spiritual leader and senior pastor at SaRang at the time, also served as the chairman of the board for OM Korea, which enhanced the mission's credibility among local churches. Extending the linkage, John Oh, current senior pastor at SaRang, had previously served as chairman of the board for OM Korean American Mission when he was senior pastor of SaRang Church of Southern California. SaRang's friendship and networking with OM leadership continues to bear fruit, and John Oh continues to be an ardent supporter of OM Korea.

The linkage between SaRang Church and OM supplies a good example of the beneficial influence that a megachurch can have on the promotion and growth of a mission organization. In an interview Su-Yong Kim, director of OM Korea, commented on the partnership between OM and SaRang: "OM Korea was able to stand on its own feet due to the faithful support and partnership of SaRang. . . . SaRang has helped OM mobilize the current generation into global mission, and OM's global infrastructure and network *have* made a positive contribution *to globalization of SaRang's ministry.*"[3]

Partnership with WEC International. As of 2014, twenty-six missionary units appointed by SaRang were affiliated with WEC, the largest number with any single mission organization. As with OM Korea, the establishment of WEC Korea was initiated and developed in close partnership with SaRang.

Trust for the partnership between WEC as an international agency and SaRang as a healthy growing church and devoted efforts on the part of WEC missionaries , all worked together to accelerate the growth of WEC Korea. In-Young Oak, an elder of SaRang church, served as the first chairman of the board for WEC Korea, which naturally encouraged the mobilization of potential missionary candidates from SaRang. In addition, WEC's prayer gatherings for missions were held at SaRang, which built up a strong partnership between it as a sending church and the mission organization.

Kyung Nam Park, the director of WEC Korea, has stated the following regarding the partnership between SaRang and mission organizations:

> SaRang has set an example for other local church bodies and mission organizations by appointing only missionaries who are affiliated with mission organizations. Although SaRang could have carried out its own ministry utilizing its own resources, it chose to recognize the importance of serving and partnering with mission organizations, which will maximize the synergy of the pastoral professionalism of local churches and the field experiences of international mission organizations. . . . Finally, the World Mission Department of SaRang has always shown a

3. Su-Yong Kim, interview by Pil-Hun Park, September 28, 2014.

true willingness to communicate and maintain openness, which has enabled these partnerships to succeed.

Partnership with SIM International. SaRang Church's partnership with SIM International was initiated in 2007, when the church invited Malcolm McGregor, then SIM's international director, along with his wife, Liz, to attend SaRang's discipleship seminar "Called to Awaken the Laity" (CAL).[4] This was the seventy-sixth CAL seminar that SaRang had offered. Over the past several years, SaRang has invited leaders of international mission organizations to this seminar with the hope of sharing the church's pastoral vision of discipleship training and the results of its ministry model. From 2005 through 2014, a total of 338 church and mission leaders from twenty-eight different countries have come to SaRang Church to attend a CAL seminar.

After attending the seminar, the McGregors realized the deep need for discipleship training on the mission field and immediately began arranging for it in SIM's mission efforts in Africa. Thanks to their efforts, this emphasis on discipleship was adopted by the Kale Heywet (Word of Life) Church, an outgrowth of SIM's ministry in Ethiopia and the largest Protestant church in the country; the emphasis eventually spread across Africa. Upon SIM's recommendation, Kale Heywet leaders themselves attended the CAL seminar. Then, recognizing the tremendous need for discipleship training, in January 2013 they hosted the African Strategic Discipleship Summit, which brought together ninety leaders from twenty-four African countries for the purpose of mobilizing and training for discipleship throughout the continent.

This example of SaRang's ministry philosophy of discipleship training being extended to many church leaders in Africa through SIM's network illustrates the potential that exists for productive partnerships between mission organizations and megachurches.

Partnership with Interserve. As of 2014, seventeen SaRang missionary units were affiliated with Interserve, and that number is increasing. Such cooperative partnerships often serve to greatly

4. See "Called to Awaken the Laity," www.disciples.co.kr/english/seminar/cal/intro.asp.

enhance member care. Certain aspects of member care are best provided by sending churches, and other aspects by sending agencies. Through their joint efforts, a missionary can receive ideal member care, coming from multiple sources.

In general, Interserve's member care services encompass the totality of missionaries' life and ministry in the field, whereas SaRang offers health and welfare services for missionaries when they are on furlough in Korea. To encourage missionaries who are on sabbatical and to take responsibility for its missionaries, SaRang provides housing, health check-ups, and medical treatment during their furloughs, and partial financial support for the education of their children.

In order to effectively debrief missionaries at the beginning of their sabbatical year, Interserve has contracted with Heartstream Resources, a specialized member care institution that provides pastoral counseling and support for missionaries.[5] If a missionary sent by SaRang and affiliated with Interserve receives counseling from Heartstream, Interserve pays half of the cost, and SaRang pays the other half.

If problems arise on the mission field, Interserve and SaRang work together to determine the best approach. By maintaining ongoing communications and close cooperation, they seek to set a good example of working together in the area of missionary member care.

BENEFITS OF COOPERATION

When we examine the history of missions, we see that God has done tremendous things for missions today by establishing more mission organizations and institutions now than in any other generation. In 1991 Charles Van Engen observed that David Barrett had counted "15,800 distinct and separate parachurch agencies serving the churches in their mission through manifold ministries in the 223 countries of the world, yet organizationally independent of the churches."[6] Yet all of these mission organizations—however organizationally independent they may be—did not arise and exist

5. See "Heartstream Resources," http://heartstreamresources.org.

6. Charles E. Van Engen, *God's Missionary People: Rethinking the Purpose of the Local Church* (Grand Rapids: Baker, 1991), 39.

in isolation, all alone, somewhere out there on their own; in every case they coexisted in close association with local churches.

Issues of cooperation or the lack of cooperation between parachurch organizations and local churches are nothing new.[7] In 1995 Lesslie Newbigin wrote:

> In the "mission station" approach, as McGavran sees it, converts are detached from the natural communities to which they belong, attached to the foreign mission and its institutions, and required to conform to ethical and cultural standards that belong to the Christianity of the foreign missionary. The effect of this policy is twofold. On the one hand the convert, having been transplanted into an alien culture, is no longer in a position to influence non-Christian relatives and neighbors; on the other hand the energies of the mission are exhausted in the effort to bring the converts, or more often their children, into conformity with the standards supposed by the missionaries to be required by the gospel. Both factors have the effect of stopping the growth of the church.[8]

Our task is to strengthen points of weakness so that local churches and mission institutions grow together in harmony.

I outline here the main benefits to be found in missional cooperation between mission organizations and megachurches as presented in this chapter.

- Megachurches possess infrastructure, are well known, and have a reputation for reliability that can provide a platform for mission organizations during start-up, enabling them to grow and develop in healthy ways.
- In a partnership with a megachurch, mission organizations gain incalculable benefits through access to a treasure store

7. John W. Nyquist, "Parachurch Agencies and Mission," in *Evangelical Dictionary of World Missions*, ed. A. Scott Moreau (Grand Rapids: Baker Books, 2000; Korean ed., 2014), 727; and Ralph D. Winter, *The Twenty-Five Unbelievable Years*, 2nd ed. (Pasadena, Calif.: William Carey Library, 2005; Korean ed., 2012), 266–83.

8. Lesslie Newbigin, *The Open Secret: An Introduction to the Theology of Mission* (Grand Rapids: Eerdmans, 1995), 122.

of resources—human resources in general, professional expertise, contacts, and financial and other resources—for world evangelization.

- When missionaries are sent cooperatively by a mission organization and a megachurch, the two can share in member care, developing a mutually beneficial cooperative approach.
- Megachurches can serve as missional role models, especially in forming partnerships with mission organizations, that midsize or small churches can emulate.

Cooperation and integration of effort between megachurches and mission organizations hold out the prospect of many positive benefits. But we must remember that such results do not come "for free." They require investment of time, mutual consideration, thoughtfulness, and open communication. To achieve a fruitful spirit of cooperation, megachurches should cultivate the following attitudes:

- Megachurches must recognize mission organizations' professionalism and acknowledge the expertise they have developed related to missions; megachurches must avoid relying too much on their own resources or know-how and avoid the temptation to go their own way.
- Megachurches must invest ongoing intentional effort in strengthening communication with mission organizations.
- In partnering with a mission organization, megachurches must be attentive to the practical needs of the organization and be willing to commit time and money toward meeting those needs.

CONCLUSION

In the mid-twentieth century, Lesslie Newbigin identified a problem present in the thinking of Christians of that time: "In the thinking of the vast majority of Christians, the words 'Church' and 'Mission' connote two different kinds of society. The one is conceived to be a society devoted to worship, and the spiritual care and nurture of its members. It is typically represented by a large and ancient building. The other is conceived to be a society devoted to the propagation of the Gospel, passing on its converts to the safe keeping of 'the Church.'"[9]

Newbigin's perceptive comments challenge today's Christians and raise our awareness of the need to revive churches whose missional focus is ebbing and whose hearts no longer burn with missional fervor. David Bosch pointed out the dilemma created by the concept of a nonmissional church, an idea that creates "an abiding tension between two views of the church which appear to be fundamentally irreconcilable. At one end of the spectrum, the church perceives itself to be the sole bearer of a message of salvation on which it has a monopoly; at the other end, the church views itself, at most, as an illustration—in word and deed—of God's involvement with the world."[10]

Bosch stressed that recognizing the *missional essence* of the *church is crucial.* On the one hand, it is clear that we need to recognize that if churches leave mission solely to mission organizations, they lose their missional essence. On the other hand, we would be ill-advised and overidealistic to think that local churches are able to fulfill the entire set of duties and professional roles carried out by mission organizations. The task placed before churches today is to understand and fulfill *the Great Commandment,* while maintaining a corresponding partnership with mission agencies in carrying out *the Great Commission.* In this way the competencies and strengths of churches and mission organizations are able to compensate for each other's limitations. Cooperation between mission agencies and local churches, and especially cooperation with megachurches, is a key factor in allowing God's people to accomplish the unfinished task of world mission in the twenty-first century.

When engaging in mission, megachurches must balance two concerns: when to act on their own, and when to act in partnership with, and accountability to, the wider Christian community. On the one hand, they have roles to play and mission projects to

9. Lesslie Newbigin, *The Household of God: Lectures on the Nature of the Church* (New York: Friendship Press, 1954), 164.

10. David Jacobus Bosch, *Transforming Mission: Paradigm Shifts in Theology of Mission* (Maryknoll, N.Y.: Orbis Books, 1991), 381.

carry out that only they have the resources and infrastructure to perform. On the other hand, it is essential that they maintain a sense of accountability and serve as healthy ministry role models for midsize and small local churches. Their ministry must not be the kind that draws attention to itself but must be one that humbly fulfills practical needs on the mission fields. When megachurches hold these two aspects of mission together in their hearts, they will serve as a great encouragement and motivation for mission agencies and for other local churches.

QUESTIONS FOR REFLECTION

1. What additional benefits of cooperation and partnerships between mission agencies and local churches can you add to those mentioned?
2. What shortcomings or pitfalls might there be to cooperation between mission agencies and local churches?
3. In what ways can local churches work alongside mission agencies to maximize mission potential and mobilize resources for mission within local churches?
4. In what ways can mission agencies work alongside local churches to accomplish the vision of the agencies?
5. Who could or should play a bridge role between mission agencies and local churches to enhance cooperation and collaboration between them?

15

Response to "Megachurch–Mission Agency Interaction"

Mark Oxbrow

I am honored to be invited to respond to Pil-Hun Park's fascinating study of the developed relationships between SaRang Church and a number of different mission agencies, and especially to his powerful insights into the challenges and benefits of such partnerships. I will respond out of my own experience of building a relational network of missional churches and agencies across six continents, a network called Faith2Share.

MODAL AND SODAL MISSIONAL CHURCH

Mission and church are inseparable, and we cannot place one before the other; they belong together, but they must not be confused.[1]

As far as I know, it was in Seoul in 1973 that Ralph Winter, the great missiologist of the last century, first used the distinction between modal and sodal church. In his lecture "The Two Structures of God's Redemptive Mission," he identified the gathered communities of the New Testament church, modeled on the Jewish synagogue, as *modal*, and the missionary bands, exemplified

1. The 2004 publication within the Church of England of the report *Mission-Shaped Church* (London: Church House Publishing, 2004) sparked a very positive international Anglican conversation about the missional nature of church. It has, however, at times run the risk of overlooking the ecclesial implications of mission, the priority for building Eucharistic communities that disciple, nurture, and equip missional Christians—a priority that the report itself fully endorses.

by Paul, Barnabas, Apollos, Timothy, and others, as *sodal*.[2] In later church history, he saw the modal church within the Roman diocesan tradition, and the sodal church in the Celtic monastic tradition.[3] His appeal to us was that we should recognize the different strengths of both modal and sodal church and discover ways in which we can integrate both into our contemporary paradigms of missional church.

The most obvious manifestations of modal and sodal church today are in the local community church as distinct from the global mission agency.[4] The former may be strong in its incarnation of the Gospel within a particular community, its fellowship, and its nurture of disciples, while the latter has a stronger vision for the universality of the church, the translatability of the Gospel, and the equipping of the saints for mission. The question before us today is whether the megachurch can be both modal and sodal. While reinforcing Park's call to partnership, I will also be drawing on Augusto Rodríguez's recent analysis of what he calls New Apostolic Churches to explore how we can move beyond partnership to a model of missional church that is both modal and sodal.[5]

HARMONIZING THE RELATIONSHIP: PARTNERSHIP IN MISSION

In his study of SaRang Church, Park rightly draws attention to the relational priorities of partnership. Words that stand out to me in his text are "friendship," "trust," "communicate," "maintain openness," "humility," and "complementing each other's shortcomings."

2. His lecture was later published as Ralph D. Winter, "The Two Structures of God's Redemptive Mission," *Missiology* 2, no. 1 (1974): 121–39.

3. See Max Warren, *I Believe in the Great Commission* (London: Hodder & Stoughton, 1976), 92–93.

4. On the contemporary relationship between mission agencies and churches, see Philip James Leage, "The Mission Agency and the Local Church" (YWAM, 2011), www.ywamkb.net/kb/The_Mission_Agency_and_the_Local_Church.

5. Augusto Rodríguez, *Paradigms of the Church in Mission: A Historical Survey of the Church's Self-Understanding of Being the Church and of Mission* (Eugene, Ore.: Wipf & Stock, 2012).

Partnership in mission is not a program but rather a philosophy, a way of or approach to life. The foundations for partnership are not pragmatic, but theological.

Among many others, Timothy Tennent reminds us that "missions should never be conceptualized apart from the *missio Dei*" and that "the Trinity is the seminal *relationship* that lies behind all human relationships."[6] The character of mission is therefore relational, which applies not just to the relationship between the evangelizer and the evangelized but even more significantly to the relationships within the church universal that give witness to the nature of God.[7] At the end of his earthly ministry, Jesus prays that his followers might be united (in him) "*so that* the world may believe that you have sent me" (John 17:21). The unity of Christ's followers, their love for each other, their trust, their friendship, their honoring of the weaker sister, their forgiving of the sinful brother—it is these things that point to the God of love, the God we can trust, the God who does not trample on the weak but forgives the sinner. How can a divided church bear witness to a God who is so united that we are forced to speak of Trinity, three in one?

If we take seriously these theological insights about the mission of the triune God, then partnership is not a choice, but a given—it is nonnegotiable. The only question left to us is, How? and it is this question that Pil-Hun Park has so helpfully addressed for us.

Primarily addressing the development of missional churches in North America, Darrell Guder writes, "The primary organizational challenge for the church is to find ways to structure the life of the particular communities so that they can

6. Timothy C. Tennent, *Invitation to World Missions: A Trinitarian Missiology for the Twenty-First Century* (Grand Rapids: Kregel Academic, 2010), 59, 78.

7. Archbishop Anastasios Yannoulatos lays great stress on the Greek term *kathōs* ("as"), reminding us that Christians are always sent in mission "*as* the Father sends the Son"; the *character* of our sending reflects and gives witness to the nature of God. See Mark Oxbrow and Tim Grass, *The Mission of God: Studies in Orthodox and Evangelical Mission* (Oxford: Regnum Press, 2015), 25.

carry out faithful witness in their places, always in responsible connection to the entire church around the world."[8] Those responsible connections can often be provided by mission agencies and other sodal (relationship-building) bodies within the church. Sadly, it is not always just the churches who want to "go it alone" and organize their own cross-cultural mission engagement without reference to mission agencies. Mission agencies can also be at fault, believing that cross-cultural mission is their God-given, and exclusive, ministry and that they should be doing this on behalf of the local (modal) church. It is not uncommon for mission agencies to look at local churches, even megachurches, as providers of finance, people, and prayer, but not wanting them to be involved in the formation of mission policy or strategy. Trust needs to be built on both sides.

Turning specifically to the case of megachurch relationships with mission agencies, I was particularly interested in Park's description of the way that SIM had recognized the potential for taking the SaRang Church program "Called to Awaken the Laity" to their partner Kale Heywet Church in Ethiopia so that they could host the African Strategic Discipleship Summit for leaders from twenty-four African countries. Here we see a well-established mission agency first having the humility to recognize the resources of a Korean megachurch and then building relationships of trust both with it and with their Ethiopian partners, which allowed this successful transfer of learning and training to churches across Africa. Without SIM, this reach across so many countries in Africa would not have occurred, and without SaRang Church, the resource would simply not have existed. It is also significant that in retelling this story, Park used the personal names of the director of SIM and his wife, a sure sign that good personal relationships made this work.

Megachurches face particular challenges in building successful relationships with mission agencies, with partner churches across the world, and with smaller churches. They can be seen as a threat because of their size and wealth of resources.

8. Darrell L. Guder, ed., *Missional Church: A Vision for the Sending of the Church in North America* (Grand Rapids: Eerdmans, 1998), 234.

They themselves can be motivated by power and expansionism. Powerful personalities can get in the way. But for the sake of the kingdom, these relationships must be built.[9]

ONE, HOLY, CATHOLIC, AND APOSTOLIC CHURCH

In 381 the Council of Constantinople expanded the Nicene Creed (325) to declare the church to be "one, holy, catholic, and apostolic." The challenge for any megachurch, as indeed for smaller churches, is to determine how it is "one," how it is "holy," how it is "catholic," and how it is "apostolic." A full treatment of this challenge is far beyond the scope of this short response, but it is pertinent here to reflect on the need not only for unity and holiness but also for catholicity and apostolicity. Is it possible for a megachurch to be both catholic and apostolic?

NEW APOSTOLIC CHURCHES

The major new force in Global Christianity, the Pentecostal/charismatic church movement, standing alongside the three older traditions of Orthodoxy, Catholicism, and Protestantism, has brought with it a renewed ecclesial vision that is both catholic and apostolic. In 1994 Karla Poewe wrote of the ways in which charismatic church streams express true catholicity by linking communities around the world that cross boundaries of class, ethnicity, and wealth.[10] In a recent study of megachurch leaders in Nigeria (all but one of whom are charismatic), W. C. Ihejiriki and G. B. Okon have demonstrated the strong apostolic nature of these churches as they seek to make new disciples not only in their own communities but also in the nation as a whole and internationally.[11] In such developments

9. For a practical guide to successful relationships between churches and mission agencies, see Lausanne Committee for World Evangelization, *Cooperating in World Evangelization: A Handbook on Church/Para-Church Relationships*, Lausanne Occasional Papers, no. 24 (Wheaton, Ill.: Lausanne Committee for World Evangelization, 1983).

10. Karla O. Poewe, ed., *Charismatic Christianity as a Global Culture* (Columbia: Univ. of South Carolina Press, 1994).

11. Walter C. Ihejirika and Godwin B. Okon, "Mega Churches and Megaphones: Nigerian Church Leaders and Their Media Ministries," in *A*

we are beginning to see the merging of megachurch and mission agency as networks of churches take responsibility for their own global witness.

This process is taken much further by the New Apostolic Churches (NACs), described by David Cannistraci.[12] Augusto Rodríguez writes, "Megachurches become NACs when they begin to develop an apostolic ministry. Cell group strategy is a vehicle towards apostolic ministry because of the development and nurture of leaders."[13] Here we see a church becoming something like a church-planting network. We have now moved beyond the development of effective relationships between churches and mission agencies, beyond megachurches having their own mission structures, to something that is organically both modal and sodal, church and mission, a network that links nodes of ecclesial being with relationships of missional intent.[14]

I end by quoting Rodríguez as he describes the leadership philosophy and missional impact of NACs, descriptions that take us right back to everything positive that Pil-Hun Park has described in the partnership between SaRang Church and mission agencies, but that at the same time force us to ask whether there is a step yet to be taken beyond partnership, toward a mutuality in mission modeled for us in the Trinity. Rodríguez writes:

> Networks in the [New Apostolic Paradigm], as opposed to denominations, are built upon the base of relationships. Cannistraci says that the difference between denominations and apostolic networks is relationships, rather than "politics and rules." Relationships become the source of strength accomplished by "partnership of prayer, discussion, planning, and visionary

---

Moving Faith: Mega Churches Go South, ed. Jonathan D. James (Thousand Oaks, Calif.: Sage Publications, 2015), 62–82.

12. See David Cannistraci, *Apostles and the Emerging Apostolic Movement* (Ventura, Calif.: Renew Books, 1996).

13. Rodríguez, *Paradigms of the Church in Mission*, 115.

14. The secular parallel to this is the development of networked organizations in postmodern society that delegate leadership to "everyone," a fascinating development classically described in Ori Brafman and Rod A. Beckstrom, *The Starfish and the Spider: The Unstoppable Power of Leaderless Organizations* (New York: Portfolio, 2006).

leadership." Apostolic networks are the result of unity. They are associations of "autonomous churches and individual ministries that are voluntarily united in an organizational structure." Authority is not positional, but relational. . . . They have a "philosophy of servanthood." . . .

Missionary networking is the result of unity amongst diversity. In a missionary network, churches bring their resources together towards a common goal, where a common understanding exists of one's own abilities as well as others' abilities where one lacks. Therefore, each member of the missionary network must understand that it is a part of a team, where the joining together of all of the parts makes the network "with the whole being greater than the sum of the parts."[15]

15. Rodríguez, *Paradigms of the Church in Mission*, 65.

16

Bible Study 2. Acts 11:19–30, 13:1–3: Diaspora, Ethnic Diversity, and the Mission of the Church

Darrell Jackson

As they trudged steadily northward, Hannah and Saul balanced their few belongings on the back of the sickly mule they had been able to hastily purchase from a neighbor. Only a few days earlier those few items had proudly decorated their small home and grocery store. They had left reluctantly, as a result of a steep decline in trade. Recent political moves were making it increasingly difficult for followers of Jesus to sell food to their neighbors, who, in turn, were being pressured to adhere to strict religious regulations concerning the sale and handling of food. Observance of those regulations was being carefully monitored by the religious police and the civil authorities, working in close cooperation. Unable to sustain a livelihood, Hannah and Saul had decided to join an uncle and his family who were living in a city close to the northern border of Syria.

Hannah and Saul's story will not be unfamiliar to the many hundreds of thousands of refugees who continue to flee Iraq, Iran, Sudan, and Syria because of their Christian faith. Religiously inspired persecution may not leave you dead, but perhaps your store is boycotted, leaving food rotting on your shelves and your household income gone. In such situations, many are forced to seek a means of survival elsewhere.

Hannah and Saul were not traveling in 2015, however. They left Jerusalem in about A.D. 33. As they traveled, these persecuted followers of Jesus, forced to become economic migrants, took with them their testimonies of life-changing encounters. Jews witnessed to Jews, and thus the stories of Jesus the Messiah and of God's enduring promises to his people were spread wherever Jews gathered in diaspora situations (Acts 8:1, 4; 11:19).

MISSION AND THE DIASPORA

I understand Acts 11 as a missiologically rich historical account and will address its narrative flow rather than pay close attention to its exegesis, except where necessary. I also understand it as a narrative whose future-directed horizon is purposely left open by Luke. Elsewhere, the task of mission is similarly oriented towards an open horizon. In the New Testament Scriptures, Luke is reluctant to write in a way that concludes Paul's ministry in Rome, Paul himself anticipates the future evangelization of even the Scythians, the "barbarian's barbarian" (Col. 3:11), and the "great multitude" of John's glorious vision have yet to be gathered (Rev. 7:9). Towards this horizon, God's Spirit moves onwards and outwards, sweeping us up in his divine activity and into God's mission. To the extent that this is true, we can argue that our missional reading of the book of Acts thereby privileges the reader, not over the biblical text, but by locating him or her within the future horizon towards which the narrative remains intentionally open.

Antioch, the third largest city in the Roman Empire after Rome and Alexandria, was strategically located on the river Orontes, about twelve miles (twenty kilometers) upstream from its seaport. It had been founded by Seleucus I, a Macedonian general under Alexander the Great, in about 300 B.C. Its size and strategic importance help to explain why it played its remarkable role in the unfolding drama and story of the mission and expansion of the early church. Estimates based on contemporary accounts have the population at somewhere around 500,000. Around 10 percent of that population was Jewish, and Josephus mentions that a large number of Greek-speaking Gentiles were "attracted to [the] religious ceremonies" of the Jews, presumably as either "God-fearers" or proselytes.[1]

Mission to and through the Jewish diaspora. As suggested by my opening story, refugees fleeing economic hardship, religious discrimination, and the threat of personal violence engaged in mission to Jews already living in diaspora. These refugees scattered to cities with existing Jewish populations on the coastlines of North Africa (Acts 11:20), the eastern Mediterranean, and the island of Cyprus (Acts 11:19). As mentioned, Jews reached out to Jews who had adopted Greco-Roman culture and lifestyles and to ethnic non-Jews who had embraced Judaism as either proselytes or God-fearers.[2]

Mission through and beyond the Jewish diaspora. The narrative of Acts 11:19–30 introduces a contrasting second group of unnamed individuals with the description "some men of Cyprus and Cyrene" (v. 20). With the arrival of this group in Antioch, Luke introduces the opening chapters of an ethnically diverse church. Arriving from Cyprus and North Africa, these anonymous missionaries began to share the Good News with the Greeks (Acts 11:20),[3] forming a radically new phase of Christian mission.

These missionaries had perhaps been inspired by Peter's coastal mission to Azotus and Lydda, in the south, and Joppa and Caesarea, in the north, news of which may have spread as far as Cyrene, Cyprus, and Antioch. Peter's encounter with the Gentile Cornelius in Caesarea (Acts 10) was reported back to Jerusalem (Acts 11:1–18) and probably followed earlier work of Philip in places like Caesarea (Acts 8:40). Even so, for missionaries to reach out beyond their own ethnic grouping was, and remarkably

1. Warren Carter, *Matthew and the Margins: A Sociopolitical and Religious Reading* (Maryknoll, N.Y.: Orbis Books, 2000), 456.

2. Known in Hebrew as *yirei Hashem,* meaning literally "fearers of the Name." The Greek form used in the New Testament is *phoboumenoi ton theon,* "fearers of God."

3. This reading of "Greeks" is preferred over "Hellenists," given the context for the text and the general direction Luke gives his account.

enough still is, relatively uncommon. Tereso Casiño has outlined several arguments nationals currently make *against* engaging in mission beyond their own diasporas, thereby bolstering ethnocentric or xenophobic cultural exclusivism:

- Such mission is not part of our denominational thrust and lacks support from our denominational leadership.
- The church of the host nation can take care of its own evangelism and discipleship needs.
- Such mission is too complicated, for cultural and other practical reasons.
- We have enough mission needs to address within our own ethnic diaspora community.
- Local mission is not real mission; mission should be from the West to the rest.[4]

Can we say anything about these missionaries and why they were in Antioch? Luke describes Jews from Cyrene opposing the Gospel in Jerusalem (Acts 6:9), though by the time of Acts 11, Cyreneans are among those proclaiming the Gospel and, with the African and Cypriot missionaries, brought the Gospel to the Greek-speaking residents of Antioch sometime between 35 and 39, presumably when on business as merchants and traders.[5]

MISSION BEYOND THE DIASPORA JEWS

The mission from North Africa and Cyprus has profound implications for every believer alive today. It led, directly, within a generation, to a church with a majority of Greek-speaking members. It resulted, indirectly, in the Gospels' being preserved in Greek rather than Hebrew or Aramaic, an early example of what

4. Tereso Casiño, "Mission beyond the Diaspora" (paper presented at the Lausanne Global Diaspora Forum, Manila, March 2015), cited throughout from notes taken by the author.

5. These residents included Nicolaus, a proselyte from Antioch (Acts 6:5), and Lucius of Cyrene (Acts 13:1). Lucius's presence in Antioch prior to Acts 11:19 may help explain why Cyreneans were regularly visiting Antioch.

Lamin Sanneh has called the "concept of translatability."[6] The Gospel is a Gospel for all, written in a common tongue for use by all people, to be carried by all, through all, and to all. It is not a story about a wonder-working Messiah for the Jews only, but a story about Jesus as *our* Lord, *our* Christ, *our* Anointed One. Casiño encourages this kind of mission by listing several arguments *for* mission beyond the diaspora. As he has noted, such mission is

- Intently soteriological: every human being is precious to God and needs redemption.
- Comprehensively missiological: God draws people to himself not only for salvation but also for his redemptive mission in the world.
- Decisively ecclesiological: God forms a covenant people and empowers them to be his witnesses as light to the world and salt of the earth.
- Feasibly practical: successful and effective models of missions beyond the diaspora abound today.[7]

Before these anonymous missionaries arrived, the demarcation in Antioch had been between Jew and Gentile. This distinction was relativized, and outsiders began to refer to the emerging communities in Antioch as "Christians" (i.e., partisans of Christ, Acts 11:26). Ironically, this usage may have been resisted by early believers, who feared losing the protection that Judaism was afforded under Roman law as a *religio licita*. It is also possible that the label "Christian" was used by opponents to stigmatize the members of the early church, much as the label "Marxist" has been used. The fact that *christianus*, the term used, was a Latin word seems to underscore its origin within the Roman, and

6. Lamin Sanneh, *Translating the Message: The Missionary Impact on Culture* (Maryknoll, N.Y.: Orbis Books, 1997), 54. Also see Andrew F. Walls, *The Missionary Movement in Christian History: Studies in the Transmission of Faith* (Maryknoll, N.Y.: Orbis Books, 1996), 26.

7. Casiño, "Mission beyond the Diaspora." Luke emphasizes the strategic and numerical benefit of this innovation in mission beyond the Jewish Diaspora three times, in Acts 11:21, 24, 26.

therefore pagan, city of Antioch. This usage seems to have been characteristic of the scorn and hatred expressed during the persecution under Agrippa I.[8]

ETHNIC DIVERSITY AND THE CHURCH

In the emerging "christian" congregations of Antioch, traditional ethnic loyalties were breaking down, exacerbated by the realities of diaspora, and refocusing around loyalty to Christ. The ethnic diversity of the church became an unavoidable consequence of the missionary activity of the apostles. Three facets of the ethnic diversity of the mission in Antioch described in Acts 11:19–30 are particularly revealing as we consider the character of mission today.

An ethnically diverse church may be appropriate to its location. Unlike Peter and Philip, who carry out urban ministry elsewhere in the region, Barnabas does not come to Antioch to preach the Gospel and baptize new believers. He arrives in response to the work of other missionaries and merely acknowledges the grace of God already at work among them (Acts 11:22–23). Barnabas might easily have passed a complaint back to the Jerusalem mother church about African evangelists arriving in Antioch without proper accreditation, but instead he recognizes that the strategic location and the ethnically diverse character of the Antiochian populace mean that such developments are inevitable within the economy of God's kingdom.

Several evangelical anthropologists have recently explored the challenges that urban ethnic diversity has posed for earlier models of ethnolinguistic missiology.[9] Missiologists have interpreted Antioch as a model for an urban, ethnically diverse church that better reflects the metropolitan context (which is the context for most megachurches).[10] Indeed Luke seems oblivious

8. Rainer Riesner, *Paul's Early Period: Chronology, Mission Strategy, Theology* (Grand Rapids: Eerdmans, 1998), 112–13.

9. See, for example, Michael Rynkiewich, *Soul, Self, and Society: A Postmodern Anthropology for Mission in a Postcolonial World* (Eugene, Ore.: Cascade Books, 2011).

10. Norman E. Thomas, "The Church at Antioch: Crossing Racial,

to any obstacles that ethnolinguistic diversity might place in the way of the rapid growth of the Antiochian church (Acts 11:21, 24, 26). His enthusiastic record of growth at Antioch is surely pertinent to discussion and application of evangelical "people group" missiologies.

An ethnically diverse church may be better suited to ethnically diverse mission. Jacob Jervell has speculated that Luke belonged to the church in Antioch.[11] With greater certainty, we can say that the church leaders included a Levite from Cyprus (Barnabas), two Africans from Libya (including a black African called Simeon), and a boyhood friend of Herod Antipas (Manaen), and to these would soon be added a Pharisee educated under Gamaliel (Saul/Paul; Acts 13:1). In a short time, this company of Christians would become not only a center for discipleship (Acts 11:26) but also a center for mission (Acts 11:29–30). The multiethnic nature of the mission from Libya and Cyprus sets the pattern for the nature of the church. Arguably, the vision for mission within the Christian assemblies of Antioch sprang out of their culturally and ethnically diverse, yet reconciled, church life.

I suggest that a vision for mission, that is, of taking the Gospel to all nations, is the likely overflow of a church made up of women and men from every nation under heaven. If you want to plant multiethnic churches, do so through multiethnic teams. Model what you want the church to become.

An ethnically diverse church may be controversial. There is little evidence that change and innovation are ever universally welcome. The new emphasis on mission to the Greeks must have raised questions. Was there now a different mission, or indeed were there now two missions: one to the Jews and another to the Gentiles?

Cultural, and Class Barriers," in *Mission in Acts: Ancient Narratives in Contemporary Context*, ed. Robert L. Gallagher and Paul Herting (Maryknoll, N.Y.: Orbis Books, 2004), 144.

11. Jacob Jervell, *The Theology of the Acts of the Apostles* (Cambridge: Cambridge Univ. Press, 1996), 7. I put this view here rather tentatively, but it would help to explain the significance that Luke gives to Antioch in the narrative of Acts, in distinction to the Galilee-Jerusalem focus of his gospel account.

Jervell insists, however, that "there is no specific mission to the Gentiles, separated from the mission to the Jews,"[12] arguing that there is only one mission seen throughout the Old Testament, that of bringing the nations to the worship of the one true God. Peter O'Brien adds that, for Paul, "this gospel that he preached is identified with the promise made to Abraham (Gal 3:8). As Gentiles were brought into a covenant relationship with the living God through faith, so the promises made to Abraham were in the process of being fulfilled."[13]

One can imagine this issue remaining a point of concern for these Jewish followers of Jesus and their Greek brothers and sisters. In order to address some of the theological and strategic questions it raised, Barnabas clearly felt it was time to call in extra help.

PAUL'S APOSTOLIC CALL TO THE WHOLE WORLD

The help that Barnabas enlisted could not have been a riskier choice, for he was clearly determined to recruit the controversial convert and preacher, Saul of Tarsus. Saul (later Paul) was recruited by Barnabas to a discipleship role in Antioch only after "some men" had already spoken "to the Greeks also, proclaiming the Lord Jesus" (Acts 11:20), and after Barnabas had subsequently "exhorted them all to remain faithful to the Lord with steadfast devotion" (Acts 11:23). While Paul located his vocation to Gentile mission in the events immediately following his experience on the road to Damascus (Acts 26:15–18), it seems certain that Paul's formation as an apostolic witness and cross-cultural evangelist is largely a consequence of his experiences in the congregations at Antioch. What, then, do we learn from this passage about Paul's formation for the mission he would go on to undertake? (For a possible chronology of Paul's writings relevant to the theme of this chapter, see table 16.1).

Barnabas's recruitment of a Jewish missionary. Paul had been persuaded by the believers to flee the opposition of Greek-speaking Jews in

12. Ibid., 41.

13. Peter T. O'Brien, *Gospel and Mission in the Writings of Paul: An Exegetical and Theological Analysis* (Grand Rapids: Baker Books, 2000), 20.

Damascus and Jerusalem (Acts 9:26–30) and leave for Tarsus. Rainer Riesner suggests that Paul did not convince many of the believers in Jerusalem that God's mission included the Gentiles.[14] Indeed, Paul himself conceded that he met only a few of the apostles on his first visit there (Gal. 1:18–19), and it is entirely possible that he returned frustrated and disappointed to his native city of Tarsus.

It was in Tarsus that Barnabas found Paul (Acts 11:25), and I want to suggest that Barnabas played a part in Paul's rehabilitation,

Location	*Scripture*	*Date* A.D.
Damascus	Gal. 1:17, conversion near the city	
Arabia	Gal. 1:17	31/32
Damascus	Gal. 1:17	
after three years		
Jerusalem	Gal. 1:18	33/34
	Acts 11:26, designation "Christian" in Antioch	ca. 37
Syria-Cilicia	Gal. 1:21	34–42
Antioch	Acts 11:25	42/44
after fourteen years		
Jerusalem	Gal. 2:1	57
Paul writes to the Galatians		

Table 16.1. Paul, Galatians, and Acts: The Likely Chronological Sequence

even if, as several commentators suggest, Paul had been engaged in mission to the Jews in Tarsus.[15] In contrast to Tarsus, where Paul likely struggled with a lack of success, Antioch saw Paul's ministry develop in new ways (Acts 11:26), for which we must acknowledge the encouragement of Barnabas.[16] (For this interpretation of events

14. Riesner, *Paul's Early Period*, 264.

15. See Jervell, *Theology*, 117. Jervell believes we can talk about the Paul of Acts as a missionary to the Jews (e.g., in Damascus, Jerusalem, and Tarsus), while the Paul of the Epistles is an apostle to the Gentiles. I find his contrast, however, to be unnecessarily polarizing, and as it is dependent on Luke's silence about Paul's activity in Tarsus, it is not entirely persuasive.

16. My portrait of Paul in Tarsus is, admittedly, speculative, but it is

in Tarsus, I follow the lead of William Larkin, who surveys Luke's use of *anazētēsa* [search] in Luke 2:44–45 and Acts 11:25, as well as the references to Tarsus in Acts 9:30; 21:39; and 22:3, and then concludes that this implies a thorough search for Paul.)[17]

Paul's call to Gentile mission. Barnabas seeks Paul out precisely because he understands the relevance of Paul's theological acumen to the new patterns of missionary practice in Antioch. Paul also has practical experience to offer, albeit of an indirect kind. Terence Donaldson has argued that Paul's mission to the Gentiles rested on his previous involvement in proselytizing Gentiles into Judaism (Gal. 5:11).[18] Prior to his vision of the risen Jesus on the road to Damascus, Paul was driven by a burning desire to maintain the purity of the elect people of God. The test for this was conformity to the Jewish law, the Torah, and it was this test that precisely distinguished Jews from Gentiles. In contrast, loyalty to Jesus, as the Messiah, represented a rival way to define and delimit the people of God; inevitably and irreversibly weakening the distinctions between Jew and Gentile.[19] The threat loyalty to Jesus posed to orthodox Judaism is what had driven Paul's fierce opposition to Stephen.

Where, then, can we locate the genesis of Paul's missionary call to the Gentiles? Paul Bowers suggests that Paul "traces back his own involvement in Gentile mission not to something commonly implicit in the believer's experience of Christ, but to a quite personal summons (1 Thess 2:4; Gal 1:15, 16; 2:7–9; Rom 1:5, 6; 15:15; Col 1:23)."[20] Donaldson agrees, seeing in Paul's conversion on the road to Damascus a reconfiguration of Paul's convictional world concerning Gentiles.[21]

---

possible to imagine Paul's frustration in Tarsus at being unable to fulfill God's words of Acts 9:15, which he placed at the center of his call and vision when defending his ministry toward the end of his life.

17. William J. Larkin Jr., *Acts* (Downers Grove, Ill.: InterVarsity Press, 1995), 179.

18. Terence L. Donaldson, *Paul and the Gentiles: Remapping the Apostle's Convictional World* (Minneapolis: Fortress Press, 1997), 298–99.

19. Ibid., 251.

20. Paul Bowers, "Church and Mission in Paul," *Journal for the Study of the New Testament* 14, no. 44 (1991): 93.

21. Donaldson, *Paul and the Gentiles*, 271; see also 293–307. Donald-

For the later Paul, the term *ethnos* as a descriptor of non-Jews is extended to include "the nations," a reinterpretation that suits his self-understanding as an apostle called to "all the world" (Col. 1:23, my paraphrase; the literal sense of the Greek is "all creation under the heavens") arrayed along a representative arc from Jerusalem to Illyricum (Rom. 15:19). Paul's reference to his priestly "offering of the nations" (Rom. 15:16)[22] seems justified by his having proclaimed the Gospel to every nation located along this arc.

Antioch and the shaping of Paul. The Jewish apostle to the Gentiles is shaped in the ethnically diverse congregations of Antioch. Norman Thomas writes of Paul, "Antioch nurtured him and allowed him to experiment with new patterns," also noting that "it was in Antioch that Paul had time to develop his strategy of mission to Gentiles."[23] This mission to the Gentiles became so central for Paul that he urged the church in Corinth, "Give no offence to Jews or to Greeks, . . . just as I try to please everyone in everything I do, . . . so that they may be saved" (1 Cor. 10:32–33). His conversion to the Gentile mission becomes so complete that when James and the Jerusalem church send observers to Antioch who then join Peter and Barnabas in withdrawing from table fellowship with the Gentiles, Paul firmly condemns their action as hypocrisy (Gal. 2:11–14).[24]

---

son argues that Krister Stendahl's assertion that Paul's Damascus vision is better understood as a prophetic-apostolic calling (and thus directed "to the ends of the world") rather than as a "conversion" (see Krister Stendahl, *Paul among Jews and Gentiles* [Philadelphia: Fortress Press, 1976], 7–23.) need not deter us from using the term "conversion," as long as we understand conversion as a complex phenomenon with cultural, social, religious, and personal dimensions, not merely as cognitive. See further Lewis R. Rambo, *Understanding Religious Conversion* (New Haven: Yale Univ. Press, 1993).

22. See Arland J. Hultgren, *Paul's Gospel and Mission* (Philadelphia: Fortress Press, 1985), 132.

23. Thomas, "Church at Antioch," 146, 149.

24. It is possible that the persecution and resultant Diaspora under Agrippa delayed a decisive resolution of issues relating to the Gentile mission (first discussed in Acts 11:1–8, though not resolved until the Jerusalem Council of Acts 15). The deferral of this issue was doubtless a source of hot controversy; indeed, Paul even refers to a "circumcision faction" in Antioch (Gal. 2:12). Paul was caught up in this dynamic, most obviously

The resulting mission activity. Korean poet Kim Chi-Ha has written, "Bread is heaven. As heaven cannot be monopolized, bread should be shared and eaten by all."[25] Paul and Barnabas learn from the church in Antioch how vital it is for the sake of the Gospel that Jews eat with Greeks in a demonstration of practical reconciliation and love that transcends all ethnic and cultural divides.

This action overturned the social conventions of the day. Charitable support was rarely, if ever, given by one ethnic group to another in the ancient world. Such a love offering is radically innovative and possibly unique. This symbolic sharing of food between Greek and Jew was a staggering moment in the life of the early church. It must have seemed that the world was being turned upside down. Consequently, the church in Antioch grows in its trust and respect for Paul and Barnabas and entrusts them with mission on its behalf (Acts 11:29; 13:2–3).

This sending out into mission is what eventually, after further extensive missionary travels, will bring Paul to trial before the Gentile rulers of the nations. Paul, defending himself before Agrippa (and others), testifies that the words of Jesus to him on the road to Damascus have convinced him that he was sent to "the Gentiles" (Acts 26:17). Paul is very aware that he stands before Agrippa because of his mission to the Gentiles and the violent response it provoked from the Jews in the temple (Acts 21:27–31). Even at trial, his public defense raises a veritable storm when he concludes with a reference to his Gentile mission (Acts 22:21–22). Paul's mission is not merely an outworking of his theology; Paul's theology is a *mission* theology that propels him to the nations, to the ends of the world, to Jew and Gentile alike.[26] Ultimately, his mission theology

---

when he opposed Peter and Barnabas for withdrawing from eating with the Gentiles.

25. Cited in Thomas, "Church at Antioch," 152.

26. Some Pauline scholars have queried the extent to which Paul expected the churches, as congregations rather than individuals, to follow his example in mission. Paul Bowers ("Church and Mission in Paul") attempts to resolve this paradox with the suggestion that Paul's mission theology reflects the Jewish concept of the mission of the people of God ("a light to the nations"). Paul's missional exhortations to his congregations are typically "live such good lives before the Gentiles." Bowers concludes, "Where Paul . . . searches out, pursues, confronts, and urges men

brings him into conflict with the authorities of both the Jewish and Gentile worlds as he spreads the Gospel of Christ's sovereign rule over the whole world.

MISSION AT WORLD'S END

Diaspora and ethnic diversity are likely to remain points of attention for missiologists and mission practitioners into the foreseeable future. For students of the megachurches also, these are important issues. Some of the largest churches I have observed during my ministry have been diaspora churches (e.g., Nigerians in the United Kingdom and Ukraine), and in a large number of other churches, from Norway to Australia, from north to south, cultural diversity has shaped the content, conduct, and communication of Sunday worship.

In such instances, we see a contemporary expression of the discovery made by the church in Antioch that the Gospel is the *reconciling* good news of Jesus for Jew and Gentile alike, even to the ends of the world. The implication is clear: the migrant Christian journey into mission was a calling to encounter previously unknown ethnic groups and cultures that existed at the margins, on the edge. Unknown dangers and boundless opportunities await those who are obedient enough to enter the migrant experience at the world's end. Paul knew of those dangers and opportunities to the end, remaining faithful to Jesus as well as to the vision for mission that had been kindled and tended by the ethnically diverse diaspora church in Antioch.

---

to accept the word, his churches are expected . . . to attract, allure, respond and receive. Paul promotes a centrifugal mission; his churches are to form the focus of a centripetal movement. Paul disseminates; they assimilate" (109). I mention this position here not because I necessarily agree with Bowers but because no serious contemporary Pauline scholar would discuss Paul's theology without reference to its missionary character.

17

Hillsong Megachurch Network: Christianity in Global Cities

Miranda Klaver

Initiated by the Pentecostal Hillsong megachurch in Sydney, Australia, a rapidly growing global network of new churches has emerged in urban centers in Europe such as London, Paris, Copenhagen, and Amsterdam, and also in South Africa's Cape Town and recently in New York City and Los Angeles in the United States.[1] This transnational network of churches, characterized by entrepreneurial charismatic leadership, displays a vibrant form of neo-Pentecostal Christianity that is accessible and appealing in its use of music and multimedia.[2]

From a missiological perspective, the Hillsong megachurch and its network raise a number of questions. How are we to understand and evaluate the current expansion of global Pentecostal networks founded by megachurches that plant new churches in different parts of the world? Furthermore, since this global movement is largely an urban phenomenon, how

1. On February 8, 2015, in presenting the vision statement "Hillsong Church 2015," senior pastor Brian Houston announced the expansion of Hillsong Network into the Latin American cities of Buenos Aires and São Paulo; www.youtube.com/watch?v=22wRTk4g18I.

2. Since the 1980s, the terms "New Pentecostalism" and "neo-Pentecostalism" have been used by independent churches to distinguish themselves from denominational Pentecostal churches such as the Assemblies of God. See Allan Anderson, *An Introduction to Pentecostalism: Global Charismatic Christianity* (Cambridge: Cambridge Univ. Press, 2004), 158.

does a megachurch network such as Hillsong relate to multiple local city contexts? How is the success of Hillsong Church to be understood in light of the missiologically acknowledged importance of contextualization?

In this case study I raise the question of contextualization of global megachurch networks, based on my research in 2013–14 in Hillsong churches in Amsterdam and New York City.[3] I will argue that although Hillsong can easily be looked upon as a consumerist and commodified form of Christianity, in practice Hillsong is able to minister to a particular "tribe" encountered in global cities today. While missiological and theological reflection is not explicitly encountered within the Hillsong churches, global megachurch networks acknowledge the dynamism of global cities and the rise of a new cosmopolitan class around the world. As a consequence, the rise of transnational megachurches poses an important challenge for further missiological reflection as they introduce new issues into the discussion of contextual theology. Global churches such as the Hillsong network underscore the need for concepts of culture and context to be understood in light of the dynamic ways the world is becoming a global network.

CONTEXTUALIZATION AND GLOBAL NETWORKS

In mission studies and contextual theology, contextualization is a key concept for discussing the communication of the Gospel. Contextualization serves as a corrective to former mission methods that contained elements of cultural imperialism and exported a Western religious culture along with the Gospel. Not only is contextualization an integral part of cross-cultural ministry, but its importance for carrying out new church planting ministries in secular contexts such as Europe and the United States is also increasingly recognized.[4] The cultures and worldviews of those who have

3. My research has been conducted as a fellow of the Congregational Studies Team, funded by the Lilly Endowment, www.hirr.hartsem.edu/cong/congregational_studies_fellowship.html.

4. For example, see Timothy J. Keller, *Center Church: Doing Balanced, Gospel-Centered Ministry in Your City* (Grand Rapids: Zondervan, 2012). Keller is a Presbyterian pastor in New York City.

not heard the Gospel are no longer taken for granted; rather they now are the subject of considerable research using sociological concepts, anthropological insights, and similar research methods. Because of growing awareness of the need for contextualization, church planters in large cities today move into neighborhoods and invest in relationships and friendships. They seek to experience life together with, and live out the Gospel among, those with whom they desire to share the Gospel.

Contextualization, however, can take different forms and convey different meanings. As Stephen Bevans has argued, contextualization involves interplay among Scripture, experience, tradition, and context. The ways these four elements are valued and taken into account in contextualizing the Gospel varies among theological traditions. The prophetic call from liberation theologians in giving voice to the oppressed and marginalized is quite different from the understanding of contextualization displayed by evangelical theologians. The latter often approach contextualization via a communication model, as translating the Gospel authentically and relevantly for another culture.[5]

Within neo-Pentecostalism, the fastest growing Christian movement in the world, discussions on contextualization are rare. The rapid growth and spread of the movement in many parts of the world seem to confirm that God is at work and leave little time for theological reflection. After all, neo-Pentecostals may think (if not say), harvesttime is probably not the best season to do so. Moreover, the evangelistic zeal of Pentecostals leads to innovative practices in the use of popular culture and new media, most visible in the integration of popular music and technology into church services, evangelistic campaigns, and conferences, and in Pentecostals' being among the first to use online media for the sake of the Gospel. According to their own understanding, the message of the Gospel is the same, while the form of presenting it is adapted to the local context and unreached groups.

Interestingly, Pentecostals (and evangelicals) often regard media technology in a positive light, providing access to mass audiences for their message. The use of media enables them to

5. Stephen B. Bevans, *Models of Contextual Theology* (Maryknoll, N.Y.: Orbis Books, 2002), 47.

extend their influence and their mission of spreading the Gospel and planting churches. The current media revolution seems to accelerate this trend as religious life is expressed through a multiplicity of media practices and networks.

The emergence of successful media-saturated, multiethnic churches, found in European capital cities such as Amsterdam, as well as in the United States, but having their center in the Hillsong megachurch in Sydney, signals a trend: global cities are breeding grounds for new modes of Global Christianity. The expansion of the Hillsong network from Australia into Europe, the United States, South Africa, and now Latin America brings cities together into one theological framework having its center in Australia. The Hillsong case illustrates the ability of neo-Pentecostal churches to produce, as well as be embedded in, transnational media circuits that shape religious imaginations, messages, and modes of worship in various localities around the globe. It is noteworthy that these church networks assume a shared global context rather than acknowledging the local contexts of the cities involved.

HILLSONG'S MEGACHURCH NETWORK

Hillsong's megachurch network began as a local church in Sydney, founded in 1983 by Brian and Bobbie Houston. In the 1990s Hillsong Sydney became known worldwide among evangelical and Pentecostal churches for its music ministry. With its music albums Hillsong Sydney is one of the leading producers of contemporary Christian music today. The church has grown into a megachurch of more than 20,000 in weekly attendance and has expanded in a number of satellite churches in Australia. At the turn of the century, the first Hillsong church outside Australia was planted in London, which became the home base for further expansion in a number of capital cities in Europe. Hillsong also planted churches in South Africa (2008) and recently in the United States, in New York City (2010) and Los Angeles (2013). Although Hillsong's beliefs and practices are rooted in Pentecostalism, the church downplays its Pentecostal identity, not presenting itself as Pentecostal but rather identifying itself as a contemporary and relevant evangelical church.[6]

6. Hillsong is a member of Australian Christian Churches (www.acc

With its integration of advanced multimedia technology and its standardized music and "sound," Hillsong is unique in creating a globally shared church experience without much regard for local contexts, suggesting even a neglect of the local context and a form of decontextualization. The movement's member churches display a remarkable similarity in worship space, liturgy, sound, leadership style, and organizational structure.

Characteristic of Hillsong churches in global cities around the world is their selection of key locations for their meeting sites. For example, Hillsong New York City rents a theater near Broadway, and the London church is located at the heart of London's theater district. Hillsong Amsterdam gathers at Escape, the city's most famous club, which is nationally renowned for being the best place to party on a Saturday night. Location clearly matters for Hillsong; the physical space of the buildings advertises that church is entertaining, exciting, accessible, and fun. The locations chosen signal Hillsong's response to the urban context, with awareness of the ways that urban dwellers meet together.[7]

The liturgy followed in Hillsong church services is standardized according to the script developed at Hillsong Sydney. A typical Hillsong church service begins with four songs, followed by a word of welcome, another song, a minisermon for the offering, announcements for upcoming Hillsong events, another song, sermon, altar call, and song of closure. Use in Hillsong network churches of the same inspirational videos, identical lighting schemes and smoke effects, and even replication of bodily gestures and language expressions on stage leaves little room for experiment or improvisation on the part of the various Hillsong churches.

The way Hillsong standardizes its music is a key factor in meeting the challenge of communicating to a transnational

---

.org.au/about-us), an alliance of Pentecostal churches previously known as the Assemblies of God in Australia. Renamed in 2007 under the leadership of Brian Houston, who was president from 1997 to 2009, Australian Christian Churches has "over 1,000 churches with over 280,000 constituents."

7. Geraldo Marti, *Hollywood Faith: Holiness, Prosperity, and Ambition in a Los Angeles Church* (New Brunswick, N.J.: Rutgers Univ. Press, 2008), 114.

audience.[8] By restricting the music repertoire in church services to Hillsong worship songs, the church is able to create a "global sound," a sound defined by the annual release of studio-recorded Hillsong albums with new worship songs. Each local Hillsong church reproduces this global sound by mixing the sounds of live local worship bands with studio-recorded tracks of vocals, instruments, and other sounds supplied by Hillsong Sydney. The production of the "Hillsong sound" is perhaps the most striking example of how media technology can be functionally applied and strategically used within a global church network. The Hillsong sound plays a critical role in the construction of community and religious identity, confirming that suitable aesthetic forms are powerful modes of bonding and means for creating commitments.[9]

The performance style of Hillsong pastors is another striking similarity found across the Hillsong churches. The pastors, who foster a young and hip style of dress and body image, embody a combination of stand-up comedian, motivational speaker, and revival preacher. Although senior pastor Brian Houston occasionally wears a suit, generally the young Hillsong pastors are dressed according to the latest hipster style, with a preference for skinny ripped jeans, black leather jackets, and most likely tattoos. In 2014 CNN referred to Carl Lenz, pastor of Hillsong New York City, as New York's "hipster pastor."[10] He is known for being a friend of Justin Bieber and for being the informal pastor of New York's professional basketball team, the Knicks. And like other celebrities, Hillsong pastors use social media to present and promote

8. Tom Wagner, "Branding, Music, and Religion: Standardization and Adaptation in the Experience of the 'Hillsong Sound,'" in *Religion as Brands: New Perspectives on the Marketization of Religion and Spirituality*, ed. Jean-Claude Usunier and Jörg Stolz (London: Ashgate, 2014), 65.

9. Ibid., 63. Miranda Klaver, "Worship Music as Aesthetic Domain of Meaning and Bonding: The Glocal Context of a Dutch Pentecostal Church," in *The Spirit of Praise: Music and Worship in Pentecostal-Charismatic Christianity*, ed. Monique Marie Ingalls and Amos Yong (University Park: Pennsylvania State Univ. Press, 2015), 110.

10. See "Mega Church Made in Manhattan," CNN, June 2, 2014, http://edition.cnn.com/videos/living/2014/06/02/ac-harlow-pastor-carl-lentz-long.cnn.

themselves in different roles, juggling between pastor, husband, father, and "cool" friend among their peers.

With their informal and entertaining presentation, Hillsong pastors bring a positive and encouraging Gospel message. The topical sermons address the struggles of everyday life in light of God's promises for blessing, miracles, and a fulfilling life. The messages are accessible, exhibiting a *lingua Christiana* which assumes that attenders are acquainted with the Christian tradition. The recurring practice of the altar call underscores Hillsong's revivalist roots.

Organizationally, the Sydney megachurch is the formal power center of the Hillsong network. Brian and Bobby Houston, together with the board of elders in Sydney, supervise the Hillsong churches around the world. The daughter churches are conceived of as extensions of the mother church, an outlook given expression in Hillsong's vision statement: "One house with many rooms."[11] That most Hillsong pastors have been trained at Hillsong's Bible college enhances the central role played by Hillsong Sydney and the Houstons. Further, the Houstons' children have been appointed to key positions in the church: Benjamin Houston is pastor of Hillsong Los Angeles, and Joel Houston both is co-pastor of the New York City Hillsong church and plays a leading role in Hillsong United, the megachurch's Sydney-based band.

In terms of contextualization, the Hillsong megachurch network can be looked upon as a church that consciously accommodates the Gospel to the shapes of popular culture by integrating elements of entertainment, popular music, and celebrity culture. But to understand the dynamic growth of global megachurch networks, a closer look at global cities and their inhabitants is needed.

REACHING THE EMERGING URBAN CREATIVE CLASS

Based on my ethnographic research in the Hillsong churches in Amsterdam and New York City, it is clear that Hillsong churches are reaching a specific cultural tribe inhabiting global cities today. Visitors to both Hillsong churches are in their twenties and early thirties. The diversity of visitors is striking, with all ethnicities and cultural backgrounds represented. Hillsong's core group of volunteers and active participants reflect the so-called creative class,

11. See http://hillsong.com/vision.

a social stratum centering on professions dealing with creative tasks that has only recently gained recognition by sociologists. According to Richard Florida, members of the creative class are geographically mobile and tend to concentrate in global cities that are diverse and offer a wide range of lifestyle options.[12] They are found, for example, in the media industry, where they may be app developers, web designers, or photographers. These well-educated millennials are confronted with a labor market in which holding a college degree no longer guarantees one will find a job.[13] In order to see their dreams and ambitions fulfilled, aspiring middle-class members of this generation find it necessary to manage their own careers and often have no choice but to be self-employed. As "individuals increasingly become entrepreneurs regarding their own public selves," the flexibility and uncertainty of what is often called the "new economy" encourage millennials to "brand" themselves and engage in self-promotion.[14]

Most Hillsong attendees have a Christian background and have moved to the city to study or to find a job. They have already heard about Hillsong through the music repertoire of their former evangelical churches. Being new in the city, they find that Hillsong offers a warm welcome and easy access to a large network of new friends. The contemporary style of worship and the practical sermons are much appreciated. Interestingly, both in Amsterdam and in New York City, I regularly met students and young adults whose parents were immigrants. A recurring theme in their stories is one of outgrowing their background, including the ethnic church of their parents, and becoming uncomfortable with the cultural rules and practices of their mother church. Hillsong offered them a place where they felt at home and were able to experience a deep sense of belonging, which they frequently expressed in words like, "At Hillsong I can be myself."

In this context of geographic, educational, social, and profes-

12. Richard L. Florida, *The Rise of the Creative Class: Revisited* (Philadelphia: Basic Books, 2012), 285.

13. Neil Howe and William Strauss introduced the term "Millennial Generation" to describe the generational cohort born after 1982; see their *Millennials Rising: The Next Great Generation* (New York: Vintage Books, 2000).

14. Marti, *Hollywood Faith*, 180.

sional mobility, social networks are the key mechanism for mobilizing resources. These networks give millennials access for finding a place to live, locating jobs, meeting new people, and encountering new ideas. Hillsong definitely caters to the needs of this creative class. As an "urban tribe," creative-class millennials move in close-knit groups of friends who replace the role of family.[15] They are often to be found at so-called third places or third spaces, areas that are neither home nor work but venues in urban neighborhoods where people hang out, meet new friends, and find an experience of community.[16] While coffee shops, bookstores, and cafés often serve as third places, Hillsong meets similar needs for those who are new to the city. It is a welcoming place that they can call home, and it provides an extensive network in an unstable labor market with uncertain employment. Furthermore, Hillsong creates many opportunities for volunteers to develop various skills, for instance, creative skills by joining the photography team, technical skills as members of the production teams, media skills in the media teams, and so on. While acknowledging that a critical mass of volunteers is necessary to operate the church, the rewards for being a volunteer go beyond the advantage of learning new skills. Volunteers themselves stress the importance of belonging, the value of being with friends, and the privilege of being part of a church "where God is present and at work."

Hillsong's positive and uplifting weekly messages display a Pentecostal discourse of personal empowerment, stressing that God has big plans for your life and that your past does have to not define your future. The recurrent altar call underscores that new beginnings are always possible. This stress on the new and on a break with the past reveals Hillsong's revivalist Pentecostal roots. From a historical perspective, one could argue that Hillsong has brought the old-time revival tent meeting into the twenty-first century. It is questionable, however, whether those responding to

15. See Nancy Tatom Ammerman, *Sacred Stories, Spiritual Tribes: Finding Religion in Everyday Life* (Oxford: Oxford Univ. Press, 2013).

16. The concept "third space" was introduced by Ray Oldenburg in his book *The Great Good Place: Cafés, Coffee Shops, Community Centers, Beauty Parlors, General Stores, Bars, Hangouts, and How They Get You through the Day* (New York: Paragon House, 1989.

the altar call are new converts. During the course of my interviews and informal talks with fifty Hillsong attendees, I met only a few people who had no former church background and were first-time believers. From the missional perspective of church growth and planting churches in global—often secularized—cities, this finding is rather disappointing.

Clearly, Hillsong offers a new generation of believers a Christian community where they feel accepted and empowered and where their faith is encouraged. Indeed, for Christian members of the mobile creative class in global cities—a group in risk of leaving the church—Hillsong offers a place they can call home. But because the unstable job market fosters a nomadic lifestyle, Hillsong churches are confronted with high turnover. People are constantly coming and going, which creates a unique dynamic of dedicated short-term volunteers who are willing to invest their time and skills but who may be present for only a limited period of time. This new mode of community formation, emerging in global cities, challenges existing concepts of church growth and the church as a bounded and sustainable community.

The rise of megachurch networks indicates that in urban settings today Christianity often functions as a network of interactions in which social relationships and structures and patterns of belief become increasingly global and interconnected.[17] As a consequence, for the sake of developing a contextualized theology, church planting ministries in global cities need to evaluate the relevance and meaning of the concepts of culture and ethnicity. As the case study of Hillsong demonstrates, the dynamics and mobility of specific groups in global cities call for an approach that reaches beyond an ethnic lens.

QUESTIONS FOR REFLECTION

1. What concepts of culture and ethnicity do you use in your understanding of contextualization? How can they be fruitful in reaching the younger generation today?

17. Heidi A. Campbell, "Understanding the Relationship between Religion Online and Offline in a Networked Society," *Journal of the American Academy of Religion* 80, no. 1 (2012): 64–93.

2. What elements from the urban creative class do you observe among the younger generation in your ministry?
3. What is the impact of new media technology on your ministry? How does the ongoing development of new media technology affect the ways young people are practicing their faith?
4. As patterns of belief become increasingly global and interconnected, how is your experience and that of your congregation affected? What does this trend mean for the future of missions and local churches?

18

Response to "Hillsong Megachurch Network"

Timothy Kim

Miranda Klaver's chapter, "Hillsong Megachurch Network: Christianity in Global Cities," was of great interest to me. My own ministry of over thirty years has been with a conservative denomination in Korea and Malaysia. Despite differences in theological and pastoral background, I found the discussion of Hillsong megachurch network helpful in broadening my mission understanding and providing new insights into a megachurch network.[1]

Klaver introduces three main points: the relationship between contextualization and the global Pentecostal network, the characteristics of the Hillsong megachurch network, and the question of how to reach the "urban creative class." The characteristics she identifies give fresh insight into developing urban mission strategies, especially for reaching the urban creative class and immigrants in megacities. The positive aspects of the Hillsong megachurch network, however, must not deter us from undertaking necessary theological and missiological evaluation of such movements.

1. Timothy Kim, a Global Mission Society missionary in Malaysia, has served in St. Andrew's Presbyterian Church Penang since 2004 as an honorary senior minister. For background on St. Andrew's Presbyterian Church Penang, planted in 1851, see Robert A. Hunt, Kam Hing Lee, and John Roxborogh, eds., *Christianity in Malaysia: A Denominational History* (Petaling Jaya, Selangor Darul Ehsan, Malaysia: Pelanduk Publications, 1992), 79.

CONTEXTUALIZATION OR GLOBALIZATION NETWORK?

"Hillsong is unique in creating a globally shared church experience without much regard for local contexts, suggesting even a neglect of the local context and a form of decontextualization" (154).[2] Klaver points out the successful globalization of the Hillsong church network; such globalization is a new mission phenomenon in the twenty-first century.

Globalization has been described as "the worldwide movement toward economic, financial, trade, and communications integration. Globalization implies the opening of local and nationalistic perspectives to a broader outlook of an interconnected and interdependent world with free transfer of capital, goods, and services across national frontiers."[3] Such globalization happens not only in the business world; it is also found in local churches around the world. For example, it is easy to find the same Sunday school materials used in Europe, Asia, and North America.[4] As Christianity has expanded from the West to non-Western countries, Western Christianity has influenced the cultures and societies of indigenous peoples. Similarities to be found to Western church buildings, worship forms, and music are reasons why Christianity is often spoken of as a "Western religion." If Hillsong's overseas network of churches follows the worship format and music found in Hillsong Sydney, will it be possible for Hillsong network churches to be indigenized in their own societies? This issue raises the question of contextualization.

Harvie Conn sharply criticized Western Christian mission work that attempted to plant Christianity while avoiding the hard effort of contextualization. He wondered "what might happen in

2. In Miranda Klaver's account, Hillsong churches display remarkable similarity in worship space, liturgy, sound, leadership style, and organizational structure.

3. *Business Dictionary*, www.businessdictionary.com/definition/globalization.html.

4. This is the writer's personal experience in teaching Sunday school students with American Sunday school materials in Canada, Scotland, Korea, Indonesia, and Malaysia. Nowadays, many Sunday schools in Malaysia directly import Sunday school materials from the United States.

Korea or Japan if a truly appropriate Christianity were developed. Many Koreans, of course, have turned to Christ, but largely to a Euro-American Christianity. But approximately 70 percent of Koreans have not yet come to Christ. Would the 70 percent of Koreans respond positively to a truly Koreanized Christianity?"[5]

Moreover, the emergence of nationalism in many countries and the presence of international conflicts make globalization a complex process. As Samuel Huntington has argued, fundamental realignments are taking place in the post–Cold War era.[6] Arguments have been raised against his thesis, but after 9/11 many people, even skeptics, have begun to admit that his view has at least a degree of validity. Haw Young expects an increase in global geopolitical realignments.[7] In light of the various political and social changes, can the globalization of a "brand" such as the Hillsong network of churches be a prominent and enduring element of urban mission work, or will its success be only temporary?

NETWORK OR FRANCHISE?

Since the year 2000, Hillsong Sydney has planted Hillsong network churches in other Australian cities and also overseas. Being fresh and creative, Hillsong's urban approach is attractive to the younger generation. The high percentage of young people in Hillsong congregations reflects this attraction.

Interestingly, most Hillsong network churches use the same liturgy, the one published by Hillsong Sydney. They even use the same inspirational videos, lighting schemes, smoke effects, and gestures. These pastoral and liturgical similarities remind us of the chain store system. The relationship of Hillsong network churches to the Hillsong Sydney mother church seems to be that of a "fran-

5. Harvie Conn served as a missionary in Korea and later was editor of *Urban Mission*. See Harvie M. Conn, Manuel Ortiz, and Susan S. Baker, *The Urban Face of Mission: Ministering the Gospel in a Diverse and Changing World* (Philipsburg, N.J.: P&R Publishing, 2002), 156.

6. Samuel Huntington, *The Clash of Civilizations and the Remaking of World Order* (London: Simon & Schuster, 1997).

7. Haw Young, "Mission Trends in the Twenty-First Century," in *Fiftieth Anniversary of Korean Mission Work in Malaysia* (Kuala Lumpur: n.p., 2015), 14–15.

chise church," similar to the identity in decor and menu found worldwide among McDonalds, KFC, and Starbucks franchises.[8]

The distinctive way that Hillsong Sydney has oriented its pattern of worship raises a theological question. Can Hillsong Sydney's worship style and related activities be standardized for other Hillsong network churches located in quite different contexts and composed of quite different people? The 1978 Willowbank Report from the Lausanne Committee for World Evangelization emphasized the freedom of the church: "If each church is to develop creatively in such a way as to find and express itself, it must be free to do so. This is an inalienable right. For each church is God's church. . . . We strongly oppose such 'foreignness,' wherever it exists, as a serious obstacle to maturity and mission, and a quenching of the Holy Spirit of God."[9] Assuredly, the Hillsong network churches have the right to manage their own church ministries, although they would do well to heed the advice of the Willowbank Report.

NEUTRAL TERRITORY OR SACRED SPACE?

"Characteristic of Hillsong churches in global cities around the world is their selection of key locations for their meeting sites" (154). For example, Hillsong network churches often rent theaters or clubs for their places of worship. In Klaver's view, Hillsong network churches do this from their desire to respond to the urban context and to acknowledge the different ways that urban dwellers meet together.

Bringing people to a neutral territory in which secular people can look at Christianity without being pressured to convert strikes modern people as a reasonable approach. With that said, however, church also has need of sacred space for worship and fellowship. The church is open for everyone, but the church also meets to

8. Franchising is the practice of granting the right to use a firm's business model and brand of products for a prescribed period of time. The franchiser distributes goods to franchisees, and the two parties share business interests in common.

9. Ralph D. Winter and Steven C. Hawthorne, eds. *Perspectives on the World Christian Movement*, 4th ed. (Pasadena, Calif.: William Carey Library, 2009), 522.

reaffirm its identity as the body of Christ. Paul Hiebert and Eloise Hiebert Meneses caution: "Without sacred places and times to give expression to our experience with God, we are in danger of being drawn into the secular world of the city and forgetting God's magnificent presence among us. Or we are in danger of becoming social clubs in which Christ is only a member."[10] Roger Greenway ventures further, supporting the use of church facilities for the benefit of the local community and citing an urban church in Colombia as a model.[11]

Without question, a "church" building is not the only place worship can occur, but having control of a structure or building is important, for its facilities can be used for various purposes that benefit the community and society. The value of a church building as a place of worship should therefore not be underestimated.

URBAN CREATIVE CLASS VERSUS ORDINARY LOCAL PEOPLE

A strong point of the Hillsong megachurches is to break down barriers of tradition that wall off the church from the younger generation. Their places of worship, style, ministers' clothes, and speech are quite relevant to urban young people. Ministers in Hillsong network churches have a reputation for following the latest hipster style and even getting tattoos. They are also very progressive in their use of social networks.

Hillsong's most influential "product" is its music. They have created a so-called global sound that has been loved by people all over the world. Some conservative churches, however, still prefer traditional hymns instead of contemporary Christian music, and some churches, including my own church, do not allow certain musical instruments, such as drums and electric guitars, to be used in their services. Still, the wide acceptance of Hillsong's music constitutes a strong argument for using contemporary music in churches.

10. Paul G. Hiebert and Eloise Hiebert Meneses, *Incarnational Ministry: Planting Churches in Band, Tribal, Peasant, and Urban Societies* (Grand Rapids: Baker Books, 1995), 333.

11. Roger S. Greenway and Timothy M. Monsma, *Cities: Mission's New Frontier* (Grand Rapids: Baker Books, 1989), 236.

Though contemporary music is popular with younger people, not everyone likes it. Even when contemporary Christian music is used in church services, the question must be asked whether the musical style used is the "heart music" of the congregation. On this point, J. Stanley Moore criticized missionaries' too frequent neglect of the local music found in their mission field.

> Missionaries have not always been as sensitive to the issue of indigenous music as they should have been. . . . The most effective musical language in a cross-cultural setting is the "first" (heart) musical language of that target group. People who live in urban centers will often accept many different musical styles, which can be evidenced by musical preferences on radio stations in metropolitan areas around the world. Although people may tolerate multiple musical styles, they will probably express themselves and relate most deeply to one particular style—their "heart music."[12]

It is thus necessary to consider all groups who have different cultures and languages. If all the focus is placed on only one certain group, the universalism of the church can be lost. The church is for all generations, not just one.

CONCLUSION

The Hillsong megachurch's global network gives fresh and creative insight into how urban mission works, especially outreach to the creative class in secular contexts. Its music ministry strongly influences many different churches and young people around the world. On the down side, its pastoral guidelines for other churches in the Hillsong network can diminish the individuality and self-government of those churches. It is a delicate balance. Can they find ways to give more freedom to the other Hillsong network churches to contextualize their ministries within their cultural setting while still adhering to the same worldwide vision?

12. J. Stanley Moore, "Strategies for Music in Missions," in *Missiology: An Introduction to the Foundations, History, and Strategies of World Missions*, ed. John Mark Terry, Ebbie Smith, and Justice Anderson (Nashville: Broadman & Holman, 1998), 565.

19

Megamission in Historical Perspective: Megachurch Missions, Hope or Anomaly?, with Special Reference to Korean Cases

Kyo Seong Ahn

An abundance of literature on megachurches is available, covering almost every aspect of the phenomenon, from theology to church life, from religiosity to sociopolitical implications.[1] Yet we have very few studies of missions as practiced by these churches. Since the globalization of Christianity has been accelerated and sometimes even distorted by missions, including those of megachurches, it is natural that missiologists and mission practitioners are interested in asking, Why and how have megachurches done mission work? What is distinctive about the character of their missions? How do missions affect the megachurches and vice versa?

This chapter seeks to answer these questions. In the first place, however, we must admit that the phenomenon of megachurches is so diverse and fluid that it is hard to define it in a single statement. In this chapter I thus use the plural form "megachurches." I also introduce the umbrella term "megamission" for all aspects of missions "of, by, and for" megachurches. The characteristics of megamission will, I trust, become clear through the process of examining it in this chapter. In using this term, I mean to suggest that we consider the missions of megachurches to be a distinct subject

1. Scott Thumma and Dave Travis, *Beyond Megachurch Myths: What We Can Learn from America's Largest Churches* (San Francisco: Jossey-Bass, 2007).

for research. Second, this chapter focuses exclusively on the missions of the megachurches, not on the megachurches themselves. Third, this chapter deals with Korean megachurches, which are indispensable for any study of the missions of megachurches, for one-quarter of the world's fifty largest megachurches are located in Korea, and the Korean church, particularly around the Han River in Seoul, is deeply imbued with the spirit of "megachurchism."[2] This area has been called the Han River Bible Belt.[3]

THE RISE OF MEGAMISSION: A HISTORICAL SURVEY

The rise of megamission can be reviewed as a three-step development: the large-scale missions that were common before megamission per se, megamission arising during the 1970s, and megamission at the turn of the twenty-first century.

Large-scale missions before 1970. If we think of megamission as simply large-scale missions, we can trace its history back to the early years of Christianity. Most missions belonging to the historical churches—in particular, those with episcopal traditions—can be regarded as a kind of megamission in that the missions have been implemented by bishops or high-ranking churchmen, who represented the church on a broad scale. The Augustinian mission to Britain at the end of the sixth century, commissioned by Pope Gregory the Great, is typical of this category.

Within Protestantism, the nineteenth century saw a burgeoning of large-scale churches in cities such as London and New York, and several of these churches were enthusiastic about missions. For example, Spurgeon's College, which succeeded Pastor's College, the school established in 1856 by Charles Spurgeon, minister of the Metropolitan Tabernacle in London, still unashamedly maintains its missionary spirit.[4]

2. See Warren Bird, "The World's Largest Churches," www.leadnet.org/world/.

3. Kyo Seong Ahn, "Chonghoe Ilbaekjunyeon Majeun Oneulnal Hangukgyohoeui Myeongam" [Positives and negatives of the contemporary Korean church at the hundredth anniversary of the General Assembly], *Gidokgongbo* [PCK world], February 28, 2012, www.pckworld.com/news/articleView.html?idxno=52945.

4. See www.spurgeons.ac.uk.

The rise of megamission in the 1970s. Scholars define a megachurch as "a Protestant church that averages at least two thousand total attendees in their weekend services"; such churches proliferated beginning in the 1970s.[5] During this period, there was a rapprochement between evangelical and ecumenical missiology, which aimed both at overcoming their then-existing missiological polarization and at sustaining their respective legacies of evangelism and humanization.

Some asked whether megachurches could be a legitimate way of "being church." This question, however, is equally one about mission. That is, *esse ecclesiae* (essence of the church) fundamentally predisposes *esse missionis* (essence of the mission), and even *bene esse missionis* (best ways of mission). In other words, the mission of a church reflects the self-image of that church. As for megachurches, their implementation of missions clearly reflects their self-image.

In the task of self-authentication, megachurches continuously faced various challenges, both within and without the church. Notably, megachurches emerged in the aftermath of the decline of traditional denominational Christianity, which was giving way "under the pressures of consumerism, materialism and individualism."[6] In practice, as Mark Driscoll has noted, three types of church can be identified with distinctive responses to changing urban contexts, namely: "Church 1.0 (traditional, institutional, assumes central place in culture), Church 2.0 (contemporary, business orientation, fights marginal place in culture, pastors are CEOs marketing spiritual goods and services to customers), and Church 3.0 (postmodern, pluralistic, accepts marginal place in culture, pastors are local missionaries)."[7] Megachurches can be said to belong to the second type.

Besides wrestling with the challenges from the world

5. Thumma and Travis, *Beyond Megachurch Myths*, xviii, 6.

6. Mark Hutchinson and John Wolffe, *A Short History of Global Evangelicalism* (Cambridge: Cambridge Univ. Press, 2012), 245.

7. Hutchinson and Wolffe, *Short History*, 262, summarizing Mark Driscoll, "A Pastoral Perspective on the Emergent Church," *Criswell Theological Review*, n.s., 3, no. 2 (Spring 2006): 87–93, www.christianitytoday.com/assets/10362.pdf.

mentioned above, megachurches are forced to formulate an authentic ecclesiology, as well as a missiology, to which we shall return shortly.

Megamission at the turn of the twenty-first century. After passing through the uncertainties of their formative phase, megachurches entered into missions in earnest at the turn of the twenty-first century. They undertook to establish their own missionary structure, claiming control of their missions as a proprietary right, and thus raised new questions about the relationship between church and mission. Furthermore, in the case of the Yoido Full Gospel Church in Korea, the largest church in the world, the mission of the church itself has been implemented in parallel with the one-man mission of David Yonggi Cho, world evangelist and minister emeritus of the church. The David Cho Evangelistic Mission was established in March 2000 with the express purpose of supporting his international ministry. Those years also witnessed the rise of diverse forms of mission such as short-term mission, mission in partnership (in particular, with NGOs), and mission as migration. Megamissions are heavily involved in each of these, as well as in most other patterns of innovative missional outreach. Therefore, beyond examining megamission as such, it is necessary to investigate megamission as one of the foundations for other models of mission.

MEGAMISSION: A THEMATIC OVERVIEW

What characteristics are present in megamission? First, megamission bears the impress of its roots in evangelicalism. Second, though it now has spread globally, it is colored by its U.S. origins. Third, it is deeply rooted in the church, that is, in megacongregations. Fourth, megamission, as could be expected, is evolving in its theological self-understanding and practice.

A revival of evangelical mission. Since the megachurch movement has strong evangelical backing, it is no exaggeration to claim that megamission represents a revival of evangelical mission. In contrast to the commonplace conclusion that the age of missions ended and the age of mission has begun, it is clear that the age of evangelical missions, particularly Majority World missions, arrived in the second half of the last century.[8] In retrospect, we find that missionaries from an evangelical background have, since the 1960s, been organizing a series of worldwide missionary conferences and establishing numerous missionary structures. The rise of megachurches in the last quarter of the twentieth century enabled the dream of a flourishing evangelical mission to become reality, for these megachurches supplied the men, women, money, and logistical support for a renewed effort in carrying the Good News of salvation to those without knowledge of Jesus Christ.

Much support is available for the claim that megamission is the major force in evangelical mission today. Lamentably, not everything envisioned by evangelical missiology has penetrated the consciousness of the churches. In particular, although the Lausanne Covenant articulated a proactive stance regarding the social ministry of the church, this change in emphasis has not been sufficiently reflected in the life and mission of churches at the grassroots level. During the same period, the arrival of the winter of ecumenism seriously dampened ecumenical mission, leaving the field open to Pentecostal and charismatic groups, which have largely been the ones to create today's most innovative forms of missions. Thus it is not surprising that the contemporary missionary landscape has been gradually reoccupied by evangelicals.

U.S.-style, though now glocal, contexts of mission. Although megachurches are burgeoning in many places outside the United States, it is undeniable that they began in the United States and are part of a U.S. phenomenon. The movement's U.S. flavor is still felt in megachurches found all over the world. In this sense, the megachurch movement and megamission, the vanguard of its globalization, are open to the charge of being a unilateral reproduction of U.S.-style churches.[9] According to Lamin Sanneh, Christianity

8. Kyo Seong Ahn, "Mission in Unity: An Investigation into the Question of Unity as It Has Arisen in the Presbyterian Church of Korea and Its World Mission" (Ph.D. diss., Cambridge: Univ. of Cambridge, 2008), 146–48.

9. See Steve Brouwer, Paul Gifford, and Susan D. Rose, *Exporting the American Gospel: Global Christian Fundamentalism* (New York: Routledge, 1996), esp. 186–92.

around the world exists in two forms: Global Christianity and World Christianity, "the former referring to colonising extensions of transatlantic evangelicalism, the latter to indigenous appropriations."[10] The second is clearly the desirable option.

Nevertheless, we must remember that megamission is carried out in the context of globalization.[11] The worldwide propagation of the megachurch movement has enabled the diversification of megachurches as well as of megamission. Now that megachurches have arisen around the world—from Korea to Ukraine, Scandinavia to Latin America, Australia to Africa—they have quickly been turning themselves into mission bodies by organizing their own missionary structures. It has been gradually recognized, however, that these latecomers of the missionary movement are no more exempt from missionary malaises than were traditional Western missions. The diversification of megamission as carried out by the new megachurches raises the old specter of mission as an expression of nationalism. For instance, Korean missiologists have expressed deep concern about an unhealthy Koreanization in world mission.[12] In a similar vein, Scott Sunquist warns about the paternalism, or "Christian cultural imperialism," of non-Western missionaries.[13] And the way megachurches have exercised their initiatives in megamission reopens the question of the relationship between church and mission.

Megamission in megacongregations. How should we characterize megamission—as a church-oriented mission? a missionary society

10. Hutchinson and Wolffe, *Short History*, 250.

11. Brian Stanley, *The Global Diffusion of Evangelicalism: The Age of Billy Graham and John Stott* (Nottingham: IVP Academic, 2013), chap. 3; Karla Poewe, ed., *Charismatic Christianity as a Global Culture* (Columbia: Univ. of South Carolina Press, 1994), 1–29.

12. Jong-Pyo Lim, "21 Segileul Dojeonhaneun Haninseongyosaui Daecheo" [The response of Korean missionaries to the challenges of the twenty-first century], in *Hangukseongyoui Banseonggwa Geu Junbi* [The reflection and preparation of the Korean world mission], ed. Jong-Pyo Lim (Seoul: Korean Missionary Leadership Development Conference, 1999), 176; Ahn, "Mission in Unity," 183.

13. Scott W. Sunquist, "Asian Mission to Asians," in *Christian Mission in the Third Millennium*, ed. Charles E. Cole (New York: General Board of Global Ministries, the United Methodist Church, 2004), 39.

or board? an amalgamated mission? However we decide to categorize it, we still will need to answer several questions.

- How can self-initiated mission avoid getting caught in the same traps into which traditional mission-of-the-church thinking fell? How can it instead be faithful to the lessons of the mission-of-God (*missio Dei*) framework that superseded the earlier emphasis?
- How can this church-oriented mission keep a balance between the "contextualization value" and the "ecclesiology value," or between field-centeredness and home-base–centeredness?[14]
- How can this home-base–centered mission take into consideration the "field-directedness" of mission, as clearly manifested, for example, by Hudson Taylor in his establishment of the China Inland Mission?[15]
- How can this newly emerging mission movement meet the multifaceted tasks facing it, ranging from management of missionary organizations to training missionary personnel and to providing supervision, continuing education, and member care for missionaries and their ministries?
- How can it equip itself to guarantee professionalism as a mission body?
- How can this revived form of the mission of the church overcome the danger of reproducing a carbon-copy church in the mission field?

Among other things, the last question leads to the fundamental issue of the foundation of megamission. We must remember that the rise of the megachurch movement can be interpreted as a return, for the church, to the zenith immediately following its nadir in the post–World War II era, in particular in the 1960s and 1970s. As is well-known, during the third quarter of the last century, skepticism about the role and future of the church was

14. Jonathan J. Bonk, ed., *Accountability in Missions: Korean and Western Case Studies* (Eugene, Ore.: Wipf & Stock, 2011), 67.

15. Klaus Fiedler, *The Story of Faith Missions* (Oxford: Regnum Books, 1994), 33.

widespread. Sensational book titles such as *A Church without God* and *Gott ohne Kirche?* (God without church?) carried the message of unremitting decline.[16] Furthermore, in criticizing the mission-of-the-church outlook, the *missio Dei* movement shared, if not welcomed, the widespread skepticism of the role of the church in mission, to such an extent that an extreme advocate, J. C. Hoekendijk, revealed "his basic suspicion of 'churchism.'"[17] Against this historical backdrop the megachurch movement and megamission trumpeted the resuscitation of church and missions.

Such affirmation of church and missions, however, poses the question of the authenticity of the church and of the mission of the megachurch movement. In practice, the megachurch movement is never free from the taint of triumphalism and the gospel of prosperity.[18] It may be understandable, therefore, that the themes of power and money rise to the fore in missionary criticism of megamission.[19] When such issues can be raised, what guarantees the authenticity of megamission? When all is said and done, is self-initiated and self-directed megamission really the only way or the optimal way for mission to be carried out by megachurches? Acknowledging these concerns, however, is not to say that the problems of megamission overshadow the great contribution that megamission has made to the mobilization of local congregations for mission.

Evolving theology and practice. As with other forms and eras of mission, megamission is evolving. Briefly stated, megamission reflects the tendency in missionary understanding to move from missions to mission. For instance, thanks to its experience in mission at home and abroad, Yoido Full Gospel Church, famous for its minister

16. Ernest Harrison, *A Church without God* (Philadelphia: Lippincott, 1967); Alfred A. Haesler, ed., *Gott ohne Kirche?* (Olten, Freiburg im Breisgau: Walter-Verlag, 1975).

17. Bert Hoedemaker, "The Legacy of J. C. Hoekendijk," *International Bulletin of Missionary Research* 19, no. 4 (October 1995): 166–70, esp. 167.

18. Kate Bowler, *Blessed: A History of the American Prosperity Gospel* (Oxford: Oxford Univ. Press, 2013).

19. Roger Finke and Rodney Stark, *The Churching of America, 1776–2005: Winners and Losers in Our Religious Economy* (New Brunswick, N.J.: Rutgers Univ. Press, 2005); Jonathan J. Bonk, *Missions and Money: Affluence as a Western Missionary Problem* (Maryknoll, N.Y.: Orbis Books, 1991).

emeritus David Yonggi Cho and its message of health and wealth, has gradually expanded its understanding of the Gospel: the latest statement on mission from Yoido Full Gospel Church legitimately pays full attention to social ministry as an aspect of mission.[20] A similar change in the evolving understanding of mission on the part of Rick Warren and Saddleback Church, Lake Forest, California, could be mentioned as well. It is too early at this stage, however, to predict the direction megamission may take in the future.

ACCOUNTABILITY IN MEGAMISSION

We now comment briefly on megachurch accountability in missions. Since the term "accountability" comes from economics, we may be inclined to focus on financial responsibility, effectiveness, or integrity. The issue of missions and accountability, however, particularly when thinking of megamission, needs to be seen from wider and deeper perspectives, ranging from missiological considerations to economics and ecumenism and beyond to politics. Since extensive research in the area of missiology has already been carried out, we may focus on the other three themes.

First, we are aware that church and mission are inescapably influenced by economics. Interestingly, according to Susan Curtis, even the proponents of the social gospel, emerging as a resistance movement against sheer capitalism, were not free from the pull of the emerging consumer culture.[21] For its part, megamission, closely associated as it is with the megachurch movement, needs to use prudence in its conduct of mission. Second, according to the prayer of Jesus in John 17, church, unity, and mission cannot be separated (see esp. vv. 21–23). The megachurch movement in general, as is widely acknowledged, has become estranged from the ecumenical movement and is thus liable to pay scant attention to the issue of mission and unity. Third, as noted above, the megachurch movement emerged in the third quarter of the twentieth century. During that period the home base of mission, that is, the mainline churches

20. Yoido Full Gospel Church, *Yeouido Sunbokeum Kyohoe 50 nyeonsa* [Yoido full gospel church: Fiftieth anniversary] (Seoul: Yoido Full Gospel Church, 2008), 359–69.

21. Susan Curtis, *A Consuming Faith: The Social Gospel and Modern American Culture* (Baltimore, Md.: Johns Hopkins Univ. Press, 1991).

in the United States, struggled in its response to changes of the times, in particular, to political changes taking place. The fallout of these changes transformed the mainline churches in their thinking and practice of mission.[22] On this point, questions about the integrity of the revived mission undertaken by evangelicals, including megamission, have come to the fore.

CONCLUSION

This chapter has argued that the mission of megachurches—what I have called megamission—is a unique missionary phenomenon. We have considered the rise of megamission through three periods: before the 1970s, from the 1970s to the turn of the millennium, and since the turn of the twenty-first century. In our summary of megamission, we have seen the following characteristic features: it is (1) evangelical, (2) shifting from an American style to a global character, (3) church-centered, and (4) evolving from missions to mission. It has also been suggested that the concept of accountability in relation to megamission needs to be expanded to include economic, ecumenical, and political accountability, in addition to attending to an individual missionary's personal integrity and effectiveness or to missiological issues more generally.

QUESTIONS FOR REFLECTION

1. Can and should "megamission" (the mission of megachurches) be a unique phenomenon?
2. In what ways do you find the neologism "megamission" helpful? How less so?
3. In what ways can megachurches guarantee the accountability of megamission?
4. In general, why do you think megachurches want to do mission on their own?
5. What pros and cons do you see in megamission?

22. Daniel H. Bays and Grant Wacker, eds., *The Foreign Missionary Enterprise at Home: Explorations in North American Cultural History* (Tuscaloosa: Univ. of Alabama Press, 2003).

20

Response to "Megamission in Historical Perspective"

J. Kwabena Asamoah-Gyadu

Kyo Seong Ahn is correct in observing that the megachurch phenomenon is significant for studies of World Christianity today and that very little has been heard from mission studies on this development. Indeed, the study of megachurches has started finding its way into missiology, and it seems that, as with the study of immigrant churches, this issue might soon become the focus of serious research at the highest levels of scholarship.[1] I myself was thoroughly impressed on visiting Ukraine in 2004 to find a Nigerian pastor leading a 20,000-member congregation, with half of that number meeting in a single location. By the next decade, however, the church was losing members because of some questionable decisions made by the leadership. The success of numbers has often turned megasize church pastors into chief executive officers rather than servants of God in ministry. The rise and apparent fall of the Ukraine initiative calls for full-scale critical evaluation and also sober reflection. The need for sober evaluation and reflection is underscored by several examples in North America of highly successful megasize church pastors falling into trouble either over lack of financial accountability or moral indiscretions of a sexual nature.

One issue that needs to be unpacked is Ahn's comment that "for megachurches, their implementation of missions clearly

1. See, for example, Jonathan D. James, ed., *A Moving Faith: Mega Churches Go South* (New Delhi: Sage, 2015).

reflects their self-image" (169). It is not clear whether his statement should be understood to mean that each megachurch has a distinct way or style of doing mission work. Mission has to do with the purposes and activities of God in and for the whole universe. God's purposes are the things that God is about in the world and, as Andrew Kirk has noted, "People committed to the reality of God seek understanding of his involvement in order to be immersed in his concerns."[2] That is, we need to be able to discern what God may be doing through the ministry of the whole church, including megachurches, and allow that to inform priorities in mission.

MEGACHURCH VARIETIES AND RELATIVE VALUE

The use of the term "megamission" to define the nature of mission in these megachurches is certainly novel, but it could be presumptuous to think that these churches all think of mission in the same way. When considering the formation and existence of megachurches, it is instructive to note that Ahn's study arises from the Korean context, where David Yonggi Cho's Yoido Full Gospel Church in Seoul is one of the best-known examples of a megachurch. Though the phenomenon of megachurches has historically been associated with Protestant evangelical Christianity, it is also right to point out that there are Catholic churches, especially in non-Western contexts, that have a regular attendance far exceeding the 2,000 worshippers each Sunday that Ahn mentions as a threshold. The important thing to note is that "mega" is relative and contextual, varying by country and denomination. What is mega in Mali, one of Africa's smallest nations, for example, may not qualify even as average in Nigeria, Africa's most populous nation. The same could be said of specific denominations. Even in Latin America, where Pentecostals are taking over from Catholics, there still are Catholic parishes with more than 2,000 worshippers gathering every Sunday.

Whether we can restrict the expression "megamission" to the work of megachurches is a matter that is open to question. In any case, how does one access the volume of mission endeavors

2. J. Andrew Kirk, *What Is Mission? Theological Explorations* (London: Darton, Longman & Todd, 1999), 21.

associated with particular churches? The emergence of the non-Western world as a major Christian heartland has brought with it many heartwarming developments; one such development is the establishment of extra-large Christian congregations similar in size to those we find in North America. We need, however, to hold the size of a church in perspective, because in God's kingdom, the smallest contribution is appreciated. Remember Jesus' parable of the workers in the vineyard in Matthew 20: the hour put in by the laborers who were hired last was valued as highly as the work of those who toiled all day. Megachurches, such as are found in Korea, have become the representative face of modern revivalism, especially with the growth of Christianity in the Global South and East. The work of churches that have megasize congregations must be celebrated. We need to be cautious, however, lest we romanticize their achievements. There is a certain triumphalism that has developed, which detracts from the work of the Spirit in mission. In reflecting on the successes of megachurches it may be important, as I mentioned earlier, to pay attention also to the high-profile scandals that have often rocked the lives of its media-savvy leaders, ranging from financial misappropriations to the despicable moral choices that some have made. It would seem to me that the success of numbers often blinds Christian leaders to the very simple avenues by which the devil tries to bring the work of Christian mission into disrepute.

CHURCH SIZE AND GOD'S BLESSING

Another matter that needs attention in our celebration of megachurches is the strong link that is often made between the anointing of the Spirit and megasize churches. It is often assumed in conservative evangelical hermeneutics that churches that have the favor of God upon their leaders must grow big. I have begun to wonder why certain churches in Africa are building structures to accommodate upward of 5,000 church members when it is clear that the charisma of the founder is responsible for bringing in the numbers. We have come to a point where certain megachurch pastors do not inform their congregations when they travel because doing so will hurt attendance! What will happen when these charismatic leaders move on in the future? We know that in Nigeria, for example, the death of Archbishop Benson Idahosa in 1988 led to the decline of his once-thriving megachurch.[3] I raise these issues because all across the world, Pentecostal/charismatic Christians interpret the megasize of their churches as a sign of success that reflects God's approval and blessing. That may be the case, but we need to bear in mind that in many very difficult and unreached areas, smaller churches—often in the midst of persecution—are reaching people that megasized churches cannot and may not even care about.

The size itself and manifold programs of megachurches have been seen as signs of prosperity in the same way that material things have become prime indicators of God's blessing in many Christian communities. The danger in that outlook may be seen in the rise and fall of Jim and Tammy Bakker, who ran into problems trying to build a material empire for God. The project collapsed, leading many people to wonder whether the Lord approved of those endeavors. In the end, Jim Bakker was humble enough to write the book *I Was Wrong*. In its introduction he makes the following revealing and instructive statement: "The mistakes I made are still being perpetuated in ministries, churches, businesses, marriages, and families. The temptation to have more, do more, earn more, build bigger, emphasize material things rather than spiritual, protect the image regardless of the cost, look the other way rather than confront wrong—these are just a few of the areas in which I have a new mindset."[4]

COMPETITION AND ACCOUNTABILITY

In addition to the issues just raised, I found myself wondering as I wrote this response, What is the opposite of "megamission"? Whose mission is big, and whose is small? In Ghana, where I live, one Pentecostal church advertises itself as a "megachurch" and another as the "unbeatable church." The competitive spirit underlying such advertisements is not lost on critical observers. If churches compete by boasting of numbers, they may undermine the core element of mission, which is, to allow God to engage us

3. J. Kwabena Asamoah-Gyadu, "Doing Greater Things: Mega Church as an African Phenomenon," in James, *A Moving Faith*, 43–61.

4. Jim Bakker, *I Was Wrong: The Untold Story of the Shocking Journey from PTL Power to Prison and Beyond* (Nashville: Thomas Nelson, 1996), xiv.

in his mission in the world. Megachurches raise large amounts of money, and their strong teaching on tithes brings in enormous resources. I have yet to hear, however, about any megachurch that holds itself accountable to the people who bring in the money. We learn about some of the controversial ways in which those resources are used only when pastors preach prosperity sermons and speak about their new extravagant acquisitions—such as luxurious automobiles, personal jets, and palatial homes—as signs of God's blessing! This observation must be weighed against Ahn's comment that "the worldwide propagation of the megachurch movement has enabled the diversification of megachurches as well as of megamission" (172). Much of what one sees being done in the name of mission amounts to tokenism. Wealth is not a prerequisite for undertaking the work of God. In addition to urban middle-class missions, the church of Jesus Christ must be "the church of the catacombs, rather than of the halls of fame and power and wealth."[5]

CONCLUSION

The church as the body of Christ must celebrate the victories of the Holy Spirit and the large numbers we find in megachurches. Care must be taken, however, so as not to restrict mission to what particular churches, including megachurches, decide to undertake. One only hopes that, given the size of these churches, workable arrangements could be made to ensure that discipleship through teaching also takes place. One Pentecostal denomination in Africa—the Church of Pentecost, with headquarters in Accra, Ghana—is growing by leaps and bounds, but the leadership has consciously discouraged the establishment of megasize churches. No local assembly of this denomination is allowed to grow to more than 500 members at a single location. In some communities, therefore, the Church of Pentecost may have ten local assemblies with 500 members each where other Pentecostal churches might decide to assemble 5,000 in a single location. The advantage for the Church of Pentecost is that it is able to build community-based assemblies that are within walking distance for

5. Jonathan J. Bonk, *Missions and Money,* revised and expanded ed. (Maryknoll, N.Y.: Orbis Books, 2006), 162–63.

those who do not drive. In this way, the Church of Pentecost has attracted many ordinary people!

Megachurches with their "megamissions" too often build middle-class congregations where, in too many cases, ordinary people do not feel welcome. The mission of smaller assemblies like those of the Church of Pentecost could be described as "mega," just as can those of the "real" megachurches! Irrespective of numbers, Christian mission is always big if it is executed in God's way. As we know, the church properly has no mission of its own; it exists to carry out God's *missio*.

21

Kaneshie Church of Pentecost: A Case Study of an Ordinary-Sized Church in Missions

Opoku Onyinah

Missions over the years has been understood differently by different people. Some have conceived of missions as getting people saved from eternal damnation, others as expanding the church, and still others as transforming the world into God's kingdom.[1] For others, missions has meant activities carried on outside the life of a congregation or local church. In this view, missions has been seen more as reaching out to other geographic regions—such as Africa, Asia, or Latin America—or as ministry among particular people groups, including gypsies, vagrants, and marginalized people.[2]

Putting all of these views together, the World Council of Churches Commission on World Mission and Evangelism considers missions to be the sharing of the Gospel by word (*kerygma*), deed (*diakonia*), prayer and worship (*leiturgia*), and the witness (*martyria*) of everyday Christian life, leading to the reconciliation and strengthening of a person's relationship with God, fellow human beings, and creation.[3] In this chapter, I consider mission

1. David Jacobus Bosch, *Transforming Mission: Paradigm Shifts in Theology of Mission* (Maryknoll, N.Y.: Orbis Books, 2001), 389.

2. Lesslie Newbigin, *The Open Secret: An Introduction to Theology of Mission* (Grand Rapids: Eerdmans, 1995), 1.

3. Commission on World Mission and Evangelism, Preparatory Paper

as encompassing all that the church does locally and internationally to spread the Good News of Jesus Christ to unreached people and to support the ministry of the church's representatives (i.e., "missionaries") in another locality. The mission endeavors of megachurches and those of "ordinary-sized" churches are viewed against this backdrop.[4]

This chapter focuses on a local church in Kaneshie, Ghana, that is known as the Church of Pentecost Kaneshie local church, as a case study of the involvement of an ordinary-sized church in mission.[5] The Kaneshie local church is a congregation of the Church of Pentecost, which has its headquarters in Ghana.[6] Founded in 1952 with seven members, the Kaneshie church was established in a municipal area in Accra. By the end of 2013 the congregation and its daughter churches had grown to a total membership of 175,470. How was such remarkable growth possible? To answer that question, we look first at the history, structure, and worship of the Church of Pentecost movement. Then a brief look at its establishment and growth will prepare the way for investigation of its approach to missions.[7] Though in this chapter I do not offer a comprehensive study of megachurches, with Kaneshie church as backdrop, I do raise several questions.

THE CHURCH OF PENTECOST: BRIEF HISTORY AND CURRENT STATE

The beginning of the Church of Pentecost, of which Kaneshie is an integral part, is linked to the ministry of Pastor James McKeown, an Irish missionary sent in 1937 by the Apostolic Church,

---

No. 3: Theme, Thematic Area, and Signposts on the Journey towards the Athens Conference, May 10, 2005, www.oikoumene.org/en/resources/documents/other-meetings/mission-and-evangelism/preparatory-paper-03-theme-thematic-area-and-signposts.

4. By "ordinary-sized," I refer throughout to churches that are small to medium-sized, with no specific or exact numbers in mind.

5. Note that Church of Pentecost Kaneshie local church is not the same as Pentecost International Worship Centre–Kanashie. This latter is one of the churches that has came out of the Kaneshie church.

6. See www.thecophq.org.

7. I express special appreciation to Pastor Samuel Gakpetor of the Church of Pentecost Ghana for gathering materials for this study.

Bradford, U.K., to the Gold Coast (now Ghana). McKeown came to help a group of believers of the Apostolic Faith led by Pastor Peter Newman Anim in a town called Asamankese. Because of doctrinal differences about divine healing, the group split in 1939 into the Christ Apostolic Church and the Apostolic Church, Gold Coast. By August 1962, the Apostolic Church, Gold Coast, had split into two under the names the Apostolic Church of Ghana and the Church of Pentecost. Missionary James McKeown led the latter group. As stated, the Kaneshie local church falls under the McKeown-led group. The name "The Church of Pentecost" was said to have been given to the wider church movement during a prayer meeting at the Kaneshie local church building, hence Kaneshie's importance in the annals of the denomination.

In recent times the Church of Pentecost has become the largest Protestant denomination in Ghana.[8] In 1989 it had the country's largest church attendance and was recognized as one of the fastest growing denominations in Africa.[9] The denominational chairman's 2013 State of the Church Address, delivered at the Fourteenth Extraordinary Council Meeting in Accra, reported that the church had a total membership of 2,078,166, meeting in 17,242 local churches throughout Ghana. Internationally, it had a membership of an additional 209,185 persons in 2,456 congregations in 88 countries spread across Africa, North America, South America, Asia, Europe, and the Middle East.[10]

ADMINISTRATIVE STRUCTURE AND WORSHIP OF THE CHURCH OF PENTECOST

The administrative structure of the Church of Pentecost is founded on local churches, called assemblies, which comprise elders,

8. Emmanuel Kingsley Larbi, "The Nature of Continuity and Discontinuity of Ghanaian Pentecostal Concept of Salvation in African Cosmology," *Cyberjournal for Pentecostal-Charismatic Research*, www.pctii.org/cyberj/cyberj10/larbi.html.

9. Ghana Evangelism Committee, *National Church Survey: Facing the Unfinished Task of the Church in Ghana* (Accra: Ghana Evangelism Committee, 1989), 16–17.

10. Opoku Onyinah, *2013 State of the Church Address, Given at 14th Extraordinary Council Meetings of The Church of Pentecost* (Accra: Pentecost Press, 2014), 25.

deacons, deaconesses, and members. The head of a local church is called the presiding elder. Depending upon the town in which a local church is situated, when it grows to about 300 members it is divided into two, with another presiding elder appointed as the head. A pastor is in charge of a district, which comprises a number of assemblies, a number that can range from one up to thirty. A number of districts, from four to thirty, come together to form what is called an area, which is headed by a senior minister who may be a pastor, evangelist, prophet, or apostle. The church has a centralized structure. At the top of the organizational chart is the General Council (which consists of all pastors of the church), Area Executive Committee members, and the chairmen of boards and committees. Below the General Council is the nine-member Executive Council, which is responsible for the administration of the church. The presbyteries of areas and nations come after the Executive Council. District presbyteries, headed by pastors, follow. Last on the administrative structure of the church are the local presbyteries, headed by presiding elders.

Worship in the Church of Pentecost is similar to that of other classic Pentecostals, but with some cultural variations.[11] These variations are apparent in activities such as the giving of testimonies, praise, and special times of prayer called worship and preaching.[12] The church's pattern of worship provides opportunity for participants to express themselves before God in diverse ways, including prayer, dancing, and the giving of testimonies.

BRIEF HISTORY AND CURRENT STATE OF KANESHIE ASSEMBLY

Kaneshie, a locality about four kilometers northwest of the Accra city center, is a densely populated community of about 62,000 people. A bustling mixed-income area, it boasts the presence of the Kaneshie Market, one of the largest markets in West Africa. The Kaneshie local church is located in this community. As stated, the church began in 1952 with seven members and is now a very

11. Walter J. Hollenweger, *The Pentecostals* (London: SCM Press, 1972), 130, 149.

12. For example, during preaching someone inspired by the Holy Spirit may interrupt with a song.

healthy local congregation within the Church of Pentecost. It was established through the prayer and evangelistic ministry of what was then called the Witness Movement.[13] As of 1982 the church had a membership of 250, with eighteen ordained lay leaders (that is, ordained leaders who support themselves). Hundreds of people from Accra and the environs attended the church's dynamic Saturday prayer meetings, led by the presiding elder, at which many miracles, signs, and wonders were recorded. Teaching of the Word of God was done on Wednesdays. As an ordinary-sized church, members of the congregation were able to visit one another. These activities helped to give them a good grounding in the Christian faith. As Gary Corwin rightly observes, "Well-grounded disciples of Christ are the building blocks of any mission outreach, and only the churches can provide them."[14]

Passionate preaching of the Gospel in all the surrounding community was a natural outflow of disciples solidly grounded in Christ, which led to the opening of many other congregations, or assemblies. Meanwhile, the mother church, or base, was also growing. By the end of 2014 the membership of the Kaneshie local church had grown to 2,801 (2,533 adults and 268 children). Led by 77 lay ordained leaders (25 elders, 27 deacons, and 25 deaconesses), the congregation has increased 1,120 percent within a period of thirty-two years, not counting the many daughter churches that it has planted. The church is blessed with a completed auditorium that can seat 1,000, a pastor's residence, and a bus, among other things. The church has an educational fund that supports capable but needy students; it also supports mission in rural Ghana and internationally. The significant growth that Kaneshie church has experienced can be attributed to prayer, evangelism, discipline, and structure. Other factors include dedicated leadership, maximum utilization of lay leadership, emphasis on holiness, respect

13. The Witness Movement (now called Evangelism Ministry) was the evangelistic wing of the Church of Pentecost.

14. Gary R. Corwin, "Training for the Frontiers: Who Does What?," *International Journal of Frontier Missions* 11 (January 1994): 2, www.ijfm.org/PDFs_IJFM/11_1_PDFs/Corwin.pdf; and "The Church's Primary Role in Training for the Frontiers," *IJFM* 11 (July–August 1994): 170, www.ijfm.org/PDFs_IJFM/11_3_PDFs/12%20Corwin.pdf.

for the Word of God, indigenous spontaneous worship, strong church discipline, and a policy of financial self-support.[15]

KANESHIE CHURCH IN MISSION

Local missions. The Kaneshie church is involved in both local and international missions. Locally, it engages vigorously in evangelism and church planting. In the church, evangelism is a lifestyle, as individual members and small groups are constantly active in evangelizing their communities. As with McKeown, the founder, their philosophy is "just to evangelize." For instance, some of the members meet every Wednesday night for an all-night service, after which they move out into a community and preach the Gospel. Also, evangelistic outreaches are planned that involve the whole church for a period of three to four days. Because these outreaches are considered to be a spiritual task and because it is believed that prayer must be relied on in order to plant churches, the outreaches are preceded by intense sessions of intercessory prayer.

Church planting is a natural outflow of the Kaneshie congregation's evangelistic passion. Indeed, the strategy of the Church of Pentecost is to encourage local churches and ministers to plant churches as they grow and as they move into unreached communities. Accordingly, church planting by the Kaneshie church has both a spontaneous and a planned aspect. The church typically identifies "new grounds" where the Gospel has not been preached, gathers a team, and sends them to the area for about a week. The team prays during the period, preaches the Gospel, and subsequently establishes a local church with the converts won. Then, together with church leadership from Kaneshie local church or another mother church and in consultation with the local presbytery of Kaneshie, a team of five, for example, is made responsible for the newly established church. The mother church raises support among its members to provide basic items of equipment for the new church.

The team then ensures that for at least the first three months the new members are taught the basic doctrines of the church and are prayed with to receive Holy Ghost baptism. Potential leaders

15. Alfred Koduah, "The Church of Pentecost in a Post Modern Society," in *James McKeown Memorial Lectures: Fifty Years of the Church of Pentecost*, ed. Opoku Onyinah (Accra: Church of Pentecost, 2004), 110.

are identified, nurtured, and trained. After a period ranging from six months to one year, the church is recognized as being able to grow without external support. It is then left in the hands of the locally trained leaders, with ongoing occasional visits by mature leaders of the mother church. The new churches are also encouraged to open other churches in unreached communities. As the number of churches grows, a new pastor is sent to nurture them. This cycle is continued over and over again.

In this manner, the Kaneshie church has multiplied, producing by the end of 2013, as noted, 175,470 members who are present in 513 local churches, and 87 districts in the Greater Accra region of the Church of Pentecost. These churches are headed by 5 superintendent ministers, 92 ordained ministers, and 7,179 lay officers.[16] The growth and impact of the local church are remarkable.

International missions. Besides its involvement in evangelism and church planting locally, the Kaneshie church is also involved in missions abroad through its financial contribution to the International Missions Directorate of the Church of Pentecost.

The Kaneshie local church has a compelling vision to be mission oriented, and members are encouraged to pray regularly for and give to support missions. In practice, the Kaneshie local church has a mission team that meets to pray and make decisions in consultation with the pastor about mission activities in the church. The church encourages individual members to pray weekly for missionaries through the use of the missions calendar. At the congregational level, the first Wednesday of every month is committed to teaching on and praying for missions. Once every year, a week called McKeown's Missions Week is devoted to teaching on missions, and members are challenged to pray for missionaries and to give to missions. Also, missions offerings are collected the first Sunday of each month to support missions.

Members are encouraged to personally donate items (e.g., cash, clothes, and bicycles) to missionaries in general or to specific missionaries. From January through June 2014, all the local churches, districts, and areas birthed by Kaneshie local church

16. Church of Pentecost Information Management Department, Summary Statistics, June, 2014, pp. 19–20.

contributed, in aggregate, approximately GHS 12,090,000 (= US$3 million) through missions offerings to support the mission endeavors of the Church of Pentecost.[17] For the year 2014 the mother Kaneshie church itself contributed a total of GHS 79,000 (= US$24,000) to support the missions of the Church of Pentecost.

LESSONS TO BE LEARNED?

The Kaneshie local church is an ordinary-sized congregation of 2,801 members, but when considered together with its daughter churches, it represents a membership of more than 175,000 of Christ's followers. In the aggregate, this size membership would make Kaneshie one of the more significantly sized megachurches. As a structural choice (and in line with the practice of the Church of Pentecost in Ghana) for the sake of discipling its members as well as for missional engagement, however, the Kaneshie church has elected for its daughter congregations to subdivide and to establish new assemblies whenever they grow beyond a certain point. A greater number of smaller-sized assemblies lends itself well to discipling church members: fellowship between members can be more immediate, training and mentoring of new leaders can be more direct, opportunities for gifted members to move into leadership roles may be more abundant, and the possibility of total congregational involvement in prayer meetings, in outreach ministries, and in efforts to establish new worship centers is much greater than if the assemblies all sought to attain megachurch size and status for themselves.

The example of one congregation within the Church of Pentecost in Ghana, the Kaneshie local church, shows a route by which an ordinary-sized congregation can lead its members to engage in mission—mobilizing and motivating them, providing them with training, sending members out as well-structured and purposeful teams. Its experience shows that ordinary-sized congregations can encourage and nurture new followers of Christ, forming them into new congregations or assemblies and supplying initial leadership and operational assistance during a limited start-up phase. Kaneshie's combination of training and assistance

17. Church of Pentecost International Missions Directorate, Financial Report, January–June, 2014.

and the model of congregational structure that Kaneshie assemblies offer enable new congregations to assume responsibility for themselves quickly. This method also enables new assemblies to become engaged quickly in their own missional outreach in other communities within their environs.

Assuredly all congregations are not to be cut from the same cloth, nor are they to be sized by a cookie cutter, but are there lessons to be gained from the experience of the Kaneshie local church? Megachurches often flourish around a charismatic senior minister whose presence and activities attract many people to the church. At the same time, megachurches may have a large staff with many associate and assistant ministers playing fruitful roles in the life of the church and in ministry to the congregation and beyond. But is it therefore to be assumed that the drive toward centralization and the overriding preeminence of a single leader is to be preferred to Kaneshie's form of distributed leadership? Does one pattern or the other tend to lead toward higher involvement in mission by the membership overall—rather than primarily or preeminently by one or a few central figures?

The threshold for being labeled a megachurch varies by context. In some settings congregations with as few as 2,000 parishioners meeting weekly for worship are called megachurches; in other contexts the label is reserved for congregations larger than 10,000. The world's largest megachurch is the Yoido Full Gospel Church, with an amazing average weekly attendance of 480,000.[18] Characteristically, large megachurches have their own church buildings and may conduct two to seven services on Sunday.[19] They can be expected to run a variety of social and outreach ministries on a scale that is beyond the capability of ordinary-sized congregations.

Without a doubt, super-sized megachurches have a major impact within the communities where they are located. But they also raise questions. One question concerns the value of extract-

18. Hong Young-gi, "The Backgrounds and Characteristics of the Charismatic Mega-Churches in Korea," *Asian Journal of Pentecostal Studies* 3, no. 1 (2000): 100, 104.

19. See Hartford Institute for Religion Research, "Megachurches," http://hirr.hartsem.edu/megachurch/megachurches.html, accessed January 5, 2015, 11:00 P.M.

ing people from surrounding communities and transporting them into a privileged location versus taking the church out to multiple locations. It is a question of collection versus dispersion, one of concentration versus spreading the church's presence into multiple local communities. It is a question of the value of meeting in stadium-sized numbers and in single-location, stadium-sized auditoriums versus meeting in multiple closer knit fellowships. Admittedly, super-sized megachurches work to overcome the handicap of overwhelming size by forming numerous cell groups and house church fellowships, but would the cure be necessary if the problem of hyper-concentration were not created in the first place?

Can megachurch culture overcome criticisms such as its alleged "theological superficiality, vapid worship music, and a seeker-sensitive, consumeristic ethos"? Can megachurches rise above "church growth strategies that emphasize upward movement in attendance figures over community cohesion and discipleship formation"?[20]

THE MEGACHURCH AND THE ORDINARY-SIZED CHURCH IN MISSIONS

What type of model do megachurches provide for mission? Where does the megachurch model actually work? For instance, the issue of commuter congregants already alluded to raises a related question: does the model of super-size churches work best—or only fit—in settings of extremely high population density per square kilometer? Is the model suitable only in areas of extremely expensive property values? This question relates to super-sized churches engagement in mission. To the degree that congregations provide a model, rightly or wrongly, of what the church is for the new churches they wish to establish, how do megachurches cope with the fact that in many parts of the world their model does not fit and will not work? Not every community has the population size or the population density to be a good candidate for being the home of a 10,000, 18,000, 40,000, or 60,000 member congregation. Conversely, are super-sized churches the only form of the church that has the money and clout to buy land,

20. See "Megachurches," *Christianity Today*, www.christianitytoday.com/ct/topics/m/megachurches.

to build, and to create services in Christ's name within some of the world's most highly populated megalopolises?

It may be taken for granted that megachurches have greater resources in terms of personnel, finance, and technology than do ordinary-sized churches. But in proportion to their financial and human means, how does the involvement of megachurches in missions compare with that of an ordinary-sized church such as the Kaneshie church? Does engagement with missions seem to be mostly centered on the senior pastor and what he does around the world? How is the membership mobilized in mission? Is mission an integral part of the vision of the church? What percentage of messages preached are mission-centered? How often does the church pray for missions? How much of the church's budget goes to support missions? How are members challenged to be involved in missions?

CONCLUSION

Despite the questions raised, megachurches and ordinary-sized churches each have strengths and each have weaknesses. While ordinary-sized churches can more easily engage in enhanced outreach to various parts of a country through personal presence and church planting, megachurches by their sheer size can attract many more people. Both can be used by the Lord to win new converts into the kingdom, for which we thank God.

QUESTIONS FOR REFLECTION

1. What shows that a church is a mission-oriented church or a mission-sending church?
2. In what ways are missions the life of a church?
3. In what practical ways is your church fulfilling the Great Commission?
4. How can the members of a congregation (whether of an ordinary-sized church or a megachurch) be encouraged to see the importance of missions?
5. What are possible challenges an ordinary-sized church or a megachurch is likely to face in missions? How can these challenges be effectively addressed?

22

Response to "Kaneshie Church of Pentecost"

Kyungsool (Joshua) Kim

To see God's church stand firm in achieving God's mission toward the lost world is a privilege—nothing else so encourages our hearts! Especially because my family and I spent many years as part of the mission community in Ghana, I find great joy in seeing a Ghanaian church introduced as a model of mission involvement. I am thankful for the opportunity to respond to Opoku Onyinah's valuable chapter on the Kaneshie Church of Pentecost, located in Greater Accra, Ghana.

As described by Onyinah, Kaneshie Church is exemplary as a model of growth from dependent immaturity to maturity in missional outreach. Kaneshie Church shows that, growing from a first stage as a church planted or parented by missionaries, churches can develop to the point where they play significant roles as partners in mission. They can do so in innovative ways and in contexts where many other churches remain dependent on outside mission agencies and have little involvement in the world mission movement.

BACKGROUND AND OUTLOOK OF KANESHIE CHURCH

Drawing on a statement of the World Council of Churches' Commission on World Mission and Evangelism that summarizes historically received concepts of mission, Onyinah offers his own definition of mission as "encompassing all that the church does locally and internationally to spread the Good News of Jesus Christ to unreached people and to support the ministry of the church's representatives (i.e., 'missionaries') in another locality" (184). Based on this understanding, he offers the Kaneshie local church, as well as the Church of Pentecost, of which it is a part, as a case study of an ordinary-sized church in mission. The Church of Pentecost is an outgrowth of the ministry of an Irish missionary from the United Kingdom who was sent to the Gold Coast in 1937. Kaneshie Church itself was founded in 1952; by 2013, after six decades and including its daughter churches, it had grown to 175,470 members. What is the key to this church's spectacular growth? In his answer, drawing from the congregation's history, Onyinah points to Kaneshie Church's structure and its involvement in world mission as part of participation in worship—strengths it received from the Church of Pentecost.

The account of the church's brief history shows how Kaneshie Church, from a humble beginning, rose to became a central part of what was in 1989 the fastest growing denomination in Africa. By 2013 the Church of Pentecost had over 2 million members within Ghana and congregations in eighty-eight other countries. The denomination has grown in spite of painful divisions because of doctrinal differences on healing and other issues in the early stages of its history.

The structure and worship of Kaneshie Church is also impressive. While it follows the basic model of the Church of Pentecost, its structure is not simply a replication of the larger denomination. Kaneshie Church seeks to encourage its members to actively display their gifts and strengths in the subgroups of the church, all for the purpose of spreading the Gospel. What is also impressive is its lack of interest in becoming a megachurch. Instead, following the model of Jesus in being sent to proclaim the Gospel to other villages (see Luke 4:43), Kaneshie Church encourages each of its church plants to become an independent, self-supported assembly. In a church plant, Kaneshie appoints a presiding elder, and when the membership has grown to about 300, the new assembly is encouraged to divide and form two assemblies, for which a new presiding elder is appointed. In this way Kaneshie Church continues to grow rapidly.

DISTINCTIVE CHARACTER OF KANESHIE CHURCH

Despite the church's similarity to other classic Pentecostal assemblies, Kaneshie Church's worship style has its own distinctive character. Instead of copying the religious rituals and practices missionaries brought from their various cultures, Kaneshie has developed a style of worship that reflects its own cultural uniqueness. It gives members opportunities to express themselves before God in diverse ways, such as giving testimonies, expressing praise, and offering special prayers, which are called worship.

As has been experienced throughout Christian history, vital prayer meetings, answered prayer, Bible studies, and home visitation that lead members to grow together toward maturity have been the wellspring of the growth of the church, as well as the birth of other congregations. Other factors—such as discipling in the Scripture, passion for preaching the Gospel, dedicated leadership, lay commitment, emphasis on holiness, spontaneous indigenization, strong church discipline, and a policy of financial self-support—have also undergirded strong growth.

Kaneshie Church has been actively involved in local missions; it makes passionate evangelism an expected part of Christian life. The church organizes strategic church planting, evangelistic outreaches involving the whole church, and focused prayer by the congregation. Evangelism, planting new churches, training, assistance, and self-support are taught and practiced in various contexts. The church is involved in global mission through financial contributions to the denomination's mission activities, prayer meetings planned and led by the mission team, and a weeklong McKeown's Week, which is a yearly effort of prayer and teaching on missions.

LEARNING FROM KANESHIE CHURCH

One lesson to be learned from Kaneshie Church, Onyinah suggests, is the value of purposeful restraint on congregational size. Though Kaneshie Church could easily have become a mega-sized congregation, it made a structural decision to remain an ordinary-sized congregation, doing so for the sake of discipleship and mission involvement. Daughter assemblies are encouraged to become independent of the mother church whenever they grow to a certain point, which means becoming self-sustaining and self-propagating as quickly as possible. The smaller size of the assemblies allows for intimate fellowship within the body as a whole and for direct training of new leaders. It also opens up more leadership opportunities for gifted people.

In comparing megachurches and ordinary-sized churches, Onyinah points to weaknesses as well as strengths of megachurches and raises challenging questions. He concludes, however, by making it clear that congregations of all sizes can be used for God's kingdom.

EVALUATING THE KANESHIE CHURCH MODEL

As noted above, Onyinah's description of Kaneshie Church provides an exemplary model of a congregation that is intentional about not simply remaining in its comfort zone but is determined—through prayerful preparation and passionate evangelism—to plant new churches in other areas. Kaneshie Church also provides an example of self-support and self-propagation that new congregations can follow. Clearly, the church has proven faithful to its vision of subdividing so as to spread the Gospel to more places, rather than pursuing as a goal that the church might be able to play a larger and more significant role if it were to grow in size. Also by offering ministry training to church members and opening doors for them to take part in the church's mission, Kaneshie Church tries to avoid having members come to rely solely on their pastor(s). As Ralph Winter pointed out, one of the most serious mistakes made throughout Western-initiated mission history has been a failure to form and strengthen mission structures.[1] Newly established churches, as in the example of the Korean church, must be trained from the beginning to be forces in God's kingdom movement. Too often, however, churches in so-called mission fields take it for granted that the work of mission is only for missionaries and that

1. Ralph D. Winter, "The Two Structures of God's Redemptive Mission," in *Perspectives on the World Christian Movement: A Reader,* ed. Ralph D. Winter and Steven C. Hawthorne, rev. ed. (Pasadena, Calif.: William Carey Library, 1992), 45–57.

they do not have a part to play. In this sense, the mission involvement of Kaneshie Church is a worthy model for other churches.

Despite all the strengths of the Kaneshie Church model, some questions should be raised. First, in its mission work has Kaneshie Church limited itself by adhering to the boundaries of traditional church ministry? In other words, is the work and mission of a church restricted exclusively to saving souls and planting religious institutions? Where are the examples of ways that people in their ordinary occupations and professional work have influenced their social contexts with the Gospel and the kingdom principle as so to display God's kingdom *there in their occupations and professions*? For when Jesus mentions "my church" in Matthew 16:18, he is referring not simply to a religious institution but to a representative body of his disciples, who display his kingdom in their various life areas. Though the members of Kaneshie Church occupy various professions, no mention is made of a strategy for finding ways that the various occupational groups can use their professional expertise to "kingdomize" their occupational areas. In Ghana—where the government still finds it necessary to fight against corruption—the church needs to face directly the needs existing in politics, economics, culture, education, medical care, and law. In its saving of souls, missions must seek to see that this salvation includes the fundamental transformation so sorely needed in society.

Second, is Kaneshie Church free from the scar and folly present in wider Ghanaian Christian history, which was so greatly influenced by Ghanaian secular history? In the past, Ghana's more populous southern people groups enslaved the peoples of the northern minority. This history seriously affected the outlook of the southern churches. To some extent, evangelism of the northerners was intentionally ignored or outright rejected by the southerners. This sense of tribal superiority is present even today. For example, churches planted in the north by southerners function mostly to provide worship services for southerners who have migrated to the north. A model of reconciliation that embraces the minorities is greatly needed. In this way the church can continue to grow and can extend its model of church expansion beyond its geographic and tribal boundaries.

Third, what of interchurch cooperation? Onyinah mentions

nothing about cooperation, networking, or partnership with other churches or mission organizations. His discussion of cooperation by Kaneshie Church in mission includes only its own denomination. Current thought on mission cooperation, by contrast, focuses much more on creating partnerships and networks of ministry that cross ecclesiastical borders. Examples include the Ghana Evangelical Missions Association (GEMA; http://ghanaglobal.org/), which has been functioning for some years, and the Movement for African National Initiatives (MANI; http://maniafrica.com/), which has been formed across the continent for effective cross-cultural ministries within and beyond Africa.

CONCLUSION

My sincere desire and expectation is that Kaneshie Church—and churches that follow its exemplary model, regardless of their size—will press on toward making the kingdom of God present and real in all areas of life, will become and spread a model of reconciliation that embraces the weak even across cultural barriers, and will be in the forefront in partnering with other parts of Christ's body for the sake of his glorious kingdom.

23

Korean Megachurches in Mission: Observations of a Korean Pastor/Missionary

Chang Ju Kim

We may compare the relationship between missionaries and their sending churches to the relationship between astronauts and their spacecraft. Everything an astronaut needs is supplied by the spaceship. Without the support of the command ship, the astronaut cannot survive for even a few seconds. Figuratively, the position of a missionary is like that of an astronaut who is securely tethered to the mother ship and is looking to its commander to clarify the principles and rules of conduct by which the astronaut operates.

In this chapter I share reflections from my perspective as both a missionary and a former senior pastor in Korea about the relationship between missionaries and the megachurches in Korea to which they are tethered. I deeply appreciate this opportunity to do so. I understand that others have had experiences that differ from mine and may have opinions, evaluations, and criticisms that likewise differ from mine. In what follows I seek to report my own general assessment of megachurches—in particular, their efforts in mission, a matter that I have considered thoughtfully for a long time while on the mission field.

I must note, with gratitude, that the discussion of this topic is possible only because Korean churches have transformed themselves, by God's grace, from being missionary-receiving churches into being missionary-sending churches. The Korean church has engaged in mission work since the 1970s, and the time that Koreans have been involved in missions is brief in comparison to the mission history of Western churches. Korean missionaries, however, now serve all around the world.[1]

Honest, candid analysis of the Korean church and the accountability of megachurches in their mission efforts could bring pain or regret. It could disturb and frustrate some of us. But it also has the potential to energize our development and to provide a fresh starting point, offering a new pathway for the future of the Korean church.

For twelve years I was associate and then senior pastor of Yedarm Presbyterian Church, a midsize church in Seoul with over 1,850 members, including church school. And for the past nine years I have been a missionary in Madagascar. From my experience as a mission co-worker and as a church pastor, I am acquainted with difficulties and problems that arise between missionaries and sending churches, and I understand the differences in perspective between the two. Raising meaningful questions may not itself provide answers, but in Korea we have a saying, "If you truly know your enemy and yourself, you can win as many as a hundred battles out of a hundred." The more we know one another's ideas and expectations, the more we will be able to understand and accommodate one another—even if we are not enemies!

TOO PROUD OF NUMBERS?

Some vitally important questions are, Who is a missionary? What criteria are necessary for a person to be called a missionary? How should churches select people and call them or give them the title "missionary"? Historically, "missionary" has been an esteemed title in Korea, respected by both Christians and others. Now, it seems,

1. The percent of Christians in South Korea is the second largest percentage in East Asia, next to the Philippines. Among countries sending Protestant missionaries to other countries, Korea ranks second, behind only the United States.

Korean churches have made it too easy to become a missionary, and the title has been losing some of its positive connotations.[2]

Over the years I have met missionaries whom Korean megachurches have commissioned for service in many places throughout the world. Regrettably, some of these missionaries are neither qualified nor trained by a missionary training course. One diplomat I met in Africa introduced himself as a missionary who was sent by a megachurch in Seoul. Upon his diplomatic appointment by the Korean government, his senior pastor called him and gave him a certificate issued by a Korean mission organization. That certificate, given at a commissioning service during a Wednesday evening prayer meeting, granted him the title "missionary."

Another missionary I met was jointly commissioned by a church and an international mission organization. Thus from the beginning he had dual membership. After his first term, a problem developed with his sending church, leading the church to discontinue its financial support. While searching for new sponsors, he used his professional career as a medical doctor as a means of credentialing himself. Many churches were attracted by his title and agreed to commission him. He soon acquired appointments from megachurches and mission societies, as well as associate memberships from further organizations plus obtaining support from NGOs. Each church and organization counts him and his wife in its list of missionaries. Unfortunately, this practice of multiple mission memberships gives an inaccurate count of the number of Korean missionaries.[3]

The desire of megachurches to increase the number of their missionaries definitely influences the process of evaluating, preparing, and sending missionaries overseas. Embracing the slogan "Make all members missionaries, and send them to the world,"

2. In 1979 Korea sent out 93 missionaries. In subsequent years this number grew to 511 (1986), then 1,645 (1990), 2,576 (1994), 8,103 (2000), 12,159 (2004), 19,413 (2008), and 25,745 (2013). For the years 1979–2000, see Kookil Han, *Mission Embracing the World* (Seoul: PCTS Press, 2004), 19; for later years, see Myungsoon Cho, "2013 Seonkyosa Pasong Hyeunhwang / Statistics of Missionaries in Various Nations as of 2013," KWMA document, p. 2; www.kwma.org.

3. This medical missionary and his wife are counted as at least twelve missionaries in the count of Korean missionaries!

some churches give the name "missionary" to any church members who work abroad as business persons, diplomats, or resident officers of a company, calling them "professional global missionaries" (PGMs).[4] The large number of unqualified persons who introduce themselves as missionaries and ask people to call them missionaries increases the apparent number of Christian missionaries.[5] Unrealistic figures for the number of missionaries are definitely unhelpful.

Many churches pray for their missionaries every Sunday and announce in their bulletins the mission fields where their missionaries work. Clearly, they are proud of the number of missionaries and the countries in which their missionaries work. Some churches exhibit the flags of the countries where their missionaries serve and list the names of unreached peoples and tribes. Such activities challenge church members to be concerned with mission and evangelism and encourage them to participate as missionaries themselves one day. But even with all this enthusiasm, it is appropriate for Korean churches to reevaluate the qualifications of missionaries and the process of recruiting, training, and sending them out. It is indeed a blessing—also a matter of pride for the Korean church—to send a great number of missionaries. But it definitely is time to curtail the overissuing, even mass producing, of Korean megachurch missionaries.

TOO EAGER TO SEE FRUIT?

During the past fifty years, Korea's economy and society have changed dramatically. Korea is now one of the most rapidly developing countries in the world. In general, the Korean mentality is one of "Bbally! Bbally!" (Hurry up, hurry up). Not just megachurches, but most Korean churches expect speedy results from their missionaries.

4. Megachurches give many different titles to missionaries: full-time long-term missionary, short-term missionary, cooperative missionary, associate missionary, lay-professional missionary, senior missionary, overseas servant, and more.

5. Members of Christian NGOs who serve overseas for one or two years, even some members of KOICA (Korea International Cooperation Agency), are called missionaries.

In 1945, following thirty-six years of Japanese colonialism, Korea became independent. Five years later North Korea invaded South Korea. For three years, one month, and two days, the two sides fought each other, destroying everything. Korea's rapid transformation from the ashes of this conflict is indeed astonishing. From a situation of great poverty in 1953, South Korean's economy grew steadily, and today it is the tenth largest in the world. Like its rapidly changing economy, everything else in Korea changed quickly too. Without its "hurry-up spirit," Korea's economic recovery and social changes could not have been accomplished with such amazing speed. During this era, the Korean churches had great influence on the modernization and development of our country.[6]

When Korean churches send missionaries to other countries, they typically expect the same type of results. They want the same transforming and developing story to unfold there that they have experienced in other areas of their national life. This expectation places quite a burden on missionaries to start huge projects and to report good results quickly. Before missionaries can even settle down in their new environments, they must deal with the stress of how to send reports of fruit as big as the sending church expects from them. In the estimation of many international mission organizations, Korean missionaries indeed work hard, but they often are overeager to attempt high-visibility projects, unrealistically expecting to quickly display much fruit.

TOO HASTY TO SEND RETIREES AS MISSIONARIES?

Because of current shifts toward early retirement, a pool of healthy and talented human resources exists in many countries. The same is true in Korea, and Korean churches especially have many deeply devoted retirees who often aspire to be resources for world mission. Most Korean Christians have clear memories of receiving aid and relief from abroad; many therefore wish to return this love by giving to others. As Christians, they find it natural to share their blessings.

6. Heekuk Lim et al., eds., *Christianity in Korea: Historical Moments of Protestant Churches* (Seoul, NCCK, 2013), 6.

Many megachurch leaders seek to persuade church members to use their life skills and specialties as missionaries, either short-term or long-term. These churches typically have a large number of people who are retiring or have just retired, including pastors, teachers, technicians, diplomats, medical doctors, and specialists in various areas. With their accumulated experience and special licenses, devoted retirees with a passion for missions are able to go anywhere and to serve others. To recruit these people as missionaries, churches use slogans such as "Won't you consider becoming a 'going missionary'"? Such people are referred to as "lay-professional global missionaries" or "silver missionaries." Again we must ask, How have these people been specially prepared and trained to do mission? How will they communicate with partners while in the mission field? Even though they are specialists in Korea, do their Korean licenses qualify them for specialist service in the field? Are these Korean retirees good communicators in foreign languages? Do they speak any local field language? Megachurches need to consider these priorities before so eagerly recruiting silver missionaries. Omitting the normal process of preparation causes many conflicts and difficulties once such recruits reach the mission field. Everyone will benefit if megachurches consider more thoughtfully all these steps, beginning with motivation and recruiting, and continuing throughout training, commissioning, and support.

The picture is not totally negative. I am aware of some good examples of retired people who were well trained and were fluent speakers of a foreign language before being sent as missionaries. These lay/professional missionaries were dispatched to the right place to work with good senior missionaries settled in a mission field. Their cooperative spirit produced fantastic synergy and wonderful results.

DRAWBACKS OF SHORT-TERM MISSIONS

By and large, Korean Christians are devoted people with a strong religious passion and enthusiasm for mission. In many ways, the Korean church is unusual in Christian history. Buoyed by the growth of the Korean economy, some churches take great pride in allocating large sums for the poor, for mission, and for evangelism.

Korean Christians think that churches that devote a significant portion of their budget for others are good, right, and healthy. It is not surprising, therefore, that mission and evangelism are emphasized and are priorities in church life. Church members are interested in the mission field and missionary work because their churches support and pray for them in every service. They make plans to visit mission fields throughout the world, doing so under the label "short-term mission."[7] Through this experience the participants, especially the younger generations, gain a missionary vision and receive many educational benefits.

There are drawbacks, however. The person who meets and welcomes the so-called short-term missionaries is himself or herself a missionary. Some churches plan to send a group of short-term missionaries to visit "their missionary" as soon as a year after the missionary has arrived on the field. The missionary must prepare the schedule for these short-termers, as well as arrange accommodations and transportation for their ten- to fifteen-day stay. I know of a Korean megachurch that sends out more than 100 teams a year, totaling about 1,300 short-termers.[8] If six or more short-term mission groups visit a missionary in a year, for example, these visits seriously impede the missionary work of that person. I have met a few missionaries who complained that they had had more than ten short-term mission groups in a year.[9] The missionaries are not able to refuse the short-termers' requests to visit, however, because of the close relationship between the short-term mission groups and the missionaries' sending church or organization.

Some missionaries have even said that they consider them-

7. Short-term groups use various names: short-term mission, vision trip, mission tour, visiting mission field, searching out the land, spying (Joshua 2), walking the land (*ddang barb ki*), and so forth.

8. Approximately 1,000 short-term missionaries go out from this one church in the summer, 300–400 in the winter. They go to approximately fifteen countries every year. First, however, they typically must undergo two or three months of training and preparation.

9. I have met many missionaries who ask persons who want to come for short-term mission trips to make their requests well in advance. Most of them are serving in Southeast Asia and East Asia, including China and India. Nowadays, many other short-termers travel also to Kenya and South Africa, which can be reached by direct flights from Korea.

selves more as tour guides than as missionaries. Sadly, short-term visitors often evaluate long-term missionaries on the basis of how well the short-termers' schedules and itineraries are arranged and how well their visiting time is planned. If the short-termers' time goes well, the long-term missionary is evaluated to be a good and capable missionary. If the missionary did not plan well enough or arrange as much as the short-term visitors might have wanted, the missionary is reported to be an incompetent missionary. It is true that mission visitors typically donate some money for mission work, medicine, clothes, or miscellaneous necessities of life. But it is with shame that I mention that, though these relationships can make missionaries feel corrupted, it is still difficult for the latter to reject the visits of short-termers.

This dilemma is an uncomfortable reality on the mission field. How do missionaries find wisdom to deal with it? Numerous Korean missionaries in the field have discussed the issue of short-termers among themselves for many years. They have not been able to propose a solution or answer to it, however, because it is not an issue that can be resolved by missionaries alone. It is a sensitive topic, difficult for missionaries to raise in public for discussion with their sending churches. If churches and mission organizations will take the initiative to discuss this matter with missionaries, however, I believe that together we can find a solution. The expectations regarding programs for short-term mission groups will not be easy to change, but restraint, self-control, and understanding will go a long way toward preparing a solution.

DOMINANT INFLUENCE OF THE SENIOR PASTOR

In Korean Protestant churches, the senior pastor is the most important person, structurally and hierarchically. This is especially true in megachurches. Protestant churches in Korea are extremely individualized, that is, local-church centered, and each church has a great deal of autonomy. The result is that each local church is like a fortress, with the senior pastor as the bulwark. He (the senior pastor is only very rarely a woman) is the great decision-maker in the church, and his ideas and authority are often absolute. When the senior pastor decides to emphasize overseas mission, all the passion and energy of the church tend to flow in that direction.

In the 1980s and 1990s, the senior pastor of one Korean megachurch demonstrated great concern for African mission. This megachurch raised huge budgets for mission in Africa and prepared many mass revival movements on the African continent. The church also invited many church leaders from Africa to Korea to participate in seminars and mission conferences and to share stories of Korean success in evangelism and church growth. After two decades, however, the senior pastor's concern and pastoral emphasis shifted from Africa to other issues. Gradually, financial support and the church's concern for Africa declined. It is clear what has happened to the churches that were planted by this megachurch and to projects that were started with financial aid from the Korean church. This flowering then decline of spiritual and financial investment has happened over the last thirty years, well within a single lifetime, in Africa.[10]

Whenever I visit the African places involved, people ask me why the Korean church no longer supports them and their churches the way they once did. These churches nearly always need continuing assistance from the Korean church. How does the missionary explain to them that the megachurch has changed its mission policy? The missionary is the bridge of interpretation between the two churches, facilitating cooperation between them. But the missionary has to heed the home church and to follow the policy of his or her sending church when it shifts. Whenever the basic mission strategy of the home church changes, the change has a ripple effect on the mission field and can create unwanted results and difficulties there. Under these circumstances, missionaries feel frustrated and helpless, with no ability to control outcomes. This whole story simply illustrates the fact that when a leadership change occurs in the sending church, the influence, whether positive or not, goes directly to the mission field.

10. In Kibera (one of the largest slums in Nairobi) and Namanga (a town in the south of Kenya, 240 km. from Nairobi, across the border from Arusha, Tanzania), I have met many Kenyan pastors and church leaders who have had connections to Korean megachurches and have visited Korea. Also I have seen commemorative plaques and stone monuments bearing the name and title of a Korean senior pastor that have been removed because of this loss of support.

CONCLUSION

Although Korean churches have faced, and still face, many problems and complexities, and though they are still learning by trial and error, grounds for hope are evident. On the positive side, the Korean church is engaged in a concerted effort toward improvement. At the same time, we must recognize that the Korean church is no longer growing numerically. The church faces both internal and external criticism over secularization, pastoral hereditary rights, and materialism. Some are concerned that the Korean church is weakening rapidly. Protestant missionaries came to Korea with the Gospel 130 years ago, but Korea's participation in global missionary work reaches back merely 40 years. In this relatively short period of time, Korean Christians have been unparalleled in terms of their faith and their passion for missionary work. They are imbued with an extraordinary sense of duty to spread the Gospel, and this devotion, we are confident, will continue in the future.

Korea's experience historically prepared it for its current role in mission. Being a colonized nation, as well as a destination for missionaries, helped equip it to send out missionaries of its own with the Gospel. It is the privilege of the Korean churches—and a special ministry—to spread the Gospel to African and Asian countries that have similarly suffered through the hardships of colonization. As a missionary in Africa, I have noticed that Africans are more willing to show a sense of kinship and intimacy toward the Korean churches and missionaries than toward those from the West. What explains this difference in attitude? Since Korea and Africa have both experienced a painful history of colonization, the local populace is more willing to open up to the Korean church. The love and grace of God that the Korean church has experienced are what African nations need. Similarly, many nations of the world are eager for missionary engagement from the Korean church, including teaching unreached tribes about the Gospel, adopting unengaged people groups, planting churches, operating social development programs, opening schools and providing education, and building hospitals and medical schools.

The sacrificial efforts and attitude of the Korean Christians will spread throughout Communist countries as well, with missionary work in North Korea and other cultures. Korean megachurches are aware of this calling and will be able to form the basic policies that are necessary. Given their internal potential to provide training and to give direction for new forms of mission, and if appropriate missionaries are mobilized and sent out, the advantages and possibilities are endless. Along with the professional missionaries they continue to send out, megachurches should display equal concern for the well-being of current missionaries by providing adequate member care. Medical treatment needs to be available for the health and safety of missionaries, as well as plans for their retirement years.

Megachurches also have a role to play in the education of Korean missionary children. Although the Korean church has the world's second largest number of Protestant missionaries, the infrastructure of the Korean church for educating the children of those missionaries has not kept pace. It would be ideal if the Korean churches were to share in the support and operation of schools that have already been established for missionary children, but that are having difficulty. The financial and human resources of megachurches position them well for providing this type of assistance. By encouraging missionaries, such investment would both directly and indirectly strengthen missionaries and world missions.

The strong faith and passion of Korean Christians stimulate them to pray and to release members of their churches for evangelism, world mission, and sharing the love of God with others. I hope that what has been presented in this chapter will encourage more cooperation between megachurches and missionaries. May it help to clarify expectations and responses, as well as responsibilities and duties, in ways that are specific, practical, and mutually helpful so that the strengths and gifts of each can be enhanced.

QUESTIONS FOR REFLECTION

1. Given the diversity in mission strategies and methods of Korean Protestant churches, what steps could be taken toward forming a model of mission that would embrace all churches, denominations, and mission organizations?

2. What would a broad model for mission look like? What problems do you foresee for the future of mission work by Korean churches if they fail to pursue such a model?
3. How can missionaries and churches (especially megachurches) maintain their passion for short-term missions? How can they fruitfully discuss and develop policies for short-term mission efforts? What can churches do to make their members' experience of mission more engaging and satisfying?

24

Response to "Korean Megachurches in Mission"

Joseph Shao

The candid observations and reflections of Chang Ju Kim, an experienced pastor and missionary, identify many important issues related to the Korean megachurches in mission. Such issues are relevant not only to the Korean megachurches, but also to most if not all Korean churches engaged in mission. With clarity and commendable honesty, Kim takes a hard look at the reasons and problems of sending missionaries into the field, the support that is needed, and the interest of senior pastors in supporting mission.

NUMBERS AND PREPARATION

Despite a comparatively brief history of mission endeavor, Korean missionaries are now found across all the continents of the world. As statistics show, Koreans are now serving in more than 170 nations. They represent a large and impressive force that is available to be utilized for the kingdom of God. With growth in the number of missionaries, however, also come concerns about the level of excellence of the missionaries' service. Kim gives a frank appraisal of the problems caused by hastily credentialing Korean Christians working abroad as "professional global missionaries" (PGMs), even though the individuals may be largely unqualified for the intercultural challenges posed by today's global societies.

Preparing believers for intercultural ministry requires time. Kim's label "traditional missionaries" presupposes men and women carefully trained in skills of both ministry and enculturation.

Sending persons with adequate training (i.e., the so-called traditional missionaries) decreases the risk of premature failure in difficult circumstances. Furthermore, persons who serve as missionaries must possess a degree of creativity with other professional skills, in addition to their biblical training. The kind of commitment shown by traditional missionaries is needed, that is, persons who can acknowledge and understand the cultural challenges and variety of religions that they are called to face.

In today's globalized world, if traditional missionaries and PGMs can be integrated with each other, it may be possible to develop synergy for the global missionary task that will benefit the kingdom of God. If PGMs are recruited and trained with basic skills of sharing God's message, they can stand alongside and profit from the expertise of traditional missionaries. In many nations of the 10/40 Window and in creative access nations (CANs), traditional missionaries do not find it easy to enter and share the Gospel of Christ by conventional means. In such settings PGMs who are willing to be bivocational in their calling and willing to share their faith openly yet discreetly may become a real force. They should be recruited, trained, and sent. I have personally witnessed an executive banker who is able to gather people together and to lead a Bible study in an Asian nation that imposes Islamic Sharia law and that normally allows no Christian witness at all. Korean multinational firms, however, go to all continents of the world. They can become much-needed ministry conduits for sending both traditional missionaries and PGMs. Fully committed disciples in all vocations who are living out their faith in our Master and Lord Jesus Christ in the marketplaces of our global village can become the fulfillment of the Great Commission. The answer is not either/or: either full-time traditional missionaries or PGMs; they can both serve together. With careful planning, PGMs can even be the primary mission force in many CANs, where doors are already closed to traditional missionaries.

RESULTS

Missionaries who are well taken care of in the field, who are assured that we are praying for them, and who receive adequate financial support will be more stable in the field. Kim rightly reminds us that missionary support should not be tied to results. This reminder is valuable, for in many Islamic countries, leading people to Christ is often a slow and demanding process of relationship building. At times, tilling the soil becomes the priority as God's messengers seek to establish trust. Friendship and lifestyle evangelism may not lead to speedy or even substantial results. Senders should show appreciation for and validate the long-lasting impact of missionary work by the commitment of all necessary support.

Working today in the Islamic countries may not lead to large numbers of new followers of Jesus. Working among unreached people groups, which is a strong emphasis in modern missionary endeavors, may not see converts multiply easily. Like Kim, who is knowledgeable about the real situation on the ground, we need to be wise champions of the advance of the Gospel in difficult places. We need to hold fast to the confident faith of pioneers such as William Carey, who exhorted God's people to "expect great things from God, and attempt great things for God," even though we may not see results quickly.[1]

RETIREES

Unless retirees have special skills and helpful technical know-how, we should not overemphasize recruitment of them into mission work. At the same time, given the good health and longer lives common today, it is understandable that there should be a group of "silver" citizens in churches who can be tapped to do mission work.

If the total needs of a given mission field are assessed, undoubtedly opportunities for valuable contributions by silver citizens can be found. Their mature Christian lifestyle and life experiences can provide models from which young missionaries can often benefit. Supportive work is often a nuts-and-bolts need in missionary settings. For example, silver citizens can be tapped to do supportive work such as serving as dormitory "dad" and "mom." Some

1. We need to reread the biographies of William Carey and other great missionaries, which can show us how they faced similar issues regarding results: they continued to work faithfully without anticipating human praise.

may be equipped to fill frequently needed and essential administrative positions such as field treasurer, business manager, or data entry person. With clear plans on the part of missionaries and with appropriate training, silver citizens can be a real force and blessing in the field.

SHORT-TERM MISSIONS

An important issue that Kim addresses is the pitfalls posed by short-term missions. Pitfalls exist both from the perspective of those who go on short-term mission trips and of the missionary hosts who receive them. Too often we hear horror stories of short-term "goers" who are unprepared for cultural entry, are immature in life, are self-serving, or see the experience primarily as a cultural adventure. Missionaries in the field, as "receivers," commonly acknowledge the added workload of preparing to receive, manage, and care for the teams that come.

The greater question is how to create a "win-win-win" situation for the senders-goers-receivers. A consortium of more than 800 church leaders, missionaries, and researchers has established seven standards of excellence that may permit the short-term experience to be valued by all concerned:

- God centeredness: centering on God's glory and his kingdom, rather than focusing on accomplishment, funds, or cultural tourism.
- Empowering partnerships: establishing healthy, interdependent, ongoing relationships between the sending and the receiving partners.
- Mutual design: collaborative planning intended to benefit all participants so that plans take into account mutual expectations and responsibilities of the senders, goers, and receivers.
- Comprehensive administration: exhibiting integrity through reliable setup and administration of all activities, including truthfulness in promotion, finances, and reporting results; appropriate risk management; and adequate support logistics.
- Qualified leadership: led by capable leaders screened and

trained for team ministry, including mentoring, cultural awareness, crisis management, and debriefing procedures.

- Appropriate training: Achieving excellence in equipping participants with relevant skills for the task, including team building, preparing for spiritual battle, and modeling exercise of the spiritual disciplines of prayer and time in God's Word.
- Thorough follow-through: Assured evaluation, debriefing, and appropriate follow-through for all participants.[2]

CONTINUITY

As Kim notes, senior pastors of many Korean churches exercise considerable power and strong leadership. But as he points out, problems can arise when a leader is succeeded by a new leader or a leader's passion in mission changes direction. As a safeguard, a system of built-in, long-range goals for mission work is needed, perhaps a five- or ten-year plan. Such a system should include responsible collaboration between senders and receivers, acknowledging and incorporating mutual expectations and intentionality for advancing God's work in specific settings.

Korean churches do have many strengths. Possessing abundant missionary passion, many Korean megachurches have established churches on the mission field. Some Korean churches even establish and support seminaries. Such passion and unselfish love are praiseworthy in global missions.

The question for any missionary endeavor is how well the newly established receiving churches flourish in their cultural setting. Do these churches offer a kind of church life that embraces the felt needs of believers there (e.g., in style of worship, cultural sensibilities to music, language, and local values)? Korean missions and megachurches in mission face the same challenge found throughout the history of Protestant missions: how to establish indigenous churches that uphold the fundamentals of the Christian faith, yet have the opportunity to express themselves in ways that will continue to stimulate authentic growth within their local communities.

We need to go back to Paul's model for establishing churches

2. Adapted from http://globalmissionspodcast.com/002.

in the mission field. The churches that we aim to establish should emulate the New Testament church, which provides a model that is consistent and continues to glorify the living God. Let us yoke the strength of the Korean churches consistently with the biblical model of mission. We need to link with one another and to partner with like-minded mission organizations so as to bring about the best practice of missionary work that is consistent with New Testament principles.

25

The Megachurch and the Mission Agency: A Case Study in Missiological Symbiosis

Christopher DeWelt

"What is the way forward?" This was the question posed to me by a returning missionary as we surveyed the landscape of our mission agencies, colleges, and local churches within the particular movement of churches that forms my context: the American grouping commonly known as "Christian churches and churches of Christ" (Cc/coC).[1] It was a valid question in light of the factors and trends involved, not only for our particular churches, but for the entire evangelical spectrum as well.

The Western mission agency struggles for survival. Today's agency is faced with serious competition for resources, a sociologically shifting candidate pool, and a deep tendency on the part of the supporting churches and individuals to be more connected to what is closer to their own front door. Hard challenges such as these threaten the present fiber of traditional missions and cast a long shadow on the ability of the mission agency to lead strong initiatives into the future.

1. This phrase refers specifically to the generally recognized evangelical church grouping that uses the same name(s). It should be noted that "churches of Christ" here does not refer to the "non-instrumental" churches of Christ, nor does "Christian churches" refer to "Disciples of Christ" churches, even though all three groups share a common historic heritage. "Christian churches / churches of Christ" comprise about 1.2 million congregants in a little more than 5,400 churches in the U.S. West and Midwest.

The political dimensions of the relation between megachurch and mission agency are undeniable. The Western church, led by the megachurch, receives a never-ending stream of requests for resources from local, domestic, and international initiatives. Those resources held by the church include material matters such as funding, human resources such as missionaries and support care, and the sometimes overlooked spiritual resources of wisdom, prayer, and the leading and direction of the Holy Spirit.

Meanwhile, the highly influential (and powerful) megachurch component of the Western church is active in the mission world, sometimes reinventing the wheel of effective partnership, often doing so without the benefit of adequate missiological reflection. The role of the megachurch in missions is of particular interest to those of us from the Cc/coC because of the relatively high proportion of megachurches within our ranks.[2]

In the United States a congregation with 2,000 or more in weekly attendance is counted as a megachurch. The total number of U.S. megachurches across the evangelical spectrum was 1,210 in 2005 and stood at roughly 1,600 in 2015.[3] To the missions scholar, the impact of the megachurch movement upon the traditional missions support and sending process is substantial. The unprecedented proliferation of the megachurch is a recent phenomenon within the Cc/coC network, coinciding numerically and chronologically with evangelical data.

Although very large churches have been in existence for centuries, the scale of the contemporary megachurch movement dwarfs all previous scenarios. This sudden shift has occurred within the last three decades of the twentieth century (see fig. 25.1), particularly since the founding of Bill Hybels's Willow Creek (1975) and

2. Cc/coC have a ratio of megachurches to nonmegachurches that is at least double the national average for evangelical churches. On a given Sunday, 21 percent of Cc/coC congregants are worshipping in a megachurch setting. See Kent Fillinger's overview "Megachurches: A Year in Review," *Christian Standard* 145, no. 15 (April 2010): 280–81.

3. Hartford Institute for Religion Research, http://hirr.hartsem.edu/megachurch/definition.html.

Rick Warren's Saddleback (1980) congregations, with all of their associated networks of leadership and influence.[4]

Noted sociologist Robert Putnam speaks of the American megachurch as being the "most interesting social invention of late twentieth century."[5] Peter Drucker asks his readers to "consider the pastoral megachurches that have been growing so very fast in the U.S. since 1980 and that are surely the most important social phenomenon in American society in the last 30 years."[6]

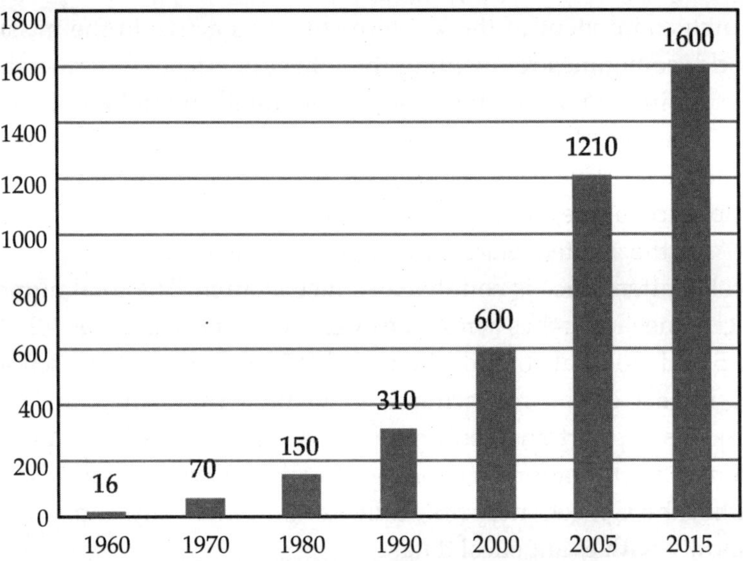

Figure 25.1. Total number of Protestant megachurches in the United States, 1960–2015

Scott Thumma and Dave Travis state their conviction that the megachurch movement has altered the entire religious landscape in America. "They [the megachurches] have superseded formerly

4. For important data on the American megachurch and common reactions to it, see Scott Thumma and Dave Travis, *Beyond Megachurch Myths* (San Francisco: Jossey-Bass, 2007).

5. Madeleine Bunting, "Capital Ideas," *The Guardian* (July 2007), http://society.guardian.co.uk/communities/story/0,,2128343,00.html. See also Robert Putnam, *Bowling Alone: The Collapse and Revival of American Community* (New York: Simon & Schuster, 2000), 407–10.

6. Peter Drucker, "Management's New Paradigm," *Forbes*, www.forbes.com/global/1998/1005/0113052a.html.

key influences such as denominations, seminaries, and religious presses and publishing. Indeed, a large part of the resistance to megachurches comes from leaders of these organizations who see their own influence waning."[7] The issues of power come to bear specifically on institutions such as the mission agency, which is by nature entirely dependent upon the church at large for support and operation.

MEGACHURCH MISSIONS SENDING PROCESSES AND PRACTICES

In my research I found virtually no literature on the subject of missionary sending or support by the megachurches within the Cc/coC network. In the world of evangelical megachurches at large, a smattering of material addresses the subject of megachurch missions programs. Even so, very little focuses on the specific aspect of missionary sending from the megachurch. In contrast, significant literature exists on the roots of the Western evangelical megachurch itself, a phenomenon of the late twentieth century in the United States, and on the history of its development.

In regard to the relationship of the megachurch and the broader missions community, particularly the mission agency, Robert Priest, Douglas Wilson, and Adelle Johnson identify specifically the lack of scholarly information about megachurch involvement in mission.

> Megachurches and their pastors are forging influential new patterns of North American congregational involvement in global mission. Their influence on mission patterns often surpasses the influence of denominational leaders, mission executives, or leading missiologists. And yet neither in missiological scholarship nor in the emerging new research on megachurches do we find a systematic treatment of megachurch involvement in global mission.[8]

Drawing from their own research in late 2007, Priest, Wilson, and Johnson identify a notable shift taking place as "the locus of

7. Thumma and Travis, *Beyond Megachurch Myths*, 2.

8. Robert J. Priest, Douglas Wilson, and Adelle Johnson, "U.S. Megachurches and New Patterns of Global Mission," *International Bulletin of Missionary Research* 34, no. 2 (2010): 97.

agency and decision-making" is moving from the field and in the direction of the sending congregation.[9] With respect to long-term missionaries supported through traditional mission agencies, when one takes into account the economic realities involved, this shift is nothing less than tectonic. The aggregate income of American megachurches today is estimated to be $7 billion; of that amount they expend between 10 percent and 13 percent on missions and benevolence.[10] If we utilize the simple sociological method of "following the money," we see that much of the resulting $700–$900 million does not flow in the direction of supporting traditional mission agencies. To say that this issue is a concern to those agencies is a significant understatement. My own research confirms this analysis. Within the ranks of the Cc/coC, the modest decline in the movement's overall membership, placed in juxtaposition with the strong growth of the megachurch, makes the crisis even more acute for the mission agency.[11]

MEGACHURCH MISSIONS DATA

In 2010 I set out to discover what I could concerning megachurch missions programs. Thanks to a sabbatical in 2011, extended to me by Ozark Christian College, I began conducting interviews among megachurch missions leaders, as well as with mission agency personnel. My principal point of research was to determine how, or to what extent, the megachurches among the Cc/coC cooperated with mission agencies in sending missionaries out to the field.[12]

9. Ibid., 102. Priest, Wilson, and Johnson provide four focal areas of shifting priorities: (1) the megachurch and short-term missions, (2) church-to-church partnerships, (3) priorities of social engagement vs. priorities of Gospel communication, and (4) the key role of the missions pastor.

10. Thumma and Travis, *Beyond Megachurch Myths*; Priest, Wilson, and Johnson, "U.S. Megachurches"; Scott Thumma and Warren Bird, *Changes in American Megachurches: Tracing Eight Years of Growth and Innovation in the Nation's Largest-Attendance Congregations* (Hartford, Conn.: Hartford Institute for Religion Research, 2008).

11. Fillinger, "Megachurches."

12. My research was in fulfillment of the requirements for a doctorate in missiology at Biola University, La Mirada, California. Readers wishing to receive a free link to the dissertation should send me an e-mail request at cdewelt@occ.edu. The only condition is that readers requesting this link should provide some feedback after looking through what I have written.

Since my principal research method was qualitative, interviews played a significant role. In all, I conducted fifty-five face-to-face interviews—twenty-nine with mission agency personnel, and twenty-six with megachurch missions staff leadership. On the megachurch side, the interviews encompassed roughly 50 percent of the Cc/coC megachurches.

Agency leadership personnel interviewed included leaders of Team Expansion International, Christian Missionary Fellowship International, Pioneer Bible Translators, Mustard Seed Global Fellowship, New Missions Systems International, The Alliance of Christian Missions International (ACMI), Kontaktmission USA, Frontiers, and several small "micro-agencies."[13] I also interviewed a variety of other people related to agencies and involved with agencies, including some leaders of indigenous agencies (mainly from India).[14] In reflecting on this research, I drew the following conclusions.

The megachurch in fact has a deep and abiding interest in missions. One of the fears of many is that the megachurch exists primarily to take care of itself and has little interest in anything that could be viewed as altruistic. This misconception unhelpfully compares the megachurch to a selfish child. It is true that every church, large or small, struggles with self-interest, yet it is clearly unfair to make such a generalization. Indeed, the data indicate the opposite to be true.[15] The fact that the American megachurch

13. Mustard Seed Global Fellowship, which worked primarily in Japan, has since been merged with Orchard Group (see orchardgroup.org), a church-planting organization. "Micro-agencies" are very small mission agencies, usually comprising one or two missionary units. Their board make-up is often a very close (and closed) group. They were the means by which my wife and I went to the mission field in the 1970s and early 1980s. These micro-agencies grew out of the direct-support missionary movement, which is a part of our Cc/coC ecclesiastical history.

14. I traveled from Ohio to California. Some interviews involved more than one person. These interviews typically lasted about twenty-five minutes and produced in all approximately 900 pages of single-spaced transcription. Although I utilized traditional avenues of research (libraries and other forms of archival research), the main body of my research was found in the data derived from the interviews.

15. See Thumma and Travis, *Beyond Megachurch Myths*, especially 78–90.

is interested in missions is borne out not only by my research but by that of others as well. In the early years of the megachurch, some megachurches seemed to have little interest in missions, especially foreign missions, and though this may still be true of an isolated few, broadly speaking, megachurches within the Cc/coC are committed to a worldwide focus. In particular, I found a corresponding deep interest in church planting, both domestic and international.

The megachurch missions pastor is indeed the "gatekeeper." "Missions pastor" or "missions minister" is a new term.[16] Missions committees and missions ministries in local churches have long been familiar, but much like the youth minister, the missions minister is a recent phenomenon. The research of Priest, Wilson, and Johnson among evangelical megachurches led them to call the person filling this role in megachurches a "gatekeeper."[17] The same gatekeeping function is true for Cc/coC. As a rule of thumb, the label holds true especially when it comes to accessing the financial resources for mission found in the megachurch.

It bears noting that the missions pastor is directly responsible to the "lead pastor," and this relationship was an invariable in my research. When the missions pastor wishes to create his or her own particular missions program without its coming directly from the lead pastor's leadership team, the missions pastor's relationship with the lead pastor is key. Missions pastors who wish to introduce innovative programming in missions must possess sufficient "chutzpah" to push back in the face of the leadership tension typical of the megachurch leadership structure in order to create space for it that they can "own." In this space they can build their program. This type of space creation and innovation does in fact occur, particularly in very large megachurch missions

16. I use the terms "missions pastor" and "lead pastor" simply because those were the terms most frequently used by the interviewees. Some referred to themselves as "missions minister," but they were a minority. Many used the two titles interchangeably.

17. See Priest, Wilson, and Johnson, "U.S. Megachurches."

ministries and among churches that have their own missionary sending processes.

The megachurch is moving rapidly toward increasing embrace of nationally led overseas church networks. One mission agency leader commented that he felt that the megachurches viewed the mission agency as a kind of "dating service." I assumed that he meant between the church and the missionary and said as much. He quickly corrected me, saying that he meant the relationship between the church and nationally led networks.

It seems clear that the clock of globalization is irreversible. The growth of communication, ever-increasing mobility, delivery systems that are unparalleled in human history, and the general shrinking of the planet form the framework of the future.[18] An interesting feature of the megachurch/national-network connection is the emotional connection felt and expressed by megachurch missions pastors on numerous occasions. Time and again I heard stories of the effectiveness and the strong work ethic of national church leaders worldwide. A good portion of this relational nexus had been generated by the ability of a lead pastor to get on a plane and in a few hours find himself standing alongside a national pastor in almost any corner of the world.

The megachurch desires a stronger missions education process. My on-site observations almost uniformly revealed men and women who were refreshingly open to learning and improving their missions acumen. In fact, I was frequently asked for recommended reading.[19] It would behoove the mission agency (as well as the Bible colleges) to assist the megachurch with this stated need. Doing so requires an agenda-less approach on the part of those bringing the help.

18. See Robert Wuthnow's work on missions coming from the American church, *Boundless Faith: The Global Outreach of American Churches* (Berkeley: Univ. of California Press, 2009), 244–50.

19. The book most frequently mentioned unsolicited by missions pastors was Steve Corbett and Brian Fikkert, *When Helping Hurts: Alleviating Poverty without Hurting the Poor—and Yourself* (Chicago: Moody Publishers, 2009).

When it comes to "who is leading this dance," it is the mission agency that must adjust. In some cases mission agencies have already adjusted to the new realities, but mission agencies that sit on the sidelines and choose not to engage in dialogue strongly imply that they are the only true experts on the subject and that they should be regarded as such. Such an approach has not fared well; a spirit of patronization is lethal to partnership. Most agencies readily recognize this caution and, to one extent or another, are adapting. The days of institutional thinking are now in the rear-view mirror.

Many megachurches do have an interest in sending out "traditional" missionaries. Of the twenty-six megachurches that I interviewed:

- eight were actively recruiting and/or sending their own people to the field;
- six were significantly interested in doing so;
- six were favorable but had no immediate plans to do so; and
- six were not interested in sending their own but exclusively viewed their missions program in terms of supporting national networks.

MEGACHURCH/MISSION AGENCY TENSION

Here, then, is the potential for symbiosis. The data indicate that the megachurch makes use of the mission agency for its own perceived needs in a largely pragmatic manner. At the same time, the mission agency looks upon the megachurch as a desirable, though capricious, partner in the fulfillment of the agency's goal of placing effective missionaries on the mission field. Recent research shows the presence of significant tensions between the megachurch and the mission agency on this point regarding sending missionaries to the field. The core tension is one of power and influence. The mission agency has been accustomed to leading in all things related to missions. But the presence of the megachurch has undeniably changed the playing field, both by the force of the megachurch's economic presence and by the force of its wide-ranging influence. Although the agency was originally created in order to serve the church in carrying out the church's mission activities, today that same church has radically changed. The megachurch in particular has acquired far more economic power and influence than was seen previously in the church in general. In consequence, the megachurch is able to carry out its own wishes, with or without the cooperation of the agency. The assertiveness of the megachurch in economic terms directly impacts both the immediate work of the mission agency and its long-term survival as a sodality of the church.

SUGGESTED TAXONOMY OF MEGACHURCH/MISSION AGENCY TENSIONS

One way of examining megachurch/mission agency tensions is to plot them on a two-axis matrix, which involves placing variables on a graph. The first variable shows the level of commitment on the part of the megachurch to sending out missionaries. The variable runs from a low level of commitment to sending at the far left (labeled "weak church initiative in mission") to a high level of commitment to sending at the far right (labeled "strong church initiative in mission").

The second variable plots the willingness of the megachurch to work with mission agencies collegially during the sending process. The variable moves from minimal interest in agencies' contribution at the low end, upward to a high interest in heavy agency involvement at the upper end. (See fig. 25.2.)

This simple axial analysis of the megachurch's level of commitment to sending held in tension with the megachurch's level of interaction with mission agencies provides a means by which a given megachurch missions program can be charted in relation to the focus of my research. As with all graphs of this type, the variables create four quadrants that can be interpreted as a taxonomy of megachurch missionary sending. (In fig. 25.2, note the four numbered types of churches.) The same four quadrants can also be interpreted as showing the following four philosophies of church/agency relationships as they relate to sending missionaries.

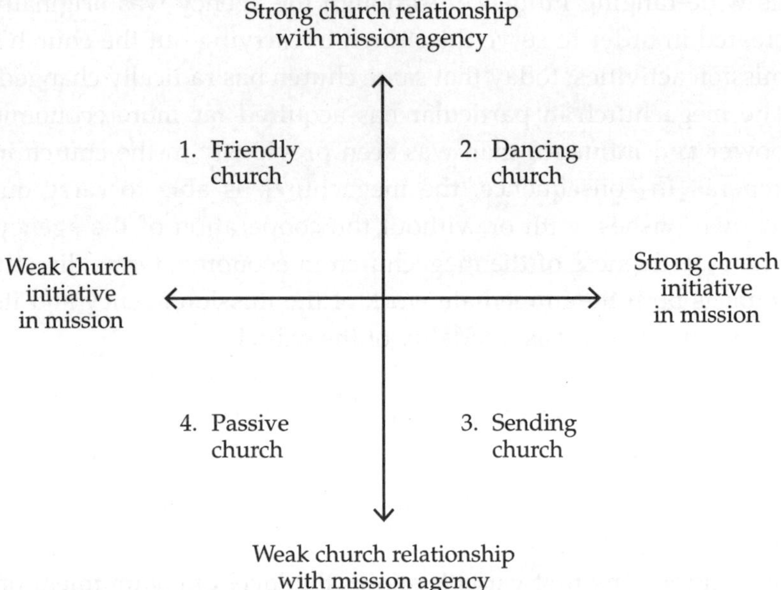

Figure 25.2. Interaction of megachurch and mission agency with regard to a megachurch's sending of missionaries

1. *A church that likes missions but does not send missionaries*. This church may be involved in supporting missionaries, but it does not become engaged with the sending process. Commitment and participation are low. In the case of megachurches, research bears out that their interaction with agencies will often be in terms of nonsending projects.

2. *A church that is a sending partner*. Churches in this category are attempting to dance with the agencies and to assume an increased role in the sending process. This attempt at partnership brings with it a number of associated tensions.

3. *A church that engages in church-based sending*. Churches that are committed to sending but prefer to go it alone and to minimize or completely bypass agency involvement fall into this category. In some cases, such churches create their own micro-agency to care for existing missionary partnerships that need more formalized accountability processes.

4. *A church that is passive*. Churches of this type essentially send a check and display low interest either in sending missionaries themselves or in agency activity. Missionaries in the field

receive little, if any, energy from this church, and mission agencies even less.

CONCLUSION

That today's megachurch within the Christian churches and churches of Christ movement is significantly involved in missions is readily apparent from my research. The relationship of the megachurch with mission agencies (and other parachurch ministries) is one that requires work. Better communication, especially on the part of mission agencies, can provide a basis for improved mutual support as the agency finds resources for increased programs and as the megachurch finds valuable resources for upgraded missiological insight.

Embedded in the triangular relationship of missionary, church, and mission agency are many common values, including a shared commitment to seeing God's will be accomplished among the peoples of the earth. May the communication increase, and may the people have a will to work . . . together!

QUESTIONS FOR REFLECTION

1. How can communication between megachurch missions personnel and mission agencies be improved so as to stimulate open discussion, particularly concerning philosophical issues of direction and strategy? Are there specific ways for creating communication opportunities? If so, what would be some possible scenarios?

2. How can U.S. megachurch interactions with non-Western mission agencies and networks be strengthened and improved? How do these relationships differ from typical relationships between U.S. megachurches and Western mission agencies?

3. What are the top three or four similarities among U.S. megachurch missions programs compared with those of non-Western megachurches? What are the top three or four differences?

4. What qualities characterize an effective partnership between a mission agency and a megachurch? How can

effective partnerships be identified, assessed, or measured? Who are the important individuals in these partnerships? What levels of engagement could emerge?

5. In what ways can the interaction between a mission agency and a megachurch mature into more than mere political discussion? In particular, how can economic issues be dealt with in a manner that recognizes the tensions inherent in them, without having these tensions dominate the entire conversation?
6. What areas of interaction between megachurch and mission agency need further research?

26

Response to "The Megachurch and the Mission Agency"

Myung Soo Park

Korea has long had a high number of megachurches. In a 1983 article, Elmer Towns noted that four of the world's ten largest megachurches were in Korea.[1] This ratio no longer holds true, but for Korea, such churches are more than just a matter of numbers or bragging rights; they are a significant force within Korean Protestantism and have a decisive impact upon denominations, union movements, and foreign missions.

Though Koreans recognize the presence and influence of the megachurches, their evaluation is not always positive. Problems associated with financial mismanagement and nepotism have brought them under criticism. Some critics have even argued that it would be better if megachurches were to disappear from Korean Christianity. Such criticism, coupled with the real influence they have in the country, poses a problem for Korean Christianity.

Before making an ethical evaluation of Korean megachurches, however, I think we should view them from a historical and social perspective. The rise of megachurches in Korea is due to urbanization of Korean society and to a kind of popularization. With urbanization, the country's population has become highly concentrated, and popularization has brought about an increase in consumer goods of all kinds—including churches!—to suit the taste

1. Elmer Towns, "The World's Ten Largest Churches," *Christian Life*, January 1983, pp. 60–66.

of the public. We can say that, in a sense, evangelical Christianity has adapted well. The Christian Gospel has been simplified for mass delivery to an urban society. Furthermore, evangelical and Pentecostal Christianity in Korea has offered a unique message of hope mixed with optimism, which has provided a counter to the strong current of pessimism in Korean society, thereby supporting the industrialization of South Korea, as well as contributing to the birth of megachurches.

I found Christopher DeWelt's discussion of the relationship between megachurches and foreign missions very informative. While the specifically American context of megachurches and missions in the United States lies outside my expertise, in reading his chapter I found myself asking, Does what he presents match the current situation we find in the church in Korea?

DIFFERENCES BETWEEN U.S. AND KOREAN MEGACHURCHES

First, I agree with DeWelt's claim that the megachurch plays an important role within the contemporary church. Just as changes in the past transformed the state church into an age of denominationalism, we have now entered the megachurch era. But I do think that the situation in Korea differs somewhat from that found in the United States. The emergence to prominence of megachurches in the United States has come about in a context that has seen a rising trend of independent churches set in the midst of declining denominational institutions. In the United States, as many as 40 percent of megachurches are independent churches.[2] In Korea, however, nearly all megachurches have remained within their denomination. The pastor of a megachurch in South Korea can serve as the head of a denomination. In fact, most of them have served as leaders of the denominations to which they belong. In this regard, megachurches in the United States and their counterparts in Korea are structurally different. U.S. megachurches become distinctive self-contained organizations, while Korean megachurches exist within the various denominations and transform their denominations' structures in ways amenable to the megachurches.

DeWelt points out that the reach of megachurches extends

2. See http://hirr.hartsem.edu/megachurch/definition.html.

even further, for they have taken over not only the role of denominations but also the formative influence traditionally held by seminaries and religious publishers. On this point I totally agree, but I should note that the influence of the megachurch in Korea is even greater. The Korean church depends more on megachurches as contributors to the denomination than is the case in the United States. In fact, in Korea all major events of the church and the construction of theological seminaries are directly dependent upon the megachurches. Professors in theological seminaries hold membership in megachurches and, in some cases, receive their regular salaries from their church. Certainly the influence of megachurches on the Korean church is higher than that of any other organization or individual.

Churches in the United States have benefited from ongoing research on megachurches conducted by the Hartford Institute for Religion Research.[3] Korea, however, even with its large number of megachurches, does not have an active research institute for megachurch studies. At this level, the Korean church has something to learn from the U.S. church.

For their part, Korea's megachurches have especially carried forward a keen interest in foreign missions. DeWelt notes that churches in the United States initially were engaged in mission through traditional means and mission agencies, but at a later date, megachurches made a significant paradigm shift by creating their own institutions for carrying out foreign mission. The situation in Korea is quite different. In fact, the rise and growth of foreign missions in Korea occurred at the same time as the emergence of megachurches there. In Korea, megachurches started foreign missions in the name of the denomination.

The case of the Yoido Full Gospel Church illustrates this point well. Yoido was involved in foreign missions first, ahead of its denomination. Yoido currently has its own mission agencies with a stronger mission force than that of the denomination itself. In the same way, Antioch Church (Presbyterian) in Jeonju (North Cholla Province) developed an independent mission organization called Paul Mission. The Paul Church (Holiness) in Jeonju, another megachurch, worked with the denominational mission department and

3. See http://hirr.hartsem.edu/.

other mission societies. Thus, it appears that Korea does not have a major conflict between denominational mission agencies and the megachurches such as is apparently found in the United States. The megachurches are so strong that they bend the mission agencies to their will, and the mission agencies dare not enter into conflict with them.

DEWELT'S CONCLUSIONS

DeWelt summarized his findings in a handful of conclusions. First, megachurches in the United States, at least those within the Christian Churches and Church of Christ tradition, do indeed have a deep interest in missions. Many people assume that a megachurch, because of its size, must be selfish and inward looking. But in fact, U.S. megachurches have an active interest in missions. The same is true of the megachurches in Korea. In reality, the accusation of selfishness, I believe, comes from people outside the megachurches. Viewed from within, megachurches are seen as acting responsibly, handling all the problems and challenges faced by large churches. According to the latest statistics in Korea, megachurch members are satisfied with their own churches' work for Korean society and Christianity.

Second, megachurches, with the help of mission agencies, form networks with national churches in the mission field and carry out many activities such as building schools and hospitals that might be recognized as part of to a national agenda. On the mission field the power of a U.S. megachurch pastor is equivalent to that of the leader of a denomination, and that of a megachurch pastor in Korea can even surpass this level. David Yonggi Cho, pastor emeritus of Yoido Full Gospel Church, is often treated as a state guest on the mission field. Similarly, Samwhan Kim, pastor of the MyeongSeong Presbyterian Church, has performed state duties at the national level.

Third, megachurches can learn much from mission agencies about how to go about doing mission. When their churches plan to develop a new ministry, megachurch leaders need to know the exact needs in the local context. South Korean churches remember the difficult times they experienced in the past. In many situations they are better able to understand the needs of local churches in other nations than are Western churches that have not had comparable experience, something that enables South Korean churches to make mission more practical.

Finally, for the sake of adapting well to a variety of mission contexts, megachurches and mission agencies overall need to learn to cooperate better. We could say that they need to learn new dance steps together. In this area the Korean church can provide an example, for in Korea the megachurches have been leading the dance from the start, and mission agencies there have already adapted to the new relationship.

RELATIONS BETWEEN MEGACHURCHES AND MISSION ORGANIZATIONS

DeWelt divides the relationship between megachurches and mission organizations into four types: friendly churches, which help mission organizations but do not themselves become active in missions; "dancing churches," which work hard to be involved with mission agencies as partners in mission outreach; sending churches, which work for mission but do not view relationships with mission agencies highly; and passive churches, which neither assist mission agencies nor view missions as vital to the church.

Though a study similar to that of DeWelt has not been carried out in Korea, I am sure that his four types can be found among the Korean churches. Of the four types he identifies, the dancing church is to be preferred, since in it megachurches and mission agencies form a symbiotic relationship and complement each other. It would be well for mission agencies to exercise initiative in strengthening partnerships with megachurches in order to convince them of the benefits that such a relationship can bring.

CONCLUSION

Other than the United States, Korea has more megachurches than any other nation in the world; the level of research on Korean megachurches, however, is quite unsatisfactory. At the most elementary level, a clear definition of what constitutes a megachurch is lacking. In the United States, megachurches have been defined as ones that have an attendance larger than 2,000 adults in Sunday worship. Statistics are not available to tell us how many churches in Korea fit that minimal definition. Finally, the megachurch community and Korean culture need to be studied to find the exact impact of the megachurch on Korean Protestantism. While such study is mainly historical, it should be extended to provide understanding of all related social perspectives.

Such study will show more detailed relationships between megachurches and mission agencies than has been previously done. Up to now, megachurches and mission agencies have worked together, but further study is necessary if even better working relationships are to be developed. In my view, DeWelt's research will act as a catalyst for such further study.

27

Bible Study 3. Prayer: The Fuel of Mission

Charles Agyinasare

> *The spirit of Christ is the spirit of missions. The nearer we get to Him, the more intensely missionary we become.*
>
> —Henry Martyn, missionary to India

Missions is reaching the unsaved with the Gospel and discipling those who are then saved to do likewise. As reaching the unsaved is the heartbeat of God, missions has God's complete approval. If the spirit of Christ is the spirit of missions, then who better to understudy than Christ himself, who was the world's greatest missionary? The discussion that follows draws from Christ's perfect example.

THE GOD FACTOR

To be effective, mission requires the power of God upon the souls of humankind, for salvation is a product of the supernatural intervention of God. The missionary must therefore know that his or her success in missions will take nothing but God himself and God's power. Remember the words of Psalm 127: "Unless the LORD builds the house, those who build it labor in vain" (v. 1). Paul, one of the greatest missionaries of all time, said, "I planted, Apollos watered, but God gave the growth" (1 Cor. 3:6). It is God who *builds* the house, and it is God who *gives the growth.*

Humankind's efforts must therefore be accompanied by the power of God to get the job done. This power comes through the force of prayer. A. B. Simpson, founder of the Christian and Missionary Alliance, famously observed, "There is no missionary force more prevailing than prayer," noting also, "The world is to be evangelized by the Church on her knees."[1] And we know that our Lord and Savior Jesus Christ prayed: "In the morning, while it was still very dark, he got up and went out to a deserted place, and there he prayed" (Mark 1:35). Only after Christ had prayed did he say to his disciples, "Let us go on to the neighboring towns, so that I may proclaim the message there also." Following his prayer, Jesus "went throughout Galilee, proclaiming the message in their synagogues and casting out demons" (1:38–39).

Christ prayed, and then he preached. No wonder he was such a powerful preacher and great physician of souls. No wonder he was so successful in his missionary work. Prayer is the only thing that moves the hand of God. We receive no result if we do not ask in prayer.

How did Christ get such power? He prayed. But what did he pray for? What should we pray for? The following sections address the major prayer points for missions.

PRAY FOR MORE LABORERS

Matthew writes of Christ, "Then he said to his disciples, 'The harvest is plentiful, but the laborers are few; therefore ask the Lord of the harvest to send out laborers into his harvest'" (Matt. 9:37–38). Similarly, Jesus said, "I tell you, look around you, and see how the fields are ripe for harvesting" (John 4:35).

The scope of the Great Commission covers "all the world" and "the whole creation" (Mark 16:15), including "all nations" (Matt. 28:19). But the laborers, those who are sent forth by Christ to the lost, are few, and therefore God needs more laborers to reach all nations. He needs laborers, not entertainers or jesters, not the eloquent or loquacious, and certainly not those who are "in royal palaces" (Matt. 11:8). Laborers are those who work together with God in the ministry of reconciliation.

1. A. B. Simpson, as quoted in Jonathan Graf, "Passionate Prayer for Missions Is Biblical," Church Prayer Leaders Network, www.prayerleader.com/resources/prayer-leader-central/missions-prayer/prayer-for-missions.

When we need laborers to help in our missionary efforts, our first approach is often to look for human qualifications. Many churches today are faced with leadership challenges because they have looked simply at scholastic credentials when appointing workers.

When our Master, who sent us to do this work, was faced with appointing apprentices or missionaries to be trained to carry on his work, he spent the whole night in prayer (Luke 6:12). Likewise, the Antioch church worshipped the Lord and fasted before choosing missionaries to take the Gospel to the Gentiles (Acts 13:2). Only after the church had prayed were Saul and Barnabas sent out as missionaries by the Holy Ghost. Prayer for the laborers should be:

- that they receive a heart of genuine compassion for the lost;
- that they receive moral courage to speak for Christ when suitable opportunity is offered;
- that they speak the Word with great boldness (see Acts 4:29, 31).

PRAY FOR MORE SOULS TO BE SAVED

John Hyde, missionary to India, begged the Lord, "O God, give me souls, or I die!" Likewise John Knox cried out, "Give me Scotland, or I die!" and George Whitefield exclaimed, "O Lord, give me souls or take my soul!" The common denominator for these well-known missionaries was fervent prayer for souls to be saved. Through prayer they all asked God for souls.

The Lord says, "Ask of me, and I will make the nations your heritage, and the ends of the earth your possession" (Ps. 2:8). This prayer is for souls to be converted, that "sins may be wiped out, so that times of refreshing may come from the presence of the Lord" (Acts 3:19–20).

The principal object of missions—successful soul winning—must also be taken up in prayer. Prayer for souls should be:

- that all hostility, opposition, and indifference be broken down;
- that the soil of people's hearts be prepared for the sowing of the seed;

- that their blind eyes be opened (see 2 Cor. 4:4); and
- that they be liberated from the power of Satan.

Simpson agreed, observing, "The great art of prayer in all the fullness of its power has been learned only by a few. God has His priests and priestesses who stand with holy hands at the footstool of the throne, sharing the intercession of the great High Priest, and some day it will be found that these are the greatest missionaries of all."[2]

PRAY FOR NEW CONVERTS

In the Epistle to the Philippians, Paul writes, "I am confident of this, that the one who began a good work among you will bring it to completion by the day of Jesus Christ" (1:6). Yet although many new converts and visitors come to church or to our evangelistic crusades, only a few of them are retained. One of the greatest challenges in missions is shutting the back door of evangelism.

Remember that a person's coming to Christ is just the beginning of the Christian life. A process whereby the new convert is established and helped to grow in Christ must follow. The apostle Paul did not leave off his work until he had formed Christ in the lives of his converts. He addressed the Galatians as "my little children, for whom I am again in the pain of childbirth until Christ is formed in you" (Gal. 4:19). He knew that one of the key factors in preserving the souls of new converts was prayer, and so he was "again in the pain of childbirth" for them.

Similarly, a missioner must pray for his new converts:

- that they be conformed to the image of Christ;
- that they grow to spiritual maturity, attaining "the measure of the full stature of Christ" (Eph. 4:13);

2. A. B. Simpson, "New Testament Missionary Types," chap. 3 in *Missionary Messages*, www.swartzentrover.com/cotor/e-books/holiness/Simpson/Missionary/Missionary%20Messages.pdf.

- that they resist the devil and overcome sin;
- that their hearts be open to teaching and training;
- that they discover and utilize their gifts for the kingdom of God and God's church; and
- that they be established and stable in a church family.

Let us undertake this business to help ground the people we reach.

PRAY THAT HEAVEN BE OPENED

Between the last prophet and the coming of Christ—that is, between the Book of Malachi and the Gospel of Matthew—there were no prophets or people of God to bring the Word of the Lord. Their absence was a sign that there was a closed heaven. In other words, we can conclude that, when the voice of God is rare, there is a closed heaven. Furthermore, among the rulers of the cities we want to take for Christ, some oppose the work (1 Cor. 16:9) or send hindering spirits (1 Thess. 2:18). Without an open heaven, authority cannot be exerted over such adversaries. Church growth therefore needs an open heaven.

When heaven is opened, the angels ascend and descend (Gen. 28:12; see also John 1:51). The angels take up prayers and bring down answers, revelations, authority, blessings, and breakthroughs. Under an open heaven, five loaves and two fish can feed "five thousand men, besides women and children" (Matt. 14:21). Under an open heaven, in other words, the littlest resource can be enormously useful for the greatest tasks.

Even Jesus, before he was launched into his successful missionary work, had the heaven opened over him: "Now when all the people were baptized, and when Jesus also had been baptized and was praying, the heaven was opened. . . . And a voice came from heaven, 'You are my Son, the Beloved; with you I am well pleased'" (Luke 3:21–22). Likewise, church growth and effective missions are possible only when we have an open heaven, and an open heaven is possible only when we pray. As I stated in *Ambassadors of Heaven*, "A prayerless pastor will have the heavens shut over his ministry. Ministry doors are shut when we don't pray. Closed heavens make it difficult to make good use of opportunities that God brings."[3]

HEAVENLY DELIVERANCE

The missioner is not automatically accepted or liked by those to whom he or she is sent. Neither is the missioner free from the attacks of wicked and unreasonable men. The apostle Peter experienced an open heaven, ministering to the first Gentile convert, Cornelius (Acts 10), but the experience did not grant him immunity from opposition and attack, and he was arrested and imprisoned. Some may even rejoice in the missioner's harm or demise, as was the case for the apostle James (Acts 12:2–3).

Paul wrote to the church in Rome, "I appeal to you, brothers and sisters, by our Lord Jesus Christ and by the love of the Spirit, to join me in earnest prayer to God on my behalf, that I may be rescued from the unbelievers in Judea" (Rom. 15:30–31). Showing us the importance of such prayer, the apostle echoed his request to the Thessalonians: "Finally, brothers and sisters, pray for us, so that the word of the Lord may spread rapidly and be glorified . . . and that we may be rescued from wicked and evil people" (2 Thess. 3:1–2).

Peter experienced the results of prayer:

> While Peter was kept in prison, the church prayed fervently to God for him. The very night before Herod was going to bring him out, Peter, bound with two chains, was sleeping between two soldiers, while guards in front of the door were keeping watch over the prison. Suddenly an angel of the Lord appeared and a light shone in the cell. He tapped Peter on the side and woke him, saying, "Get up quickly." And the chains fell off his wrists. (Acts 12:5–7)

When we pray, our brethren too will experience great deliverances, for example, from tragedies as they journey, from unreasonable and wicked men and from those who do not believe, and from every scheme and device of Satan set against them.

Prayer is the fuel that drives missions. Without prayer,

3. Charles Agyinasare, *Ambassadors of Heaven* (Accra: Charles Agyinasare, 2013), 60.

missions would be merely impotent drudgery and sweat-filled endeavor. It takes the force of prayer to resist the gates of hell, to send forth and preserve passionate laborers, to cause the heaven to open, and to invite heaven to intervene in the salvation of lost souls.

Luke recounts the words and experiences of the believers in Jerusalem:

> They raised their voices together to God and said, ". . . And now, Lord, look at their threats, and grant to your servants to speak your word with all boldness, while you stretch out your hand to heal, and signs and wonders are performed through the name of your holy servant Jesus." When they had prayed, the place in which they were gathered together was shaken; and they were all filled with the Holy Spirit and spoke the word of God with boldness. (Acts 4:24, 29–31)

May we take our place as leaders in the place of prayer. It is a new season. Let us pray, pray, pray!

28

From Hartford to the Ends of the Earth: The Mission Mobilization Initiatives of the First Korean Presbyterian Church of Greater Hartford

Sun Man Kim

Given the steadily rising worldwide migrant population, which in 2013 stood at 232 million, Stanley John has rightly described our era as the "Age of Migration."[1] Domestic migrants total more than 1 billion. About 2.5 million Afghani refugees are living in Iran, 3 million in Pakistan. Approximately one million Syrian refugees are living in Turkey, 620,000 in Jordan, and 1.1 million in Lebanon. A community of Cambodian refugees lives in Philadelphia, and Karen refugees from along the border of Myanmar and Thailand have settled near us in Hartford, Connecticut.

In response to this migration of peoples around the world, the 2010 Lausanne Congress on World Evangelism proposed three directions for missions: "Missions to the Diasporas, Missions through the Diasporas, and Missions beyond the Diasporas."[2] We

1. Stanley John, "Missiology" (unpublished lecture material on missiology, Alliance Theological Seminary, New York, 2014). See U.N. Department of Economic and Social Affairs, Population Division, "International Migration," www.un.org/en/development/desa/population/migration/publications/wallchart/index.shtml.

2. Lausanne Committee for World Evangelization, *Scattered to Gather: Embracing the Global Trend of Diaspora* (Manila: LifeChange Publishing, 2010), 24–28.

are living in a time when people in diaspora ought to understand the plight of other diasporas and reach out to help, in this way reflecting God's concern for all peoples. "From heaven the LORD looks down and sees all mankind; from his dwelling place he watches all who live on earth" (Ps. 33:13–14 NIV). By the providence of God, for the expansion of his kingdom, people in diaspora are living in all corners of the world.

This "age of migration" (Stanley John)—"of a multinational church and multidirectional mission" (Christopher Wright) and of "the next Christendom" (Philip Jenkins)—requires a multicultural approach to biblical hermeneutics and a missional hermeneutic.[3] This chapter outlines the initiatives taken by one Korean immigrant church as it seeks to mobilize its congregation to participate in missions.

Hartford, the capital city of Connecticut, has a population of approximately 125,000 people (2010 census). Its economic base lies in the insurance, manufacturing, and military defense industries. The state's population of 3.59 million (2013) includes 11,760 (2010) Korean residents, of whom 2,396 are biracial. An estimated 5,000 Koreans live in the Hartford region.

The First Korean Presbyterian Church of Greater Hartford (FKPC) was established in 1984, with Manpung Kim as inaugural head pastor. Today, the church has 586 baptized members, 138 nonbaptized members, and 53 nonconfirmed infant baptized members. As of 2014 around 450 people, including children, attend church each week. On average, the missions budget is about 25 percent of the annual budget.

PRAYER: MISSIONAL MOTIVATION IN THE LOCAL CHURCH

The biblical meaning of missions, argues Marc Spindler, needs to be reevaluated. "It is . . . anachronistic and hence meaningless to attempt to base all modern 'missionary' activities on the Bible, that

3. Christopher J. H. Wright, *The Mission of God* (Downers Grove, Ill.: IVP Academic, 2006), 38; Philip Jenkins, *The Next Christendom: The Coming of Global Christianity* (Oxford: Oxford Univ. Press, 2002).

is, to seek biblical precedents or literal biblical mandates for all modern missionary activities. Mission today must, rather, be seen as arising from something fundamental, from the basic movement of God's people toward the world" with the good news of salvation through Jesus Christ.4 As Spindler points out, all missionary activities should be reassessed to correct human mistakes and errors. We dare not overlook prayer, however, both in worship and in intercession, as a crucial element of biblical missions, on which the early church clearly placed great importance.

If the church in Jerusalem was meant to be scattered, the church at Antioch was meant to be established by those who were scattered. The church at Antioch became the center of missions because it prayed for God's command to do missions. Acts 13:2 says, "While [the church at Antioch was] worshiping the Lord and fasting, the Holy Spirit said. . . ." When they were fasting, they were also praying. During their time of worship and prayer, they heard the voice of the Holy Spirit to send off Barnabas and Saul as the first missionaries. The Bible may not tell us the grounds for all missions activities, but prayer is essential for understanding the biblical significance of missions and for participating in missions more effectively and with fuller obedience. Before Barnabas and Paul obeyed the call, the church at Antioch engaged in further prayer.

As a church, FKPC strives to pray nonstop for missions. It incorporates prayer during the Sunday worship service, Wednesday service, and Friday prayer meeting and through its daily intercessory prayer rooms. Each Sunday during the worship service, before the sermon, the entire congregation prays out loud for the missionaries with whom we partner around the world. We print the missionaries' prayer letters in the bulletin and share them on the digital wall screen as well. Through this time of prayer, we attempt to share in the suffering and partake in the ministry of missionaries, as well as to foster awareness of missions.

In July 2014 our partnering missionary in Paraguay shared in

4. Wright, *The Mission of God*, 37; Marc R. Spindler, "The Biblical Grounding and Orientation of Mission," in *Missiology: An Ecumenical Introduction*, ed. A. Camps, L. A. Hoedemaker, and M. R. Spindler (Grand Rapids: Eerdmans, 1995), 124–25.

his missions letter news about locals being displaced by heavy rains and the spiritual stress that he and his wife were experiencing after their home had been burglarized. In October 2014 our partnering missionary in Turkey informed us about 200,000 Kurdish refugees at the closed border of southeastern Turkey who were fleeing the genocide being committed by ISIS. The entire congregation prays for these and similar needs, in this way sharing the pain of others and participating in the call to missions. The church continues to pray for missionaries and for nations throughout the week.

According to Oswald Chambers, intercession is "a hidden ministry that brings forth fruit through which the Father is glorified."[5] Prayer for missions is not just a preparatory act for missions but a ministry of missions in and of itself.

MISSIONS MOBILIZATION IN A LOCAL CHURCH

First and foremost, the missions mobilization initiatives of the local church are closely related to the vision of a biblical church. This vision includes God's work of deliverance, which started in Genesis and began to be fulfilled through Abraham. When God called Abraham, he gave Abraham a missional promise, "All peoples on earth will be blessed through you" (Gen. 12:3 NIV). And to all Christians, who through Christ have become descendants of Abraham, Jesus commands, "Go and make disciples of all nations" (Matt. 28:19 NIV). God reveals his vision for the eschatological fulfillment of missions in the Book of Revelation: "A great multitude that no one could count, from every nation, tribe, people and language," stands "before the throne," praising the Lamb of God "in a loud voice" (Rev. 7:9–10 NIV). Insofar as local churches embrace this biblical vision, they will open the door of the Gospel for all peoples. In the words of Won Sang Lee, "The church was established for missions. A church without missions is not a church."6

5. Oswald Chambers, *My Utmost for His Highest* (Grand Rapids: Discovery House Publishers, 1992), June 7.

6. Won Sang Lee, "Mission Mobilization Initiative of the Korean Central Presbyterian Church of Washington" (responses to interview questions from Sun Man Kim, September 29, 2014), 7; Christopher J. H. Wright, *The Mission of God's People* (Grand Rapids: Zondervan, 2010), 73; Patrick Johnstone, *The Church Is Bigger Than You Think* (Pasadena, Calif.: William Carey Library, 1998), 23.

The church is part of God's missions strategy to spread the Gospel to all nations.

Initiatives taken by local churches for missions mobilization vary. Initiatives at FKPC include Missions Mobilization Revival Meeting, Missions Revival Conference, Missions School, Missions Bazaar, and Missions Concert. The Missions Mobilization Revival Meeting, a three-day event, takes place each year during the second weekend of January. We invite missionaries from all over the world to speak on missions and topics that relate to issues the church is facing. Listening to their missions reports and their preaching raises awareness about missions and spurs voluntary participation among church members. Missions conferences by themselves, however, are not enough to provide missions mobilization for all the believers. Repeated and continuous missions mobilization initiatives must be utilized.

Past Missions Mobilization Revival Meetings have considered various themes which have blessed and challenged our church. In 2005 the theme was "The Father's Passion to Find His Children," followed by "Why Do Missions in North Korea?" (2006), "Follow Me" (2007), "I Shall Send You Also" (2008), "The Life of the Church, Missions" (2009), "The Church's Calling, Missions" (2010), "Missions, the Work of the Holy Spirit" (2011), "Missions, the Realization of God's Kingdom" (2012), "Missions, the Work of God" (2013), and "Missions, God's Grace" (2014).7

On the last day of the Missions Mobilization Revival Meeting, a video clip shows our partnering missionary families being placed on a world map, followed by a time to make commitments to support missions financially. It is a solemn time in which the commitment to participate in missions is expressed in terms of material wealth. After a time of fervent prayer, we commit ourselves to the call of missions. As a concrete expression of one's commitment, each person writes down the amount he or she feels called to give,

7. Heeyeol Lee, "Prayer Symphony on Mission" (unpublished seminar handout in the First Korean Presbyterian Church of Greater Hartford, January 2008); Sangbae Park, "Mission as a Realization of the Kingdom of God" (mission mobilization revival meeting of the Korean Presbyterian Church of Greater Hartford, January 2012). Park now serves as director of Global Partners (GP) southeast region in Malaysia.

using forms that have already been passed out. Deciding as individuals to commit to the call of missions can take place suddenly by the work of the Holy Spirit, but a commitment to missions by the local church requires a long process, as well as the sanctification of individual believers.

COMMITMENT TO MISSIONS IN A LOCAL CHURCH

During the three days of the 2011 Missions Mobilization Revival Meeting (January 7–9), the Hartford region experienced two very heavy snowfalls. The snow, however, did not stop people from making a commitment to missions during the meeting. By providential timing, both snowfalls happened after, not before or during, a worship service. God gave us a priceless opportunity to help save lives by participating in missions. The church was blessed greatly through missionary Heungsoon Park, who serves in Turkana, Kenya, and the church committed to missions with gladness. We were particularly blessed by seeing his great love for the local church in Kenya, as well as for FKPC in the United States.

God's will is to build the church in all nations (Rev. 7:9; Matt. 24:14). Here, "all nations" does not refer to political nations as we think of them, but to God's desire for churches to be planted in every people group.[8] In Revelation 7:9, it is "every nation, tribe, people, and language"(NIV) that stands before the throne and the Lamb. What is clearly seen in the account is that our God really desires to save not only individual people but also ethnic peoples from all over the world.

John Stott points out that the church is not only called together as a body of worshipers but is also sent out into the world to testify and serve. To be true to its "double identity," the missional church must avoid the danger of becoming a passive "come-structure," in which people are satisfied with expecting non-Christians to find their way to the assembly. It must, instead, strive to take on the character of a "go-structure" for carrying out missions. In other words, the missional church is a church for others.[9] According to Craig Van Gelder, four theological perspectives mark missional

8. John Piper, *Desiring God* (Portland, Ore.: Multnomah Press, 1986), 192.

9. John Stott, *The Living Church* (Downers Grove, Ill.: IVP, 2007), 55.

churches: "God is a missionary God who sends the church into the world. God's mission in the world is related to the reign (kingdom) of God. The missional church is an incarnational ministry sent to engage a postmodern, post-Christendom, globalized context. The internal life of the missional church focuses on every believer living as a disciple engaging in mission."[10] A truly missional church must therefore never confuse its missions program with its basic identity as *a church that God is sending out on mission*.

SHORT-TERM MISSIONS OF THE LOCAL CHURCH

In a lecture entitled "Short-Term Team for the Mission Field? or for Self and the Church?," missionary Jaehwan Lee spoke about the blessings and dangers of short-term missions.[11] More important than the length of the trip, the size of the missions team, or even whether the word "missions" is used are the motives and objectives behind short-term missions. Ralph Winter called for realistic assessment of the goals of any short-term mission project: "Would we increase the number of doctors if we sent thousands of young people into hospitals for two or three weeks? The answer is 'yes' if they were enabled to understand what is really going on and got to know the workers they encountered. The answer is 'no' if they thought they were supposed to heal people while there those two weeks."[12]

We believe that one of the objectives of short-term missions, in addition to serving the local people in the mission field, is training the believers of the sending church. This objective requires much preliminary consultation and prayer with the field missionary, as well as thorough ministry preparation. The visiting team must cooperate with the missionary, especially regarding specific

10. Craig Van Gelder and Dwight J. Zscheile, *The Missional Church in Perspective: Mapping Trends and Shaping the Conversation* (Grand Rapids: Baker Academic, 2010); Rick Richardson, "Emerging Missional Movements: An Overview and Assessment of Some Implications for Mission(s)," *International Bulletin of Missionary Research* 37, no. 3 (2013): 131.

11. Jaehwan Lee, "Mission Possible" (unpublished syllabus on missional strategy for pastors, 2004), 46–52.

12. Ralph D. Winter, "Editorial Comment," *Mission Frontiers* 26, no. 2 (2004): 5.

instructions given, as they are based on the local customs, culture, and circumstances.

Since sending its first short-term missionary, Elizabeth Lee, to Gambia for one year in 1992, FKPC has sent both a short-term missionary and a missions team to Oaxaca, Mexico (1994), as well as a short-term team to Micronesia (June 5–July 25, 1995). On July 30, 1995, FKPC sent out a missionary who served one year in Micronesia. Since then, the church has sent out short-term missionaries to China (1998, 2003), Alaska (2001), Eritrea (2004, 2007), Indonesia (2008), Peru (2011), Kenya (2011), Thailand (2011), and Mexico (1996, 1998, 2010–2014). These ministries have heightened the church's sense of responsibility toward missions and expanded the church's participation in missions.

Before 1999, short-term missions at FKPC was limited to one location per year. Since then, however, the church has sent teams to multiple locations: Russia, China, Philippines, Eritrea, and, in the United States, Atlanta (Georgia) as urban mission, Alaska, and an Indian reservation in New Mexico. In 2004 we started to serve Yucatán, Mexico, and the Cambodian refugee community in Philadelphia. In 2007 a total of fifty people volunteered to serve in eight different regions (Russia, Eritrea, Mexico, Peru, Thailand, China [Changbai, Harbin, and Henan], Philadelphia, and New Mexico). From 2008 to 2014 a total of 322 people served short-term in five regions. Originally, college students made up the majority of short-term missions teams, but increasingly, we have seen high school students and adult members of the congregation participating. From 1992 to 2014 a total of 561 people went on short-term missions trips (average: 24.4 annually).

These short-term missions have also served as a catalyst for building relations with missionaries from other countries. As of 2014, FKPC has established a cooperative missions relationship with forty-four overseas missionaries in as many mission fields, twenty-eight countries, six international missions organizations (LAMP, MOM, SEED, WEC, A Cup of Water, OMSC), and four specialized mission ministries (JOY [disabled ministry], AGAPE [homeless ministry], Hope Chapel [a campus ministry in the Boston area for Korean students with an F-1 visa]).

As Glenn Schwartz points out, short-term volunteers need

to remember the greater importance of being over doing. "Before sending out His disciples on a short-term ministry assignment, Jesus told them, 'Be wise as serpents and harmless as doves' (Matt. 10:16b). Short-termers and all missionaries would do well to remember these words when venturing into a cross-cultural situation. They will find that listening, learning, and 'being' are essential to an effective ministry."13 Jesus' instructions to his disciples remind us what it means to participate in short-term missions and missions in general. As they go out, Jesus wants people to be wise and pure.

PURSUING UNITED MISSIONS BY THE LOCAL CHURCH

In a lecture at the Overseas Ministries Study Center entitled "The Story of a Missional Diaspora Church, Hong Kong Korean Missions Church," Hyung Joong Yoon shared ways that a local church can contribute effectively to world missions.14 Since its establishment in Hong Kong in 1984 as a branch of Choonghyeon Church in Korea (Hapdong), the Hong Kong Korean Missions Church has sent more than sixty missionaries to Central Asia. Furthermore, in 2001 the church launched the Life Road Exodus Mission Society, a ministry that seeks to make missions a part of daily life. At the lecture, one participant, Myeongseok Lee, a missionary to Ghana, made the good point that missions by local churches should be done in unity and cooperation with other churches. To provide examples, he mentioned ecumenical missions ministries such as the Ghana-Korea-Germany Church Mission, of which he was a part, and other joint ministries such as Korean-German youth missions leadership ministry, and ministries for fellow workers at local churches.

Won Sang Lee, pastor of Korean Central Presbyterian Church

13. Glenn Schwartz, "Short-Term Mission Trips: Maximizing the Benefits," *Mission Frontiers* 26, no. 2 (2004): 12. See, also, John R. W. Stott, "The Living God Is a Missionary God," in *Perspectives on the World Christian Movement*, ed. Ralph D. Winter and Steven C. Hawthorne (Pasadena, Calif.: William Carey Library, 1981), 17–18.

14. Hyung Joong Yoon, "A Diaspora Story of a Missional Church: The Hong Kong Korea Mission Church Story" (Korean pastors and church mission committee members luncheon, Overseas Ministries Study Center, New Haven, Conn., September 22, 2014).

of Washington (KCPC) in Virginia, stated that the SEED International missions organization was born because of the lack of united missions by local churches. "By June 2000, Central Missionary Fellowship (CMF) had grown into a missions organization that had sent 25 families as missionaries in 12 countries. . . . This may have been a great achievement by one singular church, but in the interdenominational, church-wide perspective, it was problematic."[15] In 2006 KCPC (which is a member of the Presbyterian Church in America) and New York Korean Presbyterian Church joined together to establish SEED International, which gradually developed and expanded its ministries to include SEED USA, SEED Korea, SEED Canada, and SEED Brazil.

Established in 1973 in the Washington D.C. area, KCPC is one of the largest Korean immigrant churches in the United States; in 2014 it had a weekly attendance of more than 5,000 people. In 1986 the church invited Gwangcheol Ko, a missionary in Paraguay, to talk about the mission field there. The church members were blessed and challenged, and in July 1987 they sent a short-term missions team to Paraguay and have been doing so nearly each year since. About this time the church held missions revival meetings, inviting missionaries from Hong Kong, Thailand, and Indonesia to speak. According to Won Sang Lee, missions mobilization initiatives by the local church reflect the senior pastor's deep understanding that Jesus established the church as a missions strategy to fulfill the Great Commission.[16]

In 2008 FKPC took over an unfinished project to build a missions center in Yucatán, Mexico. We completed construction of the missions center and the worship hall in October 2009 and dedicated the buildings. The vision of the missions center is threefold:

- For Yucatán Christians: Raise up pastors, missionaries, and local leaders (augmenting vocational and spiritual training).
- For our church: Build the missions training center as a base for missions in Central and South America.

15. Won Sang Lee, "Mission Mobilization Initiative," 8.
16. Ibid., 6.

- For North American churches: Vitalize spiritual resources of Koreans in the United States and South/Central America (e.g., develop the center as a short-term missions center, making the center available to other churches).

Along with this threefold vision, we set four goals:

- Expand the spiritual training center (operate a large dormitory).
- Enrich the vocational training and education curriculum (add more classes, along with classes run by the current state government).
- Operate welfare centers (e.g., an orphanage and a Christian academy).
- Develop short-term missions/spiritual training programs for Korean immigrant churches in the United States and in Central and South America.

In 2014, ten Korean churches (eight in the United States, one each in Mexico and Paraguay) established the Latin America Mission Project (LAMP). These churches united in wanting to escape the limitations imposed by missions working only at the level of individual churches.

MISSIONS AS GOD'S VISION

Loren Cunningham has said—in loving encouragement to Korean Christians with regard to missions—that for America, Britain set the pattern for missions in the nineteenth century; that for Asia, the United States set the pattern in missions in the twentieth century; and now the Korean churches are the ones setting the pattern in twenty-first-century missions.17 We must be humble, however, and give special attention to the extraordinary divine work that has taken place in the Global South during an age of numerous diasporas. Fundamentally, Jesus' objective for estab-

17. Loren Cunningham, "People of Destiny," in *The Sixth Korean World Mission Conference Manual* (Valley Cottage, NY: Korean World Mission Council, 2008), 4–13.

lishing the church is to spread the Gospel to "all nations" (Matt. 28:19).18 The Great Commission, given in the last three verses of Matthew 28, which Jesus imparted to the disciples before his ascension into heaven, is also a missions strategy imparted to the church. In response, the local church ought to embrace the eschatological vision of heaven and do everything possible so that the Gospel can be spread to "all nations."

The Bible and history show us what it cost the disciples to carry out Jesus' Great Commission. They devoted themselves to obeying that command, risking their lives in doing so. For all believers, the surest way forward in our walk of faith is to engage fully in missions. Missions is God's vision for this world and for us all.

QUESTIONS FOR REFLECTION

1. As local churches seek to follow the example of the church at Antioch in Acts 13:2, what missional motivations and what initiatives for mission mobilization should they consider?
2. What are some of the initiatives for missions mobilization that a local church could undertake? How might these initiatives differ by church or by situation?
3. According to Craig Van Gelder, what four theological perspectives mark missional churches? To what extent are these perspectives true of your church?
4. As short-termers (and all missionaries) become involved in cross-cultural situations, what advice or caution does Glenn Schwartz recommend that they remember? Why?

18. According to Won Sang Lee, "The fundamental objective of the church's establishment is to carry out the Great Commission; it is the Lord's strategy" ("Mission Mobilization Initiative," 8).

29

Response to "From Hartford to the Ends of the Earth"

Ben Torrey

Sun Man Kim has done an excellent job of describing the very commendable efforts of the First Korean Presbyterian Church of Greater Hartford (FKPC), in Manchester, Connecticut, to respond to the Great Commission of Matthew 28:19. It is a great encouragement to see this church of the Korean North American diaspora engaging directly in that for which, according to Won Sang Lee as quoted by Kim, Christ established his church—for the work of missions (247). He also points out how the church is deeply engaged with what the 2010 Lausanne Congress on World Evangelism proposes as "missions beyond diaspora" (244). As a church of one primary ethnicity (Korean) located in a larger majority culture (the United States), the congregation is well aware of the many challenges of ministering cross-culturally. Not only have they taken their responsibility seriously, they have been somewhat successful in generating "commitment to missions by the local church," something that, as Kim states, "requires a long process, as well as the sanctification of individual believers" (249).

FKPC is doing well in responding to the call to missions. Church members are increasingly involved in overseas missions, as well as in reaching out to other diasporas within the United States. Throughout his chapter, Kim draws attention to the biblical framework and imperatives that form a great part of the congregation's motivation. He also writes of missions as incarnational ministry. I wish to explore this point, for incarnational ministry fueled by love is, I believe, the fundamental motivation for missions.

MOTIVATION: OBEDIENCE? LOVE?

One might posit two fundamental motivations for missions—obedience and love. Ultimately, both obedience and love are essential, but if the fundamental motivation of love is lacking, obedience comes up short. In addition to obedience and love, many other motivations, largely psychological, can be identified, but they are secondary, ultimately inadequate in themselves to sustain missions over the long haul.

Obedience is being yielded to God in submission to Christ's command to "go . . . and make . . . ," his final word of sending to his apostles, his "sent ones." Certainly they, and we as their successors, have our marching orders. How can we not obey?

JOY, KOINONIA, AND LOVE

Yet, I would like to draw attention to another passage, one that speaks of a very different motivation: "What we have seen and heard we proclaim to you also, so that you too may have fellowship with us; and indeed our fellowship is with the Father, and with His Son Jesus Christ. These things we write, so that our joy may be made complete" (1 John 1:3–4).[1]

The word translated here as "fellowship" is the Greek word *koinōnia*. In its various forms, this word appears almost fifty times in the New Testament and is translated by such words as "fellowship," "sharing," "partaking," "having in common," "communicating," "communion," and "contribution." A thorough examination of the use of this word in Scripture shows that it involves a very deep commitment. In ancient Greek it was used to refer to the bond of marriage or a legal contract between persons. Because so many different terms in English (as well as in Korean, Chinese, and

1. Unless otherwise noted, Scripture quotations in this response are from the New American Standard Bible (La Habra, Calif.: Lockman Foundation, 1995).

other languages) are used to translate koinonia, the weight and power of the concept behind the word is obscured. I often express the meaning of koinonia as equivalent to absolute, to-the-end commitment to one another. I then add that Christian koinonia is this type of commitment within the bond of love. The encompassing presence of love enables koinonia.

John is saying that his joy is made complete when his readers receive his words and join with him in this totally committed relationship of love. And because this is the nature of his relationship to God the Father, through sharing in love with him, John's readers will come to know the Father's love as well. John's motivation for preaching the Gospel is, in short, love. He wants to have more people that he can love. His entire motivation is love and the koinonia that comes from love. Not a breath of duty or obedience surfaces here, only love for one another.

Let us look at a few more passages that connect love and joy with sharing the Gospel:

> A new commandment I give to you, that you love one another, even as I have loved you, that you also love one another. By this all men will know that you are My disciples, if you have love for one another. (John 13:34–35)

> If you keep My commandments, you will abide in My love; just as I have kept My Father's commandments and abide in His love. These things I have spoken to you so that My joy may be in you, and that your joy may be made full. This is My commandment, that you love one another, just as I have loved you. Greater love has no one than this, that one lay down his life for his friends. (John 15:10–13)

> I do not ask on behalf of these alone, but for those also who believe in Me through their word; that they may all be one; even as You, Father, are in Me and I in You, that they also may be in Us, so that the world may believe that You sent Me. The glory which You have given Me I have given to them, that they may be one, just as We are one; I in them and You in Me, that they may be perfected in unity, so that the world may know that You sent Me, and loved them, even as You have loved Me. (John 17:20–23)

THE LOVE OF GOD AS MOTIVATION FOR MISSION

Through our love for one another, the world will know that we belong to Christ and, through this knowledge, will come to know his Gospel. Not only will they see the evidence of God's love in our lives, but they will also be drawn to it and want to experience it for themselves. Such love is not just any love, however; it is not an "old commandment" love that enjoins us to love our neighbors as ourselves (e.g., Lev. 19:18, Matt. 5:43–44). Jesus says that he is giving a "new commandment" and that, by our obedience to this new commandment, all people will know. . . . What does "new-commandment love" consist of? It is the love that Jesus has for us—love to the death, death on the cross. This point is made explicit in John 15. The importance of this love, as expressed in unity, is again emphasized in Christ's prayer to his Father on behalf of his disciples and for us who come to believe through their words.

This is what it means to be incarnational—to love as the three Persons of the triune God love one another, the love expressed in John 3:16: "For God so loved the world, that He gave His only begotten Son, that whoever believes in Him shall not perish, but have eternal life."

This is the love that is God's motivation behind the Great Commission. This is the love that makes obeying the Great Commission a great joy. This is the love that makes it easy to sacrifice our comfort, our pleasures, even our lives in order that others may come to join us in this love. If we are caught up in this love of God, all else becomes easy, second nature, and our only concern is to understand all that we need to in order to be effective in the mission of Jesus Christ's body, his church. We will seek to understand, we will prepare, we will study. Think of how a young man, caught up in love for a young woman, will study and plan and sacrifice to bring her joy. This love of God goes far beyond that in power and passion. It is also an eternal love that will sustain us in our mission throughout our life.

When my wife and I were called to return to South Korea in order to prepare for the eventual opening of North Korea, Paul's words in 2 Corinthians 5 expressed what God had impressed upon my wife's heart: "For if we are beside ourselves, it is for God; if we are of sound mind, it is for you. For the love of Christ controls us" (see more fully vv. 13–15). Or as this last sentence is translated in the New International Version, "The love of God compels us." It was this compelling of love that motivated her, and me, to respond to this call of God.

So, how do we get this love? Where does it come from? Truly, it does not seem that we love this way very much—and, truth be told, we do not. Nor is it possible for us to manufacture this love in ourselves. This is indeed the love of God, and as such, it must come from him. In his chapter Pastor Kim writes of the importance of prayer. Prayer is a key factor. The other key factor is that we look to God himself to pour this love into our hearts by his Holy Spirit. As Paul writes, "Hope does not disappoint, because the love of God has been poured out within our hearts through the Holy Spirit who was given to us" (Rom. 5:5).

If we would motivate for missions, it behooves us to pray for, seek, and practice love. I thank Pastor Kim and FPKC for demonstrating this love in their efforts for missions.

30

Mission Initiatives by Korean American Megachurches: Current Trends

Won Sang Lee

I cannot help but thank God, who showed his love for Korea, the Hermit Kingdom, by sending missionaries to the country to spread the Gospel of Christ. The Koreans, surrounded by giant nations, were truly without hope when in 1866 Robert Jermain Thomas was executed at the age of twenty-seven in the Taedong River near Pyongyang, North Korea.[1] His selfless blood shed on Korean soil was not meaningless but served as an impetus for the dawn of a new era of Christian mission in Korea.[2] With the signing sixteen years later, in 1882, of the Treaty of Peace, Amity, Commerce, and Navigation between Korea and the United States, the way was opened for Horace Allen, the first medical missionary, to enter Korea in 1884. This landmark event presaged the arrival of Horace Underwood and Henry Appenzeller and their families, pioneer missionaries who landed in Korea on Easter Sunday, April 5, 1885.[3]

The tombstone of Ruby Kendrick (1883–1909), another missionary to Korea, carries the inscription, "If I had a thousand lives

1. Stella Price, *Chosen for Choson (Korea)* (Essex, Mass.: Emmaus Road Ministries, 2010), 87.

2. Kenneth Scott Latourette, *A History of Christianity* (Peabody, Mass.: Prince Press, 1999), 2:1327.

3. Nak Joon Paik, *Korean Protestant Church History, 1832–1910* [in Korean] (Seoul, Korea: Yonsei Univ. Press, 1998), 116–18.

to give, Korea should have them all."[4] The precious lives sacrificed by the missionaries for Korea in obedience to God's command have been remembered by our Lord. The psalmist sang, "Those who sow in tears shall reap with shouts of joy!" (Ps. 126:5 ESV). Truly, the missionary pioneers sowed the seeds in tears, and now we are reaping the fruit in joy. We are reaping the fruit not only through the countless multiplying of Korean churches, but also through a strong partnership for world missions by sending 26,677 missionaries to 170 countries.[5] But the spread of Christianity through Koreans has not been limited to the work of formal missionaries sent by Korean churches. Koreans have carried the Gospel through emigration. Dr. Allen, later working as a U.S. diplomat, was the first person to introduce Korean immigration to Hawaii. He dealt with Emperor Kojong of the Chosun Dynasty and visited Hawaii personally to assist in setting up arrangements. Through contacts Allen made, the first 102 Korean immigrants to U.S. territory arrived in Honolulu, Hawaii, on January 13, 1903.

The Immigration Act signed by President Lyndon Johnson in 1965 opened the door for further growth of the Korean population in the United States, which now has reached more than two million. In 2003, President George W. Bush proclaimed words of celebration: "As we commemorate the centennial anniversary of Korean immigration to the United States, we recognize the invaluable contributions of Korean Americans to our Nation's rich cultural diversity, economic strength, and proud heritage."[6] Not the least of this heritage has been the 4,303 Korean American churches established in North America throughout Koreans' 112-year history of immigration to the continent. The number of churches founded is exceptional when compared with that of other ethnic communities.[7] It is hard to deny the significant role that Koreans immigrating to America have played in the expansion of the king-

4. Ruby Kendrick's tombstone is in the Foreigners Graveyard, Yang Hwa Jin, Seoul, Korea.

5. The figure of 26,677 comes from an announcement made by KWMA Mission Research and Development Department, December 31, 2014.

6. See http://2001-2009.state.gov/p/eap/rls/ot/16606.htm.

7. *Christian Today Weekly*, January 1, 2015.

dom of God.[8] This is a missional phenomenon in which we practice what we have learned from the pioneer missionaries to Korea, who left a spiritual legacy through their biblical teaching and sacrifices.

The first 102 immigrants to arrive in Hawaii included fifty people from the Naeri Methodist Church of Incheon, Korea, a church started by Henry Appenzeller on July 29, 1885, just three months after he arrived in Korea. Naeri Methodist Church commissioned Pastor Seung Ha Hong to go to Hawaii to provide pastoral care for their fifty immigrants. There this group founded the Christ United Methodist Church, which held its first worship service on November 10, 1903. That service marked the beginning of the Korean American churches, which now number more than four thousand.

Since Korean American churches are the fruit of the labor and sacrifices of the American missionaries in Korea, it is impossible to think about Korean American churches apart from these American missionaries. But a century has passed, and Korean American churches have been defining their own identities as they have undergone the process of adjusting to the new culture and people. In all too many cases, Korean Americans view themselves, or are viewed by others, still as foreigners, even if they come from several generations of Korean Americans.

In what follows I present missional issues facing Korean American churches, including megachurches, which in many cases find themselves struggling for growth.

THE SILENT EXODUS

Without the next generation, we cannot continue to carry out Christ's missional mandate. This truth poses a fundamental challenge, to which the dying churches in Europe testify. Next-generation Korean Americans are not exempt from this historical reality. For this reason, as early as twenty years ago we heard suggestions, such as that by Minho Song, of sending missionaries to "the mission field" of Manhattan to work with "young urban Korean professionals who are no longer interested in spiritual

8. Sang Cheul Oh, *Immigration Theology* [in Korean] (Seoul: Qumran Press, 2008), 16–17.

things."[9] In 1996 Helen Lee wrote of a "silent exodus of church-raised [Korean American] young people who find their immigrant churches irrelevant, culturally stifling, and ill-equipped to develop them spiritually for life in the multicultural 1990s."[10] What was a concern two decades ago has become a reality today. A surprising 82 percent of Korean American youth desire to leave the church after graduating from high school.[11] For this reason, Danny Changsoo Ro, pastor of the largest Korean American megachurch, quoted John Maxwell's maxim—"Success without a successor is not success at all"—in setting "Building Up the Next Generation" as his church's theme for 2015.[12]

Mission and building up the next generation should go hand in hand. The Korean Central Presbyterian Church (KCPC) in Centreville, Virginia, for example, invited Peter Cha and Steve Kang for a two-day conference with the theme "Next Generation."[13] They pointed out two main reasons for the silent exodus of youth: a biblically unhealthy church and parents' hypocritical practice of their faith. A growing number of second-generation Korean Americans, ironically, return to their mother churches for the sake of the identity formation of their (third-generation) children. If second-

9. Minho Song, "Constructing a Local Theology for the Second Generation Korean Ministry," Urban Mission 15, no. 2 (December 1997): 24, www.torontoyoungnak.com/bbs.php?table=board_67&home=song_en&query=view&uid=3.

10. Helen Lee, "Silent Exodus: Can the East Asian Church in America Reverse the Flight of Its Next Generation?," *Christianity Today* 40, no. 12 (August 12, 1996); reprint in *Asian American Christianity Reader*, ed. Timothy Tseng and Viji Nakka-Camma (Castro Valley, Calif.: Pacific Asian American & Canadian Christian Education Project and the Institute for the Study of Asian American Christianity, 2009), 99–103; also available at www.christianitytoday.com/ct/1996/august12/6t9050.html.

11. See Sang Cheul Oh, *Christian Times*, May 17, 2012. See also Jeff Schapiro, "America Is One of the Fastest Growing Mission Fields in the World," *Christian Post*, October 10, 2012, www.christianpost.com/news/america-is-one-of-the-fastest-growing-mission-fields-in-the-world-82985.

12. Danny Changsoo Ro, Annual Congregational Report, Sa-Rang Community Church, Anaheim, Calif., October, 2014.

13. The conference was held March 13–14, 2015, at the Korean Central Presbyterian Church, Centreville, Virginia. Peter Cha teaches at Trinity Evangelical Divinity School, Deerfield, Illinois, and Steve Kang at Gordon-Conwell Theological Seminary, South Hamilton, Massachusetts.

and third-generation Korean Americans are to be embraced and are to become missional in obedience to the Great Commission, we must grow as a healthy Korean American church. The church's identity is not only as the sender, but also as the one being sent.[14] The church should become missionary in the power of the Holy Spirit in obedience to the Great Commission.[15] The church has a responsibility for the sake of its missional mandate to encourage parents to take seriously their duty to bring up their children in Christian faith.[16]

UNREACHED PEOPLES—RIGHT IN OUR NEIGHBORHOOD

Finishing the Task (www.finishingthetask.com) updated its list of Unengaged, Unreached People Groups (UUPG) on February 6, 2015, showing more than 722 groups with populations over 10,000. But in another scale, "across the globe, there are more than 3,000 UUPGs; about 230 of those people groups live in the Americas."[17] In 2003 KCPC adopted one of the UUPGs—a group of about 3,000 Kurdish people living in the Washington, D.C., area—and commissioned a missionary. One member of the Kurdish group became a follower of Jesus Christ and continues to attend our Sunday services. The adoption became an opportunity to open our arms to embrace Muslims living in our neighborhood and to encourage immigrant house churches to reach out to their own groups. Some

14. David Jacobus Bosch, *Transforming Mission: Paradigm Shifts in Theology of Mission* (Maryknoll, N.Y.: Orbis Books, 1991), 370. Bosch believes that the *missio Dei* changes our understanding of the identity of the church from that of being the sender to being the one sent in mission. I believe, however, that both concepts are biblical. The person or one being sent into the world must have holiness of character, reflecting Christ. The church, the people of God, must be genuine disciples of Christ, imitating his character through the Holy Spirit.

15. Charles E. Van Engen, *God's Missionary People: Rethinking the Purpose of the Local Church* (Grand Rapids: Baker, 1991), 133.

16. See Christopher J. H. Wright, *The Mission of God's People* (Grand Rapids: Zondervan, 2010), 72.

17. See www.finishingthetask.com. See also Emily Pearson, "Church 'Embraces' Unreached People Group at Home and Abroad," http://stories.imb.org/americas/stories/view/church-embraces-unreached-people-group-at-home-and-abroad.

Korean American missionaries are coming back to the United States to serve the people whom they could not contact freely in the mission field. Korean American megachurches are mature enough to see the harvest fields in their neighborhoods, which bring UUPGs closer and make them more accessible. Korean American megachurches have a great advantage in engaging in the center city Gospel movement, which Tim Keller describes as being part of world mission.[18] It is also time for them to invest time, talent, and resources in reconciliation among diverse ethnic groups for the sake of the Gospel.[19]

DEVELOPING KOREAN AMERICAN MISSION AGENCIES

Our calling is to discern the voice of God, who is sovereign and has a reason for everything he does. For the Korean American Christian diaspora, the challenge is to realize the missional reason we are here in a foreign and diversified culture. What course should we pursue?[20] Take the example of the Urbana Student Missions Conference, held every three years and sponsored since 1946 by InterVarsity. For the 2012 conference, 7,000 of the 16,000 students attending were Asian Americans, as was the conference director, Tom Lin. During Urbana many attendees feel God's call to missions, but several steps lie ahead of them before they reach a mission field: missionary training, home church commissioning, fund-raising, and appointment by a mission agency. As Korean American diaspora churches have grown, the need for establishing Korean American mission agencies in which these students can work has become apparent. Many Western mission agencies working in Korea have incorporated independent Korean mission agencies under the

18. Timothy J. Keller, *Center Church: Doing Balanced, Gospel-Centered Ministry in Your City* (Grand Rapids: Zondervan, 2012), 21.

19. Chadler H. Im, "The Korean Diaspora Churches in the USA: Their Concerns and Strengths," in *Global Diasporas and Mission*, ed. Chandler H. Im and Amos Yong (Eugene, Ore.: Wipf & Stock, 2014), 146.

20. Missiologist Enoch Wan interprets the Korean American diaspora as "clearly God's way of scattering them from the 'Hermit Kingdom of Korea' for the divine purpose of kingdom ministry." Enoch Wan, "Korean Diaspora: From Hermit Kingdom to Kingdom Ministry," in *Korean Diaspora and Christian Mission*, ed. Sŭng-hun Kim and Wonsuk Ma (Eugene, Ore.: Wipf & Stock, 2011), 106.

umbrella of the international board in order to avoid cultural and strategic differences. Independent Korean mission organizations also have become successful. Examples include University Bible Fellowship (established in 1961), with 1,670 missionaries working in 99 countries; Intercorp Mission (1983), with 900 professionally qualified lay missionaries in Central Asia and the Middle East; and TIM (Tyrannus International Mission; 1987), with 511 missionaries in 50 countries.[21] The Korean vision for missional engagement is spreading; 3,358 laypeople and 592 pastors attended the Intercorp Vision School in Korea in 2014, with an additional 530 at the school held in the United States.[22]

In a similar vein, passionate Korean American megachurches have developed strategic plans to train and commission people called as missionaries at Urbana and other gatherings. In 1986—under the triple motto "Mission is prayer, mission is war, mission is martyrdom—Grace Korean Church, Los Angeles, initiated Grace Ministries International (GMI), a mission agency focused especially on the countries of the former Soviet Union. The church has supported the mission with 50 percent of its annual budget; by 2013 it had commissioned 256 missionaries to 58 countries. Currently the church has a vision to send 1,000 missionaries by year 2020.[23] All of these efforts became possible because (1) Grace Korean Church itself established GMI, (2) KCPC established Central Missionary Fellowship in 1990, and (3) New York Presbyterian Church founded Reaching Out to the World in 1993. Won Sang Lee and Young Hee Lee, senior pastors of KCPC and New York Presbyterian Church, respectively, agreed to merge the two mission agencies, since both churches shared the same vision of letting the church become a missionary church in obedience to the Great Commission. From this merger, SEED International was born in 2000. SEED International, which includes

21. Yook Hwan Doh, "Between Two Hours," in *Tyrannus International Mission* [in Korean], ed. Yong Jo Ha (Seoul: Tyrannus Press, 2015), 6–8.

22. I thank Dong Chan Seo for supplying these statistics, which he obtained from Yong Hoon Lee, Intercorp Planning Department, February 23, 2015.

23. Daniel Taichoul Yang, *Called Out for Witness* (Oxford: Regnum Books International, 2014), 67–75.

SEED USA, SEED Korea, SEED Canada, and SEED Brazil, is a member of Missio Nexus and has 136 missionary units serving in 36 countries. Another example is Professionals for Global Missions (PGM), established by the Antioch Church of Philadelphia in 1999. PGM began with a vision that was focused on diaspora, was church centered, and was for professionals; in 2015 it had 121 missionary units (229 people) in 30 countries. Promise Church in New York initiated the 4/14 Window Mission Movement in 2009 to focus especially on children and youth ages four to fourteen. Using Luke 15:7 as a basis of its vision, Open Door Presbyterian Church in Herndon, Virginia, has developed a unique model of an interdependent congregation of first- and second-generation Korean Americans, with special emphasis on medical missions.[24]

All of these Korean American megachurches realize that the primary purpose of the church is to accomplish the Great Commission at home and abroad. If the missional goal is omitted, the church cannot grow, and members of the congregation may not commit their lives to the church, the body of Christ.

Three Korean American megachurches in Canada—Young Nak Presbyterian Church of Toronto (Minho Song, pastor), Light Presbyterian Church (Hyeon Soo Lim, pastor), and Grace Community Church (Shin Il Park, pastor)—merit special mention because of the missional achievements of the senior pastors. The conception of the missional church they are pursuing is one of holistic mission. The vision of each church is well-defined so that no one can miss the direction the church is heading. Young Nak Presbyterian Church set aside 25 percent of its 2015 budget for missions and evangelism, something that is unusual for a megachurch. The church has specific missional goals, with special emphasis on adopting unreached groups, such as groups in countries of the former Soviet Union, and on Muslims and Buddhists. With its holistic missional philosophy, Grace Community Church's comprehensive plan, Grace Mission Target 2030, sets a goal of commissioning 200 missionaries from the church. As a church, Light Presbyterian Church is truly missional, with the entire congregation concentrating

24. Yong Hoon Kim, Church Directory, Open Door Presbyterian Church, Herndon, Va. (2014), 5.

on North Korea, North India, and China by adopting four unreached people groups.

INCREASE IN SHORT-TERM MISSIONS

Not only megachurches, but Korean American churches in general are becoming more active in promoting mission engagement. In particular, they are finding that an emphasis on short-term mission trips is useful for involving their entire congregations. Such trips are particularly effective in motivating youth, college students, and young adults to share their own salvation experiences with other people so that in doing so they may grow deeper in faith with Christ. They typically spend two weeks with people of a different culture or with the underprivileged. Through these experiences, some of the youth commit to a career in missions and go on to serve as long-term missionaries. In the process of training and fund-raising activities, the entire congregation becomes mobilized for the missional goal. An outcome may be spiritual growth in the people as they realize the heart of God for seeking the lost. Korean Americans are well-equipped for this kind of mission, as they are already multicultural and live in a multicultural society.

MOBILIZING SILVER MISSION

Global trends include an increasing number of people in the upper age brackets, which provides an opportunity, with proper training, to mobilize this group for missions.[25] If members of the senior population are well-equipped spiritually, they constitute the best resources available as support groups for the mission field. MK schools welcome highly qualified senior professionals. Korean American megachurches are excellent sites for mobilizing, recruiting, training, and placing such seniors in the right settings.

CONCLUSION

Overall, Korean American churches are biblically healthy churches that understand missions to be the primary purpose of the church

25. See-Young Lee, "Mobilizing Senior Christians in Korea and among the Korean Diaspora for Mission," in *Korean Diaspora and Christian Mission*, ed. Kim and Ma, 260–63.

of Christ. This understanding of the church comes from the mission spirit that the Korean diaspora inherited from the very beginning from the early Protestant missionaries in Korea. But as part of the global trend toward secularization and because the United States has been in the process of becoming a secular nation, Korean Americans have increasingly tended to focus only on the next generation. As a result, we can say that, on the one hand, if the next generation is lost, Christian missions may not continue. On the other hand, unreached and unengaged people groups are all right here in the United States, within easy access in our neighborhoods. Social, cultural, and global changes alert us to the need for new strategies in mission.

To pursue specialized missions and to better invest their resources, Korean American megachurches are establishing mission agencies and concentrating on particular areas or groups of unreached people. They have also adopted mission strategies that emphasize ongoing short-term missions and more fully engaging the generation of retired Christians. Churches are becoming more specialized in their approach to missions and their pursuit of a holistic approach to mission in order to achieve the Great Commission. Modern churches are definitely under attack and will be utterly defeated unless the Holy Spirit empowers them to truly make missions their primary goal. Korean American megachurches would be well advised, however, to cooperate more closely with mission agencies and with other churches. Although the megachurches have resources sufficient for developing their own professional mission organizations, cooperation and networking with other churches and mission groups will lead to more efficient missionary member care and to more professional planning in carrying out global frontier missions.

QUESTIONS FOR DISCUSSION

1. The "silent exodus" of young people from their churches is a global trend. What steps could churches take in cooperation with parents to encourage young people not to leave the church?

2. In fulfilling their God-given purposes, churches and mission agencies are interdependent. Since the primary purpose of the church is world mission (Matt. 28:18–20, John 20:21), what are concrete ways mission agencies can effectively help local churches to achieve their missional goal?

3. Short-term mission teams sometimes cause harm on the mission field. What are some issues that local church mission teams should be aware of so as to avoid having a negative effect on the work of missionaries in the field?

4. The "silver-aged" population continues to grow. How can mission agencies and local churches work together to motivate and train this group for effective missions at home and abroad?

5. About 4,000 Korean diaspora churches are located in the United States. Members of the younger generation found in them are bilingual and bicultural and therefore are well equipped to serve on the mission field. What strategies might mission agencies, local church pastors, and lay leaders find effective in motivating them for mission?

31

Response to "Mission Initiatives by Korean American Megachurches"

Carlos L. Malavé

Church father Tertullian famously commented that the blood of the martyrs is the seed of the church, a statement whose truth the Korean church confirms. Christian contacts in Korea go back to the seventeenth century. Historical accounts show that more than 10,000 martyrs died in persecutions that extended for over a century. The growth and strength of Christianity in Korea was forged by the work, witness, and blood of these heroes of the faith. In the twenty-first century, not only do Christians in South Korea possess the freedom to freely exercise their faith, but according to Pew research as of 2014, they also constitute about 30 percent of South Korea's population.[1]

As we consider the contribution of these pioneers of the faith, we reflect on the countless martyrs who have lost their lives even in this twenty-first century, including in North Korea, in other countries in South Asia, and particularly in Africa and the Middle East. Today, we have much to learn from the history of our Korean brothers and sisters. The sustaining empowerment of the Holy Spirit has enabled and will continue to enable the followers of Jesus to rise up from the greatest trials and move on toward the full coming of God's promised kingdom. The stories of the Korean

1. Phillip Connor, "6 Facts about South Korea's Growing Christian Population," Pew Research Center, Fact Tank, August 12, 2014, www.pewresearch.org/fact-tank/2014/08/12/6-facts-about-christianity-in-south-korea.

church and other persecuted churches must be heard by the new generations of Christians. These stories will serve to strengthen the resolve of those being persecuted today. Even more important, those of us who live easy and undisturbed lives in the West need to wake up to our complacency. Like the churches of Sardis and Laodicea in the Book of Revelation, we need to repent and to wake up from our long spiritual nap. I wish the history of the church would be different, but it seems that persecution and martyrdom are the norm rather than the exception. Koreans, Korean Americans, and American Christians from all ethnic backgrounds should maximize the freedoms we have today, freedoms that we cannot take for granted.

THE SOCIOPOLITICAL INFLUENCE OF MEGACHURCHES

We consider here the intersection of politics and religion. As noted by Won Sang Lee, the signing in 1882 of the Treaty of Peace, Amity, Commerce, and Navigation between Korea and the United States opened the way for the first medical missionary to enter Korea in 1884. It is very important for the church not to alienate itself from the political life of the country where it finds itself. We should not exercise our power or influence to sway the political process merely in order to benefit us, but vigilance is needed that our basic rights are protected.

This point is particularly relevant because there is a tendency for megachurches in the United States to stand aloof from political life. Church involvement in the sociopolitical arena, or the lack of it, can have critical and far-reaching consequences. As we witness in the Korean experience, Christians can benefit from the right kind of political decisions, which can have an enormous effect for good. The church must be vigilant and exercise its proper role in the sociopolitical debates of the country. Megachurches sometimes have a tendency to criticize and condemn political decisions contrary to their theological positions. What is needed, rather, is an active, wise, and strategic involvement in the political life of the community. This is of particular importance given the numbers and the possible influence of megachurches. Won Sang Lee describes three churches in Canada whose conception of the missional church includes pursuing a holistic mission. Such a mission includes proper involvement of churches in the political life of the community or the country.

SPIRITUAL HERITAGE AND CURRENT PRACTICES

Won Sang Lee speaks of the spiritual heritage bequeathed by the early missionaries to Korea. He reminds us that they "left a spiritual legacy through their biblical teaching and sacrifices" (263). The early Korean Christians also left a valuable legacy. Today, Christians around the world recognize and admire the commitment of Korean Christians to prayer, which in many ways is unique. Prayer is practiced by individuals daily throughout the day, many churches offer early morning or night prayer opportunities, and there are even mass prayer rallies. Koreans in the United States often celebrate prayer rallies. On November 11, 2014, approximately 6,000 people gathered at the Verizon Wireless Amphitheatre in Irvine, California, and prayed for eight hours on behalf of the nation.

Most Koreans believe that churches that do not pray for growth, in most cases simply do not grow. Prayer for them is essential in moving not just God's heart but also their own. It can be said that the foundation of the Korean believer lies in a daily prayer communion with God. This prayer life is common to most Korean Christians, regardless of the size of the congregations in which they worship.

When asked, most Korean Christians will claim that the vibrancy of their Christianity is found in their faithfulness to daily prayer. Congregations of other traditions or ethnicities, both large and small, have much to learn from their Korean brothers and sisters. There is a perception that most American Christians today struggle to maintain prayer as a daily practice. According to a 2013 Pew Research Center survey, more than half of Americans (55 percent) said they pray every day.[2] I do not question the validity of the Pew Forum survey, but at

2. Michael Lipka, "5 Facts about Prayer," Pew Research Center, Fact Tank, May 6, 2015, www.pewresearch.org/fact-tank/2015/05/06/5-facts-about-prayer.

the same time, based on my experience as a local pastor, I can attest that my parishioners found it a challenge to set aside time to pray regularly.

I feel very strongly that American Christianity in general has much to learn from the past and current examples of the prayer life of our Korean brothers and sisters. I often wonder what would be the impact of American Christians in the United States if we devoted ourselves to prayer as Korean Christians do. Megachurches, because of their large size and complex structure, seem to be the least likely environment in which to develop a strong sense of communal prayer. This reality poses a challenge to these churches. At the same time, many megachurches have been able to develop vibrant and strong networks of small groups. It is in these small familiar units that prayer can flourish; many Korean megachurches have been very successful in accomplishing this level of prayer.

NEW GENERATIONS UP FOR GRABS

I concur with Won Sang Lee when he states that "without the next generation, we cannot continue to carry out Christ's missional mandate. This truth poses a fundamental challenge, to which the dying churches in Europe testify" (263). According to the data provided by Lee, "A surprising 82 percent of Korean American youth desire to leave the church after graduating from high school." The exodus of millennials and younger generations from our churches is well documented. Studies show that fewer young adults today belong to any particular faith than do older people. Young adults today are also less likely to be affiliated than were their parents' and grandparents' generations when they were young. One in four members of the millennial generation are not affiliated with any particular faith.[3]

The reasons for this retreat from church life are many and complex. I agree with Won Sang Lee that "the church has a responsibility for the sake of its missional mandate to encourage parents to take seriously their duty to bring up their children in Christian faith" (265). The role of parents in shaping the faith and spirituality

3. Allison Pond, Gregory Smith, and Scott Clement, "Religion among the Millennials," Pew Research Center, Religion and Public Life, February 17, 2010, www.pewforum.org/2010/02/17/religion-among-the-millennials.

of their children is critical. One very important factor, often overlooked in Western Christianity, is the lack of a sense of community. Today's younger generations have a strong need for belonging. The strong emphasis in the Korean culture on the importance of the family and the inclusion of the older generations provides a healthy model for us. Not that this model has been perfect or always successful, but it provides a strong foundation.

In our current cultural scene, and because of their lavish and media-rich content, it seems that megachurches are better positioned to reach out successfully to the younger generations. Media themselves, however, will not satisfy the needs of young people. Most research shows that millennials are engaged in a search for meaning and authenticity. They look to the past as a guide to a present that is so filled with change. A Pew Forum study reveals that "millennials respect their elders. A majority say that the older generation is superior to the younger generation when it comes to moral values and work ethic. Also, more than six in ten say that families have a responsibility to have an elderly parent come live with them if that parent wants to."[4]

Megachurches are well positioned to attract younger generations, but once they bring them in, they must provide a holistic faith and a spiritual experience that emphasize life in community. They must be communities in which both young and old grow together in the likeness of Christ.

CHURCHES THAT WORK WELL TOGETHER

Won Sang Lee recognizes the need for Korean Christians to "invest time, talent, and resources in reconciliation among diverse ethnic groups for the sake of the Gospel" (266). I agree, in that Koreans, as well as any other ethnic group, have a responsibility to promote racial unity and reconciliation. For the purposes of this reflection, I would like to suggest that Christian unity and reconciliation are also necessary. From my perspective, a negative contribution of Korean Protestantism is its fragmentation into hundreds of denominational groups. This fragmentation represents a challenge to the

4. Paul Taylor and Scott Keeter, eds., *Millennials: A Portrait of Generation Next* (Pew Research Center, February 2010). www.pewsocialtrends.org/files/2010/10/millennials-confident-connected-open-to-change.pdf.

unity of the church as portrayed by Jesus and the apostles (John 17:20–23). In 2012 I had the opportunity to attend the World Council of Churches Assembly in Busan, Korea. While there, I was saddened to witness the strong divisions among Korean Christians.

I am also not encouraged by the tendency of megachurches to minister in isolation from other Christians. Because of their affluence and access to all kinds of resources, megachurches have a tendency to turn inward. As Pastor Lee has indicated, "Korean American megachurches would be well advised . . . to cooperate more closely with mission agencies and with other churches" (pp. 270). The future growth of the church in the United States depends to a great extent on our capacity to reach new generations, who have, for the most part, left behind old ethnic, social, and theological divisions.

A FINAL WORD

In conclusion, I generally agree with Lee's concern that "modern churches are definitely under attack and will be utterly defeated unless the Holy Spirit empowers them to truly make missions their primary goal" (270). I also hope that we are able to recognize that the primary goal is not just missions, but people.

Today we have access to all the technological and organizational means necessary to present the Gospel to all people. The one important area in which we are lacking is our commitment to preach and live a faith that is communal in nature. Author Christian Piatt identifies five reasons why we need intentional community: (1) we long to be known, to share our lives with one another; (2) we need to share each other's burdens; (3) we need to mark sacred time; (4) we need to hold each other accountable; and (5) we long for sanctuary.[5] We want something set aside that is peaceful, different, quiet, and special.

Our mission should not just be to grow the church but to be the church in a world that is in desperate need of meaning, belonging, and wholeness.

5. See Christian Piatt, "Five Reasons We Still Need Intentional Community (Regardless of Your Faith)" (Patheos: Hosting the Conversation of Faith, July 16, 2015), www.patheos.com/blogs/christianpiatt/2015/07/five-reasons-we-still-need-intentional-community-regardless-of-your-faith.

32

Megachurches and Mission: Lessons and Challenges

Six mission and church leaders were asked to prepare brief written statements related to the topic of megachurches and mission. The topics for their presentations were chosen for them—or assigned to them—by the forum's coordinators. Following, in the order in which they spoke at the forum, are the texts of their remarks.

Editors

◇◇◇◇◇◇◇◇◇◇◇◇◇◇◇◇◇◇◇◇◇◇◇◇◇◇◇◇◇◇◇◇◇◇◇◇◇◇

The Theme of Megachurch Accountability in Missions

J. Nelson Jennings

For this panel, I have been asked to respond to three questions related to the theme of the consultation. I will answer each in turn.

What led me two years ago to propose megachurch accountability in mission as the theme for KGMLF 2015?

The Overseas Ministries Study Center has played an important role in bringing together various mission-related people who otherwise would not ordinarily meet. One prime example is the way in which, starting in the 1970s, Roman Catholic scholars and practitioners have been brought into what had been a strictly Protestant OMSC. Another vitally important initiative also began in the 1970s, this one called the Study Group (later the Mission Leadership Forum). This semiannual, invitation-only, off-the-record weekend gathering has involved evangelical and mainline mission leaders—who in those days did not commonly meet together—discussing concerns they shared in common and, as a result, becoming trusted friends. For its part, OMSC maintained its nonexclusionary embrace of various Christian traditions. Combined with its small and nonthreatening organizational status, OMSC could thus invite various people for periods of rest, discussion, and fellowship.

Another OMSC hallmark has been the study of important yet sensitive mission topics that others might not be in a position to tackle. Again, OMSC's nonaffiliated position with respect to any particular denomination or Christian tradition has freed it from ecclesiastical turf wars and political landmines that can cripple the capacity to discuss sensitive matters honestly and openly. The first two KGMLF gatherings addressed crucial topics for Korean missions, namely, accountability in missions generally and accountability in missions in relation to missionary families.

A topic that I understood to be urgent, vitally important, and extremely sensitive for Korean churches and mission agencies concerned megachurches. Indeed, the explosive sensitivity of the subject was made evident by the consternation shown among the planning group participants during our lunch together two years ago in Seoul. By God's grace, the importance and urgency of considering the topic prevailed over fears of backlash or damaged relationships.

In what ways have my hopes for this consultation been fulfilled?

First of all, the very fact that any forum whatsoever about the sensitive yet crucial topic of megachurch accountability in mission—with a particular focus on Korean megachurches—has actually become a reality is cause for much rejoicing. I had some doubts along the way that this consultation would ever take place, including more than once during that memorable planning luncheon two years ago. Moreover, we were aiming toward including a much broader range of non-Korean participants than the primarily North American list in the first two KGMLFs. The current group is indeed more worldwide than the earlier ones, although I admit I was hoping for representation from almost every region even greater than what we were able to assemble. I would like to have seen more participants from China, India, Southeast Asia, Latin America, Francophone Africa, and Japan, to name just some of the most obvious examples. Even so, best efforts were put forth and much prayer was offered, so in the end I believe the very best group according to God's leading has been gathered.

The quality and worldwide range of participants for this KGMLF, including the various presenters and respondents, have largely met my hopes and expectations. We were not able to secure representation from a few areas that would have been helpful, but that failure was not due to a lack of effort. Furthermore, having seen the forum's subtopics take shape, I am very pleased with the scope of essays contributed by presenters and respondents. The projected headings have largely been addressed by the essays, such that KGMLF participants and readers of the resulting books should come away with a much broader understanding of the themes associated with megachurch mission initiatives.

Originally, I had hoped that representatives from several other widely known non-Korean megachurches, such as Saddleback Church and Hillsong Church, could be present. I realize, though, that a more extensive focus on world-famous megachurches would have prevented the invaluable information about others that are not only major actors in their own right, but are also in positions to wield tremendous influence in the foreseeable future. Yet again, the wisdom of God has proven greater than my foolish aspirations.

That most of the essays are already edited for publication (at least in English) in time for the forum meeting actually exceeds what I had anticipated. The faithfulness of Jinbong Kim in gathering the essays and of Dwight Baker in spearheading the English copyediting are to be gratefully acknowledged and highly commended. So is the work so far by Abe Kugyong Koh on the Korean version of the forthcoming book. Having served in Onnuri Community Church since early September, I have had a front-row vantage point for appreciating the logistic preparations involved in hosting this particular international conference. As big as Onnuri Church is, it does not have infinite personnel or finances. A great deal of diligent work has gone into the myriad details involved in facilitating a comfortable, meaningful, and memorable consultation. I could not have hoped for a better and harder working group than the staff members of Onnuri Community Church who have tirelessly given of themselves to make this KGMLF more than fulfill everyone's hopes.

What are some major themes that need further exploration?

I will mention three themes related to this forum's topic centered on megachurches, then raise two topics that extend the reach of our vision.

First, even though one central goal of this KGMLF has been to cultivate trust among mission leaders who are either directly involved in or variously related to megachurch mission initiatives, this major theme of trust is undoubtedly going to need more examination. Mistrust that has developed over many years cannot be bridged by a single forum. The mistrust concerning megachurches in general, including mission efforts, runs deep and wide enough to require significant time and prayerful attention. I am deeply encouraged by the meeting among megachurch mission pastors that has been planned for a time soon after this conference ends.

Second, megachurch missions and ministries among the world's poor, marginalized, and oppressed populations will likely require much more focused study than this particular KGMLF can provide. The theme of megachurch accountability lends itself to attention by nonmegachurch mission participants, especially including missionaries, mission agencies, and medium- and smaller-sized churches. That theme is obviously crucial, but so is mission among marginalized peoples. Megachurches by nature approach the world's lowliest peoples from a position of greater resources of people, money, and programs. How that happens well, including through megachurch-established NGOs, will need ongoing attention.

Third, one theme that has emerged through the case studies and discussions is the combined particularity and complexity of megachurch mission involvements. For example, Australia's Hillsong, Guatemala's Christian Fraternity, and Kenya's Mavuno are all quite different from each other. Making general characterizations about megachurches and mission, therefore, is difficult, but the traits shared among various megachurch activities beg for common examination.

One major mission theme that a future gathering might address is that of the missionary's national and cultural identity: self-understood, actually practiced, and perceived by others. That matter is vitally important in all cases, but it seems particularly vital for how Korean missionaries function, given the criticism that often arises concerning their Korean ways.

A second topic is multidenominational cooperation. Many conservative Christians dislike the term "ecumenical" because of its connotations of unfaithful compromise. Nevertheless, the term itself should be useful for all Christians in speaking about partnering with those beyond their own ecclesiastical confines.

A third topic worthy of consideration, I believe, concerns how Christian traditions, agencies, churches, and missionaries are perceived by others. As Christians on mission, we stand to learn a great deal about ourselves through the eyes of those who do not yet share our beliefs or approve of our goals. For example, we might come to see that some of our internal differences may not be as great as we think they are. We might also better realize some of our hidden motives, regardless of how pure we might believe them to be.

Overall, KGMLF 2015 has raised more questions rather than providing simple answers. I hope that through this greater process clarity has emerged concerning what actually are the meaningful questions we face.

◇◇

Similarities and Differences among Megachurches in Latin America

Jorge H. López

Even though I am not expert on the subject of missions, the invitation to be part of this panel made me think about a dinner I had with Ralph Winter in the early 1980s. Luis Bush, an expert on mission mobilization, asked Winter to convince me to get involved in missions. Winter responded: "Every pastor of a megachurch is already involved in missions because he is reaching lots of people through his ministry."

At my request, Carlos López, rector of the Central American Mission's theological seminary, prepared the following observations on megachurches in Latin America, which I now present to you.

"Megachurches in Latin America: A Very Brief Analysis," by Carlos López

This brief analysis arises from considering two questions: In what ways are Latin American megachurches similar to each other? and, In what ways are they different from one another? The perspective that follows comes from that of an external observer. I am not the founder of a megachurch, nor am I a minister in one of the many Latin American megachurches. I am, however, an eyewitness of this phenomenon, which began in the decade of the 1980s and has radically changed the image of evangelical Christians and their way of "being church." It is impossible to speak about the evangelical Christian church in an informed way without taking note of the divide between the period before and the period after the rise of the megachurches. It is an important historical marker.

Before answering in summary form the questions posed at the beginning of this brief analysis, I mention five important marks that megachurches have imprinted on the evangelical church of our time. The points are important because it is from them that the similarities and differences among megachurches today emerge. I mention these marks in terms of traits that megachurches today have rejected from traditional evangelicalism.

Much-overused evangelical improvisation. Through use of a contemporary and well-prepared liturgy, megachurches have challenged the "spirit of evangelical improvisation." The current style of contemporary music and use of (semi)professional musicians, top-quality musical instruments and sound systems, with the very best in audio, lights, podium, and platform, all reflect a professionalism that is the envy of other churches. Since the arrival of the megachurches, the liturgy of the church today is no longer the same.

"Kilometric services," which only the Spirit and the preacher know when will end. The dynamics of megachurches ensure that their meetings are brief. Large screens save time during the inevitable ads and announcements. The assistants know what they are there for: to praise God and to listen to the preacher. Everything else can be deferred to other times and places, such as the annex areas of the temple or worship sanctuary (e.g., conversations, eating together as a church family, and participating in additional ministries of the church). Services or meetings in urban churches today do not last as long as they did before the arrival of the megachurches.

The bad taste of "decorating committees." Megachurches have rediscovered the value of aesthetics in the decoration of their places of worship. Everything seems to be designed with the theme of the preaching or teaching for the day or month in view. Many brothers and sisters who are professionals in the art of design now offer their time to provide aesthetic advice so as to visually convey to the audience what is wanted. The temples of urban churches today are more concerned than before with their aesthetics.

The taboo on women's ministry. Megachurches have revalued the profile of women in the evangelical church. Women's ministry, beginning with that of the female pastor, is an important axis in the leadership structure of megachurches. The magnitude of the shift is seen in the participation of women in preaching, in public teaching—despite resistance on the part of the leadership of certain ministries—and in leading Sunday worship. Despite much gnashing of teeth, women's ministry is finding its rightful place in the new urban churches.

The lethargic preacher's sermon. Megachurch preachers are skillful and dynamic communicators. They speak in a language that everyone can understand. They speak of realities faced by the people to whom they minister. They do not go wandering through the bushes. They do not use their words to beat their members down. Even if a preacher is not a skilled and dynamic communicator, the time allotted for the sermon is not long enough to put people to sleep. From the megachurches, preachers in urban churches have learned to speak with understandable, short words—in sermons that do not exceed forty minutes.

For these and many more distinguishing marks, we thank God for the megachurch movement. From the very beginning of this movement of God, the evangelical church has not been the same. We can easily speak of a before and an after, marked by the upsurge of the megachurches.

SIMILARITIES AND DIFFERENCES

Based on personal observation, I list below several similarities and differences of megachurches in Latin America.

Similarities:

1. They use contemporary liturgy.
2. They have well-organized and brief meetings.
3. They feature musical instruments and professional sound systems and lighting.
4. They show a refined aesthetic in their facilities.
5. Their women's ministries enjoy freedom in exercising leadership.
6. Their pastors are founders or remain for a long time in their pastorate.
7. Their parking facilities are as expansive as their facilities for attendees. (That is, most people drive to services.)
8. They utilize a technological platform that allows them to multiply their services, whether by radio, TV, or social networks.
9. They have full-time staff to meet people's needs.

10. They offer a variety and multiplicity of ministries to meet the needs of all members (e.g., children, youth, adults, young couples, single, widowed, divorced, and elderly).

Differences: Not all megachurches:

1. are Pentecostal, neo-Pentecostal, or charismatic.
2. belong to the New Apostolic network.
3. have a tendency toward a prosperity theology.
4. have schools or provide other services to society.
5. are independent; some depend on movements abroad.
6. have pastors with theological training.
7. have their own institutes or seminars.
8. owe their growth to small groups.

◇◇◇◇◇◇◇◇◇◇◇◇◇◇◇◇◇◇◇◇◇◇◇◇◇◇◇◇◇◇◇◇◇◇◇◇

Missional Roles of the Megachurch, Illustrated by Missionary Works of the Yoido Full Gospel Church

Tae Wook Um

Baptism in the Holy Spirit is an empowering experience for Christians who are evangelizing. Spirit baptism also unites Christians from different backgrounds, bringing them to become one in the Spirit. The experience of Spirit baptism creates a vision of a community of believers in Christ, transforms people, and produces communal cultural values.[1] The Holy Spirit enables believers to love and serve their neighbors through various spiritual gifts.[2]

The contributions of Yoido Full Gospel Church (YFGC) to the Holy Spirit movement in Korea and the rest of the world have been monumental in the past, and the church continues to be active in the movement today. The Holy Spirit movement of YFGC is a continuation of the broader characteristics of Korean

1. Shane Clifton, "Ecumenism from the Bottom Up: A Pentecostal Perspective," *Journal of Ecumenical Studies* 47 (2012): 578.

2. Jeffrey T. Snell, "Beyond the Individual and into the World," *PNEUMA: Journal of the Society for Pentecostal Studies* 14 (1992): 44.

revival movements.[3] The Holy Spirit movements of Korean churches, which were started by the revivals of 1903 and 1907, established a tradition of going beyond denominations and doctrines to become one as Christians and to engage in social issues. From the beginning, the Holy Spirit movements of Korean churches included not only the salvation of individuals but also a communal heart for all people, as well as a spirit of social service as an important way for Christians to practice the love of Christ. Inheriting the legacies of Korean Holy Spirit movements, YFGC remains enthusiastic about evangelism and active in the ministries of loving and sharing, and it continues to mature in both individual and social dimensions. Since its founding in 1958, YFGC has sent 661 missionaries to 64 countries and planted 1,187 churches over the world which are attended by 127,330 church members. I share here the ministries of YFGC in three aspects: the church (1) with its neighbors, (2) in society, and (3) for the nation.

CHURCH WITH ITS NEIGHBORS

YFGC has actively performed works of service inside and outside Korea through Good People, the NGO that it established in July 1999 as a means of providing international relief and development. Good People not only lets all people know about the needs and realities of their neighbors around the world, but also provides systematic and professional help. Its services include child protection, education, prevention of disease, emergency relief, one-to-one overseas child affiliation, and efforts to relieve poverty in areas neglected by existing governments and programs.

The works of Good People at home are for North Korean migrants, multicultural families, and foreigners staying in the country. And by dispatching an emergency relief agency when natural disasters such as typhoons, droughts, earthquakes, and tsunamis occur anywhere in the world, it carries out disaster relief, rescue of human lives, and excavation of disaster sites, as well as medical services and anti-epidemic measures.[4] Also, through

3. Young-hoon Lee, *The Holy Spirit Movement in Korea: Its Historical and Theological Development* (Oxford: Regnum Books International, 2009).

4. The Good People Emergency Relief Agency, begun in 1999 with relief activity for refugees in Kosovo and the sufferers in Turkey.

follow-up services like water-well purification and the construction and operation of child care centers, it helps in the rapid restoration of devastated areas. Good People took a major role in the work of recovery in the areas damaged by the 2004 Indonesia tsunami, the 2005 Pakistan earthquake, and the 2010 Japan earthquake which caused the destruction of a nuclear reactor.

In addition, the work of Good People overseas includes educational work, medical service, community development, and child support. Its educational work is mainly concentrated in Southeast Asia. For instance, in 2012 Good People established a large secondary school in Lan Xang, Laos, as well as a kindergarten in Vietnam.[5] Also it has built Good People Yeon-shim Lim's Mission School, in Turkana, Kenya, in honor of missionary Yeon-shim Lim, known as the Mom of Turkana, who devoted twenty-eight years of her life to the people there.

Medical work by Good People includes building the Capas Municipal Hospital for the Ita minority ethnic group in the Philippines (2009), building a treatment center for cholera patients in Haiti (2010), and sending medical devices to a Mombasa health care center in Kenya (2012).[6] It has provided free cataract surgery for 1,619 patients who were in danger of blindness in nine different countries, including Vietnam, Mongolia, and Tajikistan. Good People also has sponsored surgery for children suffering from heart disease in various foreign countries.

Good People has been active in other worldwide ministries as well. It established an IT education center as a rehabilitation project in Iran after the country suffered considerable damage from an earthquake. It has built and operated an orphanage in Sri Lanka, and it reconstructed a destroyed school in Jakarta, Indonesia. In January 2012 it constructed seventy modern houses and seven septic tanks, as well as installing a solar power system for the Ita people in the Philippines.[7] In April 2010 it launched a

5. *Kukmin Daily*, May 12, 2012; September 27, 2012. All articles cited from *Kukmin Daily*, *News Power*, and *Newsis* are in Korean.

6. "Good People Opened Mombasa Health Center," *News Power*, December 19, 2012.

7. *Kukmin Daily*, March 1, 2012.

well-drilling project for residents of Ilmarba, Kenya.[8] In all these ways, YFGC expresses the love of Christ beyond Korea and its region through Good People. Through such practices, the church has been fulfilling the vision of unity in the love of Christ, while overcoming discrimination, jealousy, and enmity between the haves and the have-nots.

CHURCH IN SOCIETY

YFGC has carried out various social welfare activities for its neighbors troubled by poverty and disease. First, since 1992 the church has conducted Sharing Bread of Grace, which is a layman-initiated service led by the Senior Deacons Fellowship. They distribute a little bread-shaped coin bank to people in the church to collect money for this ministry. These coin banks can hold three hundred 100-won coins, or a total of 30,000 won about $25), which can provide food for a month for a child in Africa. This little coin bank conveys the love of Christ to many African children who are at risk from poverty, disease, and warfare.

Since 1984 YFGC has provided free surgery for children with heart disease. This program was first started by the church when it raised the full amount needed for surgery for a child in poverty dying from heart disease. Since then, church members have participated in the movement by collecting wastepaper, milk cartons, and old clothes to raise money for the surgery fees needed for children with heart disease. Since the year 2000, this service has been expanded to children in other countries such as China, Cambodia, Mongolia, the Philippines, Iraq, and Malaysia. As of January 2014, a total of 4,532 children with heart disease had been given a new chance in life through this service of free surgery.[9]

In December 1985 YFGC decided to give aid to young people and elderly persons who had no one to rely on. The next month the church launched Elim Welfare Directorate and began to construct Elim, an entire welfare center, or town. On July 26, 1988, this welfare town was completed. It included a senior citizen center, the Elim Vocational Training Institute, a hall, a welfare center, and apartments. Since then, by opening a mission center in 1994 and a

8. *Newsis*, April 5, 2010.

9. *Full Gospel Family Newspaper*, February 2, 2014.

nursing center in 1997, this town has become the largest welfare center in Asia. Elim Vocational Training Institute offers technical training to young people, providing room and board for them while simultaneously inculcating vision and concrete goals for the future, all in a context of Christian faith. For students, there is no cost whatsoever. Those who complete the whole course receive certification as second-level national technicians and then receive help in finding jobs.

Full Gospel Hospice, begun in January 2001, carries out education of volunteer hospice caregivers. So far, 1,272 volunteers have received hospice training, and of that number, 612 have entered active volunteer service. Currently, trained workers care for patients in Sem Mool Hospice, Korea Cancer Center Hospital, Ewha Womans University Mokdong Hospital, Soodong Senior Hospital, and Elim Welfare Town, plus fifty cancer patients currently being cared for at home under the Junggu District office and the Yeongdeungpo-gu office. Good People welfare center opened on November 23, 2012, and includes a patient room, nursing room, leisure hall, laundry room, and bathing room. In addition, with well-provisioned facilities including an ambulance and medical equipment, it cares for patients using a medical team, social workers, nurses, and pastors.

CHURCH FOR THE NATION

YFGC has performed a ministry of helping North Koreans suffering from starvation, which is an effort in preparing for North Korean missions and unification. As a part of this work, the church has implemented support in the form of providing seed corn and fertilizer, constructing and operating a soybean oil factory, donating food to North Korean children facing starvation, and providing an antituberculosis drug. It has consistently supplied ground cereals to many schools in North Korea to promote children's growth.

In December 4, 2007, YFGC began construction of the Pyongyang Cho Yonggi Hospital, which is to specialize in heart disease, part of the overall medical help it offers to North Korea.[10] This hospital, located on a site of 66,000 square meters, is budgeted at

10. See *Full Gospel Family Newspaper,* December 2 and 30, 2007, for more detailed information on the Pyongyang Cho Yonggi Hospital.

2 billion won ($1.7 million) and will have 260 beds. YFGC is providing all supplies for the construction except sand and labor; a Pyongyang construction company is doing the actual building. By treating and caring for North Korean patients with heart disease, the hospital will be expressing the love of Christ, facilitating personal exchange between North and South Koreans, and contributing toward the time of eventual unification. Now, because of heightened political tensions, construction has been discontinued, although seven stories of frame construction have been completed.

Good People established the Free Citizen Education Center to help the settlement of North Korean migrants.[11] This center has various programs necessary for the financial independence of North Korean migrants. It is not easy for these migrants to adjust to the social system of the Republic of Korea, which consists of a liberal democracy and a free market economy, for they are accustomed to the very different communistic system of North Korea. YFGC helps them to get used to the new surroundings through a customized educational system at the Free Citizen Education Center. At present, the center has completed twelve eight-month terms of education, with 520 graduates. The curriculum consists of a six-month period of basic education, aimed at helping migrants adapt to the society of the Republic of Korea, followed by two months of advanced education, preparing them for employment. The center hopes to help North Korean migrants become Christians, with a holistic faith, which will help prepare them to stand on their own feet and will also nurture future leaders for the time of unification. For their financial independence, Good People operates a project to start private businesses, called Good People Family Mart. Since the first one was launched, eighteen more have been founded.

CONCLUSION

The spirituality of sharing, collaboration with other Christians, and revivalism are the characteristics of the Holy Spirit movement of megachurch YFGC. The church's revival has been fueled

11. See the web homepage of Good People and of Free Citizen Education Center for more detailed information about Free Citizen Education Center; yfgc.fgtv.com.

by the passion of the church members to express God's love through evangelism and the power of the Holy Spirit. As a result, YFGC has produced remarkable church growth, personal conversions, spiritual growth of church members, and church members bearing spiritual fruit by serving and sharing with others. Every church does not need to be a megachurch. Large or small, though, a church needs to be faithful in carrying out the role God has given it for his kingdom.

As a megachurch, YFGC has contributed to church unity and cooperation and has practiced the love of God through social relief work and welfare activities in Korea and the rest of the world. The church continues to carry on the work of the Holy Spirit to change the world, individuals, and societies, as well as bringing the Gospel to the world through unity and collaboration with other denominations.[12]

12. A full list of YFGC outreach ministries is available on request to the Mission Department of YFGC. Send requests by e-mail to yfgcpr@hanmail.net.

◇◇◇◇◇◇◇◇◇◇◇◇◇◇◇◇◇◇◇◇◇◇◇◇◇◇◇◇◇◇◇◇◇◇◇

Mission-Megachurch Relations

Kyung Nam Park

I have been asked to comment on mission-megachurch relations, speaking from my experience as a missionary and my observations as an executive of an independent mission agency. When I worked in the mission field, I was part of an international NGO that consisted of more than thirty different organizations. Seeing how well brothers and sisters in Christ worked together was a good experience. I could see the beauty of the body of Christ and the strength of collaboration. Until I started working in Korea, however, I did not realize that collaboration should extend beyond the different mission organizations. While serving in WEC Korea during the past seven years, I have come to realize that collaboration is very important for all of us if we are to do healthy, resilient, effective ministry for God's kingdom. For mission is not only a matter of what some particular agency is doing; mission is kingdom work being done through the global church, which encompasses both mission agencies and local churches. My comments arise from my reflections during my seven years at the Korean headquarters of WEC International.

THE KEY: COLLABORATION

In *The Church Is Bigger Than You Think*, Patrick Johnston addresses the importance of collaboration among local churches, mission agencies, and training institutes for God's kingdom.[1] My experience as director of WEC Korea has also shown that collaboration is vitally important. Without it, our mission efforts will not be effective, and we will fail to achieve our goals. No matter what the size of a church, no matter how mission agencies may strive, no matter how capable each person may be, if we act in isolation, the mission cannot be carried out as Jesus commanded. What I like to call "kingdom collaboration" is essential.

In my observation, the major difference between small churches and megachurches is simply the amount of resources each has and the systems they are able to develop. Megachurches have huge amounts of human and financial resources, and thus, in general, they are able to be more active in mission. Their human and financial resources give them a large advantage in serving the kingdom. They still need, however, to be collaborative with other local churches and mission agencies. Setting up their own system might seem to be the easiest way for churches to put their conception of mission into practice, but acting alone opens the possibility of duplication with other churches or mission organizations. For example, a church purchased land in a city for the purpose of starting an educational center there, not knowing that two other educational centers were already in operation in the city. The appropriateness of the action the church took continued to raise questions for several years.

Drawing from past experience, I would like to mention

1. Patrick Johnstone, *The Church Is Bigger Than You Think: The Unfinished Work of World Evangelism*, 6th ed. (Korean edition; WEC Korea, 2010), 232–35.

several positive steps that can be taken for the sake of being more effective for God's kingdom.

In missionary equipping. First, megachurches and mission agencies can collaborate in preparing and equipping workers. Traditionally, candidates have come to a mission and started the preparation process with the agency. Toward the middle or end of this process, their local church would be informed. As a result, the mission agency will have spent a long time coming to understand who a candidate is, and the megachurch may be frustrated. To avoid such a disconnect, WEC Korea asks for church leaders' recommendation, and the candidates' mission pastors are to be consulted from the beginning.

A megachurch also can take the initiative by consulting with mission agencies regarding mission candidate selection. WEC Korea, for example, gives advice as to the kind of preparation candidates would need and tells how we go about training their candidates and how we work on the mission field. Some megachurches have a policy that all workers supported by the church should be part of an appropriate mission agency with a member care system and strategies that have been approved by the church. Through these efforts, both megachurches and mission agencies can help candidates to be better equipped.

A couple of years ago, a megachurch and WEC Korea prepared a couple of candidates and sent them out. When I met the senior pastor, his testimony was very impressive. "In the kingdom of God, we have different roles. A local church's role is to care for and nurture people; the mission agency's role is doing the task. Therefore, I am very glad that we can work together with WEC Korea and want to see more young people able to go." He emphasized the characteristic roles of modality and sodality, as well as collaboration between the two entities.

Several megachurches have this type of relationship with WEC Korea, which has proven very effective. We are expecting more megachurches to collaborate in similar fashion.

In missionary member care. Second, megachurches and mission agencies can collaborate in caring for and refreshing missionaries.

Without good member care, workers cannot serve long in their position or be as effective as they could be. One retired pastor said to me, "I sent and supported several hundred missionaries. I thought sending was important, but I did not really understand the importance of caring for and refreshing workers." After more than twenty years of mission effort, he realized that his church could not provide care and effectiveness by itself. Many workers were sent directly by the church with inadequate provision for accountability structures. The church has now set a policy that all missionaries must be part of an agency. The process has not gone well so far, however, because of resistance by the workers. This example gives just a small picture of the perspective that megachurches should have. If the church does not build up appropriate caring and accountability structures, huge amounts of human and financial resources can be misused.

Member care for missionaries should be shared between megachurches and mission agencies. Basically, mission agencies should be responsible for caring for workers on the field, and megachurches should take the lead at the home level. Through such collaboration, missionaries can become more effective and stable in their ministry.

In mission strategizing. Third, megachurches and mission agencies can collaborate in developing mission strategy and in mobilization. In the twenty-first century, the nature of world mission is changing rapidly. Most missions are aware of changes that are occurring and desire international collaboration. Local churches may be less informed about these changes, since their main role as modalities is caring for their members.

WEC Korea's strategy is to work among unengaged, unreached people groups (UUPG) and in church planting. We have received several requests for consultation from megachurches, and we try to show how our strategy can apply to megachurches. Some churches embrace our strategy actively; others are hesitant about accepting the idea. I have observed that members of megachurch congregations have various needs. Not every member's need or capability is the same. Many members want to participate in mission more actively, so megachurches should make multiple opportunities for participation available to them. Some churches develop a two-track approach: a strategy for UUPG in collaboration with UUPG-focused agencies such as WEC, and a strategy for open countries in collaboration with agencies using, for example, an NGO format.

Our experience shows that, for the sake of more effective and strategic collaboration, mission agencies should be aware of megachurches' situation. Recently, WEC Korea launched the Sender School Program for local churches. We are trying to shift our mobilization outlook from a "goer-oriented" to a "sender-oriented" paradigm. This shift focuses on encouraging ordinary church members to acknowledge their calling as senders rather than just as helpers for missionaries. The program has been well received by both small churches and megachurches. We pray that God will use this program for the kingdom.

CONCLUSION

Without local churches, it is not possible to do ministry in a cross-cultural context. In the first century, the church was both a modality and a sodality. The Holy Spirit, however, guided and empowered the church to take on three roles: that of the local church (e.g., the Antioch church), the apostolic band (e.g., Paul and Barnabas's missionary band), and the training organization (e.g., Paul's lectures in the Hall of Tyrannus).[2] Originally, these three elements were part of the church and thus had organic relationships with each other. In our time, megachurches and mission agencies should seek better ways to work together for the kingdom and try to build deeper relationships, so that they glorify God in unity in one spirit. Kingdom collaboration is key to mission in the twenty-first century.

2. Ibid.

◇◇

A Lesson from the Korean Methodist Church

Dong Hwa Tae

Based upon my personal experience at the headquarters of the Korean Methodist Church (KMC), I would like to offer practical reflections on how mission agencies and churches currently cooperate with the General Board of Missions (GBM) of the denomination.

UNIQUENESS OF THE KMC

As a denomination, KMC has characteristics that differ from those of the Methodist Church in the United States or in Great Britain. Briefly, KMC maintains an episcopal system but, as much as possible, ensures the autonomy of individual congregations. In episcopacy, the bishop typically holds the power to appoint ministers and to own and use property. This arrangement centralizes power and can promote consistency throughout the entire denomination. Structurally and legally, KMC is episcopal in its ownership of church properties, but it allows its individual churches to operate more congregationally in terms of nominating their own pastors and carrying out local ministerial functions. Similar characteristics can be seen in KMC's approach to missions: while GBM is in charge of the administrative and legal aspects of the installation, dispatch, and management of missionaries, sending of missionaries and managing their mission work in the countries to which they have been sent are the responsibility of the local churches. Thus, it is important for KMC to take the lead in assigning the roles to be played by local churches and mission agencies, as well as for KMC to cooperate with them. So far, this cooperative relationship between KMC and local Korean Methodist church and mission agencies has worked well.

GBM'S COOPERATION WITH KMWMA AND OTHER MISSION SOCIETIES

In practice, KMC missionaries are responsible for finding sponsoring churches and for cooperating with them to carry out their own missions. For instance, all missionary candidates are required to pay for the expenses of their own mission training. During the missionary selection process, they are expected to submit a ministry plan and budget consistent with the financial support of their sponsors. If appointed, they carry out their ministry in the mission field in cooperation with their sending churches.

This approach led naturally to the formation of the Korean Methodist World Mission Association (KMWMA), which is the body that sends and supports missionaries in KMC. KMWMA discusses and evaluates issues of practical cooperation in the organization and formulates plans for the future direction of Methodist missions, while GBM supports the activities of KMWMA administratively and legally. GBM seeks to promote and actualize KMC missions in cooperation with KMWMA. Megachurches join in supporting this project.

GBM cooperates with mission study centers such as M-Center, a recently established mission research center at Methodist Theological University, in analyzing the current status of global missions, establishing a missiological framework, researching new strategies, and seeking to implement them. GBM also cooperates with internationally recognized mission NGOs, such as the Methodist oriented NGO LoveWorld, so as to engage in holistic mission outreach projects that are not easily carried out within denominational boundaries. Such cooperative relationships are extremely helpful for missions in creative-access countries, where churches or denominations as such are denied official access. They are also important for mission work and reunification efforts directed toward North Korea and for larger-scale missions that involve governments or businesses. In addition, GBM works together with nondenominational mission agencies such as WEC, COME, and others.

GBM IS A PLATFORM

The unique situation of KMC positions GBM to function not as a centralized institution but as a platform. Institutionally, KMC offers itself as a platform on which churches, mission societies, and missionaries that need official designation in Wesleyan missions are able to associate together and network with one another. GBM seeks to provide a strategic platform and a network that will help participating churches and agencies to proceed from an attitude of "individualistic battle-style missions" to being "united holistic missions."

Once mission agencies and missionaries gather on a common platform of Wesleyan missions and are networked, so-called economies of scale arise, synergism is formed, and the effect of mission efforts is increased. Scattered resources are able to be redistributed, God-given talents can be shared, and a great flow of blessings will be seen. In such a grand mission ecosystem, each unit will be able to cooperate in evangelism, discipleship training, church planting and growth, missionary training and support, and the expansion and carrying forward of the kingdom of God. Without the platform, the individual units could not engage in such a diverse array of ministries.

CONCLUSION

Each mission society has both strengths and weaknesses. A weakness of KMC is that, in some respects, it lacks centralization of power and unity, which is normally a strong point of an episcopacy. When GBM designs and suggests mission projects for churches and agencies, it often lacks the influence over churches and mission fields to carry them out. And in cases of conflict between churches and mission societies, GBM's influence is often ineffective and settlement is delayed. GBM has also had difficulty in resolving issues of overlapping work in a single mission field and in relocating missionaries.

A strength of the smaller GBM and of KMC's network of small mission agencies is their size. In today's diversified and fast-changing global missions, small-sized specialized mission units are vital for responding quickly and effectively to the needs of rapidly changing situations. We note also the role of megachurches in giving financial support to KMC and GBM. In this way, KMC's decentralized missions, though small, also have strength. With GBM providing the official platform, these mission units network, cooperate, and work synergistically with one another.

◇◇◇◇◇◇◇◇◇◇◇◇◇◇◇◇◇◇◇◇◇◇◇◇◇◇◇◇◇◇◇◇◇◇◇◇◇◇◇

Global Missions at Our Doorsteps

Woosung Calvin Choi

Today, megachurch status is often viewed as a sign of successful ministry. While pastors know that not every church will become a megachurch, many nevertheless wish to pastor such a church. Jesus warns us, however, that with "mega-size" comes much accountability ("To whom much has been given, much will be required," Luke 12:48). The issue of accountability becomes equally relevant when megachurch missions are in view. According to a survey reported on in "U.S. Megachurches and New Patterns of Global Mission," U.S. megachurches reported an average annual expenditure of $690,000 on global missions, an amount representing just over 10 percent of their total annual budget.[1] While the significant contribution of megachurches to global missions can be celebrated, is it time to rethink missions in light of the global realities of the church today? That is, if the primary focus of global missions has been to build bridges to distant shores, must we now also recognize the need to make inroads into the globalizing communities all around us?

IT'S AT OUR DOORSTEPS!

Two centuries ago, John Wesley passionately said, "I look upon all the world as my parish." Today, however, the world is at *our* doorsteps. The impact of globalization is widespread, affecting every sector of society, and the Christian community is not immune from its influence. Churches are awakening to diversifying pews, and neighborhoods are finding it difficult to insist on strict homogeneity in the face of the massive influx of immigrants from the Southern and Eastern Hemispheres.

Todd Johnson and Albert Hickman make several important observations concerning migration in their article "Religious

1. Robert J. Priest, Douglas Wilson, and Adelle Johnson, "U.S. Megachurches and New Patterns of Global Mission," *International Bulletin of Missionary Research* 34, no. 2 (April 2010): 102.

Demography and Mission Strategy."[2] One is that currently more people (at least 720 million) are living outside their homeland than ever before. The increasing rate of migration will continue to produce religious and ethnic diversity around the world.

Another observation is that Christianity is no longer viewed as a Western religion. As missiologist Dana Robert recognizes, "During the second half of the twentieth century, Christianity became a non-Western religion, concentrated in the Global South."[3] In 1910 the Global North had more than 80 percent of the world's Christians; by 2010 the Global North's proportion had fallen to less than 40 percent. In particular, Europe's portion of the world's Christians experienced a sharp decline from 66 percent in 1910 to 26 percent a century later.

Another surprising trend found in Christian mission is that most Christian outreach never reaches non-Christians, even though more Christians are now living in places with a higher concentration of non-Christians. Despite that fact, Johnson and Hickman's survey makes clear that most Christians have limited contact with Muslims, Hindus, and Buddhists. As many as 86 percent of Muslims, Hindus, and Buddhists do not have personal acquaintance with a Christian.

Johnson and Hickman also stress the increasing importance of mission to the major cities of the world because they are precisely where the greatest religious diversity exists, including Buddhist, Hindu, Muslim, or nonreligious majorities. Additionally, the survey reveals that true religious diversity is found in Korea, where five religions in South Korea each claim more than 10 percent of the country's population.

These trends suggest the inevitability of cultural change and diversity in North America, as well as other parts of the world. More

2. Todd M. Johnson and Albert W. Hickman, "Religious Demography and Mission Strategy," *International Journal of Frontier Missiology* 29, no. 1 (Spring 2012): 14–20.

3. Dana L. Robert, "Missionaries Sent and Received, Worldwide, 1910–2010," in *Atlas of Global Christianity, 1910–2010*, ed. Todd M. Johnson, Kenneth R. Ross, and Sandra S. K. Lee (Edinburgh: Edinburgh Univ. Press, 2009), 259.

important, given their locations and resources, megachurches are called upon for serious engagement at the forefront of global mission by viewing their diverse communities as legitimate mission fields, as well as by taking intentional missional steps to provide a relevant witness to a global society.

"POSITIVE MARGINALITY" AS ONE STRATEGY

While some resist diversity and others simply tolerate it, Christians are encouraged to look for ways to build bridges of respectful understanding and have a positive impact on people. Instead of avoiding or simply ignoring their diversifying neighborhoods, Christians are called to interact with peoples of diverse ethnic and religious origin. At this point the role of megachurches becomes critical. Megachurches can take an approach of "positive marginality" as they strategically mobilize and empower their congregations and other local churches to engage in religiously and ethnically diverse communities.

Positive marginality is the ability to *embrace* two or more ethnic or cultural groups, *engage* in intentional cross-cultural dialogue, and *establish* relationships with others by fully utilizing the assets and strengths of those groups—and thereby to *embody* a communal identity that is renewed, redefined, and rooted in the Gospel and come to *exhibit* a renewed vision for society.[4]

Megachurches are called to mobilize and train their diverse congregations and resources to embrace and engage their diverse community. Accommodating a separate ethnic worship service may be a good start, but it is not enough. Congregations need missional strategies to be developed that will equip them to engage with people of different religions and traditions and will encourage them to build cross-cultural relationships. Today, every Christian must be viewed as a missionary. Carrying out missional tasks in the community by partnering with local churches is an effective way to make the Gospel visible

4. Woosung Calvin Choi, *Preaching to Multiethnic Congregation: Positive Marginality as a Homiletical Paradigm* (New York: Peter Lang, 2015), 32.

as we strive to be, as Newbigin put it, "a community that does not live for itself but is deeply involved in the concerns of its neighborhood."[5]

CONCLUSION

Today's increasing globalization requires churches to engage biblically, theologically, and culturally. The concept of positive marginality provides a framework for the church to think of itself as a missionary church in an effort to engage and transform our globalizing society.

The congregations of megachurches are more diverse today than ever before. What will happen when those diverse Christians living in diverse communities are discipled and trained to interact with their diverse communities? Opportunities for overseas mission will remain an important consideration. Nevertheless, we must not forget that a greater opportunity may lie at our own doorsteps. Megachurches are well resourced and providentially located to make a greater impact by offering mission strategies that will be effective in their diversifying communities.

5. Lesslie Newbigin, comp. Paul Weston, *Lesslie Newbigin: Missionary Theologian: A Reader* (Grand Rapids: Eerdmans, 2006), 154.

33

KGMLF 2015: A Summation

Hyung Keun Choi

The theme of KGMLF 2015, "Megachurch Accountability in Missions: Critical Assessment through Global Case Studies," is appropriate, given the significance of churches and mission agencies working together in genuine partnership for the sake of the kingdom of God. The fourteen plenary papers presented in this forum include case studies of churches around the world: in Korea (5), the Korean diaspora (3), Africa (2), the United States (2), Australia (1), and Brazil (1). In carefully reading the chapters, I noticed that some authors deal only tangentially with ecclesiological or missiological themes or with accountability issues per se. Each one, however, includes critical reflection on the role of megachurches in mission. Some authors also focus on ways the church can grow, with consideration of the effects of charismatic church leaders on the expansion of their churches. I summarize here, in sequence, the main points suggested by the various authors.

In describing the changing scope of religion in the United States, *Scott Thumma* notes that megachurches and large-sized churches are becoming more directly involved in mission activities. He chooses a large church—Crossroads Community Cathedral, in East Hartford, Connecticut—to answer the question he raises: "To whom and in what ways is a megachurch accountable in mission activities?" Thumma focuses on the vision and missions-oriented ministry of long-time pastor Bishop Terry Wiles, which have brought growth and a sense of accountability among the churches this congregation has planted. The Crossroads Community International Fellowship, created by Wiles, has played a key role in allowing the church to expand its ministry to overseas mission fields. Thumma finds that the church's system of accountability is largely due to the church's overall mission efforts, including Wiles's vision and the commitment of church members in sharing in this vision. This missions mindset has become part of the culture of the congregation, which now engages in short-term mission trips and supports the Kitchen of Love (a church ministry in Guatemala). These and other ministries reinforce the relational ties that exist between the U.S. church members, the missionaries, and the pastors and church members on the fields. The questions Thumma raises remind us of the importance of a biblical understanding of the mission-church relationship and of leadership.

After briefly telling the story of Seoul's Onnuri Church (and its founding pastor, Yong Jo Ha), *Jae Hoon Lee, Daniel S. H. Ahn,* and *Tae Kyung Ham* assess its cross-cultural mission activities over the past thirty years. The authors note that from its very beginning, Onnuri has been a missional church. They evaluate various aspects of Onnuri's efforts at accountability in missions, including its use of human and financial resources and its interaction with other churches and mission agencies. Also, they mention ways the church has been self-focused and suggest a new way of establishing genuine partnership with other mission organizations. It is noteworthy that even though Onnuri has established effective programs of screening and selection, cross-cultural missionary training, member care, and mission facilities, it still recognizes problems and blind spots that can undermine the foundation for partnership with mission agencies. The authors present Onnuri's efforts to develop professionalism and training for missionaries in cross-cultural adjustment skills, in which the church has been willing to learn from other mission organizations. Onnuri has been effective in developing a variety of mission resources for cross-cultural work beyond the borders of Korea, including the evangelistic Love Sonata conferences (held in Japan), Christian Global Network TV, and Duranno Press. These ministries have had a great influence on many other churches and mission agencies. The authors conclude their discussion of this remarkable church by outlining three critical challenges. First, that Onnuri Church continue its unusual focus as a union of local church and international mission (i.e., amalgamating modality and sodality). Second, that it go beyond its successful practice of mission to develop also mission theology per se. Third, that it establish a missiological study center for the purpose of developing, with the partnership of Western and non-Western institutions, forums for self-theologizing and self-missiologizing.

The case study by *Tim Carriker* of Várzea Paulista (Brazil) Assembly of God (VPAG) offers a clear picture of a charismatic church leader's understanding of mission. Carriker's research on this church seems to support Rodney Stark's claim that "religious competition increases the level of religiousness prevailing in a society." Carriker's chapter focuses mainly on the strong leadership style and godly character of Pastor Resende, who, soon after arriving at VPAG, overcame a large church debt by immediately calling for the rapid growth of missionary giving. Another factor in the growth of VPAG that Carriker mentions is Resende's complementary skills of administration and goal-setting, which are very pragmatic and centered on efficiency. In discussing VPAG, Carriker seems quite aware of Brazilian cultural perspectives. We might ask whether the idea of competition as the key to success is not closely related to the doctrine of individual salvation and so-called church individualism. If so, what place is there for the (worldwide) kingdom of God or the one-flock teaching of Jesus (see Matt. 6:33 and John 10:16)? Also, perhaps there are cautions to be noted wherever the presence of a charismatic and authoritative senior pastor plays such a major role in the spectacular growth of a church.

Jinbong Kim introduces the history, ministries, and multicultural and multilingual context of the Hong Kong Korean Exodus Mission Church (HKKEMC), which is a good example of a missional church in a diaspora setting. The church's commitment to participation in God's mission and obedience to the Great Commission has resulted in the organization of Life Road Mission (LRM), which has trained and sent out sixty cross-cultural missionaries through the LRM training center. Kim reports that LRM has appropriate and thoughtful mission policies and strategies for the recruitment, training, and care of missionaries. Also, it supports the Silk Road Mission Strategic Forum, which meets every two years and involves other major churches. One point that might be considered in the future is the development of ongoing partnerships with other churches and mission agencies.

In his second presentation, Kim considers two ordinary-sized Korean churches and their mission work. After discussing the sharply dropping social credibility of Korean Protestant churches, he examines two local churches that have a positive story. On the one hand, the Hwangji Presbyterian Church, in Taebaek, has focused on ministries that serve its immediate community holistically, from medical help to counseling to education to evangelism. On the other hand, the Juhyanghan Church, in Seoul, though a small church, has been pouring its energy into missions to Francophone African countries. Its pastor is fully committed to that mission and has founded the Communauté Coréenne des Missions pour la Francophonie. These positive examples demonstrate that understanding of and commitment to missions on the part of the church leader play a key role in doing missions more effectively.

Mark Shaw and *Wanjiru Gitau* discuss an interesting case of an African megachurch, Mavuno Church, that has been effectively involved in urban church planting ministry both in and beyond Kenya through a culturally relevant leadership development strategy and by well-trained and properly-cared-for church planting teams. Shaw and Gitau deal seriously with the issue of the accountability of the sending church to newly planted churches and their ministers. The Mavuno story focuses on the vision and goal of Mavuno Church, as they are shared with churches planted in other areas and countries. Mavuno's vision is to raise up churches with a strong desire to reach out to the unchurched urban generation, "planting culture-defining churches in strategic capital cities" through well-developed discipleship training methods. It is impressive that the church's discipleship process—what they call the Mavuno Marathon—is summed up as "turning ordinary people into fearless influencers of society." The intent is for the whole congregation to become change agents in the public arena, which is congruent with the idea of holistic mission. The method of planting churches includes the formation of ten-week

Mizizi ("roots") classes, which are based on relationships built primarily among young adults. Shaw and Gitau present the process Mavuno's church planting ministry follows in various regions and describe different ways of practicing effective accountability with the ministers and their families based on genuine relationships, regular supervision and debriefing, provision of financial support, and norms for maintaining moral integrity. The authors rightly point out challenges and problems megachurches face today, such as a numerical, growth-centered approach and the emotional and moral problems of megachurch leaders.

Pil-Hun Park, in his chapter, shows how SaRang Church, in Seoul, effectively cooperates with mission agencies. Quoting Lesslie Newbigin, Park points to SaRang Church's relation with mission agencies as one of genuine partnership. The numbers are impressive: the church supports 211 missionary units, who are affiliated with 46 mission organizations. Altogether, 94 mission groups receive financial support from SaRang Church. Park provides good examples of the mutual benefits both for the church and for four mission agencies. The areas of partnership are observed in the various ways in which a megachurch can promote the growth of mission agencies. The main benefits in partnership between megachurches and mission agencies, Park suggests, are infrastructure as a platform provided by megachurches, various resources the megachurches can provide, cooperative member care, and the provision of missional role models for other churches. Park notes that in order for megachurches to make the partnership possible, they need to acknowledge their own strengths and weaknesses, to continually work at deeper communication with mission organizations, and to notice the practical and financial needs of the mission agencies.

In her research on the Hillsong Church network, *Miranda Klaver* emphasizes the trend that global networks such as Hillsong effectively minister to newly emerging groups in global cities. She acknowledges that the Hillsong megachurches and the Hillsong network raise many questions from a missiological perspective, mostly related to the expansion of global Pentecostal networks in the world's megacities. These networks seem not to be sensitive to local contexts; rather, they follow the globalizing tendency of spreading the values and practices of a single church. Regarding this point, Klaver points out both weakness and strength: Hillsong can be regarded as "a consumerist and commodified form of Christianity," but "in practice Hillsong is able to minister to a particular tribe encountered in global cities today." In terms of contextualization, the Hillsong megachurch network can be seen as a church trying to adopt the cultural forms of global cities while trying at the same time to retain the meaning of the Gospel. To a certain extent, however, a dangerous "watering down" of the Gospel appears in the weekly messages and the overall practices of the Hillsong network. Klaver points out the need "to evaluate the relevance and meaning of the concepts of culture and ethnicity." It should also be remembered that ecclesiology based on the biblical worldview helps us to avoid the pitfalls of syncretism.

Kyo Seong Ahn provides an overview of the megamission syndrome among Korean Protestant churches today. After analyzing the development of large-scale missions in three stages from the 1970s to the present, he discusses four characteristics of Korean "megamission" (i.e., missions of the megachurches): (1) it is rooted in the contemporary evangelical mission movement; (2) it has its origin in North America and is carried out in the context of globalization; (3) it mainly focuses on church-centered mission, emphasizing size and number; and (4) it has its own evolving understanding of mission and missional practices. Ahn briefly discusses megachurch accountability in missions in terms of the inseparable relationship between the church and mission. One of the main questions he raises is how megamissions can avoid eclipsing a sense of the *missio Dei*. In this respect, we must keep in mind that Korean churches commonly desire to become megachurches, and to that end often try to replicate the worship patterns, programs, and ministries of megachurches. Thus, this chapter can challenge us to rethink the essence of the church and the mission of God and his people. In other words, unless megachurches realize that they exist for the mission of God in serving God and the world as the people of God and the body of Christ, they will always face the temptation to indulge in self-righteous attitudes.

Opoku Onyinah presents a case study of an ordinary-sized church in missions: the church in Kaneshie, in Accra, Ghana, which is part of the massive Church of Pentecost. This church's participation in mission is based on the ecumenical definition of mission (Commission on World Mission and Evangelism) and on the author's own definition. He begins his explanation of the rapid growth of Kaneshie church with an overview of its history, structure, and worship styles. He points out eleven factors that have been significant in the growth of the Kaneshie church and describes the church's involvement in mission works, which focus mostly on evangelism and church planting as local missions efforts and on financial support for the Church of Pentecost. Though Onyinah mentions the involvement of an ordinary-sized church in missions, most of the content of his chapter is devoted to a detailed explanation of the Kaneshie pattern of church growth. In defining "mission," he highlights the church's "sharing of the Gospel by word and deed, prayer and worship, and the witness of everyday Christian life, leading to the reconciliation and strengthening of a person's relationship with God, fellow human beings, and creation." He could also have dealt with the broader dimension of the mission of God and the people in the world. This aspect involves the church's participation in the public arena. Here Onyinah rightly raises critical questions about "theological superficiality" and the tendency of megachurches to focus so intently on church growth that the need for Christian discipleship can easily be ignored.

Chang Ju Kim begins his chapter by describing the relationship between missionaries and their sending churches. As a missionary in Madagascar and former pastor of a local church in Seoul, Kim candidly discusses critical issues of the Korean church in general and megachurches in particular and their practice of mission. The three questions he raises (concerning pride in numbers, eagerness to see fruit, and readiness to use retirees as missionaries) and the two areas of concern he identifies (regarding short-term missions and the dominant senior pastor) may not be easy for leaders of megachurches and of mission agencies to face. Kim is basically urging deeper understanding and cooperation among sending churches, missionaries, and mission agencies. He is forthright in pointing out the overall problems of megachurch mission work relating to the recruiting and training of missionary candidates, and to the sending of and caring for missionaries. The issues he raises are highly relevant for Korean churches that have been involved in either overseas or domestic missions. Actually, they have been critically reviewed by Korean missionaries and missiologists since the 1990s. It seems clear that uncritical acceptance of the church growth movement and an inappropriate understanding of the church and mission have had a negative impact on the Korean church, even overshadowing the Korean mission movement. As Kim notes, we have seen an overemphasis on visible results and even a boasting of the number of missionaries sent to overseas mission fields. The reflection questions Kim raises are important in that they relate to the purpose and essence of the church and mission.

Christopher DeWelt first surveys the emergence and current tendencies of the megachurch phenomenon. In the United States, megachurches have influenced all aspects of the work of mission agencies, including missionary training and the sending, supporting, and caring for mission workers. Indeed, the role of megachurches has superseded that of denominations and seminaries. From his research, based primarily on interviews with mission agency personnel and megachurch missions staff, DeWelt draws conclusions in six areas. For example, he notes the growing interest of megachurches in forming networks with national churches overseas. Also he finds that megachurches are willing to learn from mission agencies about the overall process of missions. Such an attitude can foster deeper partnerships between megachurches and mission agencies. In terms of sending missionaries, DeWelt's research shows that megachurches and mission agencies can build symbiotic relationships and develop mutual support despite existing tensions if they are willing to serve the Lord faithfully.

Sun Man Kim discusses the First Korean Presbyterian Church of Greater Hartford (FKPC), a Korean American diaspora church that has been willing to mobilize mission resources for the accomplishment of God's vision. He describes the missional motivation of this congregation, with its emphasis on prayer in mission, as well as the congregation's methods of mobilizing for missions. Kim's report of FKPC's practice of short-term missions is positive, especially regarding ways in which FKPC members have been equipped to carry out their work on the field and how they have grasped the importance of building relationships with missionaries and mission agencies in partnership and unity. This case study will challenge other Korean diaspora churches to be properly motivated for missions.

Won Sang Lee shares current trends in mission of Korean American megachurches. He begins with a brief description of missions to Korea and then the immigration of Koreans to North America. He discusses reasons for the "silent exodus" of Korean American young people from their churches and urges Korean American churches to recognize the need to be missional toward the emerging generation of Korean Americans. Lee mentions a list of over 700 Unengaged and Unreached People Groups, about one-third of whom live in the Americas. He understands mission as "from everywhere to everywhere," engaging "all believers as missionaries being sent into the world by the triune God," but without losing the central concern for overseas mission endeavors. Lee sees the need to develop Korean American mission agencies, even as he presents the efforts of some Korean American megachurches to form mission agencies, to cooperate with existing mission agencies, and to be involved in short-term mission and the mobilization of retirees as missionaries.

KGMLF 2015 leaves to all participants the task of ongoing research and reflection on the relationship between megachurches and missions from a global perspective. It also challenges us to think deeply about how the church can develop genuine partnership with other churches and mission agencies all around the world in the cause of world evangelization, all for the mission of God. This gathering encourages us to participate boldly in God's mission as he calls us from darkness and sends us into the whole world with the Gospel of Jesus Christ, in and through the power of the Holy Spirit.

34

Megachurches, Heroes, Technology, Mission, and Accountability

Dwight P. Baker

Sometimes the value of a study or conference lies more in the musings and questions it stirs up than in those issues that it definitively lays to rest. In that spirit, here are several questions that have surfaced for me in reading though the forum's presentations and responses. It may be helpful to know in advance that my own life has passed largely within smaller, even miniscule, congregations. Since I have only heard and read, not participated in, megachurches, you may need to correct and adjust what I have to say, sifting for those parts in which you can, with charity, discern potential value.

MISSIONARY AS HERO

Does every age get the missionary hero it deserves? Does the missionary held up as a hero typify and to a degree encapsulate the spiritual temper of his or her age? Does the hero's life and ministry show in small how mission was thought about and carried out in a particular era?

Think of David Brainerd (1718–47), the solitary spiritual pioneer, introspective to the point of neurosis, working in an era and setting of pioneer living. Or consider William Carey (1761–1834), a humble village pastor, who uprooted all and transported his wife and children to India for life in an age of mercantile colonialism. What of David Livingstone (1813–73), the rugged explorer and herald of legitimate commerce as a route out of slavery for Africa, active at filling in the "gaps" in the map of Africa just as Europe's age of high colonialism was beginning to dawn? Another is John Mott (1865–1955), the consummate visionary and administrator, adopting the methods of "modern" business for mission purposes. Again, what of Jim Elliot (1927–56) and his search within (for resonances between his spirit, his pietistic immersion in Scripture, and promptings given to him by the Holy Spirit) for very personal guidance in mission, all at the outset of an age that was to become increasingly marked by unfettered individual self-assertion?

So, what of megachurches in mission? Are they today's heroes? Are they the trailblazers and trendsetters? Do they set the pace, exploring new directions and dimensions of mission? If so, the reports in this consultation would seem to indicate that they are so in a collective sense and not as individuals or as individual churches. I do not mean to slight anyone, and you can tell me if an individual megachurch leader or a particular megachurch stands preeminent, the pathfinder to whom others are simply followers. My impression from the accounts given in this forum is one of vitality, but also of diversity in character, ethos, approach, style, and practice, rather than of conformity and imitation. There is breadth of life in the Spirit, not just within these churches themselves, but also between them. Gifts differ; they are not carbon copies of each other.

MEGACHURCHES AND ACCOUNTABILITY

What of accountability in mission on the part of megachurches? We are to be encouraged, first, that the topic was even named—naming acknowledges a reality and opens the way to ownership—and that accountability was broached as an issue that ought to receive serious, extended discussion. It is far more important that it was decided, despite initial hesitation, that megachurch accountability in mission *could* be discussed, for discussions are fraught with uncertainty. Delicate issues can be raised, and perceptions of subordination and superordination can quickly come into play. Who are *you* to be questioning me or us or our church or our organization or our policy? We are not accountable to you. (As fellow members of Christ's body, are we not accountable to one another?)

Furthermore, we can rejoice that leaders of megachurches themselves have been present and taken part in this forum. The forum has been richer and truer for their participation. It has not been just a gathering of academics, outside researchers, or persons with a passing interest, expressing opinions or passing judgments. Having megachurch leaders participating, persons with a stake in the churches' health and vitality, has given grounding to the discussions. Their contributions have been able to correct mistaken impressions.

For one thing, megachurch leaders have been able to enlarge our understanding, at least mine, of the scope and complexity of the larger megachurches' engagement in mission. They are doing more in more locations and in connection with more partner organizations, as well as in a greater range of fields of expertise, than I at least was aware. This diversity brings with it complexity of administration and accountability. Who renders account and how and to whom? With whom are reports and records shared? What information is confidential? What is public, and, if public, how is it shared and how widely? What information is made available to researchers so as to develop an in-depth and trustworthy knowledge base for increased understanding of the field as a whole? Are accountability and information dissemination active, or are they limply passive, responding only when questions arise? What standards and forms of best practice in these areas have been developed or are being developed? Who is attending to those issues?

The topic for this KGMLF meeting was specifically megachurch accountability in mission, not issues of accountability within the structures and leadership of home-base megachurches. But can church and mission truly be separated? Some would draw on the language of sodality and modality to say that they can and maybe even should be separated. Individuals who think in that fashion might maintain that what happens downstairs or down the block or across national boundaries is mission and feel that it can be held distinct from the spiritual health and integrity or lack of integrity of the home church. But I doubt that such bifurcation is possible or that it would be a good thing if it were possible. In mission the spiritual health of the home church is as much a concern as is the spiritual health and performance of missionaries on the field or of churches established there. Though the topic was not a central focus in this forum, several of the reports did touch on issues related to home church accountability and on practices of leadership formation in relation to accountability. The efforts in leadership formation—which are the foundations on which leadership accountability is erected—by Mavuno Church, Kaneshie Church of Pentecost, and Várzea Paulista Assembly of God seem exemplary in their attentiveness to this crucial issue. Others could be cited as well.

MEGACHURCHES AND TECHNOLOGY

It may seem a stretch to some to bring up the topic of megachurches and technology when considering the issue of megachurches and accountability in mission, but let's not be quick to dismiss it. Numbers and the power they bring, the ways technology is used or the role it is presumed to have, and issues related to reproducibility are important considerations that also need to be taken into account. In short, how they are handled is also a matter of accountability.

Are megachurches (1) technology enabled, (2) wholly creatures of technology, or (3) a social form that for the sake of coming into existence has called and is calling the necessary technology into being? The third option asks whether megachurches are themselves technologically generative, whether they are driving technological innovation.

There is no question that megachurches are technology enabled. That is, without the enabling power of technology, there would be no regular gatherings in one place or a linked set of places, at regular intervals according to a set schedule, with multiplied thousands of worshippers. Technological systems that stand as necessary conditions for the emergence and functioning of megachurches include those of transportation (so that large numbers of people can gather) and communication (both to draw worshippers in and to send out widely the outflow of megachurches' worship, praise, and instruction). Necessary also are the antecedent technologies of construction (for building the massive structures and auditoriums in which the faithful are able to gather) and the technologies that make dense urbanization possible (these range from statecraft, to food procurement and distribution, to the power grid, to sanitation).

But if megachurches are technology dependent, are they wholly creatures or artifacts of technology? I would doubt that anyone at this consultation would be comfortable defending that position. To answer the question affirmatively would be to adopt the position of sociologist Emile Durkheim (*The Elementary Forms of the Religious Life* [1912]), but with a twist. Instead of religion being a case of society worshipping itself under another guise, as Durkheim thought, it would be a matter of congregations enshrining technology as central to life and godliness.

We can speak of a technological compulsion according to which "what can be done, will be done." No one will express a desire to live in a land contaminated by radioactive residue, but we know that, once the theoretical understanding is acquired and the technological expertise developed to build nuclear weapons, they will be built—and have been built in unimaginable numbers. Technology, however, is not only aversive; it can also be, and indeed is, benign and even benevolent. Advances in medical technology save lives through heart transplants, reconnect severed hands and arms, and reconstruct faces for burn victims. But technological capability is compulsive. We seem not to be able to say "No" to it. So once the array of necessary technologies was assembled, did the megachurch as a new form of social organization come into being as a quasi-necessary consequence? Does it embody spiritual significance and importance for mission that reaches deeper than that?

Or does the whole thing work the other way around? To what extent are megachurches themselves an originative good? That is to ask, are they a value that, once conceived of, makes it imperative for us to see that the technological support is created or assembled or configured in such a way that megachurches can coalesce and flourish? Are megachurches more than simply an artifact of our time; have they helped to create the age in which we live?

If the intertwining of megachurches with technology is seen as, in part, constitutive of them, what does that say about the temporal span of the era of the megachurch? Eiko Takamizawa reminded us, in her excellent Bible study, of the value of looking to the earliest church for the core character of megachurches, as of any other church, even today. Even if megachurches *are* a new fact of our time (a blend of sheer size or numerical mass and technology), we still rightfully expect them to be accountable for all the practical and spiritual issues that have been true from the beginning of the church—as well as for the new levels and facets of accountability that they bring into existence with them. The new will not replace or displace what has been true from the beginning, but ever-present issues of accountability can be expected to take new forms.

MEGACHURCH, MISSION, AND TECHNOLOGY

If technology has glamour—it certainly has appeal—how does that aura affect megachurches' engagement in mission? To what extent does or should technological innovation, expertise, and utilization be defining qualities of mission as practiced by megachurches?

These questions are not immaterial, since technology has to do with more than just hardware and software, with plows, tools, and machinery. It also has to do with structuring of human relationships, with education and personal and missionary formation (we now speak of educational systems and not simply of schools or tutors), and with how people (whether employees, colleagues, or supplicants) are viewed, treated, and "managed."

Technology tends toward the systematic and is weighted toward results. It privileges countable, numerable accomplishments and achievements. It sets markers and records them. Counting can be a useful tool, but it can also bend thought in particular directions, casting light on certain facets of a complex entity and encouraging us to gloss over other considerations.

Technology is a useful servant but a dehumanizing taskmaster. It can open up windows of opportunity for human encounter and interaction, or it can preempt the time and social space necessary for intimacy and trust to be built. As means of communication, it can enhance supportive contact between mission supervisors and missionaries in the field. It can also enable member care providers to be virtually present to field missionaries in times of crisis. As medical and nutritional knowledge, it can sustain missionaries in health, and as transportation technology, it can ease their comings and goings.

At the same time, technology—by providing ease of access to family, friends, and church family "back home"—can distance missionaries from those among whom they live and whom they wish to serve. By removing some of the urgency for missionaries to become deeply immersed in the lives, community, and setting in their field of service, technology can create barriers to missionary identification. In which direction is the missionary or the missionary family looking for primary relationships? Thanks especially to technology, some people—and unfortunately some missionaries among them—can live for years in a foreign setting without ever leaving home emotionally, socially, or in primary relationships.

Paul and Barnabas, after their missionary journey through central Asia Minor, reported to the church in Antioch about what the Lord was doing there. It was a gladsome time of reporting, though the news did contribute to the controversy that led to the convening of the Jerusalem council. But technology makes possible reports that are much more detailed, that are more personally probing, that occur at much shorter time intervals, and that—and this may be most onerous—can be expected, required, or even exacted. Does that possibility tend to skew the whole nature of missionary reporting? What effect does it have on relationships between missionaries and mission administrators or between them and their home churches? Does technology, in analogy to the U.S. stock market, shift the focus from long-term vision (what God is doing) to short-term performance (enumeration of missionary activities)? Does technology with its communicative immediacy lend itself to spiritual temperature-taking?

These issues are present for all churches and mission organizations, but are they particularly pressing for megachurches to consider, having, as they do, both the people power available at their disposal, through volunteers and paid staff, and the financial clout to implement their expectations aggressively? When the pressure of reports accumulates, how is the presence of the personal touch preserved—as well as openness to the Spirit's presence? Andrew Walls has written of the Gospel as prisoner and liberator of culture. Are there ways that megachurches can go beyond being shaped by technology? Are they able, by practicing self-restraint, to embody intimations of more humane uses and ends for technology?

MEGACHURCHES AS TRENDSETTERS

As the report by Jorge López has reminded us, megachurches are trendsetters in many ways—in worship styles, in the use of technology in worship, in music, in worship apparel, in preaching and pulpiteering, in theology, in Christian formation—for congregations and communities of Christ's followers who may never pass through their vestibules. They are without question cultural innovators. They can, in effect, be living experiments, offering themselves as trial runs for new modes of congregational life and of being the church together in community. What of new approaches to mission fostered by megachurches? Do they have similar carry-over value?

Take one example, that of the now ubiquitous short-term mission presence. What has been the role of megachurches in the rise of short-term-ism in missions? Technological transformations, especially in the fields of transportation and communication (along with growth in the amount of discretionary wealth), lie behind the efflorescence that we in the United States have witnessed of the shortening of mission engagement, for both good and ill, in the past half-century or so. Did megachurches set the trend for this phenomenon, which may be more strikingly present within the megachurch orbit, but is not limited to megachurches alone? Did the shift—in the United States, at least—from lifetime missionary commitment to project and short-term missions and then to mission tourism predate, parallel, or come as a consequence of the rise of megachurches? The answer would be of interest to know. Whatever the temporal or causal sequence, in what ways have megachurches taken over and set the agenda for short-term missions? How is megachurches' missional focus proportioned between long-term and short-term missions? Does the answer to that question vary by country or region?

REGIONAL VARIATION AND ELITES

An interesting question suggested by the case studies presented, but not fully answered by them, is the degree of regional variation in style between megachurches found in, say, Korea and those found in Africa, Latin America, North America, or Australia. How do megachurches in each of these regions differ structurally, theologically, ecclesiologically, organizationally, and in intent from those found in other regions? ? Do they tend to be more like each other cross-nationally than they are similar in ethos to humbler congregations in their own neighborhoods?

In their home base, megachurches might seem to be primarily an urban—and elite—phenomenon. But where and to whom is their mission outreach primarily directed? For the United States, research by Robert Priest, Douglas Wilson, and Adelle Johnson has shown that first, judged by budgeted expenditures, short-term missions have priority in the mission outreach of U.S. megachurches. Second, though U.S. megachurches rank evangelism high among their aspirations for their short-term mission teams, that does not seem to be what they do. For third, rather than "going from spaces where there is Christianity to spaces where there is not, [U.S.] megachurch short-term mission teams are going from places where Christianity is present and has comparative material wealth and going to spaces where Christianity is present in the midst of relative material constraint."[1] They are going from wealth to poverty, but staying within a Christian orbit. What would be true of megachurches in other parts of the world? Is their outreach primarily short-term? To whom is it directed? How do megachurches in different parts of the world compare on this matter? If recent globalization has largely been a flow from the United States to the rest of the world, are there lessons for megachurches in the United States to learn from their sister megachurches in other parts of the world? Do missional

1. Robert J. Priest, Douglas Wilson, and Adelle Johnson, "U.S. Megachurches and New Patterns of Global Ministry," *International Bulletin of Missionary Research* 34, no. 2 (2010): 99.

priorities found elsewhere differ markedly from those present in the United States?

CONCLUSION

From the sometimes narrow perspective of research projects: in what ways will answers to questions such as these be influenced by where one sets the threshold level for which churches fit the category of "megasize"? What regional variations appear? Is there variation by denominational affiliation? How do independent megachurches differ on style or type of missional practice—and in practices of accountability—from their sister megachurches affiliated with a denomination? Are denominationally related megachurches held to higher or tighter standards of accountability? In what ways does the size of a megachurch affect the answer to *that* question? Finally, if we will all give an accounting according to the gifts (resources) put at our disposal, what further steps in accountability should megachurches—with their awesome resources—be seeking to implement?

Looking more broadly, a friend has suggested the following questions, which I quote with appreciation in conclusion:

> Given their often surprising size, power, resourcefulness, and innovation, how can megachurches make clear their submission to church and kingdom values of the New Testament?
>
> Is it time to suggest a worldwide forum for megachurches to share in prayer, and also in brainstorming, regarding global questions, such as the following:
>
> - how to promote love globally among Christians (John 13:34–35; 1 Thess. 4:9–10)?
> - how to approach poverty?
> - how to submit to, as well as be of benefit to, government?
> - how to deal with other religions (e.g., with ISIS, on everyone's mind)?[2]

2. I thank Craig A. Noll for these questions and his perceptive comments on this chapter.

Bibliography

Agyinasare, Charles. *Ambassadors of Heaven*. Accra: Charles Agyinasare, 2013.

Ahn, Daniel S. H. "Historical Background of the Emergence and Development of Self-Theologizing and Self-Missiologizing." [In Korean.] *Korea Mission Quarterly* 14, no. 1 (Fall 2014): 38–48.

Ahn, Kyo Seong. "Chonghoe Ilbaekjunyeon Majeun Oneulnal Hanguk-gyohoeui Myeongam" [Positives and negatives of the contemporary Korean church at the hundredth anniversary of the General Assembly]. *Gidokgongbo* [PCK world], February 28, 2012. www.pckworld.com/news/articleView.html?idxno=52945.

———. "Mission in Unity: An Investigation into the Question of Unity as It Has Arisen in the Presbyterian Church of Korea and Its World Mission." Ph.D. diss., Cambridge: Univ. of Cambridge, 2008.

Allen, Roland. *The Spontaneous Expansion of the Church—and the Causes Which Hinder It*. Cambridge: Lutterworth, 2006; orig. 1927.

Ammerman, Nancy Tatom. *Sacred Stories, Spiritual Tribes: Finding Religion in Everyday Life*. Oxford: Oxford Univ. Press, 2013.

Anderson, Allan. *An Introduction to Pentecostalism: Global Charismatic Christianity*. Cambridge: Cambridge Univ. Press, 2004.

Asamoah-Gyadu, J. Kwabena. "Doing Greater Things: Mega Church as an African Phenomenon." In *A Moving Faith: Mega Churches Go South*, edited by Jonathan D. James, 43–61. New Delhi: Sage, 2015.

———. "Megachurches and Their Implications for Christian Mission." *Lausanne Global Analysis* 3, no. 5 (September 2014). www.lausanne.org/docs/LGA/Lausanne-Global-Analysis-2014-09.pdf.

"Assembleias de Deus." http://en.wikipedia.org/wiki/Assembleias_de_Deus.

Assemblies of God: World Missions. "Latin America." http://worldmissions.ag.org/regions/latinamcab/overview.cfm.

Australian Christian Churches. www.acc.org.au/about-us.

Bakker, Jim. *I Was Wrong: The Untold Story of the Shocking Journey from PTL Power to Prison and Beyond*. Nashville: Thomas Nelson, 1996.

Bays, Daniel H., and Grant Wacker, eds. *The Foreign Missionary Enterprise at Home: Explorations in North American Cultural History*. Tuscaloosa: Univ. of Alabama Press, 2003.

Bevans, Stephen B. *Models of Contextual Theology*. Maryknoll, N.Y.: Orbis Books, 2002.

Bird, Warren. "The World's Largest Churches." www.leadnet.org/world/.

Bonk, Jonathan J. *Missions and Money: Affluence as a Western Missionary Problem*. Maryknoll, N.Y.: Orbis Books, 1991.

———. *Missions and Money: Affluence as a Missionary Problem . . . Revisited*. Maryknoll, N.Y.: Orbis Books, 2006.

Bonk, Jonathan J., ed. *Accountability in Missions: Korean and Western Case Studies*. Eugene, Ore.: Wipf & Stock, 2011.

Bon-Rin, Ro, and Marlin L. Nelson. *Korean Church Growth Explosion: Centennial of the Protestant Church (1884–1984)*. Seoul: Word of Life Press; Taichung, Taiwan: Asia Theological Association, 1983.

Bosch, David Jacobus. *Transforming Mission Paradigm Shifts in Theology of Mission*. Maryknoll, N.Y.: Orbis Books, 1991; repr., 2001.

Bowers, Paul. "Church and Mission in Paul." *Journal for the Study of the New Testament* 14, no. 44 (1991): 89–111.

Bowler, Kate. *Blessed: A History of the American Prosperity Gospel*. Oxford: Oxford Univ. Press, 2013.

Brafman, Ori, and Rod A. Beckstrom. *The Starfish and the Spider: The Unstoppable Power of Leaderless Organizations*. New York: Portfolio, 2006.

Breidenthal, Thomas E. "Formation for Mission." *Anglican Theological Review* 96, no. 1 (Winter 2014): 147–54.

Brouwer, Steve, Paul Gifford, and Susan D. Rose. *Exporting the American Gospel: Global Christian Fundamentalism*. New York: Routledge, 1996.

Bunting, Madeleine. "Capital Ideas." *The Guardian,* July 2007. http://society.guardian.co.uk/communities/story/0,,2128343,00.html.

Business Dictionary. www.businessdictionary.com/definition/globalization.html.

Byassee, Jason. "Purpose-Driven in Brazil: Perspectives on Church Growth." *Christian Century*, April 4, 2006, p. 8.

Called to Awaken the Laity Seminar. www.disciples.co.kr/english/seminar/cal/intro.asp.

Campbell, Heidi A. "Understanding the Relationship between Religion Online and Offline in a Networked Society." *Journal of the American Academy of Religion* 80, no. 1 (2012): 64–93.

Cannistraci, David. *Apostles and the Emerging Apostolic Movement*. Ventura, Calif.: Renew Books, 1996.

Carriker, C. Timothy. "As contribuições do Messianismo para uma hermenêutica missiológica." In *Evangelho e cultura: Leituras para a antropologia missionária*. Lulu.com (2008), 177–99.

Carter, Warren. *Matthew and the Margins: A Sociopolitical and Religious Reading*. Maryknoll, N.Y.: Orbis Books, 2000.

Casiño, Tereso. "Mission beyond the Diaspora." Paper presented at the Lausanne Global Diaspora Forum, Manila, March 24–27, 2015.

Chambers, Oswald. *My Utmost for His Highest*. Grand Rapids: Discovery House Publishers, 1992.

Cho, Myungsoon. "2013 Seonkyosa Pasong Hyeunhwang / Statistics of Missionaries in Various Nations as of 2013." KWMA document, p. 2. www.kwma.org.

Choi, Yoonsik. *2020–2040: The Future Map of the Korean Church*. [In Korean.] Seoul: Word of Life, 2013.

Christian Ethics Movement Korea. "Data of Opinion Research on Social Credibility of Korean Protestant Church 2013." [In Korean.] http://cemk.org/2008/bbs/board.php?bo_table=2007_data_cemk&wr_id=347.

———. [Documents for download; in Korean.] http://trusti.tistory.com/938.

Christian Today Weekly, January 1, 2015.

Church of England. *Mission-Shaped Church: Church Planting and Fresh Expressions of Church in a Changing Context*. London: Church House, 2004.

The Church of Pentecost. www.thecophq.org.

Church of Pentecost Information Management Department. Summary Statistics. Accra: Church of Pentecost, June, 2014.

Church of Pentecost International Mission Directorate. Financial Report. Accra: Church of Pentecost, January–June, 2014.

Clifton, Shane. "Ecumenism from the Bottom Up: A Pentecostal Perspective." *Journal of Ecumenical Studies* 47 (2012): 576–92.

Commission on World Mission and Evangelism. "Preparatory Paper No. 3: Theme, Thematic Area, and Signposts on the Journey towards the Athens Conference." World Council of Churches, May 10, 2005. www.oikoumene.org/en/resources/documents/other-meetings/mission-and-evangelism/preparatory-paper-03-theme-thematic-area-and-signposts.

Communauté Coréenne des Missions pour la Francophonie. www.iccmf.com.

"Communauté Coréenne des Missions pour la Francophonie Has Dedication Ceremony for Publication of French-Korean Bible." [In Korean.] GoodtvNews, July 8, 2013. www.c3tv.com/newsmission/news_view.asp?seq=54646.

Conn, Harvie M., Manuel Ortiz, and Susan S. Baker, eds. *The Urban Face of Mission: Ministering the Gospel in a Diverse and Changing World.* Philipsburg, N.J.: P&R Publishing, 2002.

Connor, Phillip. "Six Facts about South Korea's Growing Christian Population." Pew Research Center, Fact Tank, August 12, 2014. www.pewresearch.org/fact-tank/2014/08/12/6-facts-about-christianity-in-south-korea.

Corbett, Steve, and Brian Fikkert. *When Helping Hurts: Alleviating Poverty without Hurting the Poor—and Yourself.* Chicago: Moody Publishers, 2009.

Corwin, Gary R. "The Church's Primary Role in Training for the Frontiers," *International Journal of Frontier Missions* 11 (July–August 1994): 170. www.ijfm.org/PDFs_IJFM/11_3_PDFs/12%20Corwin.pdf.

———. "Training for the Frontiers: Who Does What?" *International Journal of Frontier Missions* 11 (January 1994): 1–6. www.ijfm.org/PDFs_IJFM/11_1_PDFs/Corwin.pdf.

Cunningham, Loren. "People of Destiny," in *The Sixth Korean World Mission Conference Manual* (2008), 4–13.

Curtis, Susan. *A Consuming Faith: The Social Gospel and Modern American Culture.* Baltimore: Johns Hopkins Univ. Press, 1991.

Decol, René D. "Mudança religiosa no Brasil: Uma visão demográfica." *Revista Brasileira de Estudos de População* 16, nos. 1/2 (1999): 121–37. www.abep.nepo.unicamp.br/docs/rev_inf/vol16_n1e2_1999/vol16_n1e2_1999_8artigo_121_137.pdf.

Doh, Yook Hwan. "Between Two Hours." [In Korean.] In *Tyrannus International Mission,* edited by Yong Jo Ha, 6–8. Seoul: Tyrannus Press, 2015.

Donaldson, Terence L. *Paul and the Gentiles: Remapping the Apostle's Convictional World.* Minneapolis: Fortress Press, 1997.

Driscoll, Mark. "A Pastoral Perspective on the Emergent Church." *Criswell Theological Review,* n.s., 3, no. 2 (Spring 2006): 87–93. www.christianitytoday.com/assets/10362.pdf.

Drucker, Peter. "Management's New Paradigm." *Forbes*. www.forbes.com/global/1998/1005/0113052a.html.

Fiedler, Klaus. *The Story of Faith Missions*. Oxford: Regnum Books International, 1994.

Fillinger, Kent. "Megachurches: A Year in Review." *Christian Standard* 145, no. 15 (April 2010): 280–81.

Finishing the Task. www.finishingthetask.com.

Finke, Roger, and Rodney Stark. *The Churching of America, 1776–2005: Winners and Losers in Our Religious Economy*. New Brunswick, N.J.: Rutgers Univ. Press, 2005.

Florida, Richard L. *The Rise of the Creative Class: Revisited*. Philadelphia: Basic Books, 2012.

"Gangwon Land [a casino] Has Tenth Anniversary." [In Korean.] *Monthly Chosun*, April 2010. http://monthly.chosun.com/client/news/print.asp?ctcd=C&nNewsNumb=201004100052.

Ghana Evangelism Committee. *National Church Survey: Facing the Unfinished Task of the Church in Ghana*. Accra: Ghana Evangelism Committee, 1989.

Global Missions Podcast. "002: Standards of Excellence for Short Term Missions." http://globalmissionspodcast.com/002.

"Gods and Men in Greek Religion." http://faculty.gvsu.edu/websterm/gods&men.htm.

"The Government Tries to Revitalize the Economy of Taebaek by Introducing Leisure Industry. [In Korean.] Research Institute of Korean Studies. August 2011, issue 4. http://rikszine.korea.ac.kr/front/article/humanList.minyeon?selectArticle_id=74.

Graf, Jonathan. "Passionate Prayer for Missions Is Biblical." In *Church Prayer Leaders Network*, edited by Jonathan Graf. www.prayerleader.com/resources/prayer-leader-central/missions-prayer/prayer-for-missions.

Greenway, Roger S., and Timothy M. Monsma. *Cities: Mission's New Frontier*. Grand Rapids: Baker Books, 1989.

Guder, Darrell L., ed. *Missional Church: A Vision for the Sending of the Church in North America*. Grand Rapids: Eerdmans, 1998.

Ha, Yong Jo. *I, Yong Jo Ha, Have Dedicated My Life to Missions*. [In Korean.] Seoul: Duranno Press, 2008.

Haesler, Alfred A., ed. *Gott ohne Kirche?* Olten, Freiburg im Breisgau: Walter-Verlag, 1975.

Han, Kookil. *Mission Embracing the World*. Seoul: PCTS Press, 2004.

Hanciles, Jehu J. "Migration, Diaspora Communities, and the New Missionary Encounter with Western Society," *Lausanne World Pulse*, July 2008, www.lausanneworldpulse.com/themedarticles.php/975?pg=all.

Harrison, Ernest. *A Church without God*. Philadelphia: Lippincott, 1967.

Hartford Institute for Religion Research. "Fast Facts about American Religion." http://hirr.hartsem.edu/research/fastfacts/fast_facts.html.

———. "Megachurch Definition." http://hirr.hartsem.edu/megachurch/definition.html.

———. "Megachurches." http://hirr.hartsem.edu/megachurch/megachurches.html.

Heartstream Resources. http://heartstreamresources.org.

Hiebert, Paul G. *Anthropological Insights for Missionaries*. Grand Rapids: Baker Books, 1985.

Hiebert, Paul G., and Eloise Hiebert Meneses. *Incarnational Ministry: Planting Churches in Band, Tribal, Peasant, and Urban Societies*. Grand Rapids: Baker Books, 1995.

Hillsong. "Vision." http://hillsong.com/vision.

Hoedemaker, Bert. "The Legacy of J. C. Hoekendijk." *International Bulletin of Missionary Research* 19, no. 4 (October 1995): 166–70.

Hollenweger, Walter J. *The Pentecostals*. London: SCM Press, 1972.

"Hong Kong." http://en.wikipedia.org/wiki/Hong_Kong.

Howe, Neil, and William Strauss. *Millennials Rising: The Next Great Generation*. New York: Vintage Books, 2000.

Hultgren, Arland J. *Paul's Gospel and Mission*. Philadelphia: Fortress Press, 1985.

Hunt, Robert A., Kam Hing Lee, and John Roxborogh, eds. *Christianity in Malaysia: A Denominational History*. Petaling Jaya, Selangor Darul Ehsan, Malaysia: Pelanduk Publications, 1992.

Huntington, Samuel. *The Clash of Civilizations and the Remaking of World Order*. London: Simon & Schuster, 1997.

Hutchinson, Mark, and John Wolffe. *A Short History of Global Evangelicalism*. Cambridge: Cambridge Univ. Press, 2012.

Ihejirika, Walter C., and Godwin B. Okon. "Mega Churches and Megaphones: Nigerian Church Leaders and Their Media Ministries." In *A Moving Faith: Mega Churches Go South*, edited by Jonathan D. James, 62–82. Thousand Oaks, Calif.: Sage Publications, 2015.

Im, Chadler H. "The Korean Diaspora Churches in the USA: Their Concerns and Strengths." In *Global Diasporas and Mission*, edited by Chandler H. Im and Amos Yong, 130–47. Eugene, Ore.: Wipf & Stock, 2014.

Instituto Brasileiro de Geografia e Estatística. "Censo Demográfico 2010: Características gerais da população, religião e pessoas com deficiência." www.ibge.gov.br/home/estatistica/populacao/censo2010/caracteristicas_religiao_deficiencia/caracteristicas_religiao_deficiencia_tab_pdf.shtm.

James, Jonathan D., ed. *A Moving Faith: Mega Churches Go South*. New Delhi: Sage, 2015.

Jenkins, Philip. *The Next Christendom: The Coming of Global Christianity*. Oxford: Oxford Univ. Press, 2002.

Jervell, Jacob. *The Theology of the Acts of the Apostles*. Cambridge: Cambridge Univ. Press, 1996.

John, Stanley. "Missiology." Unpublished lecture on missiology, Alliance Theological Seminary, Nyack, N.Y., 2014.

Johnson, Todd M., and Albert W. Hickman. "Religious Demography and Mission Strategy." *International Journal of Frontier Missiology* 29, no. 1 (Spring 2012): 14–20.

Johnstone, Patrick. *The Church Is Bigger Than You Think*. Pasadena, Calif.: William Carey Library, 1998.

———. *The Church Is Bigger Than You Think: The Unfinished Work of World Evangelism*. 6th edition. (Korean ed.; WEC Korea, 2010), 232–35.

Keller, Timothy J. *Center Church: Doing Balanced, Gospel-Centered Ministry in Your City*. Grand Rapids: Zondervan, 2012.

Kim, Jin Bong. "Korean Missionary Retirement Survey." In *Family Accountability in Missions: Korean and Western Case Studies*, edited by Jonathan J. Bonk, 259–73. New Haven, Conn.: OMSC Publications, 2013.

Kim, Jong Eon. "The History of Hwangji Church and the Philosophy of Ministry of Jong Eon Kim." [In Korean.] Responses by e-mail to written interview questions from Jinbong Kim, November 20, 2014.

Kim, S. Hun, and Wonsuk Ma, eds. *Korean Diaspora and Christian Mission*. Oxford: Regnum Books International, 2011.

Kim, Yong Hoon. Church Directory. Herndon, Va.: Open Door Presbyterian Church, 2014.

Kirk, J. Andrew. *What Is Mission? Theological Explorations*. London: Darton, Longman & Todd, 1999.

Klaver, Miranda. "Worship Music as Aesthetic Domain of Meaning and Bonding: The Glocal Context of a Dutch Pentecostal Church." In *The Spirit of Praise: Music and Worship in Pentecostal-Charismatic Christianity*, edited by Monique Marie Ingalls and Amos Yong, 97–113. University Park: Pennsylvania State Univ. Press, 2015.

Koduah, Alfred. "The Church of Pentecost in a Post Modern Society." In *James McKeown Memorial Lectures: Fifty Years of the Church of Pentecost*, edited by Opoku Onyinah, 106–35. Accra: Church of Pentecost, 2004.

"Korean American Churches [in the United States], 4150." [In Korean.] *Korean Christian Press*, August 26, 2015. www.chpress.net/detail.asp?id=8667&cate=search.

"Korean Christians in Hong Kong." https://en.wikipedia.org/wiki/Korean_Christians_in_Hong_Kong.

Korean Residents Association H.K. "Korean Residents Association (H.K.) LTD." [In Korean.] http://kra.hk/new/home/kra/index.php.

Larbi, Emmanuel Kingsley. "The Nature of Continuity and Discontinuity of Ghanaian Pentecostal Concept of Salvation in African Cosmology." *Cyberjournal for Pentecostal-Charismatic Research*. www.pctii.org/cyberj/cyberj10/larbi.html.

Larkin, William J., Jr. *Acts*. Downers Grove, Ill.: InterVarsity Press, 1995.

Latourette, Kenneth Scott. *A History of Christianity*. 2 vols. Peabody, Mass.: Prince Press, 1999.

Lausanne Committee for World Evangelization. *Cooperating in World Evangelization: A Handbook on Church/Para-Church Relationships*. Lausanne Occasional Papers, no. 24. Wheaton, Ill.: Lausanne Committee for World Evangelization, 1983.

———. *Scattered to Gather: Embracing the Global Trend of Diaspora*. Manila: LifeChange Publishing, 2010.

Leage, Philip James. "The Mission Agency and the Local Church." B.A. diss., Univ. of Gloucestershire, 2011. www.ywamkb.net/kb/The_Mission_Agency_and_the_Local_Church.

Lee, Heeyeol. "Prayer Symphony on Mission." Seminar handout, First Korean Presbyterian Church of Greater Hartford, January 2008.

Lee, Helen. "Silent Exodus: Can the East Asian Church in America Reverse the Flight of Its Next Generation?," *Christianity Today* 40, no. 12 (August 12, 1996). www.christianitytoday.com/ct/1996/august12/6t9050.html.

Lee, Jaehwan. "Mission Possible." In "Missiological Strategy for Pastors" syllabus, Summit Lake Camp, Emmitsburg, Md., 2004.

Lee, See-Young. "Mobilizing Senior Christians in Korea and among the Korean Diaspora for Mission." In *Korean Diaspora and Christian Mission*, edited by Sŭng-hun Kim and Wonsuk Ma, 260–63. Eugene, Ore.: Wipf & Stock, 2014.

Lee, Won Sang. "Mission Mobilization Initiative of the Korean Central Presbyterian Church of Washington." Responses to interview questions from Sun Man Kim, September 29, 2014.

Lee, Young-hoon. *The Holy Spirit Movement in Korea: Its Historical and Theological Development*. Oxford: Regnum Books International, 2009.

Lim, Heekuk, et al., eds. *Christianity in Korea: Historical Moments of Protestant Churches*. Seoul: NCCK, 2013.

Lim, Jong-Pyo. "21 Segileul Dojeonhaneun Haninseongyosaui Daecheo" [The response of Korean missionaries to the challenges of the twenty-first century]. In *Hangukseongyoui Banseonggwa Geu Junbi* [The reflection and preparation of the Korean world mission], edited by Jong-Pyo Lim, 167–95. Seoul: Korean Missionary Leadership Development Conference, 1999).

Lipka, Michael. "Five Facts about Prayer." Pew Research Center, Fact Tank, May 6, 2015. www.pewresearch.org/fact-tank/2015/05/06/5-facts-about-prayer.

Marti, Geraldo. *Hollywood Faith: Holiness, Prosperity, and Ambition in a Los Angeles Church*. New Brunswick, N.J.: Rutgers Univ. Press, 2008.

Mavuno Church. "Our Mission." www.mavunochurch.org/new/content.php?id=50.

Mavuno Leader's Day Bulletin, 2010.

"Megachurches." *Christianity Today*. www.christianitytoday.com/ct/topics/m/megachurches.

"Mega Church Made in Manhattan." CNN, June 2, 2014. http://edition.cnn.com/videos/living/2014/06/02/ac-harlow-pastor-carl-lentz-long.cnn.

Monteiro, Duglas T. "Um confronto entre Juazeiro, Canudos e Contestado." In *História geral da civilização brasileira*, vol. 3/2, edited by Boris Fausto. Rio de Janeiro: Difel, 1978.

Moon, Steve Sang-Cheol. "The Protestant Missionary Movement in Korea: Current Growth and Development." *International Bulletin of Missionary Research* 32, no. 2 (2008): 59–64.

———. "Missions from Korea 2014: Missionary Children." *International Bulletin of Missionary Research* 38, no. 2 (April 2014): 84–85.

———, Hee-Joo Yoo, and Eun-Mi Kim. "Missions from Korea 2015: Missionaries Unable to Continue Ministry in Their Country of Service." *International Bulletin of Missionary Research* 39, no. 2 (April 2015): 84–85.

Moon, Sungmo. *The Story of Pastor Yong Jo Ha*. [In Korean.] Seoul: Duranno Press, 2010.

Moore, J. Stanley. "Strategies for Music in Missions." In *Missiology: An Introduction to the Foundations, History, and Strategies of World Missions*, edited by John Mark Terry, Ebbie Smith, and Justice Anderson, 559–71. Nashville: Broadman & Holman, 1998.

Negrão, Lísias Nogueira, and Josildeth Gomes Consorte. *O messianismo no Brasil contemporâneo*. São Paulo: FFLCH-USP/CER, 1984.

Newbigin, Lesslie. *The Household of God: Lectures on the Nature of the Church*. New York: Friendship Press, 1954.

———. *Lesslie Newbigin: Missionary Theologian; A Reader*. Compiled by Paul Weston. Grand Rapids: Eerdmans, 2006.

———. *The Open Secret: An Introduction to the Theology of Mission*. Grand Rapids: Eerdmans, 1995.

Ng, Peter Tze Ming. "'Globalization' as a Key to the Interplay between Christianity and Asian Cultures: The Vision of Francis Wei in Early Twentieth-Century China." *International Journal of Public Theology* 1 (2007): 104–15.

Nyquist, John W. "Parachurch Agencies and Mission." In *Evangelical Dictionary of World Missions*, edited by A. Scott Moreau, 727. Grand Rapids: Baker Books, 2000; Korean ed., 2014.

Oak, John H. *Called to Awaken the Laity*. London: Christian Focus, 2006.

O'Brien, Peter T. *Gospel and Mission in the Writings of Paul: An Exegetical and Theological Analysis*. Grand Rapids: Baker Books, 2000.

Oh, Sang Cheul. *Christian Times*, May 17, 2012.

———. *Immigration Theology*. [In Korean.] Seoul: Qumran Press, 2008.

Oke, Ruth O. "Paradigm Shift in Mission from Biblical Perspectives." *Ogbomoso Journal of Theology* 15, no. 1 (2010): 147–57.

Oldenburg, Ray. *The Great Good Place: Cafés, Coffee Shops, Community Centers, Beauty Parlors, General Stores, Bars, Hangouts, and How They Get You through the Day*. New York: Paragon House, 1989.

Onnuri Church, *Talk and Talk: Twenty-Five Years of Onnuri Church*. [In Korean.] Seoul: Onnuri Church, 2010.

Onyinah, Opoku. *2013 State of the Church Address, Given at Fourteenth Extraordinary Council Meetings of the Church of Pentecost*. Accra: Pentecost Press, 2014.

Overseas Koreans Foundation. "Overseas Koreans Foundation." [In Korean.] www.okf.or.kr/portal/OkfMainView.do.

Oxbrow, Mark, and Tim Grass, eds. *The Mission of God: Studies in Orthodox and Evangelical Mission*. Oxford: Regnum Books International, 2015.

Paik, Nak Joon. *Korean Protestant Church History, 1832–1910*. [In Korean.] Seoul: Yonsei Univ. Press, 1998.

Park, Kiho (Timothy). "The Big Picture: Accountability from a Korean Missiologist's Perspective." In *Accountability in Missions: Korean and Western Case Studies*, edited by Jonathan J. Bonk, 53–65. Eugene, Ore.: Wipf & Stock, 2011.

———. Lecture. Overseas Ministries Study Center, New Haven, Conn., January 2012.

Park, Sangbae. "Mission as a Realization of the Kingdom of God." Mission mobilization revival meeting of the Korean Presbyterian Church of Greater Hartford, January 2012.

Pearson, Emily. "Church 'Embraces' Unreached People Group at Home and Abroad." http://stories.imb.org/americas/stories/view/church-embraces-unreached-people-group-at-home-and-abroad.

Pew Research Center: Religion and Public Life. "Historical Overview of Pentecostalism in Brazil: Origins and Growth." www.pewforum.org/2006/10/05/historical-overview-of-pentecostalism-in-brazil.

Piatt, Christian. "Five Reasons We Still Need Intentional Community (Regardless of Your Faith)." Patheos: Hosting the Conversation of

Faith. July 16, 2015. www.patheos.com/blogs/christianpiatt/2015/07/five-reasons-we-still-need-intentional-community-regardless-of-your-faith.

Piper, John. *Desiring God.* Portland, Ore.: Multnomah Press, 1986.

Poewe, Karla, ed. *Charismatic Christianity as a Global Culture.* Columbia: Univ. of South Carolina Press, 1994.

Pond, Allison, Gregory Smith, and Scott Clement. "Religion among the Millennials." Pew Research Center, Religion and Public Life, February 17, 2010. www.pewforum.org/2010/02/17/religion-among-the-millennials.

Price, Stella. *Chosen for Choson (Korea).* Essex, Mass.: Emmaus Road Ministries, 2010.

Priest, Robert J., Douglas Wilson, and Adelle Johnson. "U.S. Megachurches and New Patterns of Global Mission." *International Bulletin of Missionary Research* 34, no. 2 (2010): 97–104.

Putnam, Robert. *Bowling Alone: The Collapse and Revival of American Community.* New York: Simon & Schuster, 2000.

Rambo, Lewis R. *Understanding Religious Conversion.* New Haven: Yale Univ. Press, 1993.

Ribeiro, René. "Brazilian Messianic Movements." In *Millennial Dreams in Action: Studies in Revolutionary Religious Movements,* edited by Sylvia L. Thrupp, 55–69. 2nd edition. New York: Schocken Books, 1970.

Richardson, Rick. "Emerging Missional Movements: An Overview and Assessment of Some Implications for Mission(s)." *International Bulletin of Missionary Research* 37, no. 3 (2013): 131–36.

Riesner, Rainer. *Paul's Early Period: Chronology, Mission Strategy, Theology.* Grand Rapids: Eerdmans, 1998.

Ro, Danny Changsoo. Annual Congregational Report. Anaheim, Calif.: Sa-Rang Community Church, October, 2014.

Robert, Dana L. "Cross-Cultural Friendship in the Creation of Twentieth-Century World Christianity." *International Bulletin of Missionary Research* 35, no. 2 (2011): 100–107.

———. "Global Friendship as Incarnational Missional Practice." *International Bulletin of Missionary Research* 39, no. 4 (2015): 180–84.

———. "Missionaries Sent and Received, Worldwide, 1910–2010." In *Atlas of Global Christianity, 1910–2010,* edited by Todd M. Johnson, Kenneth R. Ross, and Sandra S. K. Lee, 259. Edinburgh: Edinburgh Univ. Press, 2009.

Rodríguez, Augusto. *Paradigms of the Church in Mission: A Historical Survey of the Church's Self-Understanding of Being the Church and of Mission.* Eugene, Ore.: Wipf & Stock, 2012.

Rynkiewich, Michael. *Soul, Self, and Society: A Postmodern Anthropology for Mission in a Postcolonial World.* Eugene, Ore.: Cascade Books, 2011.

Sanneh, Lamin. *Translating the Message: The Missionary Impact on Culture.* Maryknoll, N.Y.: Orbis Books, 1997.

Schapiro, Jeff. "America Is One of the Fastest Growing Mission Fields in the World." *Christian Post,* October 10, 2012. www.christianpost.com/news/america-is-one-of-the-fastest-growing-mission-fields-in-the-world-82985.

Schwartz, Glenn. "Short-Term Mission Trips: Maximizing the Benefits." *Mission Frontiers* 26, no. 2 (2004): 12–13.

Simpson, A. B. "New Testament Missionary Types." In *Missionary Messages*, by A. B. Simpson, chap. 3. www.swartzentrover.com/cotor/e-books/holiness/Simpson/Missionary/Missionary%20Messages.pdf.

Snell, Jeffrey T. "Beyond the Individual and into the World." *PNEUMA: Journal of the Society for Pentecostal Studies* 14 (1992): 43–57.

Song, Minho. "Constructing a Local Theology for the Second Generation Korean Ministry." *Urban Mission* 15, no. 2 (December 1997): 23–34. www.torontoyoungnak.com/bbs.php?table=board_67&home=song_en&query=view&uid=3.

Spindler, Marc R. "The Biblical Grounding and Orientation of Mission." In *Missiology: An Ecumenical Introduction*, edited by Arnulf Camps, L. A. Hoedemaker, and Marc R. Spindler, 123–43. Grand Rapids: Eerdmans, 1995.

Spurgeon's College. www.spurgeons.ac.uk.

Stanley, Brian. *The Global Diffusion of Evangelicalism: The Age of Billy Graham and John Stott*. Nottingham: IVP Academic, 2013.

Stark, Rodney. *The Triumph of Christianity: How the Jesus Movement Became the World's Largest Religion*. New York: HarperCollins, 2011.

Stark, Rodney, and William Sims Bainbridge. *A Theory of Religion*. New York: Lang, 1987.

Stark, Rodney, and Roger Finke. *Acts of Faith: Explaining the Human Side of Religion*. Berkeley: Univ. of California Press, 2000.

Stendahl, Krister. *Paul among Jews and Gentiles*. Philadelphia: Fortress Press, 1976.

Stott, John. *The Living Church*. Downers Grove, Ill.: IVP, 2007.

———. "The Living God Is a Missionary God." In *Perspectives on the World Christian Movement*, ed. Ralph D. Winter and Steven C. Hawthorne, 17–18. Pasadena, Calif.: William Carey Library, 1981.

Sunquist, Scott W. "Asian Mission to Asians." In *Christian Mission in the Third Millennium*, edited by Charles E. Cole, 21–43. New York: General Board of Global Ministries, the United Methodist Church, 2004.

"Tabela 1.4.1." ftp://ftp.ibge.gov.br/Censos/Censo_Demografico_2010/Caracteristicas_Gerais_Religiao_Deficiencia/tab1_4.pdf.

"Taebaek's Population Drops to Less Than 50,000." [In Korean.] March 7, 2012. http://blog.daum.net/pm21234/15862358.

Taylor, Paul, and Scott Keeter, eds. *Millennials: A Portrait of Generation Next*. Pew Research Center, February 2010. www.pewsocialtrends.org/files/2010/10/millennials-confident-connected-open-to-change.pdf.

Tennent, Timothy C. *Invitation to World Missions: A Trinitarian Missiology for the Twenty-First Century*. Grand Rapids: Kregel Academic, 2010.

Thacker, Justin. "Opening Address at the World Evangelical Alliance." *Journal of Latin American Theology* 5, no. 2 (2010): 8.

Thomas, Norman E. "The Church at Antioch: Crossing Racial, Cultural, and Class Barriers." In *Mission in Acts: Ancient Narratives in Contemporary Context*, edited by Robert L. Gallagher and Paul Herting, 144–56. Maryknoll, N.Y.: Orbis Books, 2004.

Thomas, Norman E., ed. *Classic Texts in Mission and World Christianity: A Reader's Companion to David Bosch's "Transforming Mission."* Maryknoll, N.Y.: Orbis Books, 1995.

Thumma, Scott. "Megachurches." Hartford Institute for Religion Research. http://hirr.hartsem.edu/megachurch/megachurches.html.

Thumma, Scott, and Warren Bird. *Changes in American Megachurches: Tracing Eight Years of Growth and Innovation in the Nation's Largest-Attendance Congregations*. Hartford, Conn.: Hartford Institute for Religion Research, 2008.

Thumma, Scott, and Dave Travis. *Beyond Megachurch Myths: What We Can Learn from America's Largest Churches*. San Francisco: Jossey-Bass, 2007.

Towns, Elmer. "The World's Ten Largest Churches." *Christian Life*, January 1983, pp. 60–66.

2011 Population Census Office, Census and Statistics Department. "Thematic Report: Ethnic Minorities." Hong Kong: HKSAR Government Printing Office, 2011. www.census2011.gov.hk/pdf/EM.pdf.

"2014 General Assemblies of Major Denominations of South Korea." [In Korean.] *Kukmin Daily*, September 29, 2014. http://news.kmib.co.kr/article/view.asp?arcid=0922799465&.

U.N. Department of Economic and Social Affairs, Population Division. "International Migration." www.un.org/en/development/desa/population/migration/publications/wallchart/index.shtml.

U.S. Department of State. "Archive." http://2001-2009.state.gov/p/eap/rls/ot/16606.htm.

Van Engen, Charles E. *God's Missionary People: Rethinking the Purpose of the Local Church*. Grand Rapids: Baker Books, 1991.

Van Gelder, Craig, and Dwight J. Zscheile, *The Missional Church in Perspective: Mapping Trends and Shaping the Conversation*. Grand Rapids: Baker Academic, 2010.

Wagner, Tom. "Branding, Music, and Religion: Standardization and Adaptation in the Experience of the 'Hillsong Sound.'" In *Religion as Brands: New Perspectives on the Marketization of Religion and Spirituality*, edited by Jean-Claude Usunier and Jörg Stolz, 59–73. London: Ashgate, 2014.

Walls, Andrew F. *The Missionary Movement in Christian History: Studies in the Transmission of Faith*. Maryknoll, N.Y.: Orbis Books, 1996.

Wan, Enoch. "Korean Diaspora: From Hermit Kingdom to Kingdom Ministry." In *Korean Diaspora and Christian Mission*, edited by Sŭng-hun Kim and Wonsuk Ma, 101–16. Eugene, Ore.: Wipf & Stock, 2011.

———. "Mission among the Chinese Diaspora: A Case Study of Migration and Mission." http://missiology.org/missionchina/ChineseDiaspora-Missiology.pdf.

Warren, Max. *I Believe in the Great Commission*. London: Hodder & Stoughton, 1976.

Wei, Francis C. M. *The Spirit of Chinese Culture*. New York: Scribner's Sons, 1947.

Winter, Ralph D. "Editorial Comment," *Mission Frontiers* 26, no. 2 (2004): 4–5.

———. *The Twenty-Five Unbelievable Years*. 2nd ed. Pasadena, Calif.: William Carey Library, 2005; Korean ed., 2012, pp. 266–83.

———. "The Two Structures of God's Redemptive Mission." *Missiology: An International Review* 2, no. 1 (1974): 121–39.

———. "The Two Structures of God's Redemptive Mission." In *Perspectives on the World Christian Movement*, edited by Ralph D. Winter and Steven C. Hawthorne, 244–53. Pasadena, Calif.: William Carey Library, 2009.

———. "The Two Structures of God's Redemptive Mission." In *Perspectives on the World Christian Movement: A Reader*, rev. ed., edited by Ralph D. Winter and Steven C. Hawthorne, 45–57. Pasadena, Calif.: William Carey Library, 1992.

———. "When Jesus Said. . . ." *Mission Frontiers* 17, no. 11–12 (1995): 56.

Winter, Ralph D., and Steven C. Hawthorne, eds. *Perspectives on the World Christian Movement*. 4th ed. Pasadena, Calif.: William Carey Library, 1981, 2009.

Wright, Christopher J. H. "Confronting Idols." Lausanne Cape Town 2010, Plenary Session 2. www.youtube.com/watch?v=gZ57kCNQ6oQ.

———. *The Mission of God*. Downers Grove, Ill.: IVP Academic, 2006.

———. *The Mission of God's People*. Grand Rapids: Zondervan, 2010.

Wuthnow, Robert. *Boundless Faith: The Global Outreach of American Churches*. Berkeley: Univ. of California Press, 2009.

Yamaguchi, Noboru. "Shitono Hataraki" [Acts of the apostles]. In *Shin Seisho Chukai* [New Bible commentary], vol. 2, *Acts to Ephesians*, edited by Yoshio Masuda et al. Tokyo: Inochino Kotobasha, 1986.

Yang, Daniel Taichoul. *Called Out for Witness*. Oxford: Regnum Books International, 2014.

Yoido Full Gospel Church. *Yeouido Sunbokeum Kyohoe 50 nyeonsa* [Yoido full gospel church: Fiftieth anniversary]. Seoul: Yoido Full Gospel Church, 2008.

Yoo, Seung Kwan (David). "Accountability in a Local Church's Ministry of World Mission: SaRang Community Church as a Case Study." In *Accountability in Missions: Korean and Western Case Studies*, edited by Jonathan J. Bonk, 88–139. Eugene, Ore.: Wipf & Stock, 2011.

Yoon, Hyung Joong. "A Diaspora Story of a Missional Church: The Hong Kong Korea Mission Church Story." Korean pastors luncheon, Overseas Ministries Study Center, September 22, 2014.

Young, Haw. "Mission Trends in the Twenty-First Century." In *Fiftieth Anniversary of Korean Mission Work in Malaysia*. Kuala Lumpur: n.p., 2015.

Young-gi, Hong. "The Backgrounds and Characteristics of the Charismatic Mega-Churches in Korea." *Asian Journal of Pentecostal Studies* 3, no. 1 (2000): 99–118.

Participants

Jones Junior Adzrah
Personal Assistant to the Presiding Bishop
Perez Chapel International
Accra, Ghana

Charles Agyinasare
Founder and Presiding Bishop
Perez Chapel International
Accra, Ghana

Kyo Seong Ahn
Professor of Historical Theology/Church History
Presbyterian University and Theological Seminary (PUTS)
Seoul, Korea

Daniel S. H. Ahn
Professor of Intercultural Studies/Practical Ministries
Tyndale Theological Seminary
Badhoevedorp, Netherlands

J. Kwabena Asamoah-Gyadu
Baëta-Grau Professor of Contemporary African Christianity and Pentecostal/Charismatic Theology
Trinity Theological Seminary
Accra, Ghana

Dwight P. Baker
Former Associate Director
Overseas Ministries Study Center
New Haven, Connecticut, USA

Jean Bonk
Former missionary in Ethiopia
Winnipeg, Canada

Jonathan Bonk
Executive Director Emeritus/Mission Consultant
Overseas Ministries Study Center
Winnipeg, Canada

Charles Timothy Carriker
Missiological Consultant
Igreja Presbiteriana Independente do Brasil
Florianópolis, Brazil

Stephen S. Cha
Lead Pastor, English Ministry
Onnuri Community Church
Seoul, Korea

Peter JaeHyeok Chin
Senior Pastor
Global Mission Church
Sungnam-si, Gyeonggi-do, Korea

Hak Hyun Cho
Missionary with OMF International
Phnom Penh, Cambodia

Hyung Keun Paul Choi
Professor of Mission Studies
Seoul Theological University
Seoul, Korea

Woosung Calvin Choi
Senior Pastor
Watertown Evangelical Church
Watertown, Massachusetts, USA

Jae Chul Chung
Managing Director
Asian Mission
Seoul, Korea

Jae Ryun Chung
Associate Pastor
Onnuri Community Church
Seoul, Korea

Obed Benjamin Cruz
Regional Coordinator of Mobilization
Serving in Mission (SIM) in Latin America
Guatemala City, Guatemala

Christopher DeWelt
Director of Intercultural Studies
Ozark Christian College
Joplin, Missouri, USA

Yook Hwan Do
Lead Pastor
Vision2000/Tyrannus International Missions
Seoul, Korea

Keith Eitel
Dean, Professor of Missions and World Christian Studies
Southwestern Baptist Theological Seminary
Fort Worth, Texas, USA

Wanjiru M. Gitau
Teaching Fellow
Africa International University
Nairobi, Kenya

Wesley Granberg-Michaelson
Facilitation Team
Global Christian Forum, USA
Santa Fe, New Mexico, USA

Tae Kyung Ham
General Director, Management Department of CGN TV
Onnuri Community Church
Seoul, Korea

Darrell R. Jackson
Senior Lecturer in Missiology
Morling College
Sydney, Australia

J. Nelson Jennings
Mission Pastor-Consultant
Onnuri Community Church
Seoul, Korea

Ja Naw Jr
Associate Pastor of Yangon Kachin Baptist Church
Director of Evangelism and Mission Department
Yangon, Myanmar

Dae Su Jung
Head Elder, Mission Committee
Onnuri Community Church
Seoul, Korea

Soonuk Jung
Chief Executive Officer
Chunma Corporation
Seoul, Korea

Chang Ju Kim,
Mission Co-Worker and Professor
Ambatonakanga Faculté de Théologie
Antananarivo, Madagascar

Hong Joo Kim
Director of Mission Headquarters
Onnuri Community Church
Seoul, Korea

Jinbong Kim
Director of International Church Relations
KGMLF Coordinator
Overseas Ministries Study Center
New Haven, Connecticut, USA

Jong Eon Kim
Senior Pastor
Hwangji Presbyterian Church
Taebaek, Kangwon-do, Korea

Joshua Kyungsool Kim
Director of SIM Korea
Serving In Mission
Sungnam-si, Gyeonggi-do, Korea

Sunman Kim
Senior Pastor
First Korean Presbyterian Church
Hartford, Connecticut, USA

Timothy Kyung Joong Kim
Vice Director of Southeast Asia Islam Region
Global Mission Society Missionary
Kuala Lumpur, Malaysia

Yon Soo Kim
Associate General Secretary
World Mission Association
Seoul, Korea

Miranda Klaver
Assistant Professor
VU University Amsterdam
Amsterdam, Netherlands

Jonathan Kofie
District Pastor
The Church of Pentecost
Accra, Ghana

Abe Kugyong Koh
Senior Pastor
Detroit Vision Church
Detroit, Michigan, USA

George Iype Kovoor
Rector
St. John's Episcopal Church
New Haven, Connecticut, USA

D. David Lee
Associate Director of World Mission Center
Southwestern Baptist Theological Seminary
Fort Worth, Texas, USA

Han Young Lee
Professor of Old Testament Studies
Asia United Theological University
and Dean of ACTS International Graduate School
Yangpyoung-kun, Gyeonggi-do, Korea

Jae Hoon Lee
Senior Pastor
Onnuri Community Church
Seoul, Korea

Mong Sik Lee
Senior Pastor of Juhyanghan Church
Director of Communauté Coréenne des Missions pour la Francophonie
Seoul, Korea

Sang Joon Lee
Pastor of Yangjae Campus
Onnuri Community Church
Seoul, Korea

Won Sang Lee
Former Senior Pastor of Korean Central Presbyterian Church
President of SEED International
Centreville, Virginia, USA

Ida Suet Yeung Leung
Lecturer in Chinese Christianity
China Victory Theological Seminary
Hong Kong, China

Jorge H. López
Senior Pastor, Pastor General
Iglesia Fraternidad Cristiana of Guatemala
Guatemala City, Guatemala

Elsy López
Director of "Champions Zone," Praise/Worship Team
Iglesia Fraternidad Cristiana of Guatemala
Guatemala City, Guatemala

Calvin Ma
International Director for East Asia North Area
OMF International Headquarters
Singapore

Carlos L. Malavé
Executive Director
Christian Churches Together
Indianapolis, Indiana, USA

Steve Sang-Cheol Moon
Executive Director
Korea Research Institute for Mission
Seoul, Korea

Dennis Tak Wing Ng
Adjunct Professor
Shanghai East China Theological Seminary
Hong Kong, China

Peter Tze Ming Ng
Department Chair and Professor of Chinese Christianity
China Victory Theological Seminary
Hong Kong, China

Daniel J. Nicholas
Director of Communications, Publications, and Church Relations
Overseas Ministries Study Center
New Haven, Connecticut, USA

Stephen William Offutt
Assistant Professor of Development Studies
Asbury Theological Seminary
Wilmore, Kentucky, USA

Opoku Onyinah
Chairman of Church of Pentecost
President, Ghana Pentecostal and Charismatic Council
Accra, Ghana

Mark Oxbrow
International Director
Faith2Share
Oxford, UK

Kyung Nam Park
Director of WEC Korea
WEC International
Seoul, Korea

Myung Soo Park
Professor of Church History
Seoul Theological University
Seoul, Korea

Pil-Hun Park
Mission Pastor
SaRang Church
Seoul, Korea

Stephen Sikyong Park
Professor of Intercultural Studies
Grace Theological Seminary
Winona Lake, Indiana, USA

Yong Kyu Park
Professor of Church History
Chongshin University
Seoul, Korea

Samson
Associate General Secretary
Myanmar Baptist Convention
Yangon, Myanmar

Joseph Shao
Chair of SIM, Metro Manila, Philippines
Board President, Biblical Seminary
Manila, Philippines

Mark Shaw
Professor of World Christianity
Africa International University
Nairobi, Kenya

Nam Yong Sung
Senior Pastor
Samkwang Church
Seoul, Korea

Dong Hwa Tae
Vice General Secretary of The General Board of Missions
Korean Methodist Church
Seoul, Korea

Eiko Takamizawa
Professor of Mission/ICS Department
Torch Trinity Graduate University
Seoul, Korea

Scott Lee Thumma
Professor of Sociology of Religion
Hartford Seminary
Hartford, Connecticut, USA

Ben Torrey
Chairman of Jesus Abbey
Executive Director of the Fourth River Project
Taebaek, Kangwon-do, Korea

Tae Wook Um
Mission Director
Yoido Full Gospel Church
Seoul, Korea

Darrell L. Whiteman
Interim Executive Director
Overseas Ministries Study Center
New Haven, Connecticut, USA

Young Suk Woo
Mission Pastor
Global Mission Church
Sungnam-si, Gyeonggi-do, Korea

Chee Weng Yong
Mission Pastor
Calvary Church Kuala Lumpur Assemblies of God
Kuala Lumpur, Malaysia

Hyung Joong Yoon
Senior Pastor of Hong Kong Korean Exodus Mission Church
Director of Life Road Mission
Hong Kong, China

Contributors

Charles Agyinasare is a Ghanaian Christian minister, international speaker, televangelist, author of over fifty books, and the founder of Perez Chapel International, one of the fastest-growing Pentecostal-Charismatic denominations in Ghana. He is the senior pastor of Perez Dome. Its facility, which can seat 14,000 persons, is considered to be the biggest auditorium in Ghana. Divine healings, miracles, signs, and wonders confirm his preaching and teaching of the Word in his worldwide ministry.

Despite being promiscuous and riotous in his early years, as well as dropping out of high school, Agyinasare converted to Christianity at age eighteen in 1980, which led to a dramatic turnaround in his life. He is currently a missionary statesman, Christian scholar, autodidact, national and international leader, philanthropist, founder of many institutions, including a Bible school and a television station, and a successful family man. He is married to Rev. Mrs. Vivian Sena Agyinasare, and together they have three biological children, one adopted daughter, and a granddaughter.

Daniel S. H. Ahn is assistant professor of intercultural studies and practical ministries at Tyndale Theological Seminary, Amsterdam. He is a missiologist specializing in World Christianity and intercultural theology, and he has taught missiology in diverse places, including North America, United Kingdom, and Asia. He is also an OMF missionary, with extensive cross-cultural mission experience in East and Central Asia and Europe. An ordained Presbyterian pastor, he has served local churches in North America, Europe, and Asia. His current research focuses on so-called World Christianity, that is, on translation of Christianity into local languages and cultures. His publications include chapters in *Religious Transformation in Modern Asia* (Brill, 2015), *Korean Church, God's Mission, Global Christianity* (Regnum, 2015), and *Testing the Boundaries* (Cambridge Scholars, 2011), as well as the article "Johan H. Bavinck's Reformed Theology of Non-Christian Religions," *Bavinck Review* (2012).

Kyo Seong Ahn is associate professor of church history at Presbyterian University and Theological Seminary, Seoul, Korea. He was commissioned as a missionary by the Presbyterian Church of Korea and served in Mongolia (1992–2000). From 2000 to 2002 he was executive secretary of the World Mission Department of the Presbyterian Church of Korea.

J. Kwabena Asamoah-Gyadu is Baëta-Grau Professor of Contemporary African Christianity and Pentecostal/Charismatic Theology at Trinity

Theological Seminary, Accra, Ghana. He also serves the seminary as director of graduate studies and is the founding director of the seminary's Center for the Study of Christianity in Africa. He has served as visiting scholar at Harvard University, Massachusetts (2004); Luther Seminary, St. Paul, Minnesota (2007); the Overseas Ministries Study Center, New Haven, Connecticut (2012); and Asbury Theological Seminary, Wilmore, Kentucky (2015). Asamoah-Gyadu is a trustee of the Oxford Centre for Mission Studies and a member of the Lausanne Movement Theology Working Group. He is the author of many articles in international journals relating to Pentecostalism in Africa and Christianity as a non-Western religion. In December 2014 he was elected as a fellow of the Ghana Academy of Arts and Sciences. He is married to Theodora, and they have three children: Theophil, Griselda, and Emmanuel.

Dwight P. Baker served for thirteen years (2002–15) as associate editor of the *International Bulletin of Missionary Research*. Prior to retiring in 2011, he was also program director and then associate director of the Overseas Ministries Study Center, New Haven, Connecticut. Previously, he was director of the World Christian Foundations study program at the U.S. Center for World Mission in Pasadena, California. He is coeditor of *Serving Jesus with Integrity: Ethics and Accountability in Mission* (with Douglas Hayward, 2010) and *The Missionary Family: Witness, Concerns, Care* (with Robert J. Priest, 2014).

Tim Carriker is a mission co-worker of the Presbyterian Church (USA), a missiological consultant, and an educator for the Independent Presbyterian Church of Brazil. He has served as professor of mission and Bible at numerous seminaries in Brazil. He has been academic director of graduate studies at the Evangelical Mission Center, the Presbyterian Seminary of the South, MacKenzie University, and Fortaleza Theological Seminary, as well as serving as professor at several other theological schools throughout Brazil. He is the author of six books and over one hundred articles. In addition, he has edited seven volumes, including being general editor for the *Mission Study Bible*, published by the Brazilian Bible Society (2014). Versions of the *Mission Study Bible* are currently being prepared in Spanish and English.

Hyung Keun Choi is an ordained pastor of the Korea Evangelical Holiness Church. He served the Lausanne Movement as international deputy director for East Asia for seven years (2004–11). Currently, he is professor of mission studies at Seoul Theological University. He serves the Korea Lausanne Committee as general secretary and is also a member of the Theology Working Group of the Lausanne Movement.

Woosung Calvin Choi, by growing up in different parts of the world, has acquired a unique cultural background. Having lived in Korea, Iran, Turkey, India, and the United States, he is fluent in English, Korean, Persian, and Turkish. He now resides in Boston and currently serves as the senior pastor of Watertown Evangelical Church, Watertown, Massachusetts. He previously served as an associate pastor at SaRang Church, Seoul, Korea, and at SaRang Community Church, Anaheim, California. He is the author of Preaching to Multiethnic Congregation (Peter Lang, 2015) and has translated Preaching with a Plan (Zondervan, 2012) into Korean.

Christopher DeWelt has served since 1999 as the director of Intercultural Studies at Ozark Christian College, Joplin, Missouri. Earlier he served for eight years (1974–83) as a church-planting missionary in Santiago, Chile, and has since traveled in over eighty countries, representing various mission ministries. He has also served as the president of College Press Publishing Company and is the founder, in 1990, of Literature and Teaching Ministries, a nonprofit organization dedicated to bringing leadership resources to Christian leaders worldwide in their heart languages. More recently, he cofounded Global Research Team, an organization dedicated to providing quality research with missiological insight.

Wanjiru M. Gitau was a postdoctoral research fellow at Asbury Theological Seminary, Wilmore, Kentucky, for the year 2015–16. Born and educated in Kenya, Gitau has more than fifteen years of pastoral leadership experience within the Nairobi Chapel group of megachurches, Chinese immigrants living in Nairobi, and the IFES-affiliated student ministry of FOCUS-Kenya. She is also a researcher with Tyndale House's Africa Leadership Survey, with the Center for World Christianity at Africa International University, and with Asbury Theological Seminary's Center for World Christian Revitalization Movements. Her missions and research interests have taken her to Europe, Asia, and North America, as well as around Africa. Her teaching and research revolve around contemporary megachurches, missions, church history, and pastoral theologies. She is coauthor of a forthcoming book on World Christianity.

Wesley Granberg-Michaelson served as general secretary of the Reformed Church in America for seventeen years, from 1994 to 2011. Previously, he held the position of director of church and society at the World Council of Churches in Geneva and served as legislative assistant to U.S. senator Mark O. Hatfield. Active in several ecumenical initiatives, he was one of the founders of Christian Churches Together in the United States and serves with the international committee of the Global Christian Forum. His latest book is *From Times Square to Timbuktu: The Post-Christian West Meets the Non-Western Church* (Eerdmans, 2013).

Tae Kyung Ham is the general director in the management department of Christian Global Network TV in South Korea and a visiting professor at Korea University of International Studies and the State University of New York Korea. He studied landscape architecture at Kyunghee University and has studied economics, politics, Communism, diplomacy, and missiology of China at Seonggyungwan University, Seogang University, Taiwan Politics College, and Seoul Theological School, earning his Ph.D. in Chinese government and politics at Beijing University, China. He served as a senior editor of the newspaper *Kukmin Ilbo* and is actively serving in many other roles, including as director of the China Network Study Center, board member of Dulos Network, and executive board member of the Society for Korea-China Christianity Exchange Association. He is the author of *Mission We Knew, China We Did Not Know* (in Korean; Duranno Press, 2015).

Kyusam Han is senior pastor of Chodae Community Church, Norwood, New Jersey. A scholar and an educator at heart, he seeks tirelessly to find the true meaning of the Word as God intended. An equally dedicated pastor, he approaches his ministry with the compassionate heart of Christ.

Darrell Jackson is an ordained British Baptist minister. Following pastoral ministry, he served as national mission adviser to the Baptist Union of Great Britain, as executive researcher for the Conference of European Churches, and then as founding director of the Nova Research Centre at Redcliffe College, United Kingdom. Since 2012 he has been senior lecturer in missiology at Morling College, Sydney, and the Australian College of Theology, also in Sydney. A regular conference speaker and author, he is a mission commission associate of the World Evangelical Alliance, chairs the Lausanne International Researchers' Network, sits on the editorial board of *Lausanne Global Analysis*, is a board member of European Christian Mission International, serves the National Leadership Team of Missions Interlink (Australia), and is a theological consultant to Global Interaction (Australia). He and his wife, Beth, an ordained Baptist pastor, have two children, Kai and Karys.

J. Nelson Jennings serves as mission pastor and consultant at Onnuri Community Church, Seoul, Korea. From 1986 to 1999 he was a missionary in Japan, first in church planting (Nagoya), then in theological education (Chiba). He taught world mission for twelve years (1999–2011) at Covenant Theological Seminary, St. Louis, Missouri (USA); he also served as editor of *Missiology: An International Review* (1997–2011). From 2011 to 2015 he was associate director, then executive director of the Overseas Ministries Study Center, New Haven, Connecticut (USA), as well as associate editor, then editor of the *International Bulletin of Missionary Research*. He is the author of *Theology in Japan: Takakura Tokutaro (1885–1934)* (2005) and *God the Real Superpower: Rethinking Our Role in Missions* (2007), plus coauthor, with Hisakazu Inagaki, of *Philosophical Theology and East-West Dialogue* (2000).

Chang Ju Kim, a pastor and mission co-worker in Madagascar, was ordained in 1987 by the Presbyterian Church in the Republic of Korea. He has served as a military chaplain in the Korean Army (1987–90) and as associate pastor and then senior pastor of Yedarm Church, Seoul (1996–2007). Since 2008 he has been a lecturer at Ambatonakanga Faculté de Théologie, Antananarivo, Madagascar.

Jinbong Kim has served, since 2012, as director of international church relations for the Overseas Ministries Study Center, New Haven, Connecticut. Prior to coming to OMSC, he served for a number of years as a missionary in West Africa, beginning in 1990 as a short-term missionary in Côte d'Ivoire. Following further training at Chongshin Theological Seminary and Chongshin World Mission Graduate School, in Korea, he and his wife, Soon Young Jung, joined Korea's Global Mission Society in 1994. In 1998 they joined WEC International as well. They pursued mission studies at All Nations Christian College, Hertfordshire, England, and French language study in Albertville, France. During 1998 he served as an intern at a French church in Mulhouse, France. They then spent two terms working among Fulani Muslims in Guinea, before coming to OMSC in 2006. In 2008 Kim proposed that the Korean Global Mission Leadership Forum be organized, and he has, to the present, served as coordinator for it. He earned his doctorate in intercultural studies at Grace College and Theological Seminary, Winona Lake, Indiana (2016).

Kyungsool (Joshua) Kim and his family were involved in church planting, discipleship, leadership training, and mission training among unreached people groups in Sierra Leone, the Gambia, and Ghana, in West Africa, from 1992 until 2012. By God's grace, for the past three years Kim and his wife have served in Korea as director of SIM Korea, challenging and mobilizing Korean churches, recruiting and training new missionaries, and doing member care for SIM Korea missionaries.

Sun Man Kim is senior pastor of the First Korean Presbyterian Church of Greater Hartford, Manchester, Connecticut. He also serves as chairman of the board for the Latin America Mission Project Society and, from 2002 to 2015, served the Overseas Ministries Study Center, New Haven, Connecticut, as a member of its board of trustees. In 2014 he was president of the Korean Church Council of Connecticut. A graduate of Nyack College, Nyack, New York, and Biblical Theological Seminary, Hatfield, Pennsylvania (M.A.R., M.Div., and Th.M.), he is the author of *Expository Preaching on the Book of Revelation* (in Korean; CLC Publications, 2014).

Timothy Kyung Joong Kim has served, since 2004, one of the oldest Presbyterian churches in Malaysia. Planted in 1851 for a European congregation by the English Presbytery, the church's leadership was handed over to the Chinese Malaysian congregation in 1967. Since then the church has changed from a European church to a Chinese-centered church.

In his time, God led Timothy Kim to this church and allowed him to serve it instead of evangelizing a special people group. While serving the local church, he was reminded by God about what kind of mission work is needed in this context. God challenged him to revitalize the old church, which had been blocked by its traditions and past theological framework. The church has been transforming into a missional and incarnational church. Specifically, the church has a role to play as a platform for mission in Southeast Asia. Now it is seeking to form a network of Chinese diaspora churches in Asia.

Miranda Klaver is assistant professor of religion and media (and coordinator of the M.A. program Religion and Media) at Vrije Universiteit Amsterdam, Faculty of Theology and Religious Studies. Trained as a cultural anthropologist and theologian, she has broad teaching experience in contextual theology, cross-cultural ministry, and anthropology of religion. She has extensive research experience among evangelicals and Pentecostals in the Netherlands and recently in the United States. She is a recognized expert on evangelical and Pentecostal/charismatic Christianity, being consulted by national churches and public media. Her current research focuses on the impact of new media in the expansion of the Hillsong churches in Amsterdam and New York City.

Han Young Lee is professor of Old Testament at Asia United Theological University and academic dean of ACTS International Graduate School, near Seoul, South Korea. He grew up in Brazil and worked as a medical doctor in the United States before he was called to church ministry. His heart, however, is in missions. He is currently serving migrant workers in Korea and international students at ACTS. The author of numerous academic publications, Lee is currently writing a book on ethics.

Jae Hoon Lee has been serving as the senior pastor of Onnuri Community Church, Seoul, since 2011. He is also an adjunct professor at Torch Trinity Graduate School of Theology in Seoul. Lee received an M.Div. from Hapdong Theological Seminary and a Th.M. from Trinity Evangelical Divinity School, and is a D.Min. candidate at Gordon-Conwell Theological Seminary. In the United States, he pastored the Chodae Community Church in Norwood, New Jersey, for four years. As an evangelist, he leads what is regarded as one of the most creative megachurches in South Korea. He has been influential in both Christian and non-Christian circles throughout South Korea through innovative uses of social media, art, and publishing.

Won Sang Lee is president of SEED International and senior pastor emeritus of the Korean Central Presbyterian Church, Centreville, Virginia. He is the author of *Pastoral Leadership: A Case Study, Including Reference to John Chrysostom* (Wipf & Stock, 2015). In 2015 Westminster Theological Seminary, Philadelphia, Pennsylvania, honored him with a doctor of divinity degree.

Jorge H. López, born in 1950, began preaching at age fifteen. After attending Bible school, he became copastor of the church in which he grew up. He also assumed the presidency of the Evangelical Pastors Association of Guatemala and became involved in various ecclesiastical organizations.

In 1979 he founded a church named Fraternidad Cristiana de Guatemala (Christian Fraternity of Guatemala), which has grown from 20 members to more than 15,000. Its members have been taught to give, and remaining debt-free through every project has been a trademark of Fraternidad Cristiana. All projects have been funded by the congregation itself without any outside help.

The church has constructed a campus that includes Mega Frater, a sanctuary that can seat over 12,000 people and has become a city landmark. The campus is also home to Liceo Frater, the church's private Christian school. The church broadcasts daily sermons through TBN Enlace International, TV Azteca, and Channel 7. López's sermons are aired by various commercial radio stations. He is the author of a half dozen books in Spanish.

Carlos L. Malavé is executive director of Christian Churches Together (CCT) in the United States. CCT is the broadest organization working for the unity of the church in the United States. He previously served for ten years as assistant stated clerk at the Office of the General Assembly of the Presbyterian Church (USA). Malavé has postcollege degrees from Fuller Theological Seminary, Pasadena, California, and Loma Linda University, Loma Linda, California.

Peter Tze Ming Ng was professor of religious education at the Chinese University of Hong Kong for twenty-three years and is now professor and chair of Chinese Christianity at China Victory Theological Seminary in Hong Kong. He is concurrently serving an adjunct professor at both Fuller Theological Seminary, Pasadena, California, and the Center for the Study of Religion and Chinese Society, Shanghai University. He is the author of *Chinese Christianity: An Interplay between Global and Local Perspectives* (Brill, 2012).

Opoku Onyinah is chancellor of Pentecost University College, Accra, Ghana, where he also serves as chairman of the Church of Pentecost worldwide. He is a member of the Commission on World Mission and Evangelism of the World Council of Churches and is a co-chair of Empowered21 Africa. In addition, he is president of the Ghana Pentecostal and Charismatic Council. His publications include the books *Pentecostal Exorcism: Witchcraft and Exorcism in Ghana* (Deo Publishing, 2012) and *Spiritual Warfare* (CPT Press, 2012).

Mark Oxbrow is international director of *Faith2Share*, a global network of mission agencies focused on discipleship, collaboration, and emerging mission movements. Oxbrow also serves the Lausanne movement as facilitator for Evangelical-Orthodox relations and is a former assistant general secretary of CMS, an Anglican mission. He is president of Feed the Minds, a global literacy charity; a mission commissioner of the World Evangelical Alliance; and a member of the ministry team of his local Anglican church in Oxford. His research interests are Majority World mission movements and Orthodox missiology, and he recently coedited *The Mission of God: Studies in Orthodox and Evangelical Mission* (Regnum Press, 2015).

Kyung Nam Park, as director of WEC International Korea, has oversight of more than 400 workers from WEC Korea. He teaches medical mission, various mission courses, and the Perspectives study program in Korea. A general surgeon, he served previously as a missionary medical worker in a country in West Asia.

Myung Soo Park is professor of church history and the founder and director of the Institute for the Study of Modern Christianity at Seoul Theological University. His research has focused extensively on the Holiness-Pentecostal movements in America and Korea and the relationship between American evangelicalism and Korean Christianity. His articles on Korean Christianity have been published in English journals such as *Wesleyan Theological Journal* and *Journal of Pentecostal Studies*. He spent 2005–6 at the Overseas Ministries Study Center, New Haven, Connecticut, and as an outcome of that sabbatical year, published *Modern Society and Christianity* (in Korean; Kingdom Books, 2013), which explores evangelical aspects of the writings of John Locke, Adam Smith, and Alexis Tocqueville. In 2015 he published two books, also in Korean, on Korean nation building and its relationship with Korean Christianity: *Struggle for Nation Building* (BaekyunDongan) and *Post–World War Politics in Korea and Cho Mansik* (Book Korea).

Pil-Hun Park is currently serving as mission pastor at SaRang Church, in Seoul. Following graduation from Korea University, in 1994 he joined MV *Logos II*, gaining valuable experience in cross-cultural ministry. After two and a half years on board, he returned to Seoul to pastor the Myanmar Fellowship, a ministry among foreign workers in the city, along with completion of his M.Div. at ChongShin Theological Seminary. In 2000 he was appointed as one of the mission pastors of SaRang Church in Seoul, where he served with his family until 2005 when they were called to MV *Doulos*. On board MV *Doulos*, he served as partner ministries manager, training coordinator, and associate director until January 2010. He is one of the mission pastors and the planning team manager of SaRang Church's World Mission Department. He and his wife, MiAe, have two children, EunCheol and JiYoon.

Stephen S. Park, since 2010, has been on the faculty of Grace Theological Seminary, Winona Lake, Indiana. He is professor of intercultural studies and also director of the seminary's Korean Program. From 2001 to 2006 he served as director of the Global Mission Society's Missionary Training Institute. He previously served as a missionary in Moscow, Russia (1988–2001). He earned degrees from Grace Theological Seminary (D.Miss.), Fuller Theological Seminary (Th.M.), Chongshin Presbyterian Seminary (M.Div.), and Kyungbuk National University School of Engineering (B.S. in electronics).

Timothy Kiho Park is director of Global Connections and professor of Asian mission, School of Intercultural Studies, Fuller Theological Seminary, Pasadena, California. He is also president of the East-West Center for Missions Research and Development. He served as a missionary in the Philippines for fifteen years with the Global Mission Society (GMS), the missionary arm of the General Assembly of the Reformed Presbyterian

Church in Korea. He is a graduate of Chongshin University (B.A.), Presbyterian General Assembly Theological Seminary, Chongshin University (M.Div.), and Fuller Theological Seminary (M.A. and Ph.D.).

Joseph Shao, who is active in theological education and mission, is president of the Biblical Seminary of the Philippines and also general secretary of the Asia Theological Association, which has 285 member institutions in thirty-four nations. As a Hebrew scholar, he serves as a visiting professor in numerous seminaries in Asia, North America, Australia, and Europe. In 2014 he received a Qianbei (senior scholar) award in Hong Kong.

Mark Shaw is professor of historical studies and director of the Centre for World Christianity at Africa International University, in Nairobi, Kenya. He and his wife have worked in Kenya since 1980. He is the author of a number of books, including *Work, Play, Love: A Visual Guide to Calling, Career, and the Mission of God* (InterVarsity Press, 2014), *Global Awakening: How Twentieth-Century Revivals Triggered a Christian Revolution* (IVP Academic, 2010), *Ten Great Ideas from Church History* (InterVarsity Press, 1997), and *The Kingdom of God in Africa: A Short History of African Christianity* (Baker, 1996).

N. Yong Sung is the senior pastor of Samkwang Presbyterian Church, in Seoul. He previously served as a missionary in Nigeria and is currently also a professor of missions at Chongshin University's Graduate School of Pastoral Theology. Editor-in-chief of *Korea Missions Quarterly*, he has written several books and many articles. His books include *Research Methodology* (ChumTab Publishing, 2012), *365 Days of Missions in Prayer* (ChumTab Publishing, 2011), and *Mission Case Studies* (Life Book, 2006), all in Korean. He and his wife, Rachel, have two grown children.

Dong Hwa Tae is vice–general secretary of the General Board of Missions of the Korean Methodist Church, Seoul, Korea.

Eiko Takamizawa is the first Japanese female missiologist teaching in Asia. She is a professor and acting chaplain and dean of students at Torch Trinity Graduate University, Seoul. She has been a featured speaker and lecturer for conferences and seminars in various South East Asian and Middle Eastern countries, Europe, and the United States, as well as in Japan and Korea. She serves as vice president of the Asian Society of Missiology, adviser for the Lausanne East Asia committee, and member of the editorial board for the *Journal of the Japan Missiological Society*. She pastors a Japanese congregation at Hallelujah Church in Bundang, South Korea. She serves as an advisory coordinator for the Japanese Ministries Association in Korea. Her publications include translation of "Confess Your Sins to One Another, and Forgive One Another," "Wherever He Leads Me" (a series of articles on Christian mission), and articles on Japanese Christianity in various journals, of which the most recent is "A Vision to Transform Society by Empowering Women in Japan."

Scott Thumma is professor of sociology of religion at Hartford Seminary, Hartford, Connecticut, and directs its D.Min. program. He is also director of the Hartford Institute for Religion Research, manager of several research websites, and co-leader of the Faith Communities Today research project. He has published numerous research reports, articles, and book chapters, in addition to being coauthor of three books: *The Other 80 Percent* (Jossey-Bass, 2011), *Beyond Megachurch Myths* (Jossey-Bass, 2007), and *Gay Religion* (AltaMira Press, 2005). His ongoing research focuses on megachurches, the rise of nondenominationalism, and the impact of the Internet on congregational dynamics. Thumma frequently consults with congregations, denominations, and parachurch groups on issues of growth and spiritual vitality.

Ben Torrey is director of the Fourth River Project (www.thefourthriver.org) and the Three Seas Center (www.threeseas.co.kr). He grew up in Korea and as a teenager joined with his parents, Jane and Archer Torrey, in pioneering Jesus Abbey (www.jabbey.org), a community of prayer high in the Taebaek Mountains of Kangwon Do. He is currently chairman of Jesus Abbey. In 1969 he returned to his native United States. From 1979 until 2005 he served as a bivocational minister while working in the fields of computer systems development and knowledge management. He also served as the chairman and administrator for the King's School, a Christian middle and high school, formerly in Bolton, Connecticut. Since 2003 he and his wife, Liz, have been developing Jesus Abbey's Three Seas Training Center and the Fourth River Project in preparation for the opening of North Korea. To prepare the Unification Generation, they established the River of Life School, a Christian middle and high school.

Tae Wook Um is, since 2014, mission director for the Yoido Full Gospel Church, in Seoul, Korea. Previously, he served as a youth minister at Yoido, focusing on university students (1994–97), and as a missionary in Borneo, Malaysia, working among the Iban tribe (1997–2014).

Christopher J. H. Wright became International Director of the Langham Partnership International in 2001. He has also served as chair of the Lausanne Movement's Theology Working Group (2005–11) and as chair of the Theological Resource Panel of TEAR Fund since 2001. In 1983 he moved to India with his wife, Liz, and four children to teach at Union Biblical Seminary in Pune for five years. At this time he and Liz were mission partners with Crosslinks, an evangelical Anglican mission agency. In 1988 he returned to the U.K. as academic dean (1988–93) and then principal (1993–2001) of All Nations Christian College, Ware, Hertfordshire, England, an international training center for cross-cultural mission. Ordained in the Anglican Church of England in 1977, he served as an assistant pastor in the Parish Church of St. Peter and St. Paul, Tonbridge, Kent, England. He has written several books, including *The Mission of God* (InterVarsity, 2006) and *The Mission of God's People* (Zondervan, 2010).

Index